Globalization and Work

STEVE WILLIAMS, HARRIET BRADLEY,
RANJI DEVADASON and MARK ERICKSON

polity

The right of Steve Williams, Harriet Bradley, Ranji Devadason and
Mark Erickson to be identified as Authors of this Work has been
asserted in accordance with the UK Copyright, Designs and Patents
Act 1988.

First published in 2013 by Polity Press

Polity Press
65 Bridge Street
Cambridge CB2 1UR, UK

Polity Press
350 Main Street
Malden, MA 02148, USA

ISBN-13: 978-0-7456-5211-5
ISBN-13: 978-0-7456-5212-2 (pb)

A catalogue record for this book is available from the British Library.

Typeset in 9.5pt on 12pt Utopia by
Servis Filmsetting Ltd, Stockport, Cheshire
Printed and bound in Great Britain by Berforts Information Press Ltd

The publisher has used its best endeavours to ensure that the
URLs for external websites referred to in this book are correct
and active at the time of going to press. However, the publisher
has no responsibility for the websites and can make no guarantee
that a site will remain live or that the content is or will remain
appropriate.

Every effort has been made to trace all copyright holders, but if any
have been inadvertently overlooked the publisher will be pleased to
include any necessary credits in any subsequent reprint or edition.

For further information on Polity, visit our website:
www.politybooks.com

Globalization and Work

Contents

Figures

Tables

Boxes

Preface: about this book

There can be little doubt about the importance of globalization. We only have to look around us, at everyday consumer goods like iPods, iPhones and iPads, toys, clothing products and so on which are the product of complex processes of design, production and retail that extend beyond national borders, to get a sense of how the world has changed in a way that brings the global closer to people's day-to-day lives. As Dicken (2007: 3) observes, there has been an 'explosion of interest' in globalization; it has been sparked by a feeling that nearly all aspects of economic, political and social affairs are influenced by processes that lie beyond the national boundaries of individual countries (Hirst et al. 2009).

We have tackled the question of globalization in previous books (written with Carol Stephenson). In *Myths at Work* (Bradley et al. 2000)', we suggested that globalization could be viewed as a 'myth'. This was not because we rejected the idea that social and economic activities were becoming more interconnected on a worldwide basis. Rather, our concern was to challenge the tendency for dominant perspectives on globalization to neglect the important ways in which nation-states and social actors influence economic, political and social developments on a worldwide scale. Moreover, the emphasis on the novelty of globalization helped to divert attention away from the way in which the internationalization of economic activity had contributed to the intensification of capitalist relations of production, with adverse consequences for jobs. It also served as a pretext for governments wanting to promote competitiveness through policies of labour market flexibility.

In *Business in Society* (Erickson et al. 2009), we examined how the process of globalization has been driven by dominant economic interests, particularly those of the United States, and by corporate elites. While it has produced some benefits for some people, the adverse consequences of globalization include increased job insecurity and greater unemployment among workers whose jobs are threatened by greater international competition. That said, however, we anticipated that the rise of emerging economies such as China and India would have a profound impact on the nature and trajectory of globalization in the years to come.

Why turn our attention to globalization again, but this time at book length? Despite the extensive literature devoted to globalization, there is no single general text which draws on sociological insights to tackle the important subject of work and employment in a globalizing world. The main purpose of writing this book is to rectify this lacuna. In doing so, we are not so much concerned with evaluating the consequences of globalization for key measures of work and employment at a macro level; rather, our main aim is to explore and provide insights into how work operates, and the experience of workers, under increasingly globalizing conditions, drawing on evidence from around the world. We also take the view that globalization is not just something that happens to workers. Thus we appreciate the importance of taking a grounded, bottom-up perspective which recognizes the important extent to which workers and others – managers, governments, union representatives, labour rights activists – actively engage in producing globalization themselves in particular contexts. To a large extent, then, this means that our contribution takes the form of a challenge to what you might call actually existing globalization, a neo-liberal project advanced by governments, multinational companies, international agencies and other corporate elites.

What is meant by 'neo-liberalism'? We use the term to refer to a political and economic perspective which holds that free markets, deregulation, trade liberalization, privatization of state assets and weak trade unions are essential for improvements in economic prosperity. While international trade and other forms of cross-border economic activity have a long history (Hirst et al. 2009), the rapid development of globalization since the 1980s has been associated with a neo-liberal project of unrestrained capitalism in a way that has come to dominate policy approaches to work and employment relations around the world (Kalleberg 2009). We take this as the starting point for the current epoch of globalization. As we demonstrate, though, while neo-liberal globalization may have been dominant, it is subject to manifold challenges from below, in the form of labour protests or activist campaigns for change, for example. Moreover, there is plenty of evidence that nation-states retain a key role in coordinating and regulating economic affairs (Hirst et al. 2009). That said, in discussing globalization, and the project of neo-liberal globalization in particular, we are of course mainly concerned with capitalist globalization, a stage of economic development sometimes known as 'late capitalism'. Associated largely with the Marxist writer Ernest Mandel, who published a major book on the subject in the early 1970s (Mandel 1998), the concept of late capitalism is useful because it distinguishes the current period of capitalism, which is marked by increasing flows of goods, services and people across national borders, and by a more profound and extensive degree of internationalization of economic activity, from previous capitalist eras.

In this book we eschew the use of terms such as 'developed' and 'developing' countries when making comparisons, or drawing contrasts, between different parts of the world. Instead we prefer the labels

'Global North' and the 'Global South', a formulation for distinguishing between richer and poorer nations that has become increasingly commonplace since the Brandt Report made a distinction between the North and South in 1980 (Brandt 1980). While it is generally the case that regions of the world lying below the equator are less well-off than those above it – though Australia and New Zealand are conspicuous examples to the contrary – the terms 'Global North' and 'Global South' are more than just geographical concepts: they also signify that such a distinction is rooted in socio-economic differences that have some expression in, but are not necessarily a function of, geography (Rigg 2007: 3). Thus the 'idea of the global South is meant to identify countries in similar economic and geopolitical positions in the global capitalist system and to highlight their shared strategic objectives and interests' (Mosoetsa and Williams 2012: 4).

The book is organized into eleven chapters. In chapter 1, we draw on relevant conceptual frameworks and perspectives to explore the concept of globalization, and consider the implications of a more globalized world for work and employment. Following on from this, our focus in chapter 2 is on the topic of consumption, work and identity in a globalizing world, illustrated by two key exemplars: the Indian call centre industry and the fair trade movement. In chapter 3, we turn our attention to the role of multinational companies (MNCs), a generic term which refers to firms operating in more than one country, and of which there is a considerable variety. Although they are often portrayed as overly powerful bodies which are capable of transforming work and employment relations in ways that have all sorts of adverse consequences for workers around the world, sociological insights help us to understand the complex nature of work and employment in multinationals under globalization.

Multinationals are often castigated for the detrimental effects of their activities on workers' rights and employment conditions, particularly in the countries of the Global South. Chapter 4 is concerned with evaluating efforts to regulate labour standards on a transnational basis, and the prospects for a fairer and more equitable globalization that arise as a result. As we see in chapter 5, neo-liberal globalization poses some major challenges to labour movements which, because they are heavily rooted in specific nation-states, have struggled to respond effectively to the pressures and challenges that arise from the growing power of globalized capital. Nevertheless, the prospects for a renewed trade union internationalism, one based on unions acting more as social movements, offer labour movements a way of regaining some of their lost power and extending their influence. In chapter 6, we turn our attention to the nature of work and the management of labour in those factories based mainly in the Global South which manufacture and assemble products destined for global markets. The chapter demonstrates that we need to look beyond the use of coercive managerial techniques and recognize that globalization has led to the development of new subjects and identities among the largely female workforces, and prompted interest in the features of an emergent transnational labour process.

Clearly, one of the most notable features of globalization has been the growth of international labour migration. In chapter 7, we examine the main features of labour migration in a globalizing world and consider the main implications for work and employment. Following on from this, in chapter 8 our concern is with understanding the working lives of the growing internationally mobile cadre of highly skilled managers and professionals, who are sometimes referred to as the 'transnational capitalist class' (Sklair 2001). As we see, though, this approach neglects the highly diverse nature of the transnational elite, and the ways in which actors are differentially placed within it, depending on their identities and power within the global economy. Evidently globalization has contributed to increased levels of social and economic inequality in many parts of the world. Yet in chapter 9, which examines inequalities through the lens of the interesectionality framework, we demonstrate the complex and sometimes contradictory impact of globalization on existing relations of gender and ethnicity.

Chapter 10 deals with a topic that rarely features in conventional studies of globalization; indeed, it is even largely absent from much discussion and analysis of work and employment – labour conflict. As we demonstrate, though, challenges to neo-liberal globalization, evident in strikes, labour protests and other modes of contention, are manifold. Finally, the concluding chapter 11 reviews the main contribution the book makes to extending our knowledge and understanding of work and employment under globalizing conditions, considers some relevant current challenges and future prospects and sets out some ideas for how globalization can be made to work more effectively in the interests of working people and others whose interests have often been subordinated or neglected.

All of the main substantive chapters contain boxed examples, which are designed to highlight particularly notable cases and examples that are relevant to the main text. We also provide details of further reading suggestions, and the addresses of websites where relevant, at the end of every chapter.

In writing this book we were given strong support from the editorial team at Polity, especially Jonathan Skerrett and Emma Longstaff. We also express our gratitude to Leigh Mueller for her excellent copy-editing work, the result of which is a notably improved final product. Peter Scott of the University of Portsmouth provided helpful comments on some of the chapters. We would also like to thank the publisher's anonymous reviewers, whose comments enabled us to produce a better book.

1 Globalization and work – an introduction

1.1 Introducing globalization and work

The purpose of this book is to examine work and employment under globalization. According to the International Labour Organization (ILO), an agency of the United Nations, 'work is central to people's lives. No matter where they live or what they do, women and men see jobs as the "litmus test" for the success or failure of globalization. Work is the source of dignity, stability, peace, and credibility of governments and the economic system' (ILO 2004: 6).

Yet work is not just something which benefits economies and governments; it clearly also matters to working people themselves, in terms of providing them with income, stability and opportunities for personal development, particularly where it is of superior quality in terms of wages, skills, security and task discretion. Moreover, through their experiences at work, and during the course of their working lives, people come to develop interests which are in opposition to those of dominant corporate elites. Efforts to promote a more equitable globalization, in which its benefits are shared on a fairer basis, are often rooted in, or have close connections to, workplace-based labour struggles. Yet despite the importance of work, and notwithstanding its crucial role in a globalizing economy, the topic of globalization and work has hitherto attracted rather little scholarly interest (Webster et al. 2008) – a lacuna which is all the more surprising given how central questions of work were to the development of sociology as an academic discipline (Nichols and Sugur 2004).

We can get a sense of the importance of globalization, work and employment by looking at the experiences of African migrant workers employed in the Spanish agriculture sector. Centred on the region of Almeria, agriculture is a major industry in the south of Spain, worth some £1 billion each year. Tomatoes, cucumbers and courgettes are among the fruit and vegetables grown all year round, satisfying demand from Northern European consumers for fresh produce. As the traditional indigenous rural Spanish labour force declined, between the 1980s and 2000s agricultural employment in Southern Spain increasingly came to be dominated by migrant labourers from Africa, whose work is critical to what is a highly labour-intensive industry (Mendoza 2003). By April 2010 there were between 80,000 and 90,000 migrant workers employed in the agricultural industry around

1

Almeria, most of whom came from Morocco or sub-Saharan Africa, though the economic crisis means that numbers have dwindled since then. Most are illegal immigrants, lacking the relevant documentation to enable them to work legally. Felicity Lawrence's (2011) report for the *Guardian* newspaper demonstrates that migrant labour is vital to the functioning of the agricultural industry. She observes that the relative abundance of labour means that work is often irregular; workers assemble at dawn in anticipation of being selected for a day's employment, at substantially less than the formal minimum wage. Migrant workers endure desperately poor living and working conditions. They often live in huts, frequently without direct access to sanitation or drinking water. The work can be gruelling, with temperatures in the hothouses where the produce is grown reaching as high as 40–45 °C.

Migrant workers are reluctant to complain about the low pay and arduous conditions. For one thing, they are desperate for work, and do not want to prejudice their chances of getting further work by speaking out. Moreover, their status as undocumented, illegal workers means that raising concerns would attract the attention of the authorities, perhaps resulting in their deportation. Lawrence's (2011) report includes the observations of farmers who claim that the extensive low pay, while undesirable, cannot be avoided. They claim that big multinational supermarket chains, to whom they sell their produce, have pushed down the price which they are prepared to pay for it so far that it is not possible to pay workers the minimum wage and return a profit. Yet, although highly disadvantaged, there are signs that the migrant workers in agriculture are looking to improve their prospects. Some have organized collectively, forming a trade union, to pursue their interests from a position of greater strength.

The case of the Spanish agriculture sector encapsulates some of the key themes to be examined in this book on globalization and work, most notably the issues surrounding the employment of migrant labour. The situation in Spain is by no means an isolated example of how increasing competitive pressures in the global food industry are transmitted down the supply chain, resulting in low pay and worsening conditions for an often largely migrant workforce (see Shelley 2007). This case also illustrates the powerful role played by multinational companies in the global economy, and the way in which their activities increasingly stretch across national borders, particularly through the use of transnational supply chains and production networks to satisfy consumer demand for cheap goods in the rich countries of Europe and North America. The case of the African migrant workers in Spain also exposes some of the weaknesses of established systems of worker protection under globalization. In a more globalized world, national systems for regulating minimum labour standards, such as minimum wage laws, no longer seem to work as well as they once did. Therefore the question arises as to how, if at all, labour standards can be regulated on a transnational basis? Finally, it is evident from this case that the African migrant workers are not simply passive victims of globalization. In some cases, their experience of working in Spain has encouraged the development of a shared sense of grievance, which they have used to organize collectively and mobilize in pursuit of better conditions. Workers and other actors, then, do not simply respond to globalization, they also help to produce it, based on their experiences and their own working lives, influenced by the characteristics of their specific context.

Before going any further, we need to say something about what is meant by the term 'globalization'. For some, it concerns how societies and economies around the world are becoming more integrated – in the sense of being more deeply enmeshed with one another – as a result of increased levels of international economic activity (e.g. World Bank 2002). Others, though, put more emphasis on 'interconnectedness' (Held and McGrew 2007). This captures the way in which developments in information and communications technology make linkages – economic, social, political and cultural – between events in different parts of the world not only increasingly commonplace, but also more intense (Giddens 1990). For Held and McGrew (2007: 1), then, globalization involves the 'widening, deepening and speeding up of worldwide interconnectedness'.

The widening of interconnectedness refers to the growing extent of the links between people and organizations around the world, evident in the development of transnational supply chains for food produce mentioned above. This illustrates the greater mutual dependency that exists between people and activities from different countries, with work as 'one important way in which interdependence occurs' (Frenkel 2006: 389). As we have seen, consumers of food produce in the rich countries of Northern Europe increasingly depend upon the labour of African migrant workers who, in turn, depend on orders from multinational retailers and their customers for their jobs and livelihoods.

Globalization also involves a deepening of interconnectedness, as local events are increasingly strongly affected by global processes and vice versa. This deepening is linked to the diminishing salience of distance, with the space between different parts of the world being increasingly reduced, or compressed. As the constraints of geography diminish (Waters 2001), activities in one part of the world increasingly impact on those in other parts of the world, regardless of the gap between them. Globalization, then, 'involves the compression of space such that distance is less of a factor than it used to be in terms of knowledge, communication and movement' (Martell 2010: 14–15).

Moreover, the process of interconnectedness is becoming faster; the greater velocity, or speeding up, of global interactions is evident in the rapidity with which events in one part of the world affect other parts (Held and McGrew 2007). For example, information and communication technologies enable orders from retailers to be transmitted to different parts of their supply chain extremely quickly, with implications for the nature of work in supplier firms. Note how we can all book our hotels and air flights for travel abroad speedily via the internet!

Having briefly explored the nature of globalization, in the next section we focus in more detail on its different dimensions and their implications for work and employment. This is followed by a section in which we critically evaluate the main theoretical perspectives that have been advanced to conceptualize globalization, and assess what they contribute to our understanding of work and employment. We then offer a more bottom-up, 'grounded' view, and draw on relevant ethnographic, geographical and sociological perspectives to highlight the contested nature of work under globalization.

1.2 Globalization and work: process, project and practice

In order to examine what globalization involves in more detail, and in a way that highlights the relevant work and employment issues, we draw upon Amoore's (2002) distinction between globalization as a process, as a project and as a practice.

Globalization as a process

Clearly, it is important to recognize that globalization is an important process, one that involves increased mobility of capital and labour. There are four specific aspects of capital mobility, the first of which concerns the greater interconnectedness of financial markets. Globalization is marked not only by increased volumes of cross-border financial transactions, but also by the greater integration of financial markets on a worldwide basis (see Held and McGrew 2007: 83–9). The financial crisis of the late 2000s demonstrated the importance of globalized finance, as financial contagion spread rapidly from the United States, where difficulties arose in the market for sub-prime mortgages, to other parts of the world, especially Europe, whose banking system was strongly exposed to the risky financial products (Harvey 2011; Mason 2009).

Some, though, question whether a truly globalized financial system really exists. While finance operates on an international scale, it is nevertheless highly stratified and differentiated, and falls short of being genuinely interconnected (Thompson 2010). Whether truly globalized or not, clearly the internationalization of finance has influenced work and employment in some major ways. Perhaps most importantly, it acts to discipline workers, helping to reinforce the power of capital over labour (Peters 2011). This can be seen in the responses of many European countries, including Greece, Spain and Italy, to the 2007–9 financial crisis. In order to maintain the confidence of international investors, and thus retain access to sources of global finance, governments were required to initiate rigorous, even extreme, austerity measures, including substantial reductions in wages, pensions and welfare benefits, in order to tackle their deficits.

The concept of 'financialization' captures the growing dominance of international finance, in particular how economic life has come to be permeated by the operation of financial markets (Lapavitsas 2011). Financialization appears to be a common feature of capitalist development: at the start of capitalist industrialization in a country, the manufacturing sector is the main source of wealth and profit accumulation, but economic change towards a service-based economy is usually accompanied by a switch to financial speculation and stock-market manipulation as the major source of wealth creation. The new wealthy elite are financiers rather than manufacturers. The trend to financialization is particularly manifest in the tendency for owners of capital, including firms, to insist upon sweating their assets in order to secure short-term gains in value, thus satisfying the demands of financial investors (Froud et al. 2000). The result is a kind of 'disconnected capitalism' (Thompson 2003), marked by the inability of employers to develop an attachment with their workforce, something which has profoundly negative implications for work and employment. In particular, it results in ever more intensive demands on firms to produce short-term results, undermining workers' job security (Thompson 2011).

A second aspect of capital mobility concerns the expansion of global trade, including the greater participation of countries from the Global South, such as China, in the global trading system (Hirst et al. 2009). The growing trading presence of these countries is predicated on the comparative advantage they have as sources of low-cost production, particularly through their relatively cheap and abundant labour force. Rivoli's (2009) book, *The Travels of a T-Shirt in the Global Economy*, illustrates the functioning of the global trading system. Cotton grown in the United States is shipped to China for production into garments, before the finished goods are transported back to the US to be sold. Since the 1980s, concerted international efforts have been made to free up, or liberalize, international trade, with a view to reducing the barriers which restrict the ability of economies to grow by developing trading relations. Following years of negotiations, the World Trade Organization (WTO) was established in 1995 for the purpose of determining a global framework within which free trade could flourish (Hepple 2005). While, in theory, the liberalization of trade should have benefited countries from the Global South by giving them better access to markets around the world, in practice the way in which the international trading system operates works to the benefit of richer nations (Stiglitz 2007). Countries like the US operate a dense and convoluted system of quotas and tariffs which are designed to restrict and raise the cost of certain imported goods, with the aim of protecting their own domestic producers in the face of international competition (Rivoli 2009).

Workers and unions in the Global North often oppose trade liberalization because of the perceived adverse consequences for jobs and labour standards. Without some measure of protection, firms will be rendered uncompetitive relative to producers in countries in the Global South, putting jobs, particularly those in manufacturing, at risk. Efforts by some governments to use the WTO as a means of advancing 'fair' as well as 'free' trade, by making liberalization conditional on complying with minimum environmental and labour standards, have been unsuccessful since countries in the Global South see such rules as a disguised form of protection (Hepple 2005). Some, however, have challenged the view that trade liberalization has been directly responsible for job losses in the Global North. Rather, firms use the possibility of re-locating production to cheaper sites elsewhere to gain leverage over workers, getting them to moderate their wage demands and make other concessions. In the US, for example, job losses in manufacturing have been caused more by domestic policy decisions than by greater exposure to international competition (Doogan 2009).

A third aspect of greater capital mobility concerns the implications of rising levels of foreign direct investment (FDI) that characterize the international economy. FDI refers to cross-border investment by governments and, especially, multinational companies, for example through opening new production sites in other countries, or, as is becoming more significant, by merging with, or acquiring, businesses in foreign locations. Some state that FDI by multinationals has become a more important element of economic globalization than international trade (Dicken 2007; Held and McGrew 2007). Levels of FDI grew markedly during the 1980s, and continued to rise until the economic crisis of the late 2000s, whereupon they declined, before a gradual recovery to pre-crisis levels occurred (UNCTAD 2011). Commentators who are sceptical about globalization nevertheless accept that levels of FDI have grown substantially, while observing that they largely occur between economies in the Global North such as the US, Europe and Japan; large parts of the world, notably Africa, are excluded (Doogan 2009; Hirst et al. 2009). However, an increasing proportion of FDI is being generated by, and directed at, economies in the Global South (UNCTAD 2011). In 2010, China attracted record levels of FDI, with a value of $106 billion. Chinese firms themselves, moreover, have made substantial investments in African infrastructure projects.

Fourth, following on from this, multinational companies (MNCs) use FDI to organize the production of goods and services through supply chains and production networks which operate on an increasingly sophisticated transnational basis. See figure 1.1 for a generic depiction of a supply chain in an industry – clothing and textiles – which has become increasingly globalized. Yarns are created from raw material such as cotton and artificial fibres (e.g. nylon), which are then

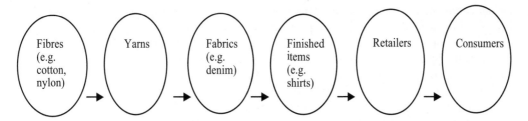

Fig. 1.1 The global supply chain in clothing and textiles

turned into fabrics – denim, for example. These fabrics are then finished, dyed and printed to produce completed goods, clothing items such as shirts, before being bought up by multinational retailers who then sell them to consumers. Between the 1970s and 2000s much of the less complex and lower value-added elements of the chain, particularly the final production of the garments, was re-located to low-wage countries in the Global South, such as China, Vietnam and Cambodia, and increasingly sub-Saharan Africa. The textile and clothing supply chain is 'dominated by large retailers, which do not own their own factories but organize and control production on a worldwide basis' (Morris and Barnes 2009: 2).

By the late 2000s, there were some 82,000 MNCs in existence, responsible for hundreds of thousands of affiliates around the world (UNCTAD 2009). It is difficult to understate the importance of MNCs to the process of globalization. They have been called the 'primary movers and shapers' of the global economy (Dicken 2007: 106). Some see their activity as prefiguring a new kind of transnational economic system, under which international firms become increasingly less dependent upon, and more disconnected from, their national home-country economies (Sklair 2001), and as an integral feature of the 'new global capitalist order' (Held and McGrew 2007: 111). The activities of MNCs have proved contentious. On the one hand, their investments have helped to generate economic growth, jobs and prosperity across the Global South, while giving consumers in the Global North access to a wider range of cheap goods. On the other hand, multinationals have often been accused of causing a range of social and environmental problems, such as the undermining of labour standards and increased pollution in their sites across the Global South, especially where effective regulation or enforcement arrangements are absent (Stiglitz 2007).

Although some contend that global multinationals have benefited from globalization by exploiting space in a way that makes them overly powerful, particularly relative to nation-states (Bauman 1998a), we need to treat claims that specific places no longer matter, and that MNCs have become 'placeless' entities, with a certain amount of caution. Most leading multinationals are far from being genuinely transnational corporations, in the sense of operating beyond the influence of nation-states, and many have strong connections to their home-country base (Doogan 2009; Hirst et al. 2009).

In addition to encompassing greater capital mobility, viewing globalization as a process means that we also have to consider its implications for labour mobility, particularly international labour migration. Compared to capital, labour has traditionally been seen as more rooted in, and committed to, particular places, and thus as more 'sticky' (Hudson 2001). However, labour mobility on an international scale, although often heavily restricted, is nonetheless an important element of the process of globalization (Standing 2011). The 'growing tide of international migrant workers . . . [is] one of the most reliable indicators of the rapid rate of globalization. Every country today is affected by international migration, whether as a country of origin, destination, transit, or all three' (Kingma 2006: 10). Even though the global economic recession of the late 2000s caused a downturn in labour migration, some signs of recovery were evident by 2010, with over 3 million people migrating to the major economies of the Global North for employment-related reasons in that year alone (OECD 2012a). Some sectors are characterized by particularly high concentrations of migrant labour. For example, nursing, domestic labour and care work in countries in the Global North often rely on work of female migrants from poorer countries such as the Philippines (Pyle 2006; Kingma 2006).

Although both are integral to the process of globalization, there is an important difference between labour and capital mobility. Whereas richer countries have encouraged the latter, and have promoted the liberalization of capital, trade and investment flows, generally international labour migration has been emphatically discouraged. The main exception is in Europe where, although certain restrictions have been imposed, workers are largely free to move throughout the member states of the European Union (EU). But the majority of rich countries operate tight, and often increasingly strict, controls over immigrant labour, mostly to the detriment of migrant workers who are rendered more vulnerable (Anderson 2010) (see box 1.1). The working lives of migrant workers are often marked by low pay, insecurity, struggles to claim unpaid wages and unhealthy working environments (Pai 2008). Yet liberalizing labour migration would do much to encourage a fairer process of globalization, one which offers greater benefits to poorer countries in the Global South, since remittances from emigrants are often a major source of family income and prosperity. The current 'asymmetry' between a highly liberalized regime of capital flows and the heavy restrictions placed on international labour migration helps to keep poorer countries poor, and is thus a leading source of global inequality (Stiglitz 2007).

Globalization as a project

In addition to being a process, globalization can also be viewed as a project: specifically, a neo-liberal project which has been operated by, and for the benefit of, multinational capital and corporate elites.

Box 1.1 Migrant labour clampdowns in the Southern United States

Efforts by some US politicians to restrict flows of migrant labour have proved to be highly controversial. It is estimated that between 8 and 12 million illegal migrants are living in the US. Many of them originate from Mexico and other parts of Latin America, and have moved to the US in search of work. In response to rising anti-immigrant sentiment, some states in the US, including Arizona and Alabama, have enacted tough laws on undocumented migrants. These give police the powers to arrest anyone they suspect is not a legal resident and, if they cannot supply proof of US citizenship, to detain them with a view to subsequent deportation. In November 2011, Detlev Hager, an executive of the Mercedez-Benz company, which has a factory in Alabama, was detained by police because he only possessed German identity documents. But the main effects of the restrictions have been felt by vulnerable Hispanic migrant workers, many of whom became scared to leave their homes, for fear that they would be picked up by police, detained and deported. Human rights and Hispanic groups have mobilized to campaign against the laws, fearing that they have helped to fuel racism. Legal challenges have resulted in federal judges blocking some of the new laws. One of the effects of the new legislation was to create labour shortages, as workers, fearful of being detained, chose to stay away from their jobs. In Kansas, employers and business groups campaigned against a proposed clampdown, suggesting instead that the state government should take steps to help undocumented migrant workers find jobs.
Sources: *The Economist* (2012); Pilkington (2012).

Seeing globalization as a project helps to capture the 'ideological function' of globalization (Nichols and Sugur 2004), which is designed to uphold the interests of the US, and US corporate interests in particular (Frenkel 2006).

David Harvey (2005: 2) defines neo-liberalism as 'a theory of political economic practices that proposes that human well-being can best be advanced by liberating individual entrepreneurial freedoms and skills within an institutional framework characterized by strong private property rights, free markets and free trade'. Central to neo-liberal ideology is the primacy accorded to free markets; regulation, including regulation of employment relations by states and trade unions, is condemned for imposing constraints on the ability of individuals and companies to contract freely with one another, impeding business competitiveness. This account of globalization as a project, then, equates it with efforts to liberalize trade and open up markets around the world (Kalleberg 2009).

It is not just globalization that we should be concerned with, but a specific kind of globalization – neo-liberal globalization – which has been promoted by international agencies such as the International

Monetary Fund (IMF) and the World Bank and reflects the success of the US, as the dominant international power, in shaping globalization (Hutton 2002). As part of what Stiglitz (2002) refers to as the 'Washington Consensus', governments, particularly those in countries in the Global South, are pressured to liberalize markets, privatize state assets and reduce taxation as a means of stimulating economic growth and competitiveness. In the area of work and employment, the neo-liberal recipe for economic prosperity emphasizes deregulatory policies said to enhance labour market flexibility. Neo-liberal reforms, often operating under the guise of 'structural adjustment programmes', have frequently been imposed on countries in the Global South, particularly in Africa and Latin America, as the price of foreign aid and development. Bolivia, for example, 'served as a social laboratory for the policies of international institutions' for over two decades between the 1980s and 2000s (Kohl and Farthing 2006: 14). Under the auspices of these institutions, successive Bolivian governments implemented a massive process of economic liberalization designed to secure economic stability, described as 'one of the most extreme neoliberal reform programmes the world has seen' (Kohl and Farthing 2006). However, the neo-liberal policies hit the poor particularly hard, and inequality grew markedly as a result of the privatization of state assets. The Bolivian trade union movement also lost much of its power and influence.

The Bolivian experience demonstrates the implications of neo-liberal globalization for work and employment. Privatizations diminish the effectiveness of union movements, whose power base has largely been concentrated in the state sector. Greater labour market flexibility can be a euphemism for reducing labour costs, giving employers more freedom to sack workers, or to erode pay and employment conditions. One of the most profound effects of neo-liberal globalization is the impact of deregulatory policies on work and employment relations. In order to remain competitive, and thus make their countries attractive for investors, governments repress independent trade unions and weaken systems of employment regulation, such as legislation on pay and working conditions, or fail to enforce it effectively. By diminishing the role of the state, and reducing its capacity to regulate employment relations effectively, neo-liberal globalization gives capital more freedom to control wages and labour conditions. From this perspective, globalization needs to be seen as a class project: by privileging the interests of corporate elites, it has been a central feature of, and indeed integral to, the broader neo-liberal effort to 'consolidate capitalist class power' (Harvey 2011: 10).

One of the main ways in which this project of globalization has affected work and employment concerns the growth of income inequality. In the US, for example, in 1975 chief executives of large firms on average earned 23 times the amount of the average pay of production workers and other non-supervisory employees. By the late

2000s, this multiple had risen to 275 (Kalleberg 2011). Globalization has diminished the bargaining power of workers whose jobs are jeopardized by growing international competition. There is a positive association between globalization, as measured by the extent of free trade, and income inequality (Bergh and Nilsson 2010). However, the consequences of globalization by no means affect all countries equally. Inequality has been moderated where relatively robust collective bargaining arrangements with trade unions as a means of determining pay have been maintained, particularly in Western Europe (e.g. Germany, Sweden) (Hayter and Weinberg 2011).

Neo-liberal globalization has also contributed to the spread of informal work and employment around the world. The informal economy is a notable worldwide phenomenon, and is a major source of employment in many parts of the world, especially Asia, Africa and Latin America. For our purposes, the central feature of work in the informal economy is that it falls outside legal and regulatory arrangements that govern employment in the formal sector. Workers are more vulnerable as a result (ILO 2002). Over half of all non-agricultural jobs in the Global South are of an informal nature, involving in excess of 900 million workers. In sub-Saharan Africa and South Asia, the proportion is even higher, with the informal sector providing more than 80 per cent of jobs outside agriculture (OECD 2009). Informal work is often commonplace in urban areas, where workers engage in various small-scale economic activities, including street selling, home-working, waste removal and building construction.

We should expect neo-liberal globalization to diminish the prevalence of informal work. This is because governments which implement market-friendly policies attract investment, thus expanding the formal sector of the economy, which becomes a more important source of employment (Biles 2009; ILO 2002; Hill 2009). In China, and parts of South-East Asia, for example, multinational investment in production facilities, particularly factories making goods for markets in rich countries, has drawn more workers into the formal sector of the economy, particularly young women. However, this has to be set against the compelling evidence that the informal economy has grown under globalization rather than diminished. Neo-liberal economic reforms seem to have played a key part in this process (ILO 2002), as they give companies more freedom to shed labour. Moreover, the restructuring and privatization of state enterprises, designed to make them more competitive, generally involves substantial reductions in employment. In India, for example, the level of informal employment has grown more quickly than the level of employment in the formal sector of the economy. It seems that 'public sector restructuring and efforts by business to maximize labour market flexibility in a bid to be globally and domestically competitive have delivered a decline in regular formal employment and significant growth in unregulated informal forms of employment' (Hill 2009: 404).

Levels of informal employment have also risen across Africa and Latin America, linked to fewer opportunities for regular employment (Biles 2009; ILO 2002). The economic crisis of the early 2000s in Argentina, the result of over a decade of rigorous application of the neo-liberal recipe of privatization and deregulation, saw a massive rise in unemployment, as employers in the formal sector shed jobs on a massive scale. Workers often faced little option but to work informally, given the absence of alternative sources of employment (Whitson 2007). In many parts of the world the expansion of the informal economy is exacerbated by population growth, especially in urban areas, since there are insufficient opportunities for employment in the formal sector to absorb the increasing labour force.

Globalization as a project has encouraged the growth of the informal sector in another way. In their quest for higher profits, multinationals have put increasing pressure on suppliers to produce goods more cheaply. One way in which the cost of labour can be reduced is through the more extensive use of casual, temporary workers, who do not enjoy the same protections as workers employed on a more permanent and formal basis. There is evidence that factories in Asia are making more use of temporary contract workers who, because their employment is more precarious, can be categorized as informal labour (D. Chang 2009). Multinational investment can produce gains for some workers. In the South African fruit industry, for example, international pressure on companies to operate in more ethical and socially responsible ways means that directly employed workers benefit from improvements in labour standards and enjoy greater employment protection. Nevertheless, there has still been an increase in the level of temporary contract labour, as multinational suppliers use informal workers as a key means of securing employment flexibility and enhancing competitiveness (Barrientos and Kritzinger 2004).

When it comes to the Global North, neo-liberal globalization has contributed to the rise of greater insecurity at work (Webster et al. 2008). Increasingly mobile capital, manifest in the growing impact of financialization and anxieties about jobs being 'off-shored' to countries where labour costs are much cheaper, has left workers in Global North countries more vulnerable, with adverse consequences for the quality of their employment. In the US, for example, neo-liberal globalization has encouraged the growth of more 'precarious' employment, as workers experience greater insecurity at work as a result of increases in temporary labour contracts, outsourcing of production and the decline of union representation and long-term benefits, such as pensions and health care (Kalleberg 2011).

Some commentators think that precarious work has become the 'dominant feature of social relations between employers and workers in the contemporary world' (Kalleberg 2009: 17), with adverse consequences for equality and economic well-being, for both individuals and communities. For Standing (2011), neo-liberal globalization has contributed to the rise of a new 'precariat', as more flexible employ-ment patterns, reduced levels of job security and weakened labour market protections render increasing numbers of workers, particularly young workers, migrant workers and black and minority ethnic work-ers, more vulnerable. Economic recession has been responsible for a marked increase in the proportion of workers in part-time and tem-porary employment on an involuntary basis, particularly in Europe. In 2010, more than 80 per cent of temporary workers in Italy, Greece and Spain would have preferred a permanent job (ILO 2012b). Yet some question the extent to which there has been a notable increase in precarious employment associated with globalization. Looking at data from the US, Doogan (2009), for example, claims that there is limited evidence that jobs have become more insecure and, even where they have, this is more likely to be connected to national policy decisions, rather than transnational developments associated with globalization.

Box 1.2 Global economic recession and the jobs crisis

The continuing neo-liberal project of globalization, evident in the emphasis placed on using austerity measures to combat the effects of economic recession, has worked against efforts to reduce government deficits through strategies which pursue growth. This has contributed to a worsening global economic climate and a poorer outlook for jobs. The ILO looks at some of the implications of the deteriorating global conditions for work and jobs around the world in the 2011 and 2012 editions of its *World of Work Report* (ILO 2011, 2012b). It finds that global economic conditions began to worsen again during 2010, some three years after the start of the financial crisis, leading to a slowing down of employment growth in much of the Global North. Elsewhere, though, the prospects for employment growth are rather brighter. Nevertheless, there is still likely to be a major global shortfall of jobs. Moreover, stable jobs, which offer good career prospects, are becoming increasingly rare. Employment is becoming more insecure and precarious, especially for young people. As a result there is potential for greater social unrest, particularly in Europe, the Middle East and North Africa. The ILO calls for governments and international agencies to put a greater emphasis on job creation measures. Whether or not this gets through to policy makers, particularly in Europe, who seem wedded to the pursuit of neo-liberal austerity measures whatever the consequences for growth and jobs, is another matter.

Nevertheless, it is clear that the project of neo-liberal globaliza-tion has had a profound impact on work and employment around the world. Yet some commentators suggest that the financial crisis of the late 2000s means that the whole edifice of neo-liberalism, and the claims it makes for global economic prosperity, have been called into question (Mason 2009). It is evident that an obsessive emphasis on promoting market forces and deregulation contributed to a lax regu-latory framework which both created and exacerbated the economic difficulties. Stiglitz (2010: 216), for example, characterizes the financial crisis as a crisis of neo-liberal globalization, with the blame for it placed squarely on deregulatory policies. Yet neo-liberalism is not to be written off so easily. The dominant interests of multinational corporations in the global economy, particularly their desire to find cheap, flexible and stable locations for production, suggest that neo-liberal policies are not going to be abandoned any time soon (Crouch 2011). Moreover, governments and international financial institutions like the IMF have used the financial and economic crisis as a means of advancing neo-liberal policy solutions – which is somewhat ironic, given that they were largely responsible for causing it! The response of the US, for example, has been dominated by policies which support the interests of finance capital (Harvey 2011). In Europe, deficit reduction programmes, sometimes involving extreme austerity measures, for the most part are based on the neo-liberal assumption that economic competitiveness, and thus prosperity, arises from cutting wages, reducing benefits and weakening employment regulation (see box 1.2).

Globalization as a practice

All that said, however, globalization and neo-liberalism are not synonymous. Whereas deregulation is central to neo-liberal globalization (globalization as a 'project'), thinking about globalization as a 'process' helps us to recognize the limits of the neo-liberal project. In some areas – environmental politics, for example, or the development of international frameworks covering minimum labour standards – globalization is linked to the development of new, transnational regulatory frameworks (Aguiar and Herod 2006; Bartley 2007). Moreover, one of the outcomes of neo-liberal globalization as a project has been the emergence of transnational campaigns and mobilizations by activists which are designed to challenge and resist it (Kingsnorth 2003). While much of the interest in globalization concerns its role as either a process or a project, we also need to recognize the role of workers and other actors in producing globalization; a perspective on globalization which sees it as a practice, one that is constructed and operated by social actors themselves, with the implication that challenges to dominant interests are also characteristics of a globalizing world. This is essentially the position taken by Amoore (2002: 2), who observes that globalization is 'not a single, universal and homogenizing process, nor is it a clearly identifiable strategic project. Rather, it is uniquely understood and experienced by people in the context of their known and familiar social practices.' Workers, managers, trade union representatives, community activists and so on will be affected by, and respond to, globalization in specific ways; and, in turn, through their own experiences and activities, they influence the nature of globalization and how it functions (Webster et al. 2008).

This is evident from factory sites in developing areas of the world, like China, which produce goods for consumers in richer countries. Here we see how the construction of specific gender identities among the largely female workforces are infused by, and yet also help to reproduce, globalization in practice (Pun 2005a). The topic of gender is covered more extensively in chapter 9. As a practice, moreover, globalization is something negotiated and contested, without necessarily having a determinate outcome (Edwards and Wajcman 2005). This is evident from Elger and Smith's study of the implications for work and employment of Japanese multinational investment in Britain (2005: 373). Management practices were not transferred from Japan to be used in the British factories in a straightforward manner. Rather, they were influenced by, and the outcome of, struggles between different groups of managers, and also through 'tacit but somewhat contested bargains with employees'.

Globalization, then, is not something that just happens to working people; it is mediated through, and produced by, the lived identities and experiences of workers themselves. This means that we have to treat resistance to dominant interest groups, and the neo-liberal policies they promote, also as manifestations of globalization. Workers and unions, for example, mobilize to protest against corporate relocation policies that result in plant closures and job losses (Jenkins and Turnbull 2011). Worker activism and resistance to dominant interests, such as multinationals, are integral features of globalization and work. When such challenges emerge, and their features where they do, are clearly related to processes of global economic restructuring and neo-liberal policy imperatives. Yet the meanings that particular groups of workers attach to them, and thus the nature of their responses, will vary from place to place. Viewing globalization as a practice, then, directs our attention to how social actors individually and collectively attach meaning to, and also interpret, broader economic and social processes, thus helping to account for resulting differences in mobilization (Silvey 2003: 150).

1.3 Theorizing globalization and work

Reviewing developments during the 1990s, David Held and his colleagues suggested that there were three main schools of thought when it comes to theorizing globalization: the 'hyper-globalist', globalization 'sceptic' and 'transformationalist' perspectives respectively (Held et al. 1999). Central to the hyper-globalist view is that economic and technological changes associated with globalization have rendered the world increasingly 'borderless' (Ohmae 1999, 2005). Growing levels of cross-border economic activity mean that places, and differences between places, have become much less important. Perhaps the best-known exponent of the hyper-globalist perspective is the US journalist and writer Thomas Friedman. In *The World is Flat*, he contends that the process of globalization, particularly the extensive interconnectedness produced by technological change, has resulted in the world becoming flatter (Friedman 2006). By this he is referring to the way in which globalization has given countries from the Global South opportunities to catch up with their richer counterparts, enabling them to compete on a more level economic playing field, thus helping to erode traditional inequalities between well-off and poorer nations.

The main problem with the hyper-globalist approach relates to the highly exaggerated claims made by its advocates, most of them journalists and management consultants, few of which stand up to close scrutiny. In particular, the extent to which the world has really become flatter is highly questionable. Whereas countries such as China have been more closely integrated into the global economy, other parts of the world, notably much of Africa, remain largely excluded. Not only is the economy highly differentiated internationally, but there is often marked variation within nation-states too, manifest in rising levels of inequality, for example (Hirst et al. 2009; Stiglitz 2010). On this basis, then, while some flattening may have occurred, the world is by no means flat, in the sense of being a level playing field upon which all countries compete on equal terms. It is becoming less flat in places. Indeed, such unevenness is integral to the success of globalization as a project. Capital thrives by exploiting geographical differences, and taking advantage of uneven development (Harvey 2011), exemplified by the extensive use made by multinationals of cheap sources of production in parts of the Global South.

The second school of thought on globalization identified by Held et al. (1999) is that of the 'sceptics', who question the extent to which a genuinely globalized economy exists and stress the pronounced differentiation that persists worldwide. Hirst et al.'s (2009) book *Globalization in Question* is the most prominent sceptical text. The authors recognize that the economy has become more internationalized; but they emphasize that this is by no means the same as saying it has been globalized in the manner described by the hyper-globalists. There has been an expansion in the level of international trade; the extent of cross-border financial transactions has increased; and the role of multinational companies has become more important. All these are signs of an increasingly internationalized economy, albeit by no means unprecedented. But we are far from seeing a genuinely globalized economy, with national borders and differences between nations being rendered superfluous. The international economy is highly differentiated and uneven. International flows of finance, trade and investment are still largely concentrated among a relatively small number of rich nations or groups of nations. Far from becoming genuinely transnational entities, in the sense of operating without recourse to national economies, multinational companies generally retain strong connections with their home-country base, particularly with regard to employment and research, and demonstrate a strong domestic orientation (Hirst et al. 2009).

The third school of thought that has been applied to understanding globalization is the transformationalist approach. As the name suggests, the focus of transformationalist writers is on the radical changes to economies and societies which globalization has unleashed. It is viewed as the 'central driving force behind the rapid social, political and economic changes that are reshaping modern societies and world order' (Held et al. 1999: 7). There is an emphasis on how the world is being transformed by globalization, and recognizing the consequences of this transformation (e.g. Giddens 1990; Castells 2000, 2001; Beck 2000; Scholte 2005). Transformationalist writers 'map the scale and complexity of worldwide social relations across all dimensions, from the economic to the cultural, arguing that their historically unprecedented extensity and intensity represents a significant "global shift" in the social organization of human affairs' (Held and McGrew 2007: 169). Given the contribution they make to extending and deepening worldwide interconnectedness, developments in information and communications technologies are seen as central to the transformation of human affairs under globalization (Frenkel 2006; Held and McGrew 2007).

Transformationalists reject the view held by globalization sceptics that the effects of global changes have been exaggerated; however, unlike the hyper-globalizers, who emphasize that the world is becoming flatter, they make no claim that globalization has a specific trajectory or end-point (Held and McGrew 2007; Martell 2010). That said, however, the transformationalist approach is marked by some specific features. Transformationalists argue that the process of globalization is producing a more complex world, one which demands new models of economic and political governance (Held and McGrew 2007; Scholte 2005). Linked to this, they emphasize how greater global interconnectedness, by reducing the significance of differences between specific national territories, has affected the way in which states regulate affairs within borders which are becoming porous if not demolished (Held and McGrew 2007). Increasingly mobile capital, for example, means that the traditional territorial basis of nation-states has become more and more redundant (Beck 2000).

Three main implications for work and employment under globalizing conditions are evident. The first concerns the development of new transnational arrangements for regulating work. Transformationalist writers are particularly interested in the rise of 'more global political forms' (Martell 2010: 22), manifest in novel and complex transnational governance arrangements (Held and McGrew 2007). This is evident from the increasing role being played by non-state and other transnational actors in regulating work and employment matters across national borders (e.g. Bartley 2007). Many multinationals, for example, operate codes of conduct designed to establish minimum labour standards across their supplier network, the content of which is often influenced by conventions of the ILO, an agency of the United Nations. The second implication of the transformationalist perspective concerns the weakened role envisaged for trade unions. Since organized labour movements largely operate within nation-states, their power and influence is bound to diminish in a more globalized environment where the traditional territorial basis of ordering society is being challenged (Beck 2000). Moreover, under globalization, work has become more individualized and flexible; this fragmentation serves to erode the established ties on which collective organized labour depended for its power (e.g. Castells 2000). Thirdly, globalization also involves the development of novel types of collective action, in the form of 'new social movements' (discussed in chapter 5), which operate within a globalized frame of action and are concerned with such matters as identity politics, environmental challenges and labour issues.

One of the most prominent features of a globalizing world, then, is the development of a more 'cosmopolitan democracy' (Held 1995), which captures the increasingly complex and multi-level character of popular participation and collective action. Perhaps the most obvious example concerns the challenge to global capitalism that has come from the 'anti-globalization' movement (e.g. Kingsnorth 2003) – an ironic label, given that, from a transformationalist perspective, anti-globalization campaigns are themselves prominent manifestations of globalization (Held and McGrew 2007). Resistance to the dominance of global capital has been driven by transnational activists, international movements and non-governmental organizations (NGOs), based around initiatives such as the World Social Forum (e.g. Tarrow 2005). In the field of work and employment, the most notable manifestation of this emergent cosmopolitan democracy is the activities of transnational networks of labour rights activists; these campaign extensively to improve labour rights and working conditions across multinationals' global supply chains (Seidman 2007) – see box 1.3.

Undoubtedly, elements of the transformationalist perspective make an important contribution to understanding globalization and work, for example by drawing attention to the development of new transnational arrangements for regulating labour. However, some of its proponents, notably Beck (2000) and Castells (2000, 2001), posit a highly exaggerated and rather misleading view of changes in labour markets, one that sees the influence of a rampant global capitalism evident in the dramatic rise of more flexible and individualized forms of employment and the decline of organized labour (Doogan 2009). Transformationalists tend to pay rather little attention to labour movements. Yet trade union organizations are currently making more determined efforts to organize effectively on a transnational basis, and to confront global capital (e.g. Anner et al. 2006; Croucher and Cotton

Box 1.3 Transnational labour advocacy – the Clean Clothes Campaign

The Clean Clothes Campaign is one of the most prominent transnational networks of activist organizations which mobilize around work and labour issues. Established in 1989, and based in the Netherlands, it operates as an alliance of fifteen national-level European organizations, and works with partners such as unions, NGOs, community activists and women's groups in garment-producing countries (e.g. Cambodia, Vietnam, Indonesia, Sri Lanka, Bangladesh) (Ross 2012). The Clean Clothes Campaign states that it is 'dedicated to improving working conditions and supporting the empowerment of workers in the global garment and sportswear industries'. It works with local partners to promote improvements in workers' rights and labour standards in factories which supply major multinational retailers, such as Tesco, Walmart and Aldi. In conjunction with Asia Floor Wage, an alliance of Asian organizations that campaigns to increase workers' pay, in February 2012 the Clean Clothes Campaign, and its UK affiliate Labour Behind the Label, helped to convene a 'people's tribunal' in Cambodia. This two-day hearing took evidence from workers about low pay, excessive working hours and unhealthy working conditions in factories making products for companies such as H&M, Gap and Adidas. As an awareness-raising exercise, the purpose of the event was to add to the pressure being put on multinational retailers and brands to ensure that garments sold under their names are produced without the extreme exploitation of workers.

Sources: Clean Clothes Campaign website, www.cleanclothes.org; Butler (2012). (Unless otherwise stated, websites cited were last accessed on 29 April 2013.)

2009). It is odd that many in the transformationalist camp, which puts so much emphasis on the indeterminate impact of globalization and on the development of more complex transnational arrangements for governing economic and political affairs, neglect the capacity for organized labour movements to operate in a more interconnected, globalized manner.

Clearly, the transformationalist perspective offers some important insights about work and employment under globalizing conditions, notwithstanding its neglect of organized labour movements. During the 2000s, though, theoretical interest has largely been concerned with explaining the persistence of cross-national diversity in work and employment relations, in the face of the strong convergence pressures which are associated with globalization. The concept of convergence is by no means new. It was originally used as far back as the 1960s to capture the way in which common economic trends and technological developments were claimed to be responsible for greater uniformity in the employment systems of countries across the Global North, particularly increases in skill levels and more consensual relationships between workers and employers (Kerr et al. 1962). Such a 'universalistic' approach was also evident in the rise of post-industrial thinking during the 1970s and 1980s, centred upon claims of a common trend of greater knowledge work and skill enhancement (Gallie 2007).

Globalization, however, has stimulated renewed interest in convergence. Greater economic interconnectedness is held to have generated increased uniformity with the deregulated, neo-liberal model of capitalism evident in Anglo-Saxon countries such as the US and UK, and propagated by international agencies like the IMF. In an increasingly open, globalized world, the capacity of individual nation-states to regulate work and employment effectively is diminished, particularly given the power of supposedly 'footloose' multinationals to secure a favourable policy environment. Countries have little option other than to pursue policies of labour flexibility, employment deregulation, decentralized pay bargaining and weakened trade unions, since these are viewed as essential to attracting multinational investment and competing effectively in the global economy. Moreover, the reduced importance of national borders allows multinationals greater scope to develop and disseminate company-specific human resource management techniques, particularly those relating to the organization of work, such as teamworking and performance management, and thus to act as agents of convergence (Frenkel 2006; Rubery and Grimshaw 2003). The more competitive environment associated with globalization means that firms come under pressure to operate a common set of 'best practice' arrangements, so-called because they are seen as the most economically efficient, for organizing and managing work activities, regardless of the context in which they operate. Consequently, national differences in work and employment have become less important under globalization (Wailes et al. 2011).

However, the persistence of cross-national diversity in the face of strong convergence pressures is a notable feature of work and employment under globalizing conditions. This implies a concern with divergence rather than, or perhaps as well as, convergence. For many psychologists and management writers, deep-rooted and intangible cultural factors, such as values, beliefs, attitudes and perceptions of authority, formality and equality, are the most important source of cross-national diversity (e.g. Hofstede 2001). For example, the existence of a distinctive 'Asian' model of managing people at work has been posited, based on a shared cultural understanding that favours collectivism and consensus.

Others, though, emphasize the key role played by nation-states, and their distinctive institutional arrangements, in upholding cross-national diversity – consistent with a sceptical take on globalization. Despite experiencing similar global economic pressures, governments retain considerable discretion over the policies they adopt in responding to them (Wailes et al. 2011). The rhetoric of globalization is often used by national governments as an excuse for failing to pursue policies at odds with the prevailing neo-liberal consensus (Hirst et al. 2009). Moreover, in some ways globalization has enhanced the power of nation-states. Global capital relies upon governments to provide supportive environments in which business can thrive. For example, the governments of Asian countries like the Philippines have developed specific sets of interventions, including policies designed to produce a quiescent labour force, in order to attract international capital (Kelly 2001). Globalization has not made the role of the nation-state redundant; rather, it has altered how states operate. Under globalization, nation-states function not so much as all-encompassing sources of regulation and law, but as legitimators of diverse sources of regulatory authority (Hirst et al. 2009). This is evident, for example, in the efforts of governments to develop and support multinational codes of conduct concerned with labour standards (Bartley 2007).

Box 1.4 The importance of divergence – the rise of New Public Management

Many countries around the world have looked to enact radical reforms to how public services (health, education, public administration, etc.) are organized, in pursuit of greater effectiveness and efficiency gains. The concept of the 'New Public Management' (NPM) has been popularly used as a generic label for such reform initiatives (e.g. Pollitt and Bouckaert 2011). An NPM approach is characterized by a number of features: the privatization and outsourcing of public services to private suppliers; the greater use of market incentives rather than bureaucratic arrangements in the delivery of public services; and the more extensive utilization of private-sector managerial techniques. It has the strong potential to undermine established work and employment relations arrangements across the public services: for example by weakening trade union organization. The rise of the NPM approach around the world would therefore seem to herald a major degree of convergence when it comes to the nature of work and employment in the public services. However, notwithstanding manifold efforts to reform public services, there is no evidence to support claims that a process of global convergence around a common NPM model is occurring. Instead, reform efforts are marked by considerable 'diversity and variation' (Bach and Bordogna 2011: 2286). Processes of reform and restructuring are 'embedded in, and mediated by, country-specific legal, institutional and cultural traditions' (Bach and Bordogna 2011: 2283). Not only does this raise the question about whether a distinctive NPM approach can be said to exist at all, but also it also demonstrates the importance of divergence in the global economy.

The resilience of nation-states, and of national-level employment regimes, implies the persistence of cross-national diversity in work and employment. There has long been a concern with how matters such as country-specific labour laws and arrangements for coordinating relationships between employers and unions (so-called 'societal effects') influence organizational practice (e.g. Maurice et al. 1986). However, during the 2000s there was much interest evinced in how institutions – 'patterns of human action and relationships that persist and reproduce themselves over time, independently of the biological individuals performing within them' (Crouch 2005: 10) – helped to sustain divergence, in the face of seemingly strong convergence pressures (see box 1.4). Rooted in the field of comparative political economy, the institutionalist perspective is principally concerned with how institutions – political agencies, legal structures, business systems, corporate governance mechanisms and employment arrangements, particularly methods of skills training and pay determination – account for the persistence of capitalist diversity. Such differentiation gives rise to different varieties, or models, of capitalism (e.g. Amable 2003; Coates 2000; Hall and Soskice 2001; Whitley 2000), from which ideal-types can be derived.

Perhaps the most well-known classification scheme is Hall and Soskice's (2001) 'varieties of capitalism' (VoC) model. Their actor-centred approach focuses on the role of firms, and how the national-level institutional environment in which they operate affects their behaviour and interactions. The principal challenge is one of coordination, across five different areas of business activity: employment relations, vocational education and training, corporate governance, inter-firm relations and the management of employees. Two broad approaches to tackling the challenge of coordination are identified, giving rise to two ideal-types – or 'varieties' – of capitalism. In liberal market economies like the UK, Ireland and the US, the emphasis is on the role of markets in resolving problems of coordination. In these countries, work and employment matters are relatively lightly regulated by law, with the emphasis on promoting labour market flexibility and on encouraging firms to take responsibility for their own arrangements in a largely decentralized system. While liberal market economies tend to have a fairly good record in creating new jobs, this comes at the expense of above-average levels of low pay and inequality, inadequate systems of employment protection and weak trade unions. In coordinated market economies such as Germany and Sweden, however, there is more emphasis on using non-market mechanisms for resolving problems of coordination. Typically such countries operate systems of work and employment which are more regulated and centralized than their liberal market counterparts, particularly over matters like skills training, with greater support evident for unions.

The VoC approach has stimulated a considerable amount of debate, and has been the subject of much analysis (e.g. Crouch 2005; Hancké et al. 2007; Hancké 2009). Gallie (2007) contends that it focuses too much on the role of employers, and the nature of their 'production regimes'. He develops an alternative method of conceptualizing cross-national diversity based on institutional differences. His concept of an 'employment regime' captures the important extent to which cross-national diversity is contingent upon matters such as the system of employment relations and the nature of the relationship between the state and organized labour movements. In countries with 'inclusive' regimes, such as Sweden, there is an emphasis on promoting equitable employment arrangements, across the workforce in general, propelled by high trade union density and widespread collective bargaining coverage. By contrast, dualist employment regimes, of which Germany is a prominent example, are characterized by a concern with promoting strong employment rights and protections for certain types of 'core' workers, generally men in full-time jobs, whereas others, such as women working part-time, tend to be more disadvantaged. In countries like the UK, which are characterized by 'market' employment regimes, trade unions are weak, and the law generally plays a limited role in regulating work and employment relationships. Drawing on evidence about job quality (e.g. skill levels, task discretion, job security) taken mainly from countries in Western Europe, Gallie (2007) concludes that a universalistic explanation, consistent with convergence, accounts for some trends, such as changes in skill levels, while the VoC ('production regime') approach is useful in accounting for variations in task discretion. Overall, however, the employment regime model is of most use when it comes to explaining cross-national differences in work quality.

Institutionalist explanations for divergence tend to attract two main criticisms. One is that they are too parsimonious (Crouch 2005). In other words, no classification scheme can ever be sensitive enough to capture the capitalist diversity evident around the world. As a result, they tend to over-simplify, being concerned mainly with a small number of countries from the Global North. Some stress the need to increase the number of categories, so that countries which are often neglected by such models, like the emerging economies of Latin America, can be included (Boyer 2005). Others, though, draw on different criteria to construct their own multidimensional approach to capturing capitalist diversity (e.g. Amable 2003). While increasing the number of categories helps to deal with the problem of parsimony, using too many will mean that the model loses its capacity to account for diversity (Hamann and Kelly 2008). A second problem with the focus on institutions is that it offers a perspective which is too static and deterministic (Crouch 2005). In other words, the nature of a particular country's model of capitalism can simply be read off from its institutional arrangements, which, given their relative durability, militates against the prospect of major challenges. This can mean that the actions of workers and unions to challenge institutional systems and bring about change come to be overlooked (Hamann and Kelly 2008).

Box 1.5 The limits of convergence – the case of Walmart

From modest beginnings in Bentonville, in the state of Arkansas, the US retailer Walmart has grown rapidly to become the largest retailer in the world. It operates some 4,000 stores in the US alone; 93 per cent of American households shop in one of its outlets at least once a year. As well as its US home base, Walmart operates stores in many countries, including Mexico, India, Japan, Canada, China and the UK, where it owns the Asda chain, employing 1.6 million workers in total (Fishman 2007). Its dominance has largely been built on being able to offer competitively priced goods, as a result of operating a low-cost model of business, which includes an emphasis on reducing employment costs. This is evident from the company's pronounced hostility to trade union organization in its US stores (Krauss 2005; Ortega 1999), and the fact that it has been the subject of numerous legal claims alleging infractions of labour legislation, including persistent allegations of gender discrimination in its employment practices. Its global dominance notwithstanding, though, Walmart has found it difficult to impose its preferred non-union approach to managing employment relations in its operations outside North America. For example, after ten years of decreasing success in Germany, in 2006 it pulled out of the country entirely, partly because it could not adapt to an environment where trade unions enjoy a prominent influence (Christopherson 2007). Walmart has been obliged to recognize unions in its stores in other countries, including Brazil and China. This illustrates the potency of national-level influences on work and employment relations arrangements, and the limits of convergence.

Whatever the problems with institutional models of capitalist diversity, their strength comes from the way in which they demonstrate that globalization does not generate a straightforward process of convergence. While we should not entirely reject the idea of convergence, we do need to adopt a more sophisticated and nuanced view of how it operates. For one thing, there may be different routes to convergence (Baccaro and Howell 2011). Moreover, the speed of convergence can vary. In countries like Sweden and Germany, for example, pressures to enact deregulatory, neo-liberal measures are evident, but their pace has been moderated by the presence of robust institutional structures which remain supportive of trade unions and collective bargaining (see box 1.5). The idea that convergence pressures co-exist with cross-national diversity is central to the concept of 'converging divergences' (Katz and Darbishire 2000). This approach recognizes that there is evidence of convergence across countries, evident in weakened trade unions for example. However, convergence is more prevalent in sectors of the economy which are more open to international competition, and marked by the presence of multinationals. Moreover, there are also different trajectories of convergence – a process of 'converging on divergence' – with the sector effect being especially prominent. In some industries, particularly in services for example, there is a greater emphasis on a low-wage, anti-union model of organizing work and employment. In others, such as vehicle manufacturing, however, the characteristic pattern of convergence is rather different, being marked by a more pronounced emphasis on firms working co-operatively with trade unions, in a way designed to enhance competitiveness. When it comes to the impact of globalization on work and employment, then, it 'is not a question of convergence or diversity, but of convergence and diversity' (Marginson and Sisson 2004: 21).

1.4 Grounding globalization and work

The approaches discussed so far all share a top-down approach to understanding globalization, focusing on the role of transnational actors, such as multinationals, international agencies and NGOs, and the implications of globalization for nation-states. A more comprehensive view of globalization and work, however, also needs to acknowledge the grounded, bottom-up implications of globalization, consistent with viewing it as a practice, rather than just a top-down process or neo-liberal project driven from above (Burawoy et al. 2000). How globalization affects workplaces and local communities cannot be attributed just to the actions of multinational companies, but is also a function of workers' and managers' own actions within specific places and contexts (Webster et al. 2008).

A grounded approach to understanding globalization and work encompasses three particular perspectives. First, the focus of 'global ethnographers' is on understanding 'globalization from below', with the emphasis placed on how working people experience globalization in specific environments, filtered through the lived relations and shared experiences of class, gender and ethnicity (e.g. Burawoy 2001; Burawoy et al. 2000). Since people's circumstances, and how they experience and attach meaning to them, will vary from location to location, there is a strong emphasis on the diversity of responses to globalization (Frenkel 2006). More than that, global ethnographers treat workers as subjects who play an integral part in producing globalization in specific places, rather than just as objects affected by it: 'Globalization is produced and consumed not in thin air, not in some virtual reality but in real organizations, institutions, communities etc.' (Burawoy 2001: 148). Perhaps the most notable example of how the global ethnography perspective has been used to illuminate the topic of globalization and work concerns studies of women factory workers in parts of the Global South, such as Indonesia and Malaysia (Ong 1987; Wolf 1994). The experiences of these women, particularly family relations, influence how they react and attach meaning to their working lives in the factory, shaping the nature of their responses to their jobs. Global ethnographers are especially concerned with understanding the complex and dynamic process of identity construction among workers in factories making products for international markets. This often involves the production of new, highly gendered identities, which draw on women's shared experiences of, and the meanings they attach to, their patriarchal family backgrounds, the nature of their work, including the management regime, and their aspirations in life (e.g. Pun 2005a; Salzinger 2003). See chapter 9 for more on the topic of gender.

Second, a grounded approach to understanding globalization and work helps us to appreciate that globalization is produced by workers and managers in specific places – workplaces and communities, in particular. This implies taking a geographical perspective on globalization, one that acknowledges the importance of space, place and scale. Writers on globalization often focus on the spatial dimensions of global interconnectedness. Multinationals, for example, enhance their power by exploiting geographical space, based on their capacity to operate in a way that transcends national borders. By re-locating to another country, or at least threatening to re-locate, supposedly 'footloose' multinationals can ensure that work and employment arrangements meet their own firm-specific requirements, eroding the discrete characteristics of different places around the world (Bauman 1998a). Yet this is rather over-simplistic. Capital still has to manifest itself in specific places; how multinationals benefit from exploiting spatial difference, and thus the nature of their particular 'spatial fixes' (Harvey 1982), is driven by variation between places (Webster et al. 2008). If place did not matter, then spatial fixes would not be needed.

Understanding globalization and work, then, means that we need to be aware of the importance of specific places, not least because they are where globalization, in its different manifestations, is produced. The 'result is that rather than location becoming increasingly irrelevant in a shrinking globe, the specificities of location actually become *more* important' (Herod et al. 2007: 250). For example, much of the economic activity associated with globalization is concentrated in specific urban centres – so-called 'global cities' (Sassen 1991) – the 'locations in which the global economy is in good part organized, serviced, and financed' (Sassen 2007: 32–3). Members of the transnational corporate class, and their associates, concentrate in such key locations as New York, London, Dubai, Hong Kong and Singapore, serviced by a host of cleaners, waiters, domestic servants and security staff (Perrons 2004). The work of cleaners, for example, is integral to the production and reproduction of globalization within global cities (Aguiar and Herod 2006).

Places are clearly important under globalization; but it is important to recognize the 'relational' nature of place (Ward 2007). What this means is that specific places do not exist in isolation from one another; rather, they are related through transnational economic and social flows, something that globalization has clearly accentuated. This does not simply mean that places are becoming more interconnected, but that they are becoming more interdependent. What 'goes into making a place unique has as much to do with distant events, processes and institutions as it has to do with those things that happen nearby' (Ward 2007: 270). Places are important, to be sure, but we need to bear in mind that work activities undertaken in them are influenced by the broader spatial relations of production that characterize worldwide interconnectedness (Jones 2008).

In order to understand globalization properly, we also need to be aware of its multi-scalar character (Herod et al. 2007). In other words, places and space combine in a complex and dynamic way that produces globalization at a variety of levels. This is evident when we consider the experience of migrant workers in London. They are generally employed in highly localized, place-specific service sector jobs, including hotel work and in hospitals, in a way that seems far removed from the globalized economy. Yet the workers are recruited on a transnational basis, from a variety of different countries; and the agencies that hire them operate at a global level: 'Thus, although consumer services by definition are tied to specific localities, the labour force involved in the production and exchange of consumer services increasingly is assembled across a wide spatial scale, and so is an international, if not global, labour force' (McDowell et al. 2008: 753).

The third way in which a grounded perspective enables us to develop a more complete understanding of globalization and work is by drawing our attention to the way in which globalization is a contested process (e.g. Edwards and Wajcman 2005). Taking a 'critical globalist' (Held and McGrew 2007) view directs our attention to how power relations and the potential for conflict are integral elements of globalization, particularly when it comes to understanding globalization and work. The key concern of the 'dominant interests' approach to understanding globalization, for example, is with identifying the power resources of multinational companies, and how they use their power to influence government policies, shape consumer preferences and undermine organized labour (Frenkel 2006). Viewing globalization as a contested process, however, means being concerned with the ways in which workers and unions resist and challenge dominant power interests. This is apparent from the experience of Electrolux, which has made full and effective use of the opportunities provided by globalization to undermine employment conditions and insecurity through its own 'spatial fix'. Yet workers across its sites mobilized to challenge the company's actions, by creating global alliances with Electrolux workers in other countries and by working alongside sympathetic community organizations to fight job-cutting measures (Webster et al. 2008). Thus a grounded view of globalization helps us to recognize that globalization involves, and indeed is the product of, struggles for power between different interest groups, particularly (multinational) capital and labour.

1.5 Conclusion

We have used this first chapter to explore the concept of globalization, and consider the implications of a more globalized world for work and employment. This involves taking a multidimensional perspective on globalization (see Amoore 2002), recognizing that it can be viewed as a process of greater worldwide interconnectedness, as a political project designed to advance neo-liberal policies and as a social phenomenon which is not just influenced and reflected by actors in distinct workplaces and communities, but actively produced and reproduced by them in dynamic ways. While the transformationalist approach offers a sophisticated analysis of social change in a globalizing world, particularly by highlighting the transnational dimension of governance structures and the development of new patterns of mobilization, its proponents' disregard for organized labour, and the exaggerated nature of some of their claims, mean that it has to be treated with a certain element of caution. Evidence of convergence pressures notwithstanding, the resilience of cross-national diversity is a notable feature of work and employment in a globalizing environment. In order to understand globalization and work properly, though, we cannot just rely on approaches which offer a top-down perspective – those concerned with how actors, processes and structures have been affected by globalization. A grounded approach is also needed, one which highlights the lived experiences of workers, managers and others, and how they produce and reproduce work activities in specific workplaces; recognizes the dynamic way in which work is related to geographical concepts of space, place and scale; and acknowledges the importance of power relations and the contested basis of work under globalization.

Further reading

For globalization in general, the key texts are Held and McGrew (2007) and Hirst et al. (2009). When it comes to theorizing globalization and work, we have drawn on some of the insights provided by Stephen Frenkel (2006). Perhaps the most insightful existing book on globalization and work is Webster et al. (2008). For specific details of work and employment developments on an international scale, the ILO publications are recommended: www.ilo.org/global/lang--en/index.htm. Its Global Reports, including an annual review of the *World of Work*, are particularly useful: www.ilo.org/global/research/global-reports/lang--en/index.htm.

2 Consumption, work and identity in a globalizing world

2.1 Introduction

In this chapter we will look at the relationship between consumption, work and identity in the context of a globalizing world. Whilst there have been a number of studies of the relationships between work, consumption and identity in the context of Global North societies – most notably Paul du Gay's *Consumption and Identity at Work* (1996) and Catherine Casey's *Work, Self and Society* (1995) – in this chapter we will attempt to look at the topic from a global and globalizing perspective. To do this we will first examine the core concepts of consumption and consumerism, then look at the consumption–work–identity relationship in the context of two globalized producer–consumer relationships.

The first is offshore call centre work, a case which, on the surface, looks as if there is a simple export of Global North labour regimes and practices onto Global South economic structures. As we shall see, this is not a simple process of imposing a new pattern on old forms, but is a complex situation in which globalization of production is engaged in by individuals and groups in different ways and, often, with resistance. The second is the emergence of fair trade and ethical consumption, a new form of consumption in Global North societies where ethics concerning the conditions of production and the rewards for production become a significant factor in consumer choice. As with the example of call centres, we see significant changes to labour practices and organization as a result of this globalized producer–consumer relationship, but these changes are often tempered by other global factors, and must always be understood with reference to local contexts.

It has become almost axiomatic to say that the Global North, and particularly the UK, have become societies characterized by consumption rather than production, that such societies are now *consumer societies* (Bauman 1998a). What do we mean by this? The idea of a consumer society has been around for a long time, and we can see how the concept has shifted and changed across the years – from being a derogatory term implying a society of indolence, to being one that describes the main imperatives that capitalism presents to us and the chief hope for global economic recovery. But such stark statements hide complexities that we need to untangle and trace if we are to produce an adequate sociological understanding of contemporary societal and global trends in work and lifestyles.

2.2 A consumer society? Consumption in a globalized world

In earlier years, when production, not consumption, was the main consideration in understanding self, consciousness and identity, we can see that questions of status and self-worth could be determined by reflecting on the way that an individual, or a group, was related to production: were they productive or unproductive? This clearly leads to one form of inequality, and is also a reflection of a determinant of inequality: those excluded from the productive process, such as pensioners, housewives or the unemployed, were likely to suffer from negative characterization by others, and from a much lower standard of living. Yet the vast majority of the adult population in most Global North countries were included in the various parts of the productive process, and could identify their position within this. Other identifiers of status could be brought to bear – gender, wealth, culture, conspicuous consumption, membership of exclusive societies – but, ultimately, these were subsidiaries to that core identifying feature: productive or unproductive. Sociologists identified the construction of self around this relationship to production; classic studies, such as the 1960s examination of the 'affluent worker' (Goldthorpe et al. 1968, 1969), alongside classical sociological theories, such as that of Karl Marx (1975) or the structural functionalism of Talcott Parsons (1937, 1951), did the same. According to these studies and theories, people understood themselves, and were understood by others, in terms of what they 'did'.

In contrast, a consumer society encourages a wholly different sense of self, self-worth, consciousness and identity, and generates quite different forms of inequality. As Bauman notes, the society of consumers is a kind of society which 'interpellates', speaks to and shapes, its members

> ... primarily in their capacity of consumers. While doing that, 'society' ... expects to be heard, listened to and obeyed; it evaluates – rewards and penalizes – its members depending on the promptness and propriety of their response to the interpellation. As a result, the places gained or allocated on the axis of excellence/ineptitude in consumerist performance turn into the paramount stratifying factor and the principal criterion of inclusion and exclusion, as well as guiding the distribution of social esteem and stigma, and shares in public attention. The 'society of consumers' ... stands for the kind of society that promotes, encourages or enforces the choice of a consumerist lifestyle and life strategy and dislikes all alternative cultural options. (Bauman 2007: 52–3)

The consequences of this shift to a mature consumer society, which took place in the post-war years and accelerated in the 1980s and 1990s, have been manifold and significant in almost all parts of social,

Box 2.1 Global consumption, global inequality

Global consumption figures are by their very nature quite staggering: private consumption by households topped $20 trillion in 2000, a fourfold increase over 1960 (in 1995 dollars) (source: Worldwatch, www. worldwatch.org/node/810, accessed 4 July 2012). Some of this rise is due to the dramatic increase in the population of the world, from 3 billion in 1960 to 7 billion in 2000, but the global consumption figure also indicates a shift towards consumerism around the globe.

Consumption growth indicates an increase in affluence, but this increase is not evenly spread across the globe, or across specific populations. World Bank figures (World Bank 2008) show that the poorest 10 per cent of the global population had a 0.5 per cent share of the world's private consumption, while the richest 10 per cent had a 59 per cent share.

Is there a link between globalization and global inequality? This is a very difficult question to answer as it depends on so many different variables, and so many different measures. Milanovic's exhaustive survey of attempts to measure global inequality and address this question concludes that it is simply not possible to say, because globalization affects inequalities among individuals in different ways. However, a consistent trend has been for income distributions to become more unequal in all societies, rich and poor, around the world (Milanovic 2005: 20). The OECD, only looking at its thirty developed member states, also found that there had been an increase in income inequality – an average increase of 2 Gini points (the best measure of inequality) in the past twenty years: 'This is the same as the current difference in inequality between Germany and Canada – a noticeable difference, but not one that would justify to talk about the breakdown of society' (OECD 2008: 15).

In the UK there has been a similar pattern over the past twenty-or-so years:

> Over the 20th century the distribution of wealth in the UK became more equal. In 1911, it is estimated that the wealthiest 1 per cent of the population held around 70 per cent of the total UK wealth. After World War Two this proportion had fallen to 42 per cent in 1960. Using a different methodology and data source, during the 1970s and the 1980s the share of the wealthiest 1 per cent of the population is estimated to have fallen from 22 per cent in the late 1970s to reach 17 to 18 per cent during the second half of the 1980s. Since the beginning of the 1990s the distribution appears to have widened again. HM Revenue and Customs estimates indicate that in 2002 the wealthiest 1 per cent of the population owned 23 per cent of total marketable wealth. (ONS 2010: 62)

cultural, political and economic life (see box 2.1). The interconnections between these facets of society are multiple and complex, and our complicated forms of consumption and attachment of meaning to consumption emerge from this interplay. At the core, however, are the economic conditions, and the rise in affluence in Western industrial societies in recent years (something which has dramatically halted and started to reverse in most European economies) has led to individuals being able to consume for purposes other than purely subsistence (Ransome 2005: 5). The consequence of this, as Slater notes, is that 'the meaningful or cultural aspect of consumption comes to predominate, and people become more concerned with the meanings of goods than with their functional use to meet a basic or "real" need' (Slater 1997: 133). The consumption of goods becomes a central component in the construction of identities, but identities themselves, like goods, are things to be 'appropriated and possessed, but only in order to be consumed, and so to disappear again. As in the case of marketed consumer goods, consumption of an identity should not – must not – extinguish the desire for other, new and improved identities, nor preclude the ability to absorb them' (Bauman 1998b: 29).

In this chapter we will focus on one specific relationship – that between the producer and the consumer. We consider how the shift to mass consumption and increasing affluence has become intimately linked with globalization. Yet consumption attached to the pleasure of consumption itself is something that serves to obscure the relationship between producer and consumer, making it difficult to get to the bottom of the relationship.

The traces and trappings of consumer society surround us: advertisements with exhortations to consume, lifestyle media productions that guide our consumption choices, increased consumer credit, a myriad of goods, services and products. But the consumption imperative goes much deeper than just providing impetus to lifestyle choices. There are three major consequences of the shift towards a society of consumers. The first is that our sense of self and identity changes as we become more focused on consumption rather than production. The second is that the consumption imperative becomes embedded in all aspects of social life including, most significantly here, employment; again, this is something that has consequences for work and the labour process. Finally, the shift towards developed societies becoming consumer societies is achieved through other societies becoming, initially, advanced production societies before, inevitably, becoming societies of consumers themselves. We can observe how this process is beginning to operate in the changing and increasingly westernized lifestyles of richer people in China and India, for example.

It is easy to forget or ignore consumption in everyday life, particularly in a society which is infused with imperatives to consume, and crammed full of opportunities to do so. The spread of the consumption imperative from private purchasing to public-sector structures, and the change in identity orientations, from producer to consumer, has been a recurring theme in recent decades, such that we now rarely notice when it is being done to us. At a mundane level, these changes can be seen in the UK in the ways that, for example, travellers and commuters are referred to as customers not passengers, and students are reminded that they are 'consuming' their degree courses through paying ever higher fees. Not only that, consumer spending in many Global North countries is seen as the salvation for economic, and even political, crises. Following the 7/7 suicide bomber attacks in London, British Prime Minister Tony Blair exhorted citizens to rally round and keep consuming, a significant shift from the World War 2 slogan of 'digging for victory'.

At the time of writing (2012), a significant component of the UK government's strategy to revive a stalled economy is through con-sumer spending. Yet so inured are we to consuming as a part of our lives, and consuming more and different things, that we easily forget that our consumption entails someone else's production, someone else's *work*, often at a great distance from us geographically. Similarly, we rarely reflect on the form that these relationships of producer and consumer take; it is too easy to see these are being 'merely' economic or technical. Yet, as Frank Mort points out, drawing on the ideas of Michel Foucault, relations of power are external to differing types of relationships (including economic processes). This means that power relations in the field of consumption are not simply the reflection of other relations, 'they are integral to this arena: the product of the combined effect of its knowledges and strategies, alliances, social movements, resistances and forms of experience' (Mort 1997: 30). We need to see the relationship of producer to consumer in ways which will reveal these power relations.

In this chapter, we will do this by focusing on two interconnected things. The first is the export of Global North labour process regimes and practices into Global South economic structures. As stated at the beginning of the chapter, this is not a simple process of imposing a new pattern on old forms, but a complex situation of responses and changes. We will look at this in the context of the dramatic and rapid expansion of the call centre industry in India. The second object of inquiry is the emergence of new forms of ethical consumption in socie-ties of the Global North.

2.3 Consumption and identity in the workplace

The importance of identity to work, of identity construction in work-places and the complexity of identity dynamics have been well documented by sociologists of work (Kondo 1990; Casey 1995; du Gay 1996; Sennett 1998). Many commentators and research studies have found that attitudes and behaviour at work are shaped, at least in part, by the intersection of different foci of identity, most notably occupa-tional identity, gender, ethnicity and class. This has consequences for the way that the labour process is ordered and controlled, and also for the development of resistance from workers. However, there have been few studies looking at how globalization may play a part here. We can, at a very general level, observe that the proliferation of multinational corporations and strategies of integrated production across the globe, coupled to outsourcing, may have led to the emergence of shared patterns of control, at least in some sectors. But this general view lacks detail, and is too clumsy a tool for making sense of how groups of workers in specific industries and locales are experiencing work and employment relations. In particular, the shared pattern of control model focuses on managerial control in a technical sense, and doesn't consider, as we will do here, the ways that workers and managers construct and consume identities to conform to, or resist, control in the workplace.

Take, for example, a paradigmatic new form of work: call centre work has proliferated in many countries, has become a major occupational route for large numbers of people, and is closely related to globalizing trends in capitalism due to its connection to offshoring, an aspect of Business Process Outsourcing (BPO). Call centre work covers a range of different forms, although all share a common type of labour process, in which workers use telephones and computers to interact with clients, either to offer support for existing services, or to sell new goods, services or products: these are referred to as qualitative and quantitative markets, respectively. Yet although this is a 'new' form of work, it is remarkably similar, in how it is organized and controlled, to older forms of work, so much so that Taylor and Bain (1999) describe it as simply a new manifestation of a Taylorized labour process – that is, where the overall work is broken down into small repetitive tasks and workers have limited autonomy over how they perform them. The division of labour is detailed, workers must achieve targets, workers are closely supervised (often monitored using technology) and workplaces are often organized on panopticon principles so that supervisors may more easily oversee employees (Taylor and Bain 2003). Work is often stressful and there are high rates of burnout in call centres around the world.

Many studies of call centres have focused on organizations in Global North countries (e.g. Jenkins et al. 2010; Lankshear et al. 2001; Lloyd and Payne 2009; Pritchard and Symon 2011; Taylor and Bain 1999; Taylor et al. 2003). This approach implies that there may not be significant differences around the world in terms of how call centre work is arranged and experienced. However, a number of recent studies suggest that, whilst the form of work is largely similar, the content and the context of the work can give rise to quite significant differences in experience, attitude and behaviour at work through the ways that identities are constructed and adopted in workplaces. Of particular importance to understanding how globalization can have local effects in specific workplaces is analysis of the articulation and management of national, and occupational, identities by employers and managers in call centre work. Whilst the business of making and taking phone calls is fairly straightforward in terms of organization and skills required, the actual interaction itself, between caller and (potential) client, is one that needs to be very carefully managed. These interactions, the outcome of which is the core business for the employer, are often scripted (Leidner 1993), and often require the worker to adopt a manner, or even a whole persona, that may be at odds with what they want to do or feel (this 'emotional labour', whereby workers have to modify their behaviour in order to cater to the needs of consumers is, of course, not confined to the call centre industry, as we shall see in further examples in chapter 9).

Service work has been globalized in recent years and more and more companies in the countries of the Global North have turned to offshoring of call centres as a way to reduce costs. There are complex outcomes for such processes. Whilst the increase in better-paid and better-skilled jobs in countries in the Global South is an obvious positive result, there are significant other outcomes. At a general level, some have claimed that this process will lead to a homogenization of identities, a charge often levelled at globalization itself, seen either as a positive outcome, as suggested by Friedman (2006), or as negative (Ritzer 2000). This seems hard to substantiate; local/global interactions and effects have been reported variously across the years (leading George Ritzer to consider a new process – glocalization) and it may be that reports of the death of local identities have been exaggerated. Indeed, possibly the opposite is the case: as service work is increasingly globalized, issues of the nation and national identity become more significant as workers are asked to suppress their own identities in favour of a corporate identity and so national identity becomes a focal point for resistance to the labour process.

Indian call centres

The Indian call centre industry provides us with a good example of the transnationalization of service-sector work, and an opportunity to examine how globalization has an effect on individual identities and specific workplace practices. The Indian call centre sector is immense, with over 500 companies employing at least 350,000 workers directly. In a country of 1.2 billion people, with a labour force estimated at 487.6 million (CIA 2012), this may seem to be quite a small number. However, almost 95 per cent of the Indian labour forcework in unorganized enterprises. When we consider this backdrop, the figure of 350,000 workers employed in these organized enterprises assumes a new importance. The organized private sector in India employs 9.875m workers (Government of India 2012: Table A52). This makes the call centre sector responsible for employing 3.5 per cent of organized Indian private sector workers. Indian call centres provide services to some sixty-six countries, but mainly the US and UK (NASSCOM n.d) (see box 2.2). It is important to note that this industry is entirely a consequence of globalization: there was no domestic call centre market in India prior to the introduction of international call centres in the 1990s (from Greg Stitt's 2003 *Diverted to Delhi* Australian Broadcasting Corporation documentary).

Box 2.2 Business Process Outsourcing in India

The BPO industry in India has expanded dramatically in recent years and now, according to NASSCOM – the industry association for the IT-BPO sector in India – contributes $16.9 billion to the Indian economy and employs, directly or indirectly, 4.5 million people (www.nasscom.in, accessed 23 January 2012). Projections for annual growth suggest 15–16 per cent in India, a figure that indicates the dominance of India in this sector, given that global annual growth projections for the sector run at 5.1 per cent (TechNavio report 'Global BPO Market 2011–2015', published 12 June 2012, www.technavio.com/content/global-bpo-market-2011–2015, accessed 9 July 2012).

However, the Indian BPO Information Technology / Information Technology Enabled Services (IT/ITES) sector faces some threats. The first is from new entrants to the BPO sector, notably the Philippines. With a US colonial heritage and a large English-speaking population, BPO in the Philippines, particularly directed towards US clients, is growing. The second threat is, perhaps paradoxically, the growth in IT literacy and online experience of Global North citizens. Clients are more likely to accept help and support from an online 'chat'-based operator, cutting out the need for the specific English accents and assumed Global North identities that call centres require. Currently, the ratio of voice- to non-voice-based services in Indian BPO stands at 60:40 per cent (BPO India – same source as above).

See also chapter 9 for an account of Indian women call centre workers.

A significant feature of Indian call centre work is the way that clients, often large US multinationals, require call centre workers, often even those who are not in direct contact with US customers, to adopt a 'false' persona – an Americanized identity, an American or British name, and a European or American accent when talking to customers. Poster, whose qualitative research in India was based on in-depth interviews with a wide range of call centre staff and ethnographic study inside four call centres (2007), notes that the depth of this American identity was profound: the training of operatives was extensive, over a period of months, and required them not only to change their accents and language articulation, but also to construct American identities, fictitious friends and relations, to have knowledge of American popular culture (training included watching episodes of *Friends* and *Baywatch*), politics, society and geography. Whilst the labour process in Indian call centres was similar to that of UK call centres, this additional component of identity change and emotional labour marks a significant difference, not least due to the colonial legacy of India.

This legacy has had obvious political effects, not only in terms of the formation of Indian nationalist political parties such as the Bharatiya Janata Party (BJP) (Lukose 2009), but also in terms of the construction of identities. Fanon's *Black Skin, White Masks* (1967) examined the emergence of inferiority complexes amongst colonized peoples and this theme also appears in the work of other postcolonial writers, notably Homi Bhabha (1994).

The tensions and even psychological traumas that emerge from contested cultural identities, and from the requirements to look and act in a way that conforms to the desires of those in power, are not new discoveries. As Nadeem points out (2009), there is a striking parallel between the demands of the nineteenth-century colonial power for Indians to conform to English values, mores and ways of being, and the demand of global corporations for Indian employees to adopt Western personae. Two significant questions emerge from this: why do Global North companies require this hiding of national identity and adoption of a new, false identity, and what are the effects on workers who perform this form of labour?

There are obvious benefits to Global North companies associated with offshoring BPO to India. There is a large, well-educated English-speaking workforce available, and wages are significantly lower; Poster reports that labour costs are one-tenth of those in the US for similar employees (Poster 2007: 291). But this doesn't explain why the workers have to pretend to be calling from America or to be US nationals. There is an assumption being made, on the part of clients, that smooth and consistent customer service that will be experienced similarly around the globe can only be achieved by adopting and replicating the identity of the customer base. This may be the case, although, given the very high levels of racist abuse that Indian call centre workers experience (Poster 2007; Nath 2011), it seems that the strategy either is not working or is easily seen through by customers. We could conjecture that Global North clients ask their Global South subcontractors to adopt these identities to ease communication inside the business network, but given the fact that there are no language barriers to overcome and that business-level discussions will, most likely, be confined to mission-specific matters, the adoption of an alter-identity seems unnecessary.

Poster's explanation for this phenomenon is more subtle: the deliberate effacing of the identities of these workers is the global corporation's strategy for controlling labour *and* customers. Hiding the identity of the employee also hides a bigger problem from the customer, namely the outsourcing and removal of jobs from the Global North, thus suppressing potential public opposition (see box 2.3). But it also 'conceals the neo-liberal project of exploiting workers in the Global South' (Poster 2007: 291). These corporations are deliberately misleading their customers so that they will retain customer loyalty: 'In a Foucauldian sense then, national identity management allows

Box 2.3 Indian call centre workers face a barrage of racist abuse

Poster's research found significant levels of racist abuse faced by call centre workers. There is evidence that this abuse is not on the spur of the moment, but is actually planned. A *Times of India* report from 2005 included an interview with a US citizen who deliberately called help-line numbers to abuse the workers:

> I have inside knowledge of call centres, having worked in several. It's crucial that the agents be efficient. Barraging them with 60–second calls will ruin their stats and also lower their morale. Eventually, they'll start thinking 'another damn rude American a******' every time a call comes up. All of this will have a cumulative effect. If 100 people across the US would commit to spending 10 minutes a day, we could cripple them, and bring those jobs back to the US. (*Times of India*, 11 January 2005)

Outsourcing call centre operations to India and other Global South countries is controversial in the USA. The economic downturn has led to a backlash against companies that have outsourced 'American' jobs, and this became a significant topic in the 2012 US presidential election. Democrat Barack Obama accused Republican candidate Mitt Romney's finance company, Bain Capital, of supporting the export of 'American' jobs overseas and relying on 'Asian labour' (Obama's *Washington Post* column, 21 June 2012). Campaign adverts describe how Obama believes in 'insourcing' and favours tax cuts that will bring jobs back to the US ('Obama campaign launches new ad in key battleground states casting Romney as an outsourcer', *Washington Post*, 4 July 2012).

these firms to hide the exercise of power on the consuming public. Ultimately, they are managing the consumers' reality as much as that of workers' (Poster 2007: 291).

In contrast, the benefits for workers are slim. Poster does note that workers derived some benefits from adopting an American persona – a few reported receiving preferential treatment in local businesses, and many thought that other benefits may accrue in terms of career opportunity. Murphy's research (2011) finds that Indian call centre workers are part of a growing middle class and that they share lifestyles and values with their Western counterparts. But 87 per cent of Poster's research participants identified some form of conflict with the national identity requirements of their workplace (Poster 2007: 290). This is hardly surprising given the levels of extreme abuse that these workers experienced in their everyday work:

> Workers repeatedly told me that 'people only like to be helped or served by their own kind.' They reported many incidences of customers who refused to be served by an Indian, and demanded to talk to

a 'real' American agent. It was quite a sobering experience for me to listen to as an American – that is, the steadfast composure and professionalism of Indian employees as American consumers said things like, 'How do I spell my name? F-U-C-K-Y-O-U!' Employees reported this happens in about 1 in 30 calls. In my observations, it happened at least once an hour. (Poster 2007: 283)

Das et al.'s (2008) survey research of Indian call centres confirms the finding that Indian call centre employees are subjected to sustained and unpleasant verbal attacks on their national identities. In examining the intersection of different identities, specifically the interplay of occupational and organizational identity, they found that employees with a strong sense of organizational *and* national identity were the worst performers in workplaces:

In general the process of masking and concealing one's national identity would be devaluing this identity and would affect people for whom national identity is important. Again, for employees who are high on OI [organizational identity] and high on national identity centrality, despite the best intentions of performing on the job, the challenge posed in the form of customer abuse on their national identities leads to high levels of dissonance which affect their performance. (Das et al. 2008: 1524)

The solution to these problems for Das et al. is directed towards Human Resources (HR) managers: strengthening organizational identity and reducing national identity would improve productivity in call centres and reduce stress and burnout. This may be the case, but such a recommendation calls into question the validity of this form of quantitative research. Whilst the results do, indeed, show a strong correlation between organizational identity and work performance (table 1: 1515), no consideration is given to the work culture that these employees are immersed within, and the model presented by Das et al. is an entirely individual one in which specific employees' identities can be managed by HR strategies.

Poster's qualitative study suggests we must approach such conclusions with caution: her observations of call centres themselves revealed that many managers were actively involved in promoting national identity symbols, rituals and activities. For example, during important international cricket matches the call centres would be festooned with Indian flags, Diwali was enthusiastically celebrated and some companies have specific prayer areas. Some managers even encourage the employees to speak in Hindi instead of English when not talking to customers, something that is expressly against the companies' stipulations (Poster 2007: 288). Poster does identify a small group (13 per cent of her sample) who 'assimilate' and agree with the national identity requirements. But the majority of workers are either accommodators, objectors or resistors. Given the role of managers in also resisting, or at least confounding, the national identity requirements in call centres, it seems unlikely that an HR strategy directed simply at promoting organizational identity would be particularly successful.

The research into call centres in India and elsewhere presents a rather stark account of globalization, with identities being constructed from Global North imperatives and imposed on Global South workers, and little traffic flowing in the opposite direction. Yet there is a possibility that this is a sector effect: offshoring call centre services is itself a stark business scenario based on a hierarchic relationship between (richer) client corporation and (poorer) service organization. It may be the case that other industrial sectors show different patterns of changing identities. This would appear to be happening in the globalized software industry.

Global North – Global South relations in offshoring

Labour process-based studies of the Indian software industry show a familiar picture of knowledge economy work practices. There is an emphasis inside ODCs (offshore software development centres) on soft management and the introduction of a cultural labour process that emphasizes teamwork, collaboration and communication (Upadhya 2009). But the reality experienced by many workers, including highly skilled software engineers, is a work environment that is often coercive and exploitative. Indian software companies have adopted en masse Western HR policies that are designed to represent the corporate culture and to retain key employees (2009: 7). However, many software companies have 'developed distinctive cultures and identities that combine "global" management ideas with what is understood as Indian ethos or work culture':

> Although most managers we interviewed spoke in positive terms about this shift, many employees had a very different view, maintaining that the global corporate model exists only on paper while 'traditional Indian' organizational culture persists in the form of hierarchical structures, bureaucratic mentality and 'feudal' relationships. The reproduction of traditional management practices was often explained by reference to the habits and cultural dispositions of managers and employees who had yet to fully adapt to the culture of the 'new workplace'. (Upadhya 2009: 7)

So far, so familiar: 'new' management practices and corporate culture used to control a workforce, replicating and building on 'traditional' forms of management, is a pattern that has been identified by critical organizational theorists for some time now (Thompson and Findlay 1999; McKinlay and Starkey 1998; Willmott 1993). However, this single-country labour process approach presents a stark case, and the mode of analysis here does not consider what effects the globalization of software production may have on employees' identities in client countries.

Studies of this topic, comparative analyses of identity construction in client and offshore organizations, whether quantitative or qualitative, are few and far between. However, Zimmermann and Ravishankar's qualitative study of the construction and management of professional role identities in two software organizations, one German and one Indian, participating in collaborative projects, reveals some significant trends which are likely to be shared in similar relationships (Zimmermann and Ravishankar 2011). They found that the new offshore work arrangements had significant, but different, effects on both the German and Indian software workers. The German workers noted large shifts in professional roles and identities as the collaboration required that the more technical aspects of the project were offshored, while more conceptual tasks were retained. This phenomenon, of retaining high-end and exporting low-end work, is experienced in a different way by the Indian workers, who felt strongly about not receiving more challenging tasks from the German side, 'and also expressed their unhappiness about being treated as vendors by German counterparts, when on paper they were promised to be accorded the status of colleagues' (Zimmermann and Ravishankar 2011: 353). Some of the German software engineers struggled to identify with the change in their work tasks, and were nostalgic about the technical aspect of their job. A manager noted that 'they find it incredibly hard to detach themselves from it [the machine]' (2011: 354). Coordinating others was not seen as a challenge or even as appropriate by some German software engineers, for example: 'That's not a challenge for me, to coordinate five, six, seven Indian work colleagues here ... I have studied electronic engineering, and now I could have just as well studied something else, to conduct these tasks here and now, because the technical aspects, they are gone' (2011: 354).

The offshoring situation directly challenges the German software engineers' view of themselves as 'professional engineers-doing-technical-tasks (2011: 357). There is a certain irony here in that both groups of workers feel that they are not utilizing the skills they were trained for! This situation is mirrored across the Indian BPO sector, and many call centre workers are very highly qualified – overqualified – for their work. As German engineers find dissatisfactions with their work and occupational identities, so do Indian software engineers, who reported cases of being marginalized, talked down to or even blamed for mistakes that could not have been their fault. But a significant shared feature was that both groups identified that their professional selves were fundamentally precarious, and they felt insecure about their jobs and careers. This was for different reasons: on the German side, the sense of precariousness came from the growth of the Indian subsidiary with the possibility that their jobs might be taken from them. On the Indian side, workers felt in a precarious position due to a lack of opportunities for career and skill development, leaving them at a disadvantage in the labour market (2011: 358).

We can see a complex relationship emerging between Global North and Global South institutions, social groups and individuals through the process of offshoring. Rather than this being a simple enactment of the project of globalization through the imposition of MNC imperatives onto Indian subcontractors (globalization as process), we see globalization as practice, through multinational companies (MNCs) constructing a global strategy, and actors in the Indian subcontinent enacting globalization through localized working practices, albeit whilst acceding to the commercial demands made upon them. A similarly complex set of circumstances and practices emerges in other economic relationships, and this extends beyond the activities of organizations and institutions into the everyday practice of individuals around the world. The recent phenomenon of ethical consumption and ethical trading is a particularly good example of this.

2.4 Fairtrade production and consumption as globalization in practice

Origin and rise of ethical trade

The term 'ethical trade' has a particular resonance in contemporary society, with connotations of fairness, equity and lack of exploitation. But this general sense of what ethical trade entails subsumes a quite complex set of relations, both within a national economy and in the global economy. We first need to note that it is a relatively new phenomenon: Blowfield (1999) argues that the first use of the term was as recently as 1995, although the idea of trading in a fair and ethical way goes back considerably further, with roots in consumer boycotts, the co-operative movement and the paternalist trend in nineteenth- and early twentieth-century capitalism. The premise of contemporary ethical trade is that consumption can promote economic empowerment amongst previously disadvantaged producers, thus improving their standard of living and general well-being, through levelling the playing field (Young and Utting 2005; Micheletti 2010).

In recent years in the UK, ethical consumption and ethical trading have become synonymous with the phenomenon of the Fairtrade movement. This is a social movement that shares the aim of helping producers in the Global South to receive better incomes and develop more sustainable production processes. At its centre is the Fairtrade Foundation, a non-profit organization that licenses the use of the Fairtrade mark on products. The mark indicates products that meet the standards set out by the Fairtrade Foundation; in short, the mark indicates a trading partnership based on equity and transparency. It also indicates the application of an alternative set of values, whereby 'Third World' citizens are seen as equal partners, not as victims.

The Fairtrade mark is applied to a range of imported commodities, most notable of which are foodstuffs like cocoa, coffee, tea, sugar and bananas. In recent years, Fairtrade has expanded into other commodities such as cotton and fresh fruit. The Fairtrade market in the UK is estimated by the Fairtrade Foundation to double every two years, although recent growth has been less pronounced; a 39 per cent rise in 2010 fell to just 12 per cent in 2011 (Fairtrade Foundation, www.fairtrade.org.uk/, 2012). The Fairtrade movement has become attached to a number of corporate sponsorships (Cadbury and Sainsbury are the most prominent of these) and has also constructed a large public support base through setting up local groups and 'fair trade towns', of which there are now more than 500 (Wheeler 2012: 127). The Fairtrade organization is one of a growing number of Alternative Trade Organizations (ATOs) (see box 2.4).

Box 2.4 Alternative Trading Organizations (ATOs)

Around the Global North, there are established and emerging ethical consumption 'brands' (Fairtrade, Rainforest Alliance, Equal Exchange, UtzCertification are the most prominent), most of which operate on a shared principle of a moral economic concern to transfer more benefits of global trade to the producers in poorer countries. However, there are differences of emphasis between these organizations which make it difficult to describe them all as simply 'fair trade' or 'ethical consumption' organizations. In recent years the phrase 'Alternative Trade Organizations' (ATOs) has become the umbrella term to group these organizations. ATOs are organizations for which philosophies of social justice and/ or environmental well-being preside over mission-based marketing transactions (Geiger-Oneto and Arnould 2011: 276). ATOs have been very successful, albeit in a small range of areas, in creating new channels of trade between Global North and Global South. The original intention of many ATOs was to try to increase the amount of money going to producers through cutting out exploitative stages in the commodity chain, for example by bypassing 'coyote' coffee processors in Latin America who paid low prices for raw materials, processed these and retained considerable profits. More recently, ATOs have been less involved in direct interventions, such as purchasing infrastructure, and more involved in processes of certification and inspection to ensure that standards and rules are maintained. Whilst the increase in income going to producers is the primary concern, most ATOs also specify other benefits and values that they are attempting to promote – most notably equity, anti-discrimination practices and fair labour policies.

Interestingly, whilst there has been considerable sociological analysis of the emergence of a new form of consumption – ethical consumption or 'challenged consumption' (Halkier 2010 cited in Wheeler 2012) – which we shall examine later, there is limited sociological or business studies analysis of the labour conditions that pertain in ATO-supervised commodity chains, although interest in this area has certainly been growing. The studies that have been carried out report mixed results in terms of the employment benefits of ATO-supervised production, although all studies report significant and tangible changes for the better in the position of women in agricultural production.

Box 2.5 Fairtrade, identity, protest and globalization

Is the active choice to purchase fairly traded products a form of identity politics? A number of studies have linked such choices to identity politics and suggest that consumers are positioning themselves as ethical selves (Wheeler 2012; Varul 2009). Fairtrade ATOs often present themselves as offering an alternative, and seek to distance themselves from colonialism through a discourse of empowerment and 'anti-conquest' (Varul 2009: 187).

However, there are some significant paradoxes in these discourses. The first, perhaps obviously, is that this form of consumption takes place inside the context of global consumer capitalism, a phenomenon which has brought about widespread exploitation and environmental degradation – the things that Fairtrade aims to address. And just how far can this challenge to exploitation go? As Damani James Partridge notes: 'To protest outsourcing or globalization is to protest what one cannot imagine life without' (Partridge 2011: S107). Matt Adams and Jayne Raisborough's study of the forms of representation used by ATOs to market their products, focusing primarily on the visual representations on packaging, found a re-working of a familiar narrative of ingroup–outgroup, where the outgroup is denigrated by the ingroup: 'The fairtrade farmer of the Southern hemisphere is clearly an outgroup for the Northern consumer' (Adams and Raisborough 2011: 8.10).

This doesn't mean that Fairtrade is not making a difference; it obviously is in some areas. Not only that, it clearly contributes to identity construction for both Global North consumers (Wheeler 2012) and Global South producers (Lyon et al. 2010). Perhaps what is needed is, as Partridge suggests, a more critical perspective, and a wider global economic vision:

> In calling attention to supply-chain citizenship as a limited and limiting form of global belonging, it makes sense that one should begin to call for more supply-chain democracy – that is, political, social, and economic accountability – particularly from the perspective of those for whom ethical standards are being created without their input and without significant improvement in their lives. On the other hand, one might ask to what extent any of these options are equivalent to apartheid-era corporate accommodation. What economic alternatives exist that would make possible a more robust system of social transformation? (Partridge 2011: S107)

This is in marked contrast to studies of non-Fairtrade agricultural production. In African commercial horticulture, for example, women workers are frequently employed in informal and insecure ways, and for lower wages than male workers (Barrientos et al. 2005). Much of this employment is in agricultural production for European supermarkets. Wright and Madrid's study of the Colombian cut-flower industry, which employs 80,000–90,000 people directly and another 50,000–80,000 indirectly, found that 'Classed, racialized and gendered divisions in Colombian society are reproduced in floriculture' (2007: 257). The vast majority of the lowest-paid workers are women, and conditions are poor. Workers receive a minimum wage, but this is insufficient to meet a family's basic living costs: 'Moreover, the "surplus value" extracted is substantial: the flowers one woman picks daily retail for US$600–800 whereas her minimum wage is US$2' (2007: 259). Workers' health is threatened by intensive chemical use without adequate protection: workers report a range of problems, from headaches to repetitive strain injury (RSI), while short-term and subcontracted employment serves to expose workers to more risks (2007: 259). Workers have responded to these conditions by forming independent unions, but at immense personal risk, not just to their employment but to their own lives and those of their families, as will be explored in chapter 5 on trade unions.

Fairtrade, work and production

The application of the Fairtrade label to commodities is limited to smaller producers, a deliberate policy that ensures that most value goes directly to producers who rely, largely, on family labour. In the coffee industry, for example, the bulk of the production takes place on estates which rely wholly on hired labour. In contrast, Fairtrade coffee production takes place on individual farms where labour is provided by members of the household. The obvious benefit to the farmer is that more of the cash value of the crop is retained by those who have actually produced it. Moreover, as a number of studies have noted, there are significant non-cash benefits such as access to health and education services attached to this form of production.

Women workers throughout the Global South commonly face sexual harassment in the workplace, lower pay than men and less stable employment (often with no written contract of employment). In addition they:

> are doubly burdened, and, with little support from their governments or employers to cope with it, the stress can destroy their own health, break up their families, and undermine their children's chances of a better future. The result: the very workers who are the backbone of wealth creation in many developing countries are being robbed of their share of the gains that trade could bring. (Raworth 2005: 3; see also chapter 9)

In many Global South countries, there has been a feminization of agricultural labour and this has been particularly pronounced in Latin America (Deere 2005). Whilst the biggest growth area in women's agricultural employment has been in the non-traditional agro-export sector favoured under neo-liberalism – specifically, in the production and packing of fresh vegetables, fruits and flowers for Northern markets – there has been significant expansion in the number of women involved in the production of basic foodstuffs and commodities such as coffee. In this specific case, many women have become producers in their own right, not a result of Fairtrade interventions – although these have helped to facilitate the transformations – but as a consequence of male immigration to urban areas in the search for wage labour. There has also been a strong shift to Fairtrade coffee production and organic coffee production by small farmers in Latin America, partly due to the collapse of coffee prices from their high point in the mid-1980s (Lyon et al. 2010: 95).

Coffee production has historically shown a clear gendered division of labour, with women involved in lower-skilled tasks such as picking, and men involved in higher-skilled tasks such as grading and processing. (See chapter 9 for more on the topic of gender.) The shift towards more women-run farms and production operations has impacted on this division of labour, although this has generally been at the upstream (production) end. Lyon et al. found that more women have become involved in coffee production in general and in decision-making, specifically at the level of farm and initial production (2010). However, further downstream in the commodity chain, there has been little change in the gendered division of labour. Managerial staff among Fairtrade coffee organizations are overwhelmingly male (2010: 99) and women are still excluded from these higher functions due to sexual discrimination and a simple lack of time to become involved: women's double burden of household and agricultural labour consumes too much of their time. However, Lyon et al. did find that some women take on managerial and other skilled roles upstream in the commodity chain, often becoming Fairtrade inspectors, a position that not only provides additional income but also challenges the local discourse of women lacking skills or education to carry out these tasks. This is a result of changing local circumstances rather than Fairtrade organizations making specific efforts or enacting rules that promote gender equity. Overall, though, the combination of Fairtrade and organically evolving local habits 'constitutes a case of norms operating in tandem that, under the right circumstances, enhances participation opportunities for women' (2010).

To what extent have these changes in coffee production under Fairtrade, organic or other ATO oversight had an effect on the working lives of agricultural workers? Lyon et al. note the increase in participation, but does this itself mean that Fairtrade is 'working'? Geiger-Oneto and Arnould's (2011) study does suggest a significant change. They carried out an extensive survey to examine changes in quality of life amongst participants who either were participating in a specific coffee marketing channel (that of the American TransFair USA organization) operating in Nicaragua, Peru and Guatemala, or were operating in 'traditional' ways. The survey examined quality-of-life social indicators, and also general perceptions of how participants' lifestyle, and that of their children, had changed. In general the research found that participation in the TransFair USA programme had significant positive effects, with participants reporting a greater sense of general well-being and a more positive outlook for their future compared to those not involved in the programme. Notably, the research reported that both men and women identified increased levels of support in their lives due to participation in the TransFair USA programme; given that Transfair USA is committed to gender equity, this result may, according to the authors, 'suggest the cooperatives they support are delivering on their commitment' (Geiger-Oneto and Arnould 2011: 288).

From these studies, it would appear that ATO-controlled commodity chains provide significant benefits for agricultural workers and small farmers. However, we need to be cautious about extrapolating from one sector (coffee production) to others. A stark contrast to the success of Fairtrade coffee production is visible in Fairtrade cotton programmes. Thomas Bassett's detailed examination of this commodity chain reveals 'Fairtrade's weak potential for truly changing trading practices' (Bassett 2010: 44).

Why has a Fairtrade strategy not improved working conditions and income for cotton farmers? The problem here is the cotton sector itself, which has a much longer value chain than that of, say, coffee and is also heavily skewed in favour of producers in the Global North through state subsidies. Bassett's analysis of the Fairtrade cotton programmes of Mali and Burkina Faso, the two largest cotton-producing countries in Africa (but also amongst the poorest of African nations), exposes the vulnerability of Fairtrade strategies to much larger and more powerful global interests.

In Mali and Burkina Faso, cotton exports are a major component of overall exports (25 per cent and 50 per cent, respectively), which makes both nations very dependent on export markets. However, the volatility of the global cotton market, and the artificial deflation of the price of cotton due to US subsidies of its domestic producers (a practice which has led to other World Trade Organization (WTO) members lodging a formal complaint in 2003) and its refiners, militate against Fairtrade producers increasing their income. Put simply, cotton producers in these countries are compelled to sell their cotton to cotton companies, often the same companies that supplied the farmers with credit to grow the crops in the first place. With the global price of cotton at an all-time low (since the 1930s), cotton producers get very meagre rewards from selling their crop. Cotton growers don't receive the actual market value of their crop because cotton companies and international cotton traders are adding value through 'opaque grading and trading practices'. This has not stopped the growth of Fairtrade programmes in these countries, but the financial benefits are small compared to other Fairtrade commodity programmes.

Although the financial benefits are small, the Fairtrade programmes in Burkina Faso and Mali do produce other benefits. Growers form co-operatives that are much more democratic and transparent than other cotton groups and, significantly, women were particularly emphatic about these differences 'since they have experienced discrimination in the conventional cotton growing sector' (Bassett 2010: 51).

However, it was in the organic cotton Fairtrade programme that the most tangible benefits were realized. This is due to the introduction of targeted programmes that deliberately operated throughout the commodity chain, from organic growing to finished product. These programmes often had far more women involved, although there is some over-estimation of this, owing to the involvement of more than one family member in cotton production.

Whilst the international cotton market is distorted and global cotton prices deliberately depressed by US state subsidies, there are still significant benefits to Fairtrade producers in West African countries: improved quality of cotton, and hence higher rewards to growers, increased organic production methods that are more sustainable and transferable to other agricultural operations; and improved access for women to cash cropping opportunities (Bassett 2010). It is likely that increased Fairtrade production will have benefits throughout the West African cotton sector, although, while the global market remains distorted and dominated by Global North companies, the financial rewards for West African producers will remain meagre.

Overall, we can see that Global North ethical consumer programmes can have significant effects in Global South agricultural production systems. However, these are constrained by global value chains that fix prices for commodities to favour Global North economies and producers. Given the contradictory evidence for radical change from the examples of coffee and cotton, it is appropriate to ask whether Fairtrade and ATO programmes in general really do benefit Global South producers, or if the main beneficiaries are Global North consumers who get high-quality produce and products at the same time as salving their consciences about the inequities of global trade.

Fairtrade: ethics and benefits

There can be little doubt that Fairtrade branding and programmes have been remarkably successful in Global North markets, making the fair trade movement a 'recognized force for helping marginalized and poor producers in developing countries enter the world trading system' (Young and Utting 2005: 139). But despite this visibility, there is little research into just what the 'positive impact' has been (2005: 140). The research that has been conducted has been inconclusive, and some has revealed the problems with alternative trading systems, as in the case of West African cotton discussed above. One of the core problems with evaluating the impact of Fairtrade is the specificity of local conditions in contrast to the generality of global markets.

Whilst it is simple to identify the amounts of produce flowing through the commodity chains, and the amounts going to Fairtrade chains, actual analysis of the financial benefits accruing to individual producers or co-operative groups is scant. Johannessen and Wilhite's extensive analysis of the benefits of Fairtrade coffee production at various points in the global value chain (GVC) revealed that benefits for local producers are small. They examined the distribution of value of the Fairtrade coffee sold and consumed in Norway, and considered the income generated in the chain from production to consumption, using producer co-operatives in Nicaragua and Guatemala as a case study (Johannessen and Wilhite 2010). Norway is a good site for this study as Norwegians have the third-highest annual per capita consumption of coffee in the world (9.21 kg), behind Finland (12.12 kg!) and Denmark (9.46 kg) – for comparison, the UK per capita consumption is 3.04 kg (2010 data, International Coffee Organization, www.ico.org, accessed 15 May 2012).

As we noted above, the coffee commodity chain is straightforward, particularly when compared to that of cotton, with few side branches and split into four stages:

> The first stage is the income generated by the producer, which is the income at farm gate. The second stage is the income generated in the producer co-operative. In Guatemala this stage is divided into a sub-stage by level of co-operative (first or second level). The third stage is the income generated by the importer/roaster; in Norway the majority of large importers are also roasters. The fourth stage is the income of wholesalers, retail trade, cafés, and the state through taxation. The total income along the chain is calculated according to retail prices, or the amount a Norwegian consumer pays for the product. (Johannessen and Wilhite 2010: 531)

Johannessen and Wilhite's (2010: 535) analysis shows that the vast majority of the value of the coffee remains in the country of consumption. They broke down the value of one brewed cup of coffee sold in the cafeteria on the campus of the Norwegian University of Life Sciences and found that the producer receives 2.02 per cent of that price, the co-operative a further 1.91 per cent, but 96.07 per cent of the retail price of the coffee remains in the consumer's country: 'In summary, the distribution of value in the coffee chain from Central America to Norway is skewed dramatically in favour of the consumer country.'

But perhaps the focus on financial benefits is too restrictive? The co-operatives and producers in both Nicaragua and Guatemala were in receipt of the Fairtrade social premium which was used to improve the technical efficiency of production and the quality of the coffee, effectively a form of insurance against the free market 'coyote' coffee traders who would undercut the Fairtrade prices. However, co-operative members in both Nicaragua and Guatemala reported problems with Fairtrade, including lack of demand, strict obligation and low minimum price. In Guatemala, 16 per cent of producer co-operative members reported that they were not selling to the Fairtrade market, although they were, without being aware of it.

As with the cotton example above, the problem here is the position of Fairtrade in a global market that favours MNCs and disadvantages producers regardless of whether they are part of a Fairtrade commodity chain. Johannessen and Wilhite report the words of a Nicaraguan coffee co-operative manager describing the arrangement with Starbucks, who claim to offer credit to producers so they can postpone selling their crops until a favourable price (for whom?) emerges on the market: 'I believe, for what concerns Starbucks, Starbucks always send contracts when the New York "C" price is at the ground, when the prices have fallen. When the New York "C" price is high, Starbucks never sends contracts . . . It is the tricks of the market. They (Starbucks) are specialists on the market' (Johannessen and Wilhite 2010: 538).

Fairtrade, consumption and identity

The benefits of Fairtrade production, from the above survey, appear to be in the realm of personal and social empowerment, rather than from increased income (although some Fairtrade schemes are providing increased economic benefits). As we shift our attention from the producers in the Fairtrade commodity chain to the consumers of Fairtrade products we see a similar, non-pecuniary, aspect emerging in analyses of benefits.

A number of studies of ethical consumption in industrialized countries have found that consumers of Fairtrade and other ethically sourced products experience positive benefits in terms of feeling actively engaged in 'making a difference' or 'playing one's part'. There is a certain moral pleasure in knowing that your consumption is making a difference (Wheeler 2012: 133; Adams and Raisborough 2010). The consumption of Fairtrade products is also linked to conscious conceptualizations of the recipient of the benefits of Fairtrade – consumers aren't simply considering themselves in the act of buying these products. The conceptualization varies between countries, as Varul's 2009 research into the moral economy of Fairtrade consumers in the UK and Germany shows: 'For British respondents, the ideal mainly was to enable them to set themselves up as sustainable *business operations*, while the German respondents tended to reference them as *workers* with a set of guaranteed rights. As one German participant put it, fair trade conditions should include that "they've got social insurance and health insurance"' (Varul 2009: 187).

Although there are differences, both sets of ethical consumers are considering their position as consumers in a supply chain, and are actively conceptualizing what the consequences of their consumption choices might be. We can see a form of 'doing globalization', or globalization as practice, here, as these consumers are considering their own global belonging and connecting this to their identity. Wheeler's study of UK fair-trade activists found a high degree of awareness of world development issues, and participants were members of a range of organizations promoting development, such as the World Development Movement (WDM) and Oxfam (Wheeler 2012).

It is difficult to say that these attempts at understanding one's place in a global supply chain are solely the result of recent globalization; after all, consumer awareness and boycotts have a long history. Johannessen and Wilhite (2010) trace the particular ethical consumption movement that Fairtrade has emerged from back to the 1950s. (We could go much further back to anti-slavery and animal rights campaigns of the nineteenth century.) However, it is clear that ATOs in general, and Fairtrade in particular, deliberately construe themselves as organizations that are acting on a global scale to connect consumers and producers (Adams and Raisborough 2010). That consumers are clearly aware of this is testament to the efforts made by these organizations in this direction.

Given this, it is quite reasonable to ask whether these consumer campaigns are doing any 'real' good: 'the premises of consumer campaigns and associated codes and/or labels are worth questioning. Have workers been marginalized and misrepresented by campaigns owned and controlled elsewhere and founded on the recuperative potential of consumption? Do these initiatives privilege and legitimate consumer pleasure over and above labour rights?' (Wright and Madrid 2007: 260–1). Wright and Madrid's work exposes the cynical deployment of 'ethical codes' by the Colombian cut-flower industry, a recuperative strategy that pays great financial dividends. But we should be wary about extrapolating from the case of Colombian flowers to all cases. As the material above illustrates, participants at the production end of Fairtrade supply chains do report significant positive benefits. But, perhaps, it is not unreasonable to ask whether this is as good as it gets. Could the circumstances of commodity producers not be improved through interventions at the level of global markets? And could the supply-chain citizenship currently on offer – a form of global belonging that is both limited and limiting according to Partridge (2011: S107) – not be transformed into a supply-chain democracy in which all participants could be recognized and have a say in the relationship between producer and consumer?

2.5 Summary and conclusion

The links between consumption and identity have become stronger in recent years, as many commentators have noted, and in this chapter we have suggested that facets of globalization are intermingled with this. The control and articulation of occupational identity are specific goals for MNCs involved in offshoring work, particularly service-sector work. Yet we can see that this process of globalization is resisted through the reclaiming and consumption of national identities by workers in the Global South. Similarly, the imposition of neo-liberal values through commodity chains is resisted by the operation of a range of ATOs attempting to bring about more equitable producer/consumer relationships and, whilst the financial benefits to producers from such operations may be small, in terms of quality of life and, notably, gender identity politics the effects are considerable.

At the same time, we can see Global North consumers becoming more aware of their position in value chains; consumers consume products that make specific appeals to their ethical understanding of consumption, and this results in reconstructions of personal identities based on a consciousness of one's position with respect to other parts of the globe. Whilst it would be overblown to suggest that Global North consumers develop a global consciousness, they are certainly experiencing globalization in a direct way and enacting globalization through their consumption practices. Given this, it is unremarkable that a number of MNCs have attempted to 'buy in' to these trends, whilst retaining their primary goals of expansion into and consolidation of markets. It is to this topic that we will now turn.

Further reading

Globalization and consumption

One of the key theorists of globalization and consumption is Zygmunt Bauman, and three of his works stand out as essential reading. Bauman's main theory, that modernity has become 'liquid' and that people around the globe feel a sense of detachment, of rootlessness and flux in their lives, is not a new theory, but it is clearly expressed and applied in these books:
   Bauman (1998a, 1998b and 2007).

Consumption and identity

A straightforward introduction to the general topic of consumption and political identity is Micheletti (2010). However, a more theorized approach to the complex issue of consumption and consumerism can be found in Lury (2011).

Global work and global production

The World Bank provides very extensive, if somewhat hard to digest, data on global production, consumption, wages and benefits. The most relevant dataset to the topic of global development is the World Development Indicators & Global Development Finance dataset, published annually and available online at:

http://data.worldbank.org/data-catalog/global-development-finance.

3 Multinationals, work and employment in the global economy

3.1 Introduction

One of the founders of industrial sociology, Wilhelm Baldamus, noted in his seminal work *Efficiency and Effort* that what we really need to explain, in looking at employment and work organizations, is not how things break down, cease functioning or fall apart, but how work and organization is possible in the first place: how things keep going (Baldamus 1961). His reason for taking this view is based on two things. The first, as discussed in the previous chapter, is the corrosive aspect of much work in modern societies: for many it is dangerous, difficult, degrading, alienating, stressful and even pointless – why would anyone do this? The second is the complexity and conflictual nature of industrial organizations: given the size, disorganization, disharmony, internal inequality and range of activities of even medium-sized enterprises, how is it possible that production, and often efficient production, emerges?

The purpose of this chapter is not to answer these questions; rather to provide a sociologically informed understanding of the role and activities of multinational companies (MNCs) under globalization. But they are included at the outset to highlight two things. The first is the sheer achievement of any multinational enterprise – that such organizations can emerge and even flourish is testament to the achievement of human social organization and social action. For example, in 2009 the international oil corporation BP had 80,300 employees, an operating cash flow of $27.7 billion, and was active in thirty countries (BP 2009: 6–9). The sheer scale of the organization is startling, and yet BP employees are no different from those in any other company, and in essence BP is run on pretty much the same lines as any other.

This brings us to the second point: the need for social and sociological analysis to understand these organizations; they are social in origin, in nature, and have palpable social and political effects. Organizations emerge from human social action, not from technology or products or services or finance. It is people who form MNCs through their individual and collective effort, and if we want to understand organizations, then this is where we should look.

We start, though, with a section which examines the nature of multinationals, and how they can be conceptualized. In the following section, we turn our attention to the role of multinationals in a globalizing world, and how their activities, which are increasingly stretched across and beyond the borders of nation-states, contribute to the process of globalization. In the next section, we are concerned with the implications of MNC activities for work and employment, pointing to the ways in which multinationals, as increasingly dominant transnational actors, use their power to advance their interests, by subjugating labour unions, for example, or through the diffusion of 'best practice' management ideas and approaches across national borders. Sociologically, however, there are a number of problems with the idea that multinationals are able to operate unproblematically as rational agents of global convergence. Therefore, in the following section, we draw on appropriate sociological perspectives to consider some relevant issues and challenges with regard to the operation and activities of MNCs, including the large degree to which societal factors often influence work and employment arrangements in their foreign subsidiaries. The model developed and elaborated by Smith and Meiksins (1995) and Elger and Smith (2005), which incorporates system, society and dominance (SSD) effects, offers the prospect of a more complex and nuanced approach to understanding the management of work and employment in multinationals. We consider its application and relevance in the next section, before making some concluding observations in the final section.

3.2 Understanding multinational companies

The activities of MNCs are one of the clearest manifestations of economic globalization in action (Jones 2005). They 'span every sector of the global economy – from raw materials, to finance, to manufacturing – integrating and reordering economic activity within and across the world's major economic regions' (Held and McGrew 2007: 111). But what makes an MNC, and how can one be defined? In our minds we know what a multinational is: we think of Coca-Cola, HSBC, Siemens, Sony, Walmart, McDonald's or ExxonMobil, and other major companies emanating from the traditionally dominant economies of the Global North. See box 3.1 for the rise of multinational internet giant Google.

In terms of a specific definition, though, it is useful to regard an MNC as an 'enterprise that engages in foreign direct investment (FDI) and owns or, in some way, controls value-added activities in more than one country' (Dunning and Lundan 2008: 3). One analysis suggests that

> there are some 82,000 MNCs worldwide, with 810,000 foreign affiliates in the world. These companies play a major and growing role in the world economy. For instance, exports by foreign affiliates of MNCs are estimated to account for about one third of total world exports of goods and services. And the number of people employed by them worldwide, which has increased about fourfold since 1982,

Box 3.1 The rise of Google

Google is a US-based internet search engine company that provides additional services and generates revenue through hosting sites and from advertising. It was founded in 1998, and has expanded remarkably rapidly. It employs 23,000 people in forty countries across the globe (www.google.co.uk/corporate/, accessed 18 May 2011). Google has an annual revenue of $29 billion and made an $8.5 billion profit in 2010 (Google's revenue machine stays unstoppable in Q4, www.theregister.co.uk/2011/01/20/google_q4_2010_results/, accessed 18 May 2011).

Google, in its short history, has also faced a fair amount of controversy through its self-imposed censorship of internet search results accessed from inside China (http://news.bbc.co.uk/1/hi/technology/4645596.stm 26 January 2006, accessed 18 May 2011). The company, following online campaigns from human rights and anti-censorship activists, reversed its policy and decided to withdraw partially from mainland China in late 2010. As a consequence, a new, Chinese government-approved, search engine, Baidu, has emerged and now dominates the China search engine field, with over 75 per cent of searches going through it, compared to 20 per cent via Google (www.bbc.co.uk/news/business-13222423 28 April 2011, accessed 18 May 2011). It is difficult to say whether Google's business or share price have been affected by the controversy: with such a massive market share, Google can easily weather a storm, and given its high rate of profitability it is unlikely that corporate investors would be dissuaded from buying Google's shares. However, the company is vulnerable to losing market share to new entrants, to regional providers, specialist and human-assisted searchers, or to other service providers with different or better products: Facebook and Twitter are obvious examples here (www.newsweek.com/2007/10/27/searching-for-the-best-engine.html). In a rapidly changing and volatile market such as this, any threat to brand reputation or status is potentially harmful to a company like Google.

amounted to about 77 million in 2008 – more than double the labour force of a country like Germany. (UNCTAD 2009: 17)

During the 2000s, MNCs based in the Global South – those originating from China, India and Latin America in particular – became increasingly prominent international economic actors. The expansion of the conglomerate Tata Group, whose global portfolio of operations encompasses steel making, automobile manufacturing and food and drink production – it now owns the Tetley tea brand for example – exemplifies the growing of multinationals from India (Ramumurti and Singh 2009; Sauvant et al. 2010). The growing prominence of Chinese multinational enterprises in the global economy is also increasingly evident, being particularly manifest in Africa, the location of substantial investment activity (Alden 2007; Shen and Edwards 2006; Pearce 2011). With regard to Latin America, firms such as Brazilian oil company Petrobas and Mexican cement and building materials producer Cemex have also become major MNCs (Casanova 2009).

We need to be careful not to assume that multinationals are all the same, when in reality the MNC label can be applied to a heterogeneous mix of organizations by size, scope and orientation. For example, many multinationals employ fewer than 250 people; and service-sector MNCs often employ fewer than 100 (Gabel and Bruner 2003). Perhaps the most useful approach to classifying MNCs is that which has been elaborated by Bartlett and Ghoshal (1989), based on three broad strategic objectives of the companies: pursuing global integration; responsiveness to country-specific circumstances; and the promotion of worldwide learning and innovation, through the transfer of knowledge and expertise across their different operations around the world. On the basis of these strategic objectives, they distinguish between four different types of multinational enterprise.

- Multi-domestic firms tend to operate a portfolio of different national-level operations, concerned with being responsive to country-specific circumstances. Given that tastes vary so much from country to country, food and drink multinationals commonly take such an approach.
- International firms concentrate more on promoting worldwide learning and innovation, with the aim of transferring practices from their home-country headquarters to operations in host-country locations, adapting them accordingly. Japanese MNCs like Honda and Toyota often place a strong emphasis on diffusing their management techniques to subsidiary operations in foreign locations.
- Global firms, by contrast, focus on realizing the worldwide integration and coordination of their activities; such an emphasis is typically found in multinational enterprises in sectors like energy and oil supply.
- Transnational firms, though, concentrate on trying to realize all three broad strategic objectives. Companies like the Swiss–Swedish conglomerate ABB, for example, benefit from having robust arrangements in place to coordinate their global activities, while operating their businesses in a devolved fashion, and making use of extensive systems for transferring knowledge and expertise across their various sites.

There are three key criteria that distinguish an MNC from other forms of business organization. The first is the willingness to seek new opportunities, be these markets, resources or finance, from countries outside their country of origin. These opportunities are often combined; for example, companies using offshoring are utilizing foreign resources but are also potentially reaching or constructing new markets. Central to this is the deployment of FDI – see chapter 1. It is through directly investing abroad that MNCs expand. We need to note the quite specific nature of FDI at this point. There are a number of ways that a capitalist enterprise can expand. It can, for example, buy stocks and shares in another company: indirect investment. However, FDI is different in that it is not organized by the market and the MNC retains control of the process; it is direct, and internally controlled, investment which avoids the market.

The second criterion is the internalization of cross-border markets, whereby firms take control of international economic activities themselves. This operates in two directions. MNCs can internalize using backward integration, by using investment to obtain and control markets in, for example, raw materials. Backward integration can be described as a rational move for a multinational that wants to protect its supply chain. But MNCs also internalize markets in a forward direction, using forward integration. They often do this through acquisitions to secure control, particularly quality control, over intermediate components in the production process. In doing this, the multinational is also using forward integration to internalize the component market *and* parts of the labour market through having greater control over the skilled labour supply. An MNC, then, has 'two distinctive features. First, it accesses, organizes and coordinates multiple value-added activities across national boundaries and, second, it internalizes at least some of the cross-border markets for the intermediate products arising from these activities. No other institution engages in *both* cross-border production and transactions' (Dunning and Lundan 2008: 6).

Finally, the third factor of significance here is the size and location of the enterprise. An MNC is a sizeable enterprise with employees in more than one country and, if it is a publicly quoted company, with its stocks and shares trading on a number of stock exchanges around the world. So, FDI, internalization and size, coupled to location, are the core components of the ideal typical multinational.

When we look at our ideal-type of MNC, we can see that these three factors create three parallel sets of problems and questions. Why do companies feel the need to seek opportunities abroad, and why at this scale? Why and how do companies internalize cross-border markets and how are these regulated (if they are)? And how do companies address and reconcile the imperative for global integration with pressures to be responsive to the circumstances and conditions of different countries where they operate? We will address these questions in the following sections in an attempt to develop and consolidate our understanding of multinationals in a globalizing world, before turning to a sociological interpretation of their role.

3.3 Multinationals and globalization

Clearly, the imperative for capital accumulation lies at the heart of why companies, as profit-maximizing actors, decide to internationalize (Dicken 2007). Under capitalism, firms seek out additional means of production (e.g. raw materials, labour power) in order to grow in value (Harvey 2011). But why would they opt to develop an international dimension to their activities, as opposed to simply focusing on expanding their operations within the boundaries of specific nation-states? Since the 1960s various theorists have sought to account for the decision of firms to grow through internationalization. Hymer (1976), for example, focused on how firms gain competitive advantage by securing ownership and control of foreign operations. An alternative perspective was proposed by Buckley and Casson (1976), who suggested that companies can benefit more from organizing cross-border activities internally, through hierarchical relations within the firm, than from entering into market transactions with separate foreign enterprises. But the most well-known theoretical contribution to understanding why firms develop an international dimension to their activities is the 'eclectic paradigm', which was elaborated by John Dunning (see Dunning 1997, 2001).

It identifies three factors which, depending on how they are configured, influence the extent and degree of internationalization. These are: the ownership-specific effect, the advantages that stem from internalization, and the location-specific effect (Dunning 2001). Thus the eclectic paradigm holds that

> Firms will engage in international production if they possess ownership advantages in a particular foreign market; if the enterprise perceives it to be in its best interest to add value to these ownership advantages rather than sell them to foreign firms – internalization advantages; and if locational advantages make it more profitable to exploit its assets in a particular foreign location rather than at home.
> (Jones 2005: 12)

Whilst credit must be given to Dunning for presenting a theory of international production which enables us to account for the role and activities of multinationals, there are some significant problems. For one thing, we are using a technical model to explain a social phenomenon: MNCs, as we will see, are avowedly social in nature, and this requires at least some kind of social analysis. Simply looking at the composition of ownership (regional, national or international), location and the modes and degree of internalization does little to help us to understand how and why MNCs have expanded, and the consequences. Moreover, the eclectic paradigm explicitly avoids discussion of wider contexts: for Dunning, multinationals provide their own context through their individual actions and their current and future collective actions in a form of 'alliance capitalism' (Dunning 1997: 14). From this perspective, the nation-state, local communities, non-governmental agencies and even non-human factors such as the environment have little or no relevance to making sense of MNCs.

Marxist perspectives are useful in helping to explain the process by which multinationals take advantage of the uneven development of capitalism when it comes to selecting investment locations. In this respect, geography matters: firms are impelled to internationalize in the first place, or to extend their international presence, by the search for the most profitable locations in which to source goods, or establish production sites. Two factors are generally considered to be significant: economies of scale and economies of scope. Put simply, economies of scale mean that a firm can lower its costs by producing a greater quantity or providing a larger amount of a service. Similarly, a firm can achieve an economy of scope by diversifying and expanding its range of products or services. Often both of these economies can only be achieved by moving into a new region or country, often a location where the business infrastructure is less advanced and costs – labour, raw materials and utilities – are significantly lower than in the home nation. Harvey (1982) has dubbed the process by which MNCs use their transnational presence to find new, more cost-effective and efficient locations for production as the search for a 'spatial fix' to the key challenge of generating more value. The multinational white goods (refrigerators, etc.) company Electrolux, for example, has made extensive use of spatial fixes in order to realize efficiency gains. It re-located production activities from plants in the US to Mexico, for example, and also from factories in Western Europe to cheaper production sites in Central and Eastern Europe, part of an aggressive plan to stay competitive based on the exploitation of geographical space (Webster et al. 2008).

We need to be cautious here in ascribing agency to organizations, but in the abstract what we can see is the purported increase in power of MNCs, and the concomitant decline in power of nation-states, particularly with respect to the operation of capitalist enterprises. Why has this happened? MNCs have sought to consolidate themselves across borders, rather than within borders, through internalizing markets, and to do this they have required national norms and regulations to be replaced by international norms and regulation, or lack of regulation (see chapter 4). From the early 1980s onwards, the dominant factor underpinning changes in the world economy has been FDI, rather than international trade. It is commonly thought that firms are 'now supposed to roam the globe in search of cheap but efficient production locations that offer them the largest and most secure and profitable return on competitive success' (Hirst et al. 2009: 69). Globalization, then, is largely driven by MNCs, particularly by their investment decisions, and how these affect the geography of global production (Dicken 2007).

Traditionally, MNCs typically moved overseas in the pursuit of markets or natural resources; however, there is now a much closer integration of production chains and a greater tendency for firms to re-locate their operations, including research and development activities, away from their home-country base (Dunning 2000 cited in

Edwards and Wajcman 2005). However, the effects of globalization are perhaps most evident in the way in which MNCs operate transnational arrangements for designing, sourcing, manufacturing, distributing and retailing goods in a way that maximizes efficiency, particularly in sectors such as electronics, clothing and footwear (Dicken 2007). Multinationals rarely own or even directly control the sites where goods are made; instead, factories are owned and managed through a complex network of contractor and subcontractor firms in a way designed to minimize costs (Hale and Wills 2005). For example, the Taiwanese-owned Yue Yuen company operates the factories in China which actually make the sport-shoes designed, marketed and sold by leading global branded retailers including Nike and Reebok (Merk 2008). The terms 'global commodity chain' (GCC) and 'global value chain' (GVC) have been used to express how economic activities are outsourced around the world, particularly to countries of the Global South, rather than retained within large-scale, vertically integrated and nationally based bureaucratic organizations (Gereffi et al. 2005).

However, the concept of the 'global production network' (GPN) has increasingly come to be preferred when it comes to capturing the complex nature of the highly flexible and geographically dispersed arrangements for organizing economic activities in a globalizing world which have proved so important to the success of major retail brands such as Zara and H&M (Coe et al. 2008). In some ways, the label is irrelevant; whether these arrangements are called GVCs, GCCs or GPNs, 'they are all centrally concerned with the globally coordinated interorganizational relationships which underpin the production of goods and services, and the power and value dynamics therein' (Coe 2012: 390). Nevertheless, there are a number of reasons why the term 'network' is preferable to 'chain'. For one thing, the latter implies that activities are coordinated by MNCs in a sequential or linear fashion, whereas they are often characterized by much more complex sets of relationships (Coe et al. 2008). A second reason for preferring to use the concept of the GPN, rather than GCC or GVC, is that it is more useful when it comes to acknowledging the role of non-firm actors. Although multinationals exercise a high degree of control over GPNs (Barrientos et al. 2011), their structures and dynamics are also influenced by national governments, labour unions and non-governmental organizations (NGOs) as well as supplier firms (Coe et al. 2008).

The rise of GPNs has influenced work and employment in a number of ways. For one thing, they have generated a new and increasingly complex international division of labour (see chapter 6). In some parts of the Global South, like Bangladesh, growing numbers of female migrant workers have been drawn into formal employment as a result of MNC investment (Perrons 2004; Barrientos et al. 2011). The manufacture of popular consumer electronics devices, like Apple iPods, iPhones and iPads, is outsourced to a wide range of countries in Asia: 'While the consumption of finished products remains concentrated in the West, the production of this increasing range of commodities is increasingly conducted by workers located across the far reaches of global capital-ism' (Taylor 2008: 11). A second key implication concerns the question of how labour standards are governed within GPNs. While networks operate beyond the boundaries of nation-states, their nodes do not, and activities therein may be subject to regulatory efforts by national governments. The development of GPNs has also been associated with the rise of innovative forms of private governance, such as labour codes of conduct, which are often prompted by campaigns by consumer and labour activists (Coe 2012) – see chapter 4. This highlights the way in which GPNs are sites of political contestation (Levy 2008); through their emergent transnational structures (see chapter 5), labour unions and activist organizations often play a prominent role in shaping, influenc-ing and contesting how GPNs operate (Rainnie et al. 2011; Coe 2013).

Export-oriented industrialization strategies pursued by many coun-tries in the Global South have helped multinationals to develop GPNs. Countries such as Mexico, Taiwan and South Korea became desirable locations for investment and new factories in the 1960s and 1970s, fol-lowed from the 1980s onwards by Malaysia, Indonesia and Thailand, among others. The Philippines has become a leading manufacturing and assembly location for high-technology electronics goods (McKay 2006). In many countries, governments have established dedicated locations, sometimes known as 'export processing zones' (EPZs), within which planning, tax and labour regulations are relaxed, as incentives to attract foreign investment there. In 2006, there were some 3,500 EPZs, operating in around 130 countries (Barrientos et al. 2011). However, economic development and rising wage levels meant that they became increasingly costly places for multinationals want-ing cheap, flexible and compliant labour. Countries like China, with its large pool of potential labour, became preferred as a result (Pun 2005a). It has instituted a number of 'Special Economic Zones' in the south of the country, in places like Shenzhen for example, where factories making products for international markets are concentrated (Cantin 2008). Elsewhere, Cambodia has developed a rapidly expand-ing export-oriented textile and garment industry, and has become an important location in the transnational production process as a result (Arnold and Shih 2010).

The transnational organization of economic activity is not just lim-ited to the production of manufactured goods. As we saw in chapter 2, developments in information and communications technology (ICT) have enabled business services, call centre operations and ICT work itself to be 'offshored' (re-located) from developed economies like Britain and the US to countries where costs, particularly labour costs, are cheaper (Blinder 2006). India has become a major location for call centre work and software development activity (Hirst et al. 2009). The process of offshoring, as applied to the re-location of call centre opera-tions from Britain to cheaper sites in India, for example, is a further illustration of the spatial fix in action (Taylor and Bain 2005). Clearly, developments in ICT have made the offshoring process both easier and cheaper for multinationals to operate, leading some commentators to make lofty claims for its transformational potential (e.g. Blinder 2006), although the likely impact on jobs in the Global North may not be as dramatic as is sometimes supposed (OECD 2007).

That said, though, offshoring has become increasingly commonplace across a wide range of sectors, including many business services such as the provision of human resources support (e.g. Pereira and Anderson 2012). Some business services, such as the recruitment and staffing industry, increasingly operate on a transnational basis (Ward 2004). Even sectors of the economy which have traditionally been less exposed internationally, because they involve delivering personal services that cannot easily be re-located, have developed a transnational character. In the social care industry, for example, both Hochschild (2003) and Perrons (2004: 103–12) examine the characteristics of an emerging 'global care chain', encompassing multinational providers of care services who rely upon migrant workers to staff their operations. Its social consequences are felt both in the Global North, where it results in changes to gendered work patterns, and in the Global South, where countries are denuded of valuable skills (Hochschild 2003). We will explore this more fully in chapter 9.

The spatial reorganization of production on a transnational scale has some important implications for work and employment. Yet concerns have been expressed about the capacity for multinationals to exploit spatial differences in a way that weakens workers' bargaining power and undermines labour standards. Re-locating, or threatening to re-locate, production activities to countries which offer lower wages and weaker arrangements for enforcing workers' rights may encourage a 'race to the bottom', to the detriment of workers as a whole (see chapter 4). It also has implications for jobs in the Global North, as the developments in the clothing sector demonstrate (see box 3.2).

While acknowledging the importance of multinationals as both drivers and beneficiaries of globalization, care needs to be taken not to exaggerate the extent to which they have become genuinely transnational actors, in the sense that their operations and activities transcend national borders. As Hirst et al. (2009: 100) remind us, MNCs 'are still largely confined to their home territory in terms of their overall activity: they remain heavily "nationally embedded"'. In other words, multinationals, even those that strive to create an authentically global presence, have strong and deep-rooted connections with their respective countries of origin. Generally, they are best conceived of as 'national corporations with international operations' (Dicken 2007: 126). Major international companies like the giant retailer Walmart have most of their operations in their home country – the United States in this case (Edwards 2011).

Box 3.2 The closure of Burberry's Treorchy factory

In March 2007, the clothing company Burberry closed its plant in Treorchy, South Wales, which made polo shirts, with the loss of some 300 jobs. It claimed that the factory had become commercially unviable, and that it was more cost-effective to switch production to sites in Asia and Southern and Eastern Europe where wages and employment costs are lower. The original closure announcement sparked a vigorous campaign by Burberry workers and their union – the GMB – to keep it open. Their efforts drew support from celebrities, including the singers Tom Jones and Charlotte Church. Jenkins and Turnbull (2011: 208) observe that the 'Burberry dispute attracted remarkable public attention as workers, under their union banner, mounted a fierce campaign that encompassed skilful use of the media, direct protest, political lobbying and legal action'. A set of coordinated, international protests against Burberry's move were mounted in cities including Paris, London and New York, though they had little practical effect. More seriously, unions based in Burberry's other UK plants turned down requests for solidarity action, largely from a fear that any disruption to production would put their future in jeopardy. The campaign delayed the Treorchy plant's closure, but did not in the end prevent it. Moreover, less than two years later, Burberry announced major job losses and a factory closure among its surviving Yorkshire plants (Jenkins and Turnbull 2011).

3.4 Multinationals, work and employment

Having established the main parameters of how multinationals operate in a globalized environment, and their distinctive features, the purpose of this section is to examine how their activities impact on work and employment. One very important consequence of the rise of global supply chains and production networks has been the development of a more internationalized division of labour in the world economy. This is particularly apparent when we consider the growing importance of manufacturing as a source of employment, particularly for women, to many economies in the Global South, such as Indonesia (Caraway 2007). We look at the implications for the management of labour in the new global factories in chapter 6. Here, though, our focus is on four other key issues relating to how MNCs use their position as dominant actors in the global economy, derived from the power they accrue through being able to operate across national borders, to influence work and employment in ways that benefit their interests.

First of all, there are the implications of what is rather euphemistically known as 'regime competition' (Streeck 1997). This refers to the way in which, in a more globalized economic environment, the desirability of attracting multinational investment, and therefore jobs, means that countries feel obliged to compete with one another by offering more attractive employment 'regimes', in the form of weaker labour laws and other regulations. Governments come under pressure to relax the supposed regulatory burden for fear that, if they do not do so, multinationals will transfer their activities to countries that are more pliable. Competition between countries to attract multinational investment, based on which of them can offer the most desirable regulatory environment, operates akin to a 'beauty contest'. This was evident during the 2000s, for example, when major auto firms, such as Toyota and Hyundai, engaged in a process of selecting locations for new manufacturing plants in Central and Eastern Europe (Meardi 2012).

Multinationals can shrewdly use the threat to withdraw their operations from a country, or 'disinvestment' as it is termed, to exert pressure on the governments of countries to operate more business-friendly systems of employment regulation. The multinational white goods manufacturer Electrolux, for example, has evidently benefited from operating a policy of 'regime shopping': actively seeking out locations which offer supportive regulatory environments, in the form of lax labour laws and weak unions, as areas for investment (Webster et al. 2008). Countries in the Global South, such as Malaysia, whose economic development is centred on attracting multinational investment, advertise the advantages of their low-paid workforces and limited employment rights (Caspersz 2006). It is this that has fostered the 'race to the bottom' in labour standards (see chapter 4) as countries compete with one another to offer multinationals ever more weakened, and thus attractive, regulatory environments.

Second, multinationals also use the power that derives from their activity as international actors to undermine and challenge employment standards which prevail in particular national production sites. Multinationals often try to scrutinize, and thus be in a position to compare, the respective performance of each of their subsidiaries and plants, particularly in circumstances where their operations are highly integrated globally (Marginson and Sisson 1994). The concept of 'coercive comparisons' is used to refer to the way in which multinationals use elaborate financial, productivity and output data to make detailed comparisons of the performance of their plants operating in different locations (Mueller and Purcell 1992). These can then be used to exert pressure on workers and unions in plants that are stated to be under-performing to make concessions, such as accepting more flexible working arrangements or moderating bargaining demands, as a means of catching up.

The potency of coercive comparisons lies in the extent to which multinational employers can use the threat of re-location – moving production away from plants and subsidiaries deemed to be underperforming to other, more efficient sites – to exercise control over workers (Marginson and Meardi 2009). According to Grimshaw and Rubery (2003: 214), coercive comparisons operate most effectively 'as a disciplinary tool, and as a means of enforcing some degree of conformity with corporate policies and objectives, when the implicit threat to the continued existence of the subsidiary has some degree of credibility'.

In their study of German- and US-owned automotive plants in three Central European countries, Meardi et al. (2009) found that coercive comparisons were used extensively by the companies concerned. These comparisons were invoked in ways that demonstrated the reality of international competition to the workers on the production line. The ever-present possibility of re-location, of which workers were acutely aware, produced a climate in which concessions were viewed as necessary. While the mere threat of re-location was sufficient in itself to produce the desired results for the companies concerned, the fact that actual re-location was generally unnecessary nonetheless offered unions some opportunity to develop effective responses.

The scope globalization provides for enabling multinationals to engage in regime competition and coercive comparisons challenges the role of largely nation-based labour movements. But the third aspect of how multinationals use their power as dominant actors in the global economy often has effects which are even more severe. This concerns reports that multinationals are responsible for incidents of labour repression and violations of workers' rights around the world on a large scale (e.g. Mosley 2011). The regular survey of violations of trade union rights undertaken by the International Trade Union Confederation (ITUC) highlights manifold instances of labour repression, many of which are connected to multinational activity. In the Central American country of Guatemala, for example, companies owned by the major fruit multinational, Chiquita, have been associated with attempts to suppress legitimate trade union activity, including reported death threats against a prominent union official (ITUC 2012). The ITUC's 2012 report states that, worldwide, 90 people were killed and around 2,500 detained as a result of legitimate trade union activity in the period January to December 2010. Colombia is the world's most dangerous place to be a trade unionist; 49 people were killed there in 2010 on account of their trade union activities (see chapter 5 for more details). Allegations that it is implicated in violence against trade unionists have been levelled at the multinational beverages company Coca-Cola (see box 3.3).

Multinationals are rarely implicated directly in union repression themselves, although the same cannot always be said of their suppliers. Suppression of union activities and attacks on labour rights are often undertaken on behalf of multinationals by governments wanting to establish suitably pacified workforces which are attractive to inward investors. In the Philippines, for example, government officials have endeavoured to maintain union-free environments, in order to provide multinationals with favourable sites for investment (McKay 2006; Kelly 2001). Elsewhere in Asia, state-sanctioned repression is commonplace. In Malaysia and Sri Lanka, for example, governments

Box 3.3 Allegations of violent anti-union repression in Colombian Coca-Cola bottling plants

Since the 1980s, hundreds of Colombian trade unionists have been murdered by right-wing paramilitary forces with connections to employers; many more have been attacked, or threatened with violence, on account of their union activities. The giant US beverages multinational Coca-Cola is alleged to have been implicated in the violent deaths of trade unionists at some of its separately owned bottling plants in Colombia. In his book, *Belching out the Devil*, an account of the nefarious activities of Coca-Cola in various parts of the world, Mark Thomas talked to a former bottling-plant worker who describes how his brother was murdered by right-wing paramilitaries (Thomas 2009). The main food and drink union in Colombia, Sinaltrainal, pursued an ultimately unsuccessful lawsuit through the US courts against Coca-Cola and its bottling plants. It also called for consumers to boycott Coca-Cola products in protest against the violence, a campaign which was supported by labour unions around the world (Brodzinsky 2003; www.colombiasolidarity.org.uk/campaigns/18–coca-cola/405–coca-cola-and-the-paramilitaries-in-colombia).

The US Public Broadcasting Service has made a *Frontline World* documentary investigating the allegations that Coca-Cola and its partner bottling firms were complicit in attacks on trade unionists, including murders. The programme is available to view on its website: www.pbs.org/frontlineworld/fellows/colombia0106/.

have used 'legislation and regulation to create a climate that nullified employer–employee conflict through the use of threats and sanctions. Jailing of worker activists, blacklisting their employment and acts of violence including police shooting at worker protests were not uncommon' (Caspersz 2006: 156–7).

A fourth way in which multinationals use their power as transnational actors to influence work and employment across their network of subsidiaries concerns their ability to diffuse management practices across national borders. A key implication of this is that firm-specific, global approaches to managing people at work become more commonplace, lessening the influence of individual countries and their specific regulatory systems. One important trend is the development of global arrangements for identifying, nurturing and supporting managerial talent across borders; major multinational companies including IBM, HSBC and Procter & Gamble have invested heavily in global talent management initiatives (Schuler et al. 2011; Scullion and Collings 2011). Efforts by multinationals to develop global systems for managing people at work are often supported by corporate human resources functions, which seem to play an increasingly important part in coordinating work and employment arrangements across national borders (Farndale et al. 2010).

By diffusing so-called 'best-practice' employment techniques internationally – for example, those relating to work organization and job design or to pay and reward arrangements – multinationals act as a key driver for convergence in the global economy (Rubery and Grimshaw 2003). The work of Gamble (2006, 2011), who studied the operations of a UK retailer which had successfully established a presence in China, testifies to the capacity of multinationals to transfer corporate practices to foreign subsidiaries in a relatively unproblematic fashion.

Often, though, multinationals attempt to replicate elements of their home-country base in foreign subsidiaries; this is especially where they originate from those countries, such as the United States, which are dominant in the global economy. A good example of this concerns the way in which firms from the United States attempt to operate union-free workplaces in their foreign operations, reflecting the practice which prevails in their home-country base (Almond and Ferner 2006). The increasing prominence of Chinese multinationals in the global economy, mentioned above, provides a further illustration of the relevance of this home-country effect since they are associated with the imposition of harsh disciplinary regimes which mirror practice in China (Brooks 2010). When it comes to the mechanisms for enabling diffusion, managers undertaking international assignments often play a prominent part in enforcing control and effecting coordination across multinationals and their subsidiaries. Through the use of 'appropriate technical and personal skills', international managers also help to ensure that corporate policies and practices are transferred effectively to foreign subsidiaries (Gamble 2011: 51). By spreading 'best-practice' management ideas and approaches across national borders, multinationals and their personnel act as important agents of convergence, contributing to a more globalized system of work and employment.

3.5 MNCs, work and employment: sociological insights

There are some important sociological concerns that arise from the above discussion, one of which concerns the implications of social stratification in a globalizing world. The relationship between globalization, changes in social structure and multinationals is a complex one: without economic change, multinationals cannot emerge, and without multinationals emerging some of the social stratification effects we see today would not appear. But MNCs engender new social formations that, some argue, can themselves push for further globalization (Sklair 2001), which results in changes in social structure and the location of labour. We will briefly look at these in turn.

Complex processes of globalization, changes in political ideology leading to a reduction in the role of the state and state-controlled industries, global markets, geopolitics and general social and economic transformation have come together to create conditions within which social groupings change and emerge. For Leslie Sklair, these conditions have led to the emergence of a wholly new class formation: what he calls the transnational capitalist class (TCC) (Sklair 2001, 2002), a class that is not made up of capitalists in the traditional Marxist sense (i.e. owners) but, rather, composed of MNC executives, bureaucrats and politicians, globalizing professionals, and merchants and media. These correspond to four fractions: corporate, state, technical and consumerist (Sklair 2002: 99). The TCC is a class in itself and for itself; it 'sees its mission as organizing the conditions under which its interests and the interests of the global system (which usually but not always coincide) can be furthered within the transnational, interstate, national and local contexts' (2002: 99). Capitalist globalization has created this class, and has also created a new group of emerging, and aspiring, TCC members, usually based locally but who identify with global capitalism.

In addition, MNCs have created specific strata, notably globalizing bureaucrats, professionals and politicians, to ensure their expansion and success; these strata combine with the TCC to bring about the ends that the multinational is trying to achieve. Of course, this cannot happen without the support of wider groups in society, and, to achieve this, the TCC promotes the 'culture-ideology' of consumerism via the media. As Sklair notes, 'It is no accident that the age of capitalist globalization should have begun to flower in the second half of the twentieth century, just when the electronic revolution that heralded the age of the globalizing mass media took root' (2002: 105). From this perspective, globalization is a consequence of the actions of this self-interested social class, and becomes a self-perpetuating process as the TCC pushes its own interests, bringing about social and economic changes. In turn these result in the creation of more aspiring TCC members wanting to join the TCC and push for their own interests.

Sklair presents some powerful evidence for his thesis – we can see global struggles between indigenous state interests and MNCs combining with TCC members to bring about dramatic changes, particularly in the Global South. Yet there is a sense of reduction here, of a complex set of issues being reduced to the actions of a relatively small number of individuals who share some interests but, it should be remembered, are also often competing against one another for market share and profit. It is this point that stands out; MNCs share many interests with one another, but these do not always coincide, and this makes the idea of a unified TCC difficult to sustain.

Empirical studies would appear to confirm this. Fiona Moore's ethnography of transnational business people based in Frankfurt and London (Moore 2005) found a much more complex set of relationships and understandings of self, identity, culture and nation. Whilst sympathetic to Sklair's thesis, Moore found that multiple cultures were being formed by these workers, and many did not see their interests from a TCC perspective. In contrast, whilst they do identify with a global system, this is not a conscious identification, more a sort of habitus, or disposition, into which they drift as a result of their transnational activities (Moore 2005: 161). There is more discussion of these ambiguities in chapter 8.

The implication here is that it is the work environment, and not personal interests, that generates this TCC culture, something which undermines Sklair's argument about active agency inside the TCC pushing globalization onwards. That said, the trends of social change do conform broadly to Sklair's outline, and one feature in particular stands out – the incidence of migration, and particularly skilled migration. It is clear that there is a significant group of individuals, highly skilled, who move around the globe between contracts, or within specific multinationals (see chapter 8).

Sociologically related insights can help us to understand the role and activities of multinationals better in other ways too. In particular, they cast doubt on the extent to which MNCs operate as supremely powerful and wholly rational agents of convergence, capable of diffusing best-practice management techniques, and able to transcend, or render ineffective, the influence of national-level labour regulations and trade unions in an unproblematic fashion. Four issues are relevant here.

First of all, multinationals are often hindered from replicating corporate policies and practices relating to work and employment issues in foreign locations because they have to adapt to the circumstances and characteristics of the societies in which their subsidiaries operate. These 'societal effects' (Maurice et al. 1986) include those distinctive features of a 'host' country's institutional framework, such as country-specific labour laws and arrangements for coordinating relationships between employers and unions, which influence organizational practice. Some host countries offer institutional environments which are more amenable to transfer than others. The UK, with its relatively lightly regulated labour market, gives US multinationals keen to avoid unions a relatively free hand (Edwards and Ferner 2002; Marginson and Meardi 2010). Elsewhere in Europe, countries such as Turkey, and parts of Central and Eastern Europe (e.g. Czech Republic, Hungary), are also 'permissive' environments which allow MNCs a high level of autonomy when it comes to enacting corporate management techniques and practices (Sayim 2010; Meardi 2012).

Elsewhere, however, national-level regulatory arrangements (e.g. labour laws) and other institutional characteristics of host countries offer multinationals less room for manoeuvre. The Walmart case featured in chapter 1 demonstrates how country-specific, national-level factors hindered efforts by the company to operate a uniform firm-specific approach to managing work and employment relations across its various international operations. Multinationals often have to adapt their practices in a way that respects the characteristics of the host-country context, rather than being able to diffuse them directly to subsidiaries unaltered (Edwards 2011). The need to respect cultural differences between countries poses a further problem. Notwithstanding the expansion and consolidation of cross-border markets multinationals face a major challenge, that of coping with and controlling national differences that affect their operations. Primarily, we can see these as problems of identity. There is an extensive literature on the relative contribution that local cultural effects have on the operation and performance of MNCs (e.g. Myloni et al. 2004). The key to understanding work and employment in multinationals, then, lies in an appreciation of the competing demands that arise from, on the one hand, the standardized management practice that derives from the imperative to act as globally integrated firms and, on the other hand, the pressure to be responsive to the societies in which they operate.

Second, the question of culture points to a further area of complexity when it comes to developing a sociological interpretation of multinationals. In essence, we can see the construction and articulation of an organizational culture specific to the MNC as an important way that the organization unifies its employees and orients itself in terms of operation and extension. But how does this work in practice? Sociological studies of occupational identity versus organizational identity illustrate the ways that organizations cope with these tensions, and this process is central to understanding how it is that multinationals manage actually to operate. Occupational identity – the sense of self that emerges from performing a particular role, belonging to a particular profession or a skilled trade – is still strong for many employees, providing a sense of self and worth.

However, in recent years, many organizations, and multinationals in particular, have fostered and promoted the idea of organizational identity and culture: distinct cultures that are associated with the MNC alone, and which require high levels of commitment. In attempting to answer how it is that multinationals manage to operate, we should consider those social and cultural factors that ensure employee loyalty and commitment to a particular way of doing things. We can interpret these as procedures designed to control the labour process. Elger and Smith's study of Japanese multinationals in the UK provides a good case study of how a transnational actor – the multinational firm putting FDI into a national economy – mobilizes resources to confront and control local actors, such as organized labour and managers, with a nationally based understanding of operations and identity. The result is often a new form of organization, one that has clear roots in a distinct national culture, but one that also has evolved and innovated to cope with significant uncertainties and tensions that emerge as the MNC transplants itself into a new national setting (Elger and Smith 2005: 14).

Third, we need to be wary about ascribing too much power to MNCs, as dominant actors in the global economy, for another reason. This is because of the large extent to which multinationals, in addition to being political agents themselves, operate as political organizations, marked by struggles for power between actors within them (Ferner and Edwards 1995; Dörrenbächer and Geppert 2011). Sociological insight involves acknowledging the importance of the respective 'power capabilities' enjoyed by MNC actors, and how these influence the success of efforts by corporate headquarters to diffuse work practices to international subsidiaries (Ferner et al. 2012). In particular, subsidiary managers may enjoy some scope to resist or amend policies emanating from the company's home-country base, where they judge them to be unnecessary or inappropriate. This is often achieved by selectively drawing on elements of their host country's institutional framework, to use as a power resource when negotiating with managers in corporate headquarters (Edwards 2011; Edwards et al. 2007; Ferner 2010).

Ferner et al.'s (2005) study of equality and diversity issues in US multinationals offers a good illustration of how this process operates in practice. Managers of UK subsidiaries were able to negotiate changes in the implementation of corporate diversity policies by utilizing the specific legal framework of their own country. This rendered them more appropriate to the specific context of UK society. Clearly, we have to see multinationals as fundamentally social entities whose objectives and activities are the product of dynamic and relational processes of interaction between different actors within and around them.

Moore's (2006) case study research in a German multinational bank points to the importance of viewing the MNC as a negotiated order, one which is centred upon the self-presentation efforts of individuals. Her findings indicate 'that the practices and strategies of firms are predicated less on rational-action strategies for achieving competitive advantage . . . and more on organic, not necessarily rational, negotiation between the different parts of the group' (Moore 2006: 410).

Finally, we should recognize that multinationals are far from being all-powerful entities. A sociological perspective helps to highlight the extent to which their activities have generated a substantial amount of opposition from numerous social groups and movements around the world, at both national and transnational levels. Multinationals have been challenged by, and can be distinctly vulnerable to, pressure from transnational activist networks, international NGOs and labour unions, among others (e.g. Keck and Sikkink 1998; Seidman 2007, 2011). The international anti-sweatshop organization, the Clean Clothes Campaign, which was discussed in chapter 1, is one of the most prominent activist groups involved in mobilizing efforts to ensure that multinationals respect workers' rights in the factories of the Global South (Ross 2012). Micheletti and Stolle (2007) highlight the potency of efforts by such anti-sweatshop groups and labour rights campaigners to mobilize consumers and public opinion in a way that impels multinationals to initiate reforms. For example, the controversy attracted by Nike over allegations of poor working conditions and violations of workers' rights in the factories making its products forced it to institute remedial action, including the establishment of a corporate code of conduct setting out minimum labour standards across its supply chain together with appropriate compliance arrangements (O'Rourke 2003). In chapters 4 and 5 we examine the role of cross-border activist campaigns and labour unions under globalization in more detail.

3.6 The system, society and dominance (SSD) framework

We have seen that one perspective on the role and activities of multinationals in relation to work and employment portrays them as powerful agents of global convergence, using their dominant position to operate transnational arrangements for organizing work that maximize efficiency and undermine labour unions, while diffusing management ideas and practices around the world. In contrast, an alternative, sociologically informed perspective focuses on the ways in which multinationals have to adapt their operations in accordance with pressures deriving from the nature of the particular societies within which they operate. A further sociological perspective is concerned with understanding how MNC objectives and activities have to be viewed as outcomes of dynamic processes of negotiation between organizational actors, such as head office managers in the multinational's country of origin, and those who are based in its foreign subsidiaries.

The system, society and dominance (SSD) approach, which was initially elaborated by Smith and Meiksins (1995), before being deployed by Elger and Smith (2005) in a study of Japanese-owned workplaces in the UK, integrates these different perspectives within a single overarching framework. It attests that work and management in MNCs are shaped by a complex and dynamic set of interacting effects. While structural factors, such as specific management practices, play an important part, the SSD approach recognizes that work and employment outcomes are also the product of social relationships which mediate their influence (Smith 2008). It thus 'seeks to provide a holistic framework for understanding the complex world of management and workers within the internationalizing firm' (Delbridge et al. 2011: 497). We can use the SSD approach as the basis of a properly sociological understanding of multinationals in general, and work and employment within them in particular.

Elger and Smith's (2005) examination of Japanese multinationals in the UK led them to construct a theory that explains the relationship between external, global (or home-country) factors and local conditions of work in specific facilities. They identify three parameters: system imperatives that emerge from political economy (both local and global), societal effects, and dominance effects (e.g. local dominant solutions to workplace and work organization problems). Thus, the 'SSD framework argues that the international firm will be a site for the social interaction of these three sets of processes, and not simply a universal set of economically "efficient" organizational practices or a local set of institutional rules, customs, laws, and relations' (Elger and Smith 2005: 58).

System effects are those deriving from overarching structures and processes which operate above and beyond particular nation-states and societies, such as the broader (capitalist) political economy within which multinationals operate. The way that global capitalism functions, for example through the above-mentioned drive by multinationals for 'spatial fixes', illustrates such a system effect in action.

We discussed the importance of societal effects in section 3.5. By recognizing that work and the management of labour in multinationals are influenced by both the formal institutions and the social norms, customs and values of the different societies in which they operate, the SSD framework demonstrates that there are important limits to global convergence.

The dominance effect captures the way in which, given uneven global economic development, and notable differentials in economic power, there is a 'tendency for one society to take the lead in evolving work organization and business practices considered more efficient than those operating within other countries' (Elger and Smith 2005: 66). Multinationals originating from such dominant economies, like the United States in particular, play a key part in transferring management practices from their home-country base to subsidiaries in host countries. Sayim (2010), for example, documents how the dominance effect enjoyed by US multinationals enabled them to diffuse reward management practices to subsidiaries based in Turkey. It is not just countries that produce a dominance effect – in some sectors, certain multinationals are so dominant that they exercise an important influence over the practice of indigenous firms themselves. In Italy, for example, local fast-food companies copied the management policies and practices of US fast-food chain McDonald's, including its forceful anti-union approach (Royle 2006).

By incorporating these three sets of processes, the SSD framework clearly offers a sophisticated, sociologically informed approach to understanding work and employment in multinationals. However, Delbridge et al. (2011) contend that a fourth element – 'corporate effects' – needs to be added to the model in order to capture the influence of the parent company's strategy on the policies and practices of specific subsidiaries.

A further notable contribution of the SSD approach is that it recognizes the importance of agency, particularly how organizational actors in multinationals influence work and employment outcomes through the ways in which they interpret and act upon prevailing structural and contextual factors. According to Elger and Smith, 'It is only through micropolitical processes of argument, interpretation, conflict, and compromise that groups and individuals negotiate how these different (and perhaps competing) ways of working, standards of quality, authority relations, and methods of employment will actually shape particular work situations' (2005: 69).

As we have already seen, the UK retail multinational studied by Gamble (2011) was able to transfer corporate management practices to its sites in China in a relatively unproblematic fashion. Nevertheless, once they were in place, Chinese workers understood, interpreted and acted upon them in distinctive ways, meaning that how the practices actually operated on the ground differed in important respects from the original managerial intention. Thus management practices diffused across national borders by multinationals do 'not enter a void. The way host country employees respond to them is coloured by unique configurations of experiences, norms and expectations' (Gamble 2011: 79). See box 3.4 for a case study example of an internationalizing Chinese firm.

Box 3.4 Managing work and labour in an internationalizing Chinese firm

McKenna et al.'s (2010) case study of 'Compco' (a pseudonym), the largest maker of personal computers in China, offers some useful insights into the complex and dynamic ways in which the management of work and labour operates in internationalizing firms. In 2005, Compco bought the PC division of a major US company. This provided an opportunity to transfer North American management ideas and practices to its home-country plants in China. Because they viewed these ideas and practices as 'modern', the firm's human resource managers assumed that operating them would enhance its global competitive performance. They were also seen as desirable for another reason: they allowed managers more scope to exercise greater control over, and secure efficiency from, the workforce. Yet this was not simply a case of management ideas and practices being transferred across borders to the detriment of the workforce in a straightforward fashion. Many Chinese workers actually welcomed the new practices, not least because they were able to influence how they functioned on the factory floor; workers did not just passively consent to them, but actively shaped their operation. Compco staff 'were aware of the need to adapt both the new practices and to retain or at least keep in mind facets of the existing system. How newly introduced practices played out in the day to day reality at Compco was subject to interpretation and negotiation around their utility, relevance and value' (McKenna et al. 2010: 869).

To understand the management of work and labour in internationalizing firms, then, we should not just consider the effects of factors like the firm's capacity to transfer practices, or the influence of the host-country society, but also explore the active part which both managers and workers play in constructing those practices.

The SSD model has some distinct benefits. It allows us to examine workplace relations as emerging from a combination of local and external factors, and to identify the tension that often exists between these. The SSD framework offers both a critical and a contextualized approach to understanding work and employment in multinationals. Without appreciating the wider system imperatives and structural constraints (and freedom from constraints), we cannot simply measure FDI and take it as a marker of MNC activity. Moreover, multinationals are also embedded in societies, and themselves produce social environments. These social aspects produce societal effects which are significant in terms of creating different, and often more favourable, conditions for the further expansion of MNCs. Whether such expansion is inexorable remains to be seen. However, the SSD approach also recognizes modes of resistance to changes in both the labour process and wider community structure. Perhaps contrary to expectations, even multinationals on greenfield sites face local dominance factors, particularly in terms of resistance and non-compliance: 'Local workers and local managers deploy resources such as claims to expertise or labour market leverage, which mediate and challenge the design intentions of international management' (Elger and Smith 2005: 8).

3.7 Conclusion

Multinationals are both major drivers, and key beneficiaries, of the process of globalization. Their importance is evident not just in respect of markedly increased levels of FDI in the global economy, but also with regard to the widespread development of transnational arrangements for organizing production and consumption. Clearly, this has had a major impact on work and employment. Using the power that emanates from operating at a transnational level – above and beyond the borders of nation-states – multinationals enjoy greater scope to shape work practices in ways that suit their objectives: by stimulating competition between countries for more favourable regulatory climates; invoking cross-border comparisons of work and employment arrangements to reduce costs ('coercive comparisons'); suppressing the activity of labour unions; and diffusing best-practice management ideas and approaches. For these reasons, then, multinationals are a particularly important source of convergence in the global economy. As we have seen, though, they often have to adapt their work and employment arrangements in order to comply with the circumstances of host-country societies. Some national-level employment regimes are more 'permissive' than others. We must remember too that multinationals are also social entities themselves; their objectives and the outcomes of their activities are often the product of dynamic and relational processes of interaction between different actors within and around them. The SSD model, as modified by Delbridge et al. (2011) to recognize the role of 'corporate effects', is therefore a particularly useful tool for understanding the complex and dynamic sets of processes which influence work and employment in multinationals.

Importantly, it also helps to focus our attention on how multinationals are constituted, and the way in which they operate, as fundamentally social actors.

Further reading and useful websites

For the role and activities of multinationals in relation to globalization, see Dunning and Lundan (2008) and Jones (2005). There are also chapters devoted to MNCs in some of the more general texts on globalization (e.g. Dicken 2007; Held and McGrew 2007; Hirst et al. 2009). Ferner (2010) and Edwards (2011) provide good overviews of issues relating to the management of work and labour in multinational enterprises, especially issues relating to the cross-border diffusion of employment practices. For details of the SSD framework, and insights from its application in the case of Japanese-owned subsidiary plants operating in the UK, see Elger and Smith (2005). Delbridge et al. (2011) offer a good overview of the SSD approach, and suggest adding 'corporate effects' to it.

The United Nations Conference on Trade and Development (UNCTAD) website provides access to downloadable copies of its annual *World Investment Report*: http://unctad.org/en/Pages/Home. aspx. The 2011 edition is available at:
http://unctad.org/en/Pages/DIAE/World%20Investment%20Report/ WIR2011_WebFlyer.aspx

The ITUC publishes an *Annual Survey of Violations of Trade Union Rights*: http://survey.ituc-csi.org/.

4 Globalization and the regulation of international labour standards

4.1 Introduction

In November 2010, the self-styled 'ethical fashion chain' Monsoon faced allegations that it sources some of its products from suppliers in India that use child labour and pay illegally low wages. This is a particularly sensitive issue for Monsoon. It is a founding member of the Ethical Trading Initiative (ETI), a UK-based organization comprising retailers, non-governmental organizations (NGOs) and trade unions, whose remit is to work towards ensuring that workers in global supply chains are free from exploitative working conditions. Monsoon responded to the claims by stressing the efforts that it puts into stamping out labour abuses in its supply chain. Yet it is not the only UK high street retail chain to have faced claims that the workers in the Global South who make its products are grossly exploited. Other ETI members, including Primark, Asda and Tesco, have been accused of sourcing clothes from factories in Bangladesh where workers earn as little as 5 pence per hour, and which have poor safety standards, such as inaccessible fire exits.

Accounts like these have stimulated much interest in how far working conditions and labour rights should be protected in a global economy, and also the most appropriate means of doing so. Trade liberalization and multinational investment, allied to growing demand from Western consumers for cheap products (clothes, toys, sports-shoes, etc.), mean that many more people from around the world have been drawn into the transnational production process. Some view this aspect of globalization as an unambiguously positive development, because of the resulting jobs and prosperity it generates. Others, however, assert that global production arrangements, and particularly the demand for cheap labour they stimulate, have undesirable consequences for workers, which need remedying in some way. Traditionally, the regulation of working conditions and labour rights resided within discrete nation-states. But working conditions in global production networks (GPNs) are beyond the regulatory capacity of individual governments. Therefore, attention has increasingly been focused on transnational arrangements for regulating employment conditions and workers' rights (Tsogas 2009).

We begin this chapter by examining the reasons why the topic of international labour standards has become so important. The main arguments for and against regulating labour standards internationally are then assessed. The subsequent sections deal with the main approaches to regulating international labour standards. There has been a lot of interest in multilateral efforts involving more than one country to effect regulation, particularly under the auspices of the International Labour Organization (ILO). Moreover, the rise of private, voluntary arrangements, particularly codes of conduct dealing with labour issues, is also a prominent trend.

4.2 Why international labour standards?

While there is also a long history of efforts to regulate labour standards on a transnational basis (Brown 2001), since the 1990s the question of whether or not, and how, labour standards should be regulated internationally has become more prominent, largely in the context of globalization (Royle 2011). The key issue concerns how globalization, with all the advantages it offers to capital, particularly greater mobility, can be reconciled with effective regulation of work and employment relations in a way which ensures that the working conditions and labour rights of people around the world are protected (Hepple 2005). Many activists and campaigners contend that the pursuit of free trade, and the greater ease of movement enjoyed by capital, renders multinational companies and their associates much more powerful, and workers a lot more vulnerable (e.g. Klein 2000; Seidman 2007).

There are a number of related reasons why globalization has generated renewed interest in the question of international labour standards. First, it is contended that globalization imposes significant constraints on the ability of nation-states to control their own affairs, including the ability to regulate labour and working conditions effectively. The growth of cross-border trade, and the greater ability of supposedly 'footloose' multinational companies (MNCs) to direct investment to parts of the world which offer the most favourable conditions for capital accumulation, are seen to erode the regulatory capacities of national governments whose *political* remit is restricted to activities that occur within specific national borders which *economically* are of reduced importance (Strange 1996). As a result, national-level arrangements for regulating labour standards are seen as increasingly inadequate (Bercusson and Estlund 2008; Tsogas 2009).

The process of neo-liberal globalization is said to have 'hollowed-out' the nation-state, rendering it less influential as a regulator of labour standards, as countries compete with one another to attract MNC investment by relaxing their regulatory conditions. In many parts of the Global South, for example in Mexico and Guatemala, the state can no longer be relied upon to enforce national labour laws in a reliable manner (Rodríguez-Garavito 2005), through either incapacity or unwillingness. While African countries have, on paper at least, quite rigorous systems of labour law, the 'ideological hegemony' of neo-liberalism has sapped the political will to regulate employment conditions and labour rights effectively (Brewster and Wood 2007). International agencies such as the International Monetary Fund (IMF) and World Bank have made the enactment of so-called 'structural adjustment programmes' a condition of financial support for rescuing often debt-ridden African economies. These programmes generally consist of a neo-liberal reform package of increased privatization, reductions in state welfare provision and greater labour market flexibility. In addition to eroding the industrial capacity, weakening the skill base and reducing the employment levels of African states, these structural adjustment programmes have also diminished their capacity to regulate labour conditions (Brewster and Wood 2007). A further consequence of neo-liberal globalization in the Global South has been growth of the informal sector, as mentioned in chapter 1, where employment regulation is generally absent.

However, as we have noted earlier, there is a large body of scholarly work which criticizes the view that weakened state capacity is a necessary and inevitable consequence of globalization (e.g. Hirst et al. 2009). Tonkiss (2006), for example, questions the assumption that the nation-state is in a crisis. There is a marked variation in the respective capacities of different countries. She also points to the way in which nation-states use the various powers at their disposal to attract global investment, for example by guaranteeing favourable infrastructure conditions and an attractive legal framework, arguing that 'state capacities are re-worked under global conditions, not simply eroded' (2006: 61).

The erosion of labour standards within nation-states is often not a consequence of the incapacity of national governments in the face of overwhelming globalizing pressures – rather, it is more a question of their unwillingness to enforce the (often robust) laws that they already have in place (Barrientos 2008; Kuruvilla and Verma 2006). Yu (2008), for example, points out that in theory the system of labour law in China is rather impressive, guaranteeing certain important protections for workers, such as the right to be paid a minimum wage. However, local governments, which are responsible for overseeing and enforcing many of China's labour laws, choose to take a lax approach for fear of driving away multinational investment. In some Asian countries (e.g. Malaysia, Indonesia), firms are able to secure valuable employment flexibility, not because there is an absence of labour laws, but from a lack of effective enforcement activity (Caraway 2009).

A second reason why globalization has generated renewed interest in the question of regulating international labour standards concerns the sourcing strategies of MNCs discussed in the previous chapter. The development of GPNs (see chapter 3) has profound consequences for workers employed by the vast array of supplier firms in areas of the world such as South-East Asia and Central America who make the products sold by giant branded retailers. Importantly, such outsourcing of manufacturing activities allows MNCs to distance themselves from the production process, and also absolve themselves of any responsibility for workers' interests (Esbenshade 2004; Merk 2009). The growth of transnational production chains means heightened insecurity and vulnerability for those workers employed by subcontractors, who know that their jobs and livelihoods depend upon the continuing preferment of their factory locations as a source of cheap labour (e.g. Collins 2003).

It also challenges the viability of national-level arrangements for regulating employment and working conditions. Efforts to uphold national-level regulation are viewed as undesirable because of the implications for MNCs which, faced with the prospect of increased labour costs and thus reduced competitiveness, would look to transfer production to other, more amenable locations. Since the viability of traditional nation-state-based arrangements for regulating labour standards, which rely on national governments to monitor and enforce them, is increasingly called into question, the focus of attention switches to the potential for international regulatory initiatives of some kind (Esbenshade 2004; O'Rourke 2003).

Following on from this, the third reason for the greater attention given to the issue of international labour standards concerns the implications of MNC activities for working people in the Global South, and in particular the view discussed in chapter 3 that they have contributed to a competitive 'race to the bottom' creating very poor conditions for employees. Violations of labour standards in global supply chains, including very low wages, excessive hours of work, poor health and safety standards, child labour, harsh discipline, manifold employment discrimination and trade union repression, have been extensively documented (e.g. Mosley 2011).

Exploitative working conditions and violations of labour standards in the Global South are thus an outcome of MNC efforts to pursue ever-cheaper sources of labour in the manufacture of goods such as clothes, sports-shoes and toys (Posner and Nolan 2003). Moreover, changes in communications technology mean that there is now a much greater degree of public awareness of poor labour conditions in the countries of the Global South (Lee 1997). Workers in the Global North have been concerned that the influx of cheap goods made in locations where harsh and exploitative work environments prevail threatens their jobs and livelihoods (Gould 2003; Jenkins et al. 2002). Particular concern has been expressed about the prevalence of child labour in the global economy: the ILO estimates that in 2008 some 306 million children around the world aged between five and seventeen were in employment of some kind (Diallo et al. 2010).

Linked to this, the fourth reason for the increasing interest in the regulation of labour standards on an international basis relates to the campaigning activities of activists, NGOs and trade unions, not just in the Global North, but also in areas of the world where exploitative working conditions and violations of labour standards are most evident (see Tsogas 2009). Their efforts have played a major part in putting the question of international labour standards firmly on the policy agenda, and are often linked to, or part of, broader campaigns against neo-liberal globalization – the so-called 'anti-globalization' movement.

Box 4.1 Student-led labour rights activism

One of the most striking features of campaigns to improve international labour standards concerns the involvement of students and young people in parts of the Global North, particularly in the United States. Students led campus-based campaigns aimed at drawing to wider attention and tackling labour rights abuses in factories making goods for universities and colleges (Cravey 2004; Featherstone and United Students Against Sweatshops 2002). A prominent example of one of these anti-sweatshop campaigning organizations is United Students Against Sweatshops (USAS); you can find out more about its activities from its website: http://usas.org/. The student-led Worker Rights Consortium (WRC), established as an offshoot of USAS in 2000, has developed into an effective labour rights monitoring body, and conducts investigations of factories in the Global South: www.workersrights.org/.

In the United States, for example, during the 1990s, anti-globalization campaigners focused their campaigning efforts on high-profile MNCs in the apparel and textile industries, such as Nike and Reebok, which reportedly sourced their products from factories which used exploitative practices such as child labour (Seidman 2007). As well as NGOs and unions, some of the most active participants in US campaigning efforts to raise awareness and tackle harsh working conditions across global supply chains have been bodies of students (Elliott and Freeman 2003) – see box 4.1. This demonstrates the extent to which the debate around international labour standards has been driven from below, rather than by governments, MNCs or international agencies. A further implication relates to our understanding of how globalization operates. To be sure, the principal beneficiaries are MNCs and other powerful actors; but globalization also provides other parties, who may wish to challenge the dominant neo-liberal hegemony, with leverage which they can use to agitate and mobilize for a fairer and more equitable global economy.

4.3 The debate over international labour standards

The question of international labour standards may have become more prominent; however, a vigorous debate exists about whether or not transnational regulation of labour is desirable. Liberal economists and pro-globalization enthusiasts generally reject the proposition that globalization has generated a 'race to the bottom' and are critical of efforts to regulate working conditions and labour rights on an international basis (e.g. Bhagwati 2004; Wolf 2004). Globalization is said by these commentators to improve labour standards around the world, challenging the idea of a 'race to the bottom' (Flanagan 2006). Rather than viewing it as a threat to labour standards, globalization should be welcomed, and indeed accelerated, since a globalizing economy offers the best hope of jobs and increased prosperity for workers in the Global South.

Globalization enthusiasts contend that workers in poor countries benefit from the prosperity generated by free trade and MNC investment. While the jobs they create are poorly paid by the standards of the Global North, the opportunities globalization gives to people, especially women, who would otherwise be entrenched in poverty, means that it should be welcomed. Campaigners wanting to improve labour standards would do better to focus their efforts on indigenous firms, particularly those operating in the informal sector of the economy, which is where exploitative labour conditions are generally at their most acute (Flanagan 2006).

Moreover, the problem with operating a system of international regulation is that prevailing labour standards reflect productivity levels, and that these vary between countries depending on the stage they have reached in their economic development (see Flanagan 2003). Thus we should not expect countries from the Global South, with relatively low levels of productivity, to be able to operate with the same kind of working conditions and labour rights as those from the Global North. The 'stages of development' argument holds that attempts to raise the cost of labour through greater regulation would, if not supported by a corresponding increase in productivity, lead to job losses and a reduction in prosperity (Hall and Leeson 2007). It is argued that critics of the use of child labour in parts of the Global South should recall that, at similar stages of economic development in countries like Britain, children also worked in factories – although vigorous campaigns developed in the nineteenth century to limit child labour. Indisputably, the earnings of children can be an important element of family income in poorer countries (Brown 2001).

However, the 'stages of development' argument has been criticized for failing to distinguish between different types of labour standards. Some, like the right to associate in trade unions, can be tailored to the circumstances of a particular country (Fields 2003). Another problem with the 'stages of development' argument concerns the way in which it is used as a pretext for maintaining harsh and exploitative labour conditions, and for failing to recognize that there are moral and social justice reasons for treating workers with respect and dignity. It is doubtful how far economic development is contingent upon the practice of child labour; rather, its existence helps to keep wages low to the benefit of unscrupulous employers (Tsogas 2001).

A further reason why efforts to regulate labour standards on an international basis are viewed as undesirable is because, while seemingly altruistic in orientation, they in fact unfairly help to protect the jobs, income levels and working conditions of workers in North America and Europe at the expense of those in the Global South. Enacting international labour standards would mean that countries wishing to use one of their key competitive advantages, low labour costs, to attract investment and pursue economic growth would be prevented from doing so. Campaigns for stronger international labour standards come primarily from actors in the Global North, such as businesses and trade unions, who understandably want their interests protected and use labour standards as a means of impeding overseas competition.

Yet the argument that international labour standards are inimical to a globalized economy and, since they are a disincentive to MNC investment and a barrier to free trade, help to reduce economic prosperity is by no means accepted by everyone. Palley (2004), for example, suggests that international labour standards can be enacted as part of a more sustainable model of economic development, one which is not contingent upon attracting multinational investment. Key labour standards, such as the rights to freedom of association in trade unions and to bargain collectively with employers, instead of being seen in negative terms, as a cost on firms, and thus a challenge to their competitiveness, should be viewed more positively. By raising wages and improving working conditions, unions can help to raise productivity levels (Palley 2004). The ILO claims that compliance with international labour standards and productivity improvements go hand in hand. Effective health and safety provision, for example, reduces the likelihood of workplace injuries, reducing welfare and absence costs for firms and raising employee morale (ILO 2009).

Therefore, the assumption that a trade-off exists between labour standards, on the one hand, and productivity, on the other, has been called into question. Rather than seeing labour standards simply as a function of prevailing productivity levels, they should be viewed as a key influence on productivity, and can help to enhance it. Enacting rigorous labour standards can also give the process of globalization greater legitimacy, demonstrating that the benefits of global economic integration can be shared more widely, not just concentrated amongst multinationals, and used to forge a more equitable model of development (Elliott and Freeman 2003). A key implication, then, concerns the way in which international labour standards can be used to encourage 'a race to the top' (Hepple 2005: 24), by helping to promote positive economic freedoms for workers (Warnecke and De Ruyter 2010).

Central to the debate in this area is the distinction made between 'core' and 'non-core' labour standards. The former are process-oriented, relating to matters such as the eradication of exploitative child labour, the prohibition of forced labour, workers' freedom of association in trade unions, the right to bargain collectively with employers and the principle of non-discrimination in employment. Often articulated as labour 'rights' (OECD 1996; Breining-Kaufman 2007), they concern the organization of employment, and their presence does not imply any specific employment outcome (e.g. wages, hours) (Brown 2001). As such, they can be applied universally, and can be enjoyed by workers wherever their location and whatever stage of economic development their country has reached. So-called 'non-core' labour standards, though, are outcome-based, and relate to the substance of employment relationships – wages, hours, holidays. Whereas the presence of these non-core standards – for example a minimum hourly wage – might adversely affect a country's comparative advantage, by raising its labour costs and reducing its competitiveness relative to other countries, core standards will not necessarily be disadvantageous, and may even be economically beneficial (Gould 2003).

This raises the question of whether or not 'core' labour standards can be treated as fundamental human rights, universally accepted principles governing how workers should be treated irrespective of context. The issue of labour rights has traditionally been neglected by the international human rights movement. It tends to focus on campaigning against violations of civil and political rights, such as restraints on individual freedom of expression and liberty from state coercion (Compa and Diamond 2003; Gross 2003). Yet some scholars increasingly assert that a human rights perspective is an appropriate and useful tool for protecting and advancing the interests of workers. Gross and Compa (2009), for example, reflect on the 'new connection' between labour rights and human rights that is being articulated, particularly in the United States. It expands the scope of workers' and unions' activity by framing their goals in terms of 'rights', rather than just narrow economic objectives pursued by vested interests, which have no more legitimacy than those of employers.

Nevertheless, some in the US labour movement have expressed reservations about the efficacy of the human rights approach, and are wary of the individualist nature of the concept of rights, since it might not take into account the collective basis of effective action by workers in trade unions (Gross 2009; Gross and Compa 2009). There is also a concern that the contemporary human rights movement, rooted in the Western tradition, is less appropriate in parts of the world like Asia (Gross 2009). Perhaps the chief objection to viewing labour rights as fundamental human rights, though, is that they cannot be equated with genuine human rights, like the right to freedom of expression or the right not to be imprisoned without a trial. To be sure, the prohibition of forced labour may also be put alongside them. But are other 'core' labour standards, like the principle of non-discrimination for example, or the ability to form unions and bargain collectively, really 'rights' in a similar sense? Perhaps it is more appropriate to think of them as desirable social and economic goals rather than as fundamental human rights (Hepple 2005).

4.4 Multilateral arrangements for regulating labour standards

In this section and the next, we turn our attention to the principal approaches used for regulating international standards, beginning with multilateral arrangements – those involving more than one country. Established in 1919, the ILO is the leading international body responsible for promoting labour standards, which it does mainly by enacting conventions which member countries are encouraged to observe once they have ratified them. By 2011, 189 conventions had been enacted, covering such topics as the eradication of child labour (Convention 138, 1973) and the right of workers to enjoy freedom of association by being able to organize in trade unions and bargain collectively with employers (Conventions 87, 1948, and 98, 1949). See box 4.2 for more information about the latest (at the time of writing) Convention, No. 189, on domestic workers, adopted by the ILO in 2011.

The ILO was set up because countries in the Global North were fearful of the consequences of an increasingly internationalized economy for jobs and employment at home. Without some kind of floor of labour standards, countries from the Global South could use their cheap labour to take an unfair competitive advantage (Flanagan 2006; Gould IV 2003). It was also thought that promoting improvements in labour standards would help to maintain social peace (Kaufman 2004). The ILO's principal concern today is with reconciling economic progress with the 'creation of decent work', so that the benefits of globalization can be more equitably shared and not be achieved at the expense of workers' freedom, welfare or dignity (ILO 2009: 10).

For a specialized agency of the United Nations, the ILO is organized in rather an odd way. It is based on a tripartite structure, comprising representatives of governments, trade unions and employers' organizations from among its 183 (in 2012) member states. The involvement of employers' organizations and unions has influenced the ILO's mission in quite a significant manner. It has imbued its work with a 'labourist' ethos, one which prioritizes the interests of workers in formal-sector employment (where unions are most influential) and asserts the desirability of enhancing collective bargaining relationships with employers as a means of driving improvements in labour standards (Standing 2008). Understandably, the ILO's influence was at its peak during the 1950s and 1960s, a period when organized industrial relations was at its high point in the Global North, and spreading elsewhere (Deacon 2007; Standing 2008).

There are some major difficulties with the use of ILO conventions as a method for setting international labour standards. First, the process of enacting new standards can be rather lengthy, involving research, extensive consultation and the need to attract sufficient support from ILO delegates to proceed, a tortuous affair which is exacerbated by

Box 4.2 The ILO Convention on Domestic Workers

In June 2011, the ILO adopted Convention No. 189 Concerning Decent Work for Domestic Workers. Domestic work, involving labour which is performed by workers within the employer's own household, where they often reside, is often thought to be difficult to regulate effectively. Respect for the employer's privacy, manifest in a reluctance to intrude on households, is valued more highly than interventions by external agencies to improve working conditions of domestic workers, who are often treated harshly and suffer abusive treatment from their employers as a result (e.g. Albin and Mantouvalou 2012: 69, 74). The ILO contends that regulation of domestic work is desirable on the grounds that it 'continues to be undervalued and invisible and is mainly carried out by women and girls, many of whom are migrants or members of disadvantaged communities and who are particularly vulnerable to discrimination in respect of conditions of employment and of work, and to other abuses of human rights'. The Convention consists of 27 Articles which, among other things, concern the rights of domestic workers:

- to be provided with written information concerning their employment terms and conditions;
- to enjoy fair terms of employment and decent working conditions, including respect for their privacy if they reside within an employer's household;
- and to benefit from minimum wage protection, where such coverage exists, and equal treatment with other workers in respect of working hours, rest breaks and rest periods, and paid annual leave entitlement.

Full details of the Convention can be found on the ILO's website: www.ilo.org/ilc/ILCSessions/100thSession/reports/provisional-records/WCMS_157836/lang--nl/index.htm.

A notable feature of the Convention concerns the way in which an emphasis on protecting and promoting the 'human rights' of domestic workers which are universal in character (for example, respect for their privacy) is integrated with the desirability of specific social (labour) rights, over matters like pay and working-time arrangements. It 'reflects the belief that domestic work should be seen not only as giving rise to universal human rights issues but also, and very much so, as a type of remunerated labour that calls for regulation' (Albin and Mantouvalou 2012: 75). Some countries, though, withheld their support from this attempt to improve the rights of domestic workers. For example, when it came to the vote on whether or not to adopt the Convention, the UK government abstained, on the basis that enacting it would impose excessive regulation on private households employing domestic workers.

the ILO's tripartite structure and the need to secure support from sufficient numbers of employers' representatives, unions and governments (Flanagan 2003, 2006).

Second, once a country has ratified a convention, in theory it is obliged to uphold its provisions. However, there is no compulsion for countries to ratify any of the conventions, and many do not do so (Kuruvilla and Verma 2006). The United States is particularly culpable here; it has not ratified conventions providing for workers' freedom of association, among many others. As a consequence, there is a wide level of cross-country variation in convention ratification (Flanagan 2006).

Third, the ILO lacks an effective means of ensuring that countries which ratify a convention actually comply with it in practice (O'Brien 2002). There is a supervisory system in place which the ILO uses to tackle allegations of non-compliance, generally through a process of investigation and enquiry (see Hepple 2005: 47–56). It can point to some successes, such as getting the government of Mauritius to pass a 2005 law prohibiting all cases of child trafficking (ILO 2009). But ultimately the ILO is powerless to enforce compliance with its own standards (Kuruvilla and Verma 2006).

Fourth, there has also been a marked decline in standard-setting activity since the 1980s (Hepple 2005; Royle 2011), suggesting that the ILO's traditional approach to regulating international labour standards is increasingly irrelevant in a more globalized world economy.

For all these reasons, then, the effectiveness of ILO conventions as an approach to setting international labour standards has been questioned. Moreover, the growing tide of neo-liberalism during the 1980s and 1990s, which promoted the values of labour market flexibility and deregulation, further marginalized the ILO's role (Standing 2010). Attention increasingly focused on the opportunity that the 1995 establishment of the World Trade Organization (WTO) offered for using the trade liberalization agenda as a vehicle for enacting a multilateral set of labour standards (O'Brien et al. 2000; van Roozendaal 2002).

During the negotiations that led to the founding of the WTO, there was some anticipation that it might be induced to agree to a 'social clause', meaning that countries would benefit from freer trade as long as they complied with a minimum set of labour standards (Hassel 2008). However, at the first WTO ministerial meeting, in Singapore in December 1996, governments rejected the idea that trade liberalization and labour standards should be linked in this way, and specified that the ILO was the appropriate body for dealing with international labour matters. Many countries from the Global South objected to the principle of a social clause, viewing it as a protectionist device, impeding their ability to attract multinational investment (Fields 2003; Leary 2003). Liberal economists believe that it is profoundly misguided to penalize countries, by restricting their trading rights, for failing to comply with a floor of labour standards (e.g. Deardoff and Stern 2002).

Against this, however, some commentators argue that the campaign for a social clause is not motivated by protectionist sentiments, but rather stems from the efforts of international unions to ensure that the process of liberalizing trade, which is a key facet of globalization, does not lead to a race to the bottom (Stevis and Boswell 2008). This may well be true; but the debate is of a rather academic character now, since the WTO has not shifted from its initial position that the question of labour standards is beyond its purview (Fields 2003; Hepple 2005; Royle 2011). There are also some doubts about whether the WTO could ever be an effective vehicle for promoting labour standards, given its passion for free trade (Hepple 2005).

The failure to link trade liberalization with labour standards multilaterally, though, may encourage efforts by countries in the Global North to promote social clauses in their own trade agreements (Kuruvilla and Verma 2006). Such deals are generally of a unilateral kind; countries in the Global North impose hefty conditions, including compliance with a set of minimum labour standards for example, in exchange for access to their home market. Both the European Union (EU) and the United States operate Generalized System of Preferences (GSP) arrangements. These give certain countries in the Global South more favourable trading terms as long as they comply with certain defined minimum labour standards. There is some evidence that the GSP approach can stimulate improvements in labour standards; it helped to encourage trade union activity in Guatemala, for example (Compa 2001).

However, GSP arrangements are highly susceptible to political influences, with foreign policy considerations frequently influencing the selection of countries for inclusion (Tsogas 2009). International trade and labour standards may also be linked on a regional basis. The North American Free Trade Association (NAFTA), a multilateral trade deal involving the United States, Mexico and Canada, contains a rather feeble side agreement on labour standards (Teague 2003). It is not at all comparable with the EU's 'social dimension', which encompasses a range of legal minimum employment standards over matters such as health and safety, including the regulation of working-time issues, discrimination and information and consultation rights for employees. Based on the principle that some positive harmonization of labour standards was desirable in order to moderate the impact on workers of progress towards a single European market in goods and services, the social dimension became an increasingly prominent feature of European integration during the 1990s. It must be remembered, however, that the EU has always been primarily a vehicle for the promotion of market integration, designed to favour the large MNCs which benefit from the removal of economic and other barriers within Europe. Although pressure from trade unions has been an important influence, the main reason for developing the social dimension was that it would help to support, and add legitimacy to, the process of economic union (Meardi 2012). The financial and economic crisis and the recession it generated have undermined a social dimension that had become pretty moribund during the 2000s anyway, given the increased preference for neo-liberal, deregulatory policies at EU level. EU support for member states to help them out of the crisis has been made conditional upon their governments instituting wide-ranging programmes of labour market deregulation and austerity, including substantial cuts in wages. As a result, not only can the EU no longer be relied upon for measures that protect working people, but also it has become the main protagonist of a race to the bottom in labour standards across Europe (Barnard 2012).

A further consequence of the WTO's aversion to a social clause has been to put the spotlight once again on the capacity of the ILO to secure improvements in international labour standards (Leary 2003). In 1998 it published a *Declaration of Fundamental Principles and Rights at Work*, comprising seven (subsequently eight) conventions – covering freedom of association and the right to collective bargaining, the elimination of forced or compulsory labour, the elimination of workplace discrimination, and the abolition of child labour – designated as core labour standards. For the ILO, these core standards embody certain basic principles and rights that all countries should aspire to respecting (ILO 2009). Unlike conventions in general, which have to be ratified before they impose any duty to comply, there is an obligation on all ILO members to work towards upholding the core labour standards.

Much of the impetus for the development of the core labour standards approach in general, and the 1998 *Declaration* in particular, came from the United States. Urged on by domestic interests, the US government pressed for the inclusion of a social clause in the WTO trading regime which would lead to countries being penalized with trade sanctions for failing to abide by a minimum floor of labour rights. However, its failure to ratify many ILO conventions put it in an awkward position. By removing certain core labour standards from the standard process of convention ratification, and by emphasizing the use of softer, promotional techniques for encouraging compliance, rather than the conventional process of ratification, the ILO's change of emphasis helped to accommodate the US government's rather contradictory stance (Alston 2004; Hepple 2005).

The ILO's emphasis on the core labour standards approach since the late 1990s has three main implications. First, it represents a more flexible approach to promoting labour standards than the traditional convention-based route. There is less of an emphasis on government action to promote and ratify standards, and instead a concern with providing a set of principles which can be used more widely as the basis for improving employment conditions and workers' rights (Alston 2004). Second, following on from this, the ILO's *Declaration* provides other actors, such as NGOs and multinational companies, who are looking to develop their own regulatory arrangements, and countries wanting to insert social clauses in unilateral or bilateral trade agreements, with 'a ready set of core rights' which they can draw upon (Hepple 2005: 62). As we see below, the content of private regulatory initiatives, such as codes of conduct, is often influenced by the ILO's core labour standards.

Third, perhaps most importantly, the core labour standards approach heralds a shift in the ILO's priorities. Standard-setting efforts through conventions, and arrangements for monitoring compliance, have become less important relative to the emphasis now being placed on helping countries to improve their labour standards so that core rights are upheld, particularly through the provision of technical assistance (Alston 2004). This means that the ILO's role is becoming increasingly interventionist, concerned with securing on-the-ground change, rather than being restricted to somewhat ineffective efforts to influence the policies of governments (Cleveland 2003). Promotional interventions by the ILO can help to improve labour standards. In the Middle East, for example, ILO technical assistance has helped to promote the independent representation of workers' interests even in countries where trade unions are banned (Kuruvilla and Verma 2006). The 'Better Factories Cambodia' programme exemplifies the greater emphasis placed by the ILO on technical assistance and development work (see box 4.3).

Although some have welcomed the ILO's change in emphasis, seeing it as a way in which the agency has been able to reassert its role (e.g. Fields 2003), the focus on the core labour standards has attracted some criticism. For one thing, the emphasis placed on monitoring improvements means that the core labour standards approach lacks an effective mechanism for ensuring compliance (Standing 2008). Another problem is that the hitherto longstanding concern with regulating employment outcomes, such as working hours, seems to have dropped down the ILO's agenda (Hepple 2005; Standing 2010). A more profound criticism is that the ILO's core labour standards approach represents an attempt to accommodate, rather than challenge, neo-liberal globalization. Regulating international labour standards has become dominated by an emphasis on upholding certain broad principles rather than on enforcing substantive labour rights (Royle 2011). Asserting that exploitative child labour should be abolished, or that employment discrimination is undesirable, is not as hard as insisting upon specific measures to improve people's working conditions, which may generate greater opposition from governments and employers. As a result, many argue that the ILO has become a less effective agency for protecting and advancing the interests of workers around the world (Alston 2004; Standing 2008).

For Guy Standing (2008, 2010), the enthusiastic promotion of the core labour standards approach masks a deep and profound crisis in the ILO's legitimacy. A former ILO official, he charges the organization with failing to adapt effectively to the changing nature of work in a globalized economy. For example, it has paid little attention to the matter of labour migration.

The ILO's main weakness is that its structure is based on an outdated model of work and employment relations, one based upon

Box 4.3 The ILO – from 'Better Factories' to 'Better Work'

The growing importance of the ILO's technical assistance and development activities is best illustrated with reference to the Better Factories Cambodia project, and its subsequent influence on the development of the 'Better Work' initiative which emerged from it. Since the 1990s, Cambodia has developed an increasingly important export-oriented textile and garment industry. However, there were concerns that this growth was accompanied by a high incidence of exploitative working conditions. The imperative of a trade agreement with the United States, which was contingent upon efforts to improve labour standards, encouraged Cambodian employers to examine how they could best develop as a niche site for ethical production.

In 2001 the Better Factories Cambodia programme was launched as a joint initiative between the ILO, the Cambodian government and leading textile and garment producers. Its aim was to develop interventions that would improve labour conditions, but at the same time drive increases in quality and productivity. The ILO gave the programme a positive evaluation; it was held up as a model of sustainable development, one which reconciles better working conditions with enhanced business competitiveness. However, until 2004, Cambodia's export garment sector was partly protected from direct competition by cheaper producers by the presence of export quotas. Full exposure to global markets may undermine Cambodia's efforts to orient itself as an ethical producer by encouraging a race to the bottom. A further problem concerns the increasing tendency of many employers in Cambodia to use workers on short-term contracts, partly as a means of union avoidance. This undermines efforts to secure greater job security and promote freedom of association, both ostensibly objectives of the Better Factories Programme (Arnold and Shih 2010).

Nevertheless, it has helped to stimulate the broader Better Work initiative, a partnership between the ILO and the International Finance Corporation, a private-sector offshoot of the World Bank. Launched in 2007, it is designed to improve labour standards in global supply chains while at the same time helping to enhance business competitiveness. Pilot projects have been established in Jordan, Haiti, Vietnam and Lesotho. In the latter, for example, clothing manufacturers, who made goods largely for the US market, faced increased competitive pressures once the quota-based system ended. With the help of the ILO, they tried to tie in improvements in labour standards with the production of more expensive goods that could be targeted at ethically conscious Western consumers. However, the initiative stalled due to the diminished enthusiasm of MNCs, a lack of financial support and a more cautious ILO (Seidman 2009).

standard employment relationships and the predominance of trade unionism and collective bargaining. Standing (2010) argues that, if it is to have a successful future, the ILO needs to eschew this labourist tradition, and redefine itself as an agency which intervenes to establish arrangements that provide decent working lives for all, especially the workers in the expanding informal economy.

4.5 Private regulation and codes of conduct

The absence of effective alternative mechanisms for regulating international labour standards has left a gap which MNCs and other actors have exploited by developing their own privatized regulatory interventions, principally codes of conduct which deal with labour issues (Mamic 2004; Tsogas 2009).

Labour codes of conduct are best viewed as voluntary frameworks which, through the specification of certain defined objectives, guidelines and other criteria, in theory commit MNCs and their suppliers to the observance of certain minimum standards when it comes to working conditions and labour rights throughout their supply chains (Hepple 2005; Voss et al. 2008). They have a relatively long history in the international business arena, and are not just restricted to labour issues. The Organisation for Economic Co-operation and Development's (OECD's) *Guidelines for Multinational Companies*, which provide MNCs with a set of voluntary principles relating to how they should conduct themselves in their international operations, originated in the 1970s. However, since the 1990s there has been a marked proliferation in the use of codes of conduct covering labour issues (Barrientos and Smith 2007; Jenkins et al. 2002; Royle 2011).

In 1992 Levi-Strauss and Nike were the first major US corporations to establish their own corporate codes which covered labour issues in their respective supply chains. Since then the use of codes has proliferated, with many multinationals now operating them, often within the broader context of their corporate social responsibility (CSR) programmes. Exposés of sweatshop labour helped to raise public awareness of the harsh and exploitative working conditions experienced by many of the workers who toil in the factories of the Global South to make the products marketed and sold by Western corporations. The development of codes can be a useful way in which multinationals can demonstrate their ethical business credentials and seriousness with which they take CSR issues (Dicken 2007).

A key motivating force behind the development of codes, then, has been the pressing need for corporations to protect their reputation and safeguard the image of their brand, in the face of increasingly assertive campaigning by activists and rising consumer awareness of the harsh working conditions endured by workers who make the products sold by global branded retailers (Frenkel 2001; Frenkel and Scott 2002; Merk 2009). While reputational issues have been an important catalyst for the development of codes, some have questioned their value as a means of delivering improvements in labour standards (e.g. O'Brien 2002). Companies without strong brands, or whose reputation is relatively unimportant, will lack the motivation to develop codes.

Without any other robust incentives, codes can only ever offer a partial solution to the problem of labour regulation in the global economy. Nevertheless, they have become the most prominent mechanism for regulating international labour standards, not least because of the absence of any significant alternatives (Locke and Romis 2010).

Codes of conduct exemplify the trend towards private regulatory arrangements in the global economy (Wells 2007). The emergence of codes is part of a more general movement towards the use of voluntary, non-state arrangements for regulating economic activity under globalization such as certification schemes and other forms of 'soft' (non-binding) rather than 'hard' (legally binding) law. The distinctive feature of private regulation is the absence of a role for the state in the governance of business activities. Rather, corporations themselves, sometimes in association with NGOs, determine the regulatory framework within which they operate, in areas like environmental management and labour conditions (Cashore 2002; Pattberg 2005; Vogel 2008). This can be seen to reflect the antipathy felt by corporate business towards state intervention, seen by proponents of neo-liberalism as 'interference' in free market competition.

Privatized, or 'outsourced' (O'Rourke 2003), forms of regulation, then, are not rooted in public authority. Rather, they are seen to embody a more market-based approach to regulating business activities. This is based on the assumption that certification schemes and codes of conduct are rational and desirable techniques for securing improvements in business practices by responding to market pressure from consumers and activist campaigners (Locke et al. 2007).

It is often thought that private regulation has grown in significance because globalization has undermined the regulatory capacity of nation-states and because of the absence of effective multilateral arrangements; it is therefore helping to fill the regulatory 'gap' or 'vacuum' that exists at a global level (Everett et al. 2007). However, the work of Bartley (2003, 2007) suggests that we need to be cautious about assuming that private regulation has developed as a function of the retreat of the state. He traces the important way in which the US government encouraged, and helped to establish, private regulatory arrangements in the field of labour standards. State support for codes of conduct and certification schemes was predicated on the belief that political interventions can be an effective means of constructing market institutions (Bartley 2007). While evidently a 'market-friendly' mode of regulation – in the sense that it imposes no obligations on firms to alter their practices and implies that change is enacted as the result of the need to satisfy the demands of consumers, NGOs and other non-public actors – private regulation has to be seen as the outcome of an 'inherently political project' (Bartley 2007: 337, 336). Moreover, research on the multinational electronics firm HP's supplier network demonstrates the important ways in which labour codes of conduct, as ostensibly private forms of regulation, interact with regulatory interventions by governments (Locke et al. 2012).

Whatever its nature and origins, private regulation, in the form of codes and certification schemes, is frequently viewed as a particularly appropriate means of regulating the international activities of firms in a more globalized environment (Esbenshade 2004; O'Rourke 2003). It is portrayed as a flexible, responsive form of regulation which complements, and helps to sustain, a global production system marked by the use of sometimes lengthy and complex supply chains and the extensive use of subcontracting arrangements for organizing production activities (O'Rourke 2003). Importantly, however, while private regulation, and the monitoring activities which complement it (see below), are tailored to, and help to support, the global production activities of MNCs, essentially they do not challenge them, leaving the prevailing system of power relations intact (Esbenshade 2004: 10). Those aspects of the transnational organization of production that generate exploitative labour practices and promote worker vulnerability are registered, but not alleviated, as a consequence.

While the content of codes of conduct often varies considerably, the ILO's core labour standards tend to exert an important influence over their subject matter (Hepple 2005; Tsogas 2009). That said, code content frequently reflects the nature of its status and origins. Codes drawn up by business, for example, often pay little attention to freedom of association issues, such as the right to form trade unions. Codes that involve a broader range of stakeholders, such as unions and NGOs, generally do. There are four broad types of labour code.

- Multilateral codes: these generally take the form of non-binding guidelines produced by intergovernmental bodies and international agencies which are designed to influence the activities of multinational firms. In 1999, for example, the United Nations published its *Global Compact*. This covers a range of human rights, environmental and labour standards, with the latter modelled on the ILO's core labour standards (Frenkel and Scott 2002). The relevant part of the OECD's revised version of its *Guidelines for Multinational Enterprises*, published in 2000, is also heavily influenced by the core labour standards approach. The main problem with these multilateral initiatives, however, is that, being exhortative in character, they lack any arrangements for enforcement (Hepple 2005; Kuruvilla and Verma 2006).
- Industry-based codes: the leading example of this type of code is WRAP (Worldwide Responsible Accredited Production). Based in the United States, WRAP is an industry-led initiative which focuses on certifying apparel factories around the world, based on whether or not they comply with its twelve key principles. There is a particular emphasis placed on ensuring that certified factories comply with local labour laws and regulations. Industry-based codes, however,

have been criticized for lacking rigour and transparency, and for their narrow and limited content (e.g. Esbenshade 2004; Jenkins et al. 2002; O'Rourke 2003).

- Corporate codes: multinational companies, particularly large branded retailers such as Nike and Gap, operate their own internal codes of conduct which they use to set minimum labour standards in their global network of supplier factories. Corporate codes are marked by considerable diversity, and, like industry-based codes, have been criticized for their often narrow and limited criteria. Another problem concerns waning managerial interest. Although multinational toy manufacturer Mattel developed a detailed and ostensibly rigorous code of conduct, it was abandoned when the firm failed to identify any competitive advantage (Prakash Sethi et al. 2011).

- Multi-stakeholder codes: these are marked by the involvement of NGOs, and sometimes labour organizations, as well as private firms. One of the best-known multi-stakeholder initiatives is the ETI, which comprises leading retailers such as Tesco, Marks & Spencer and W H Smith among its members, as well as the Trades Union Congress (TUC) and major NGOs like Oxfam (see Blowfield 2002). Its 'base code' requires member companies to source their products from suppliers who, among other things, respect workers' rights to form trade unions and pay 'living wages', defined as 'enough to meet basic needs and to provide discretionary income'. Multi-stakeholder codes are generally stronger than industry-based and corporate codes, and broader in scope, being more likely to cover freedom of association issues for example (Jenkins et al. 2002). They also put more emphasis on independent scrutiny and external verification when it comes to assessing compliance with codes (Everett et al. 2007; Hassel 2008).

There are common problems which impede the capacity of codes of conduct to promote sustained improvements in labour standards. First, they are generally articulated as managerial interventions, designed to serve managerial goals (Merk 2009). For the most part, the purpose of corporate codes is not to enhance workers' interests, but to aid the management of the enterprise (Pun 2005b). Taylor (2011) suggests that it is mistaken to view codes just as technical arrangements; rather they are devices that reflect and mediate the prevailing power relationships which underpin the global division of labour.

Linked to this, a second problem with codes of conduct is that workers and their representatives generally have little involvement in their design and implementation, and are often unaware of their existence (Esbenshade 2004). While ostensibly concerned with protecting workers, codes should more accurately be viewed as a device for keeping them quiescent and avoiding unionization (Arthurs 2002; Kuruvilla and Verma 2006).

Third, codes of conduct are often highly selective in their coverage of labour issues, particularly compared with regulatory mechanisms rooted in public authority (Hepple 2005). As we mentioned earlier, few corporate codes encompass freedom of association issues, for example (Leary 2003).

A fourth problem with codes of conduct is that sanctions for non-compliance with code provisions are generally weak (Frenkel and Kim 2004; Hepple 2005; Rodríguez-Garavito 2005). While there is some evidence that multi-stakeholder codes can help to promote labour standards' improvements in some areas, by reducing the use of exploitative child labour for example, rigorous enforcement is essential, something which rarely prevails (Barrientos and Smith 2007). For these reasons, the privatization of labour regulation, whereby codes increasingly come to displace the public regulatory interventions of nation-states and international bodies such as the ILO, and deflect efforts to promote social clauses in trade agreements, may have adverse consequences for labour in the Global South (Tsogas 2009). Moreover, they do little to protect or enhance conditions for workers in the informal economy.

Effective code compliance depends upon the presence of a rigorous framework for monitoring and auditing standards, ideally through the use of independent verification arrangements. Three broad types of monitoring system exist: companies may operate their own internal private arrangements for assessing code compliance (e.g. Nike), use specialist private auditors (e.g. accountancy firms such as PriceWaterhouseCoopers) or participate in multi-stakeholder initiatives which involve NGOs in monitoring compliance. Generally, private monitoring arrangements are highly flawed (Royle 2011). Auditors may spend very little time actually in the factories that are being assessed for compliance with codes, and often miss obvious manifestations of non-compliance, such as blatant health and safety hazards. Factory managers are frequently informed of upcoming inspection visits in advance and are relied upon to provide the relevant data. While auditors will generally want to talk to factory workers, the selection process is governed by managers, who will understandably be inclined to choose those employees they think will be more likely to give a positive impression of factory conditions (O'Rourke 2002; Wells 2007) – see box 4.4.

Factories have become skilled in misleading auditors, giving a false impression that the standards contained in codes are being enforced. Workers and managers in global factories report that codes are often violated in practice (Egels-Zendén 2007; Pun 2005b). Both, moreover, have a vested interest in asserting that code compliance is satisfactory since a negative inspection report might impel a multinational to switch production to another supplier, threatening the viability of the factory and putting jobs at risk; workers are aware of the dangers of giving the 'wrong answers' to auditors (Pun 2005b: 107).

Multinational firms expect supplier factories to abide by the terms

Box 4.4 The Walmart code in China

Some of the problems with using codes of conduct as a means of regulating labour standards are illustrated by Pun and Yu's (2008) account of the experience of three toy factories in China that make products for the giant US retailer Walmart. In 1992, Walmart established a code – 'Standards for Suppliers' – which stressed that suppliers should abide by local labour laws. However, this was not a very demanding aim since, notwithstanding how rigorous they appear in theory, in practice the influence of Chinese employment laws is rather minimal, with independent trade unions prohibited. During the late 1990s, Walmart began to take a more robust approach to implementing its code, for example by establishing more rigorous monitoring procedures, including the introduction of a certification programme. However, Walmart's in-house arrangements for verifying compliance, which gave the company the power to control monitoring activities and decide whether to publish the results of audits, lacked much credibility.

A further problem was the code's punitive emphasis, which was oriented towards punishing factories for non-compliance, rather than with assisting them in finding ways to meet the terms of the code. Instead of being helped to improve, factories found to have seriously breached Walmart's code were simply cut out of its supply chain. While this punishment-centred approach helped to ensure that Walmart was insulated from bad publicity, it failed to tackle the underlying causes of exploitative labour conditions. Another problem with the process of code verification was that managers had advance knowledge of inspection visits. This enabled them to coach workers on the most appropriate answers to auditors' questions. It was made clear to the workforce that if the questions were answered 'wrongly' – in other words, if workers actually gave an accurate picture of the poor state of working conditions and labour rights violations in their factories – then it would demonstrate non-compliance with the code, with the likely loss of orders and jobs as a result.

One worker explained how this worked in practice:

> One day, the line manager sent me to the office for a talk with the Wal-Mart auditor. The auditor asked me how many overtime hours I took, how much I was paid, and if overtime work was voluntary. But I did not dare tell the truth, because right before I went to the office, the manager told me how to answer these questions 'correctly'; otherwise, the factory would lose the order and we workers would lose jobs. (Pun and Yu 2008: 121)

of their codes. However, they rarely give them sufficient resources to do so. Demands from multinationals for lower prices make it difficult for suppliers to adhere to the provisions of codes, given the potential increase in labour costs associated with compliance (Bulut and Lane 2011; Robinson 2010). Downward pressure on costs, with the implied threat that production can always be switched elsewhere if necessary hanging in the background, means that managers of supplier factories often have little incentive to comply with codes. Yu's (2008) study of a Chinese factory that makes sports-shoes for Reebok highlights some of the adverse consequences of code compliance. The factory could only afford to comply with Reebok's code by disadvantaging workers in other ways, particularly by raising the intensity of work.

Activist campaigns have succeeded in pressurizing companies such as Nike and Reebok to strengthen their respective codes, and to open them up to a greater degree of independent external scrutiny (Elliott and Freeman 2003; Frenkel and Kim 2004; Locke et al. 2007). However, they remain dominated by a 'compliance' ethos, in which factories are punished or rewarded depending on how well they are judged to meet the criteria specified in the code. This encourages factories to focus on demonstrating that they conform to codes in a 'ritual of compliance', rather than driving substantive improvements in labour standards (Locke et al. 2009: 328). Work undertaken by Richard Locke and his colleagues indicates that monitoring, on its own, is an insufficient condition for improving labour standards. Instead, they propose a 'commitment-based' approach, involving the development of more collaborative, long-term relationships between multinationals and their supplier factories. Their research with Nike and other multinationals indicates that substantive improvements in labour standards are best achieved through strengthened relations with supply-chain firms, and a shift towards the use of more advanced production processes which avoid Taylorist forms of work organization based on low-skilled narrow tasks (Locke et al. 2007, 2009; Locke and Romis 2010).

An alternative view of the potential for codes has been advanced by scholars and activists who see them as possible vehicle for worker empowerment. As they are currently constituted and operated, codes are clearly an unsatisfactory method of driving improvements in labour standards. Yet there is no reason why workers and unions cannot use them to lever more sustained and profound change. Under propitious circumstances, workers and their organizations can take control of the agenda of codes, use them to hold multinationals to account and seek to broaden the process of code design, implementation and verification. This is viewed by some as a more desirable approach to operating codes because it engenders an empowered workforce, which has the knowledge and capacity to monitor and enforce labour standards effectively itself (Esbenshade 2004).

Such a more participatory approach to labour codes, which focuses on 'enabling' workers to take greater control over their working conditions, has attracted growing interest (Rodríguez-Garavito 2005). See, for example, the code which has been elaborated by the activist organization the Clean Clothes Campaign. Its 'full package' model stresses that codes should be comprehensive in scope, subject to independent, external verification and have credibility, for example by allowing freedom of association. More importantly, however, it recognizes that codes on their own are an insufficient means of raising labour standards. Rather, it is their capacity for promoting worker self-organization and grassroots, bottom-up mobilization that is crucial (Merk 2009). In particular, codes should encourage independent worker representation through trade unions as the most effective way of driving up labour standards (Clean Clothes Campaign 2009). Codes of conduct, as they are generally constituted, are currently unsatisfactory instruments for delivering sustained improvements in labour standards. Reconfigured, though, and used in ways that empower workers, who have more control over their own working conditions as a result, their prospects seem brighter.

4.6 Conclusion

Clearly, globalization has encouraged greater interest in the question of transnational labour regulation – specifically, whether or not, and also how, international labour standards should be applied for the purpose of reconciling economic development with social justice and respect of workers' dignity and labour rights (Hepple 2005). The disdain with which liberal economists and globalization enthusiasts view transnational labour regulation largely misses the point. Pressure from below, from unions, social movement activists, NGOs and the like, means that multinationals and international agencies have been obliged to take the matter of international labour standards more seriously. The most pertinent question is not whether or not transnational labour regulation in a more globalized economy is desirable, but rather what kind of regulatory interventions are best suited to promoting workers' interests. Codes of conduct, for example, have been elaborated largely for managerial reasons and, as currently constituted, do little to improve employment conditions and labour rights. However, reconfigured, so that workers are involved in their design and implementation, codes may have more positive effects.

On their own, though, private regulatory initiatives like codes are an insufficient condition for raising labour standards globally (Royle 2011). Given the well-attested problems of multilateral approaches – the failure to secure a 'social clause' in the WTO's trading regime for example, and the weaknesses of the ILO – what other actions are necessary to secure substantive improvements in employment conditions and labour rights? For one thing, efforts to raise labour standards internationally need to engage with, and focus their efforts on, nation-states. We have criticized the view that the issue of transnational labour regulation has come to the fore because globalization renders national governments incapable of developing effective regulatory interventions. Moreover, the development of much private regulation has been influenced by nation-states (Bartley 2007). National governments, then, must still have a large role to play in implementing labour regulation under globalization. Efforts to improve the capacity of states, so that they are better placed to secure compliance with their own employment laws, would be a particularly useful way of driving improvements in labour standards (Kuruvilla and Verma 2006). Moreover, the important role played by both national-level and international labour movements in improving employment conditions and protecting workers' rights also needs to be acknowledged. In the next chapter, for example, attempts by international trade union organizations to reach agreements over labour standards with multinationals, in the form of International Framework Agreements (IFAs), are assessed. Perhaps the most effective way of bringing about sustained improvements in labour standards around the world would be to encourage robust collective worker organization in the form of independent trade unions.

Further reading and useful websites

Tony Royle (2011) offers a very useful overview of the issues covered in this chapter, while Hepple (2005) provides the most extensive and detailed analysis of efforts to build transnational forms of labour regulation. Some of the key issues and debates are also covered by Kuruvilla and Verma (2006) and Tsogas (2009). The book-length study of private monitoring arrangements by Esbenshade (2004) is also recommended. Finally, the work of Richard Locke and his colleagues (e.g. Locke and Romis 2010) is recommended for the insights it brings to understanding the implications of codes of conduct.

You can find out more about the work of the ILO from its website: www.ilo.org.

The ETI has a website, where you can find out about the activities of this multi-stakeholder organization: www.ethicaltrade.org.

Details of the UN *Global Compact* can be accessed from its website: www.globalcompact.org.

You can read the OECD's *Guidelines for Multinational Enterprises* by visiting its website: www.oecd.org/document/28/0,3746,en_2649_34889_2397532_1_1_1_1,00.html.

WRAP's website contains details of its activities: www.wrapcompliance.org.

For an example of a corporate code, access that of the Adidas Group: www.adidas-group.com/en/sustainability/suppliers_and_workers/code_of_conduct/default.aspx.

5 Globalization, labour and social movements

5.1 Introduction

In October 2006 the first meeting of a new organization was held in Vienna. The International Trade Union Confederation (ITUC) was formed out of a merger between the International Confederation of Free Trade Unions (ICFTU) and the World Confederation of Labour (WCL), together with eight other national trade union organizations which were affiliating to a global body for the first time. The ITUC, which claims to represent some 175 million workers in 153 countries, was deliberately formed as an attempt to strengthen the trade union movement in the face of globalization, as stated on its website:

> The international trade union movement is adapting in order to remain a key player in an economic climate that is creating more losers than winners. The imbalances of economic globalization are having a devastating effect on millions of workers. Off-shoring, abuse of workers' rights and increasing poverty are all examples of the negative impact of these developments.

This chapter examines such effects of globalization on trade unions and labour movements, and considers how they have responded to the internationalization of economic activity. The chapter, after a brief account of the origins and role of unions, offers an assessment of how they have been affected by globalization, looking especially at membership trends. The focus then switches to explore how unions and labour movements have responded to the challenges of globalization, at both a national and an international level. The chapter examines the main characteristics of the international union movement, including the key institutions. Finally, it assesses efforts by labour movement actors to build cross-border solidarity among workers and considers the role of new social movements and community unionism.

5.2 Trade unions in the Global North: a brief history

Beatrice and Sidney Webb provided what has become the classic definition of a trade union: 'a continuous association of wage earners for the purpose of maintaining or improving the conditions of their employment' (1920: 1). Trade unions are strongly associated with industrialization. Although there were working men's trade associations and craft guilds before the Industrial Revolution, trade unions in the form we know them now evolved subsequently to protect their members in the face of the problems they were experiencing, becoming employees who no longer owned their means of production, as characterized by Karl Marx in *Das Kapital*. Early trade unions tended to be small and locally based, but as time passed they grouped together to form national unions with better resources and the ability to unite workers around the country. By the end of the nineteenth century, they had developed into more formal and bureaucratized structures, governed by rules and constitutions. By then unions existed in most European countries and across the Anglo-Saxon world. Realizing that they could use their muscle more effectively if they combined to form a major social bloc to confront state and employers' interests, individual unions began to band together to form confederations such as the TUC (Trade Union Congress) in the UK, the AFL–CIO (American Federation of Labour – Confederation of Industrial Organizations) in the USA, and the LO in Sweden (Landsorganizationen i Sverige).

Their origins in industrialization account for the fact that initially some of the most powerful and influential unions were those who organized skilled workers, especially those deemed essential to national economies, such as the National Union of Mineworkers in the UK, IG Metall in Germany, and the Autoworkers and Teamsters in America. Often these unions of skilled workers excluded women, part-timers and Black workers, practising exclusionary tactics to protect the interests of their (predominantly) white male workers. This sectionalism has long been one of the least prepossessing features of unionism: it was countered slowly by the advent of large general unions organizing less skilled workers, along with the admission of women and minority workers. However, in most countries, white males remain dominant as union leaders, despite the fact that many contemporary unions have apparently strong equal opportunities policies (Bradley 1999).

The influence of the unions was strengthened by the two world wars, in which their leaders collaborated with governments to maintain vital production and forbore from official strikes. Consequently, their social position was strongest after the Second World War, when many European countries developed a tripartite system of industrial relations, with employers, unions and governments in partnership. Commentators have labelled this structure of governance as a 'corporatist tendency', which was seen as an important aid to postwar recovery (for example, Goldthorpe 1984). Since the 1960s, the major change has been the growth, with the decline of industrial production in the Global North, of union organization among white-collar and professional workers. One of the largest and most powerful unions in the UK, for example, is UNISON, which organizes health and local government workers, along with some other administrative groups.

Although unions have grown away from their original forms, their central function and role remain the protection, maintenance and improvement of their members' employment conditions. However, their range of activities has widened, and may include most or all of the following:

- collective bargaining over pay and conditions, such as regular negotiations for pay increases, often on an annual basis;
- representing individual members in grievances against their employers or in procedures brought by employers, including legal representation;
- working to promote equality and diversity programmes within companies and organizations;
- political lobbying of governments for employee rights and supporting political parties seen as sympathetic to their cause (usually socialist or social-democratic parties);
- providing a range of benefits for their members, for example discounts, training, legal advice.

As noted above, trade unions were first formed in Europe, spreading thence to North America and around the world. Most countries of the South did not have unions till industrial 'take-off' in the twentieth century, though some plantation workers pioneered unionization earlier. Though their basic social role of protecting workers' interests is constant, the specific nature of their activities and their political activities are highly variable between nations. Hyman (2001) suggests that union behaviour is affected by the relative influence of three broad types of activity – determining labour market outcomes, fostering social integration, and acting as a vehicle for political activism and raising class awareness.

Thus, the history of unionism in Britain, the first industrial nation (Mathias 1983), has meant it has evolved with its focus chiefly on controlling its members' economic position. A more extreme version of this, labelled 'business unionism', developed in the USA, focused firmly on trade issues and eschewing politics. In general, the Anglo-Saxon countries, including Australia and New Zealand, prioritize labour market protection over political intervention, despite occasional outbursts of militancy and waves of strikes.

In contrast, French unions are particularly radical, putting their political role before their economic role (Gallie 1978), as is also the case in Italy. Although French union membership levels are very low (7.6 per cent of the workforce in 2011), they do wield political influence. In the Global South, unions are often closely allied with nationalist independence movements or freedom parties, seeking to challenge dictatorships or right-wing regimes. This can often lead to extreme repression of union activists and violent suppression of actions such as strikes – something which has happened in countries like Indonesia and South Korea (Koo 2001; La Botz 2001) – see box 5.1 for the example of Colombia.

Box 5.1 Trade union oppression in Colombia

In chapter 3 we looked at how the multinational beverages firm Coca-Cola is allegedly implicated in violent anti-union repression in Colombia, South America. The country is considered the most dangerous place in the world to be a trade unionist. It has recently been ruled by right-wing governments and legislated by judges linked into capitalist business interests. However, the distinctive feature of the country is that it exists in a virtual state of civil war between two armed guerilla organizations, the communist FARC and a range of ultra-rightist paramilitary groupings. The latter have instigated a violent anti-union campaign. Carlos Castano, former head of one paramilitary group, stated: 'We kill trade unionists because they interfere with people working.' According to a report by the Solidarity Center, an international body set up by the US AFL–CIO trade union confederation, since the mid-1980s approximately 4,000 trade unionists have been murdered in Colombia, more than 2,000 of them since 1991. More trade unionists are killed there each year than in the rest of the world combined. In 2005, the ICFTU reported that 70 trade unionists were killed, while 260 received death threats, 56 were arbitrarily detained, 7 survived attacks in which explosives or firearms were used, 6 were kidnapped, and 3 disappeared. In 2010, 49 were murdered.

Unsurprisingly, union density in Colombia has fallen from 15 per cent in 1964 to less than 5 per cent. However, the various union groupings are affiliated to international bodies. International delegations have visited Colombia and worked to publicize and call for an end to the violent anti-union repression. The Solidarity Center asks the international labour movement to help by:

- supporting efforts of global union federations to increase bargaining power for workers in companies in Colombia;
- strengthening international alliances, networks and coalitions among unions, labour NGOs, human rights groups, legal advocacy organizations and the academic community to support worker rights in Colombia.

One British union which has been involved is the University and College Union (UCU). Teachers have been among the victims of the assassinations. In 2007, the Colombian trade union federation CUT notified campaign organization Justice for Colombia of the murder of four teachers active in the teachers' trade union, FECODE. For example, Rosalino Palacios Mosquera, an English-language teacher, was shot walking through the town of Bello. As well as visits to Colombia, UCU has pursued the case of university lecturer Dr Miguel Angel Beltran, who was wrongly imprisoned on charges of terrorism. In 2012 Dr Beltran was released from jail as the evidence against him was found to be unreliable, but he remains under threat from the Colombian right wing and has to be accompanied by bodyguards. He received a standing ovation when he visited the UCU Annual Conference in Manchester in 2012, speaking on the oppression of teachers and threats to free speech in Colombia. UCU General Secretary

Sally Hunt stated: 'we are delighted that Dr Beltran has been absolved of all charges. This vindicates the efforts UCU members have put in alongside Justice for Colombia, Amnesty International and teacher trade unionists round the world. We hope that it will be a significant step forward in the ongoing battle for human rights in Colombia.' The case of Colombia illustrates the success of specific instances of union alliances with new social movements.
Sources: *Justice For All: The Struggle for Worker Rights in Colombia, Report by the American Center for International Labor Solidarity*, Solidarity Center 2006; UCU website – www.ucu.org.uk.

German unions are particularly well integrated into government processes and were given this role as part of postwar reconstruction. In Japan there is a tradition of conservative company-based unions which collaborate with managers to preserve industrial harmony (Dore 1973). A striking case of this integrationist approach is the union movement in China, which was established to preserve the interests of the state and the Communist Party, although it may currently be evolving beyond that point. Frege (2006), commenting on unionization in Eastern Europe and Russia, opines that in repressive or authoritarian states unions do not have the capacity to become independent actors. Instead of acting to protect workers' interests, they collaborate with governments to keep workers in order, becoming, in C. Wright Mills' trenchant phrase, 'managers of discontent' (1948), rather than vehicles, or even fermenters, of dissent and opposition. All these differences have in the past been an obstacle to international union organization, as we will discuss later in the chapter.

It has been argued by some commentators that unions over the decades have become 'institutionalized' and bureaucratic, with salaried union officers even becoming closer in their culture and ideas to employers than to their members (Dahrendorf 1959; Michels 1911). Müller-Jentsch (1985) argued that the structural and legal conditions prevailing in the Global North had propelled trade unions into being intermediaries between the interests of capital and of labour, rather than advocates for the latter, picking up the earlier idea of Mills. However, many employers and companies have never accepted the role of trade unions, or been prepared to work together with them, a tendency which has been strengthened by the process of neo-liberal globalization (Gall et al. 2011).

5.3 Trade unions under neo-liberal globalization

Bieler et al. (2008) identify two major challenges for trade unions and labour movements as a result of neo-liberal globalization. First, as we have seen in previous chapters, there is a danger of workers in different countries competing against each other for jobs, as multinational companies (MNCs) and national businesses try to cut costs because of heightened international competition. Labour markets are no longer as nationally constrained as they used to be, since both labour (increased flows of migrant workers) and capital (as technologies become more portable and regulation less restricting) can more easily move between countries. For example, we saw in chapter 2 how the rise of 'offshore' call centres has involved jobs being moved out of Britain into India where highly qualified graduates can be cheaply employed. This poses real difficulties for labour movements, because, unlike capital, unions are still firmly nationally based organizations and find international collaboration, though a desirable goal, more difficult to achieve in practice, as will be discussed below.

Second, as a result of restructuring, the privatization of state-owned organizations and enterprise and the implementation of new technologies, most countries have witnessed increased unemployment, more casualized labour and the growth of the informal sector. Taken together, Bieler et al. (2008) argue, this means an alteration in the balance of power between capital and labour, in favour of the former. These trends in both Global North and Global South have contributed to the formation of what has been termed the 'precariat': a huge mass of people employed in insecure, unregulated employment (Standing 2011) – see chapter 1. Samir Amin (2008) has attempted to calculate its size: he estimates that what he calls the 'popular classes' (people who *have* to work to make a living) make up three-quarters of the world's urban population; in the Global North, he estimates that 40 per cent of the popular classes are in the precariat, and in the South this rises to 80 per cent (Amin 2008: xvi). Because of the often casual and temporary nature of their work, members of the precariat may not consider it worthwhile joining a union, and unions find it hard to organize in casualized sectors of the economy.

The concern among governments committed to neo-liberal economic policies to dismantle state protection for workers, discussed in chapter 4, may be a further factor contributing to the decline of union density – the proportion of the labour force who are in a position to join a trade union who are actually members – since its peak in the twentieth century in the countries of the Global North. Visser (2006), who calculated that there were around 320 million union members worldwide (91 million in China, 61 million in Europe and 24 million in North America), provides detailed information on union density in the early twenty-first century. He estimated that global union density (if agricultural workers were excluded) was 23 per cent, but there were major variations between continents and nations. Characteristically, density is also much lower in most countries of the Global South, where unionization is a more recent phenomenon and many workers are in the informal sector (see box 5.2). However, where unions are essentially an arm of the state rather than independent bodies, as discussed in the previous section – as in China, for example – density is high.

Box 5.2 Organizing the informal sector

Dan Gallin (2001) argues that the decline in union density can be partly explained by the growth of the informal sector, which has reached massive proportions in many parts of the Global South. In India, for example, in 2011, 92 per cent of the active population worked within the informal economy – if agriculture is included. Conditions in this sector are very poor:

> The International Labour Organization estimates that, in 2009, one in five workers worldwide – 630 million or so workers – lived with their families at or below the US $1.25 a day poverty level: 40 million more than before the global economic crisis began in late 2008. The vast majority of these working poor earn their living in the informal economy where, on average, earnings are low and risks are high. (WIEGO – Women in Informal Employment Globalizing and Organizing – website 2011)

It is hard to delineate the informal sector, but it generally implies workers who are not directly employed within a recognized company or organization. It includes the self-employed, subcontracted workers, unpaid workers in family businesses, homeworkers, domestic servants, street vendors, independent farmers and fishermen, freelance and casual workers. Often people think of these as traditional and atypical occupations, but Gallin points out that they are often a function of how MNCs operate, and are thus thoroughly modern.

Gallin describes the practice of many MNCs as the organization of production actually carried out by others. The core of the enterprise, usually located in a major global city, contains managers, administrators, and staff dealing with finance, marketing, and research and development, with perhaps a few highly skilled technical employees. Most manufacturing work is carried out elsewhere, through all sorts of contractual arrangements: for example, United Brands transformed the labour force in its banana plantations into 'independent farmers' who grow the fruit and sell it to the company. This serves to avoid the regulation which protects workers in formal employment and to cut labour costs and overheads (such as heating, insurance and building maintenance). Contracted workers often have to provide their own tools. In this way, MNCs can maximize profits for their shareholders.

If unions wish to increase their membership and retain any control over the labour market, argues Gallin, they must start to organize the vast armies of these scattered and hard-to-reach workers, many of whom are women. This can be done by existing unions or by associations set up directly to organize informal-sector workers. For example, the Textile, Clothing and Footwear Union in Australia organizes homeworkers, commonly employed in garment industries. Two of the best-known organizations in this field are Kalayaan, which organizes domestic workers in Britain, and SEWA, the Self Employed Workers' Association in India, which formed in 1972. SEWA organizes street vendors, domestics, homeworkers and refuse collectors, among others. It encourages the formation of workers' co-operatives and study circles, and helps with finance, education and training. SEWA has been notably successful and has steadily built up its membership. Along with similar organizations, it is now part of a global network set up in 1997, WIEGO, which works to get better conditions for informal workers, for example by researching and publicizing their situation and by campaigning for improvements in international labour standards. WIEGO is affiliated to the ITUC.

Thus, with the loss of jobs and the growth of precarious labour, it is unsurprising that in many countries trade unions have seen their membership in steady decline. Table 5.1 shows the extent to which union density in the Global North has declined since the 1980s during the phase of neo-liberal globalization. The fall has been particularly marked in liberal market economies like the UK, Australia and New Zealand. In the two ex-Soviet Bloc countries – Estonia and the Czech Republic – there was a very sharp decline in union density between 1999 and 2009. Elsewhere, though, it was far less marked – in Canada, for example. Although the Nordic countries did not experience union decline during the 1980s and 1990s (in Finland and Sweden, density even increased), this has changed in the twenty-first century, as these

Table 5.1 Union density, selected OECD countries 1980–2009

Country	1980 (%)	1999 (%)	2009 (%)	% change 1980–2009
Australia	50	25	19	−62
Austria	57	37	29	−49
Belgium	54	51	52	−4
Canada	35	30	29	−17
Czech Republic	n/a	30	17	
Denmark	79	75	69	−13
Estonia	n/a	16	8	
Finland	70	76	69	−1
France	18	8	8	−56
Germany	35	25	18	−49
Iceland	n/a	87	79	
Italy	50	30	30	−40
Japan	31	22	18	−42
Netherlands	35	25	19	−46
New Zealand	69	22	21	−70
Norway	58	55	54	−7
Sweden	78	81	68	−13
UK	51	30	27	−47
USA	20	13	12	−40

n/a – not available
Source: OECD statistics 2012.

countries found it hard to resist the global political climate, and some returned right-wing governments. Nonetheless, unionization remains high. These countries, with their characteristically egalitarian values and highly developed welfare policies (Esping-Andersen 1990), demonstrate the importance of national economic and social policies in resisting the global trend to individualism encouraged by neo-liberal globalization.

Although Frege (2006) concludes that globalization has indeed contributed to the overall trend of union decline, she highlights the significance of the national variations mentioned above, and points out that unions in different countries react differently to the threats from globalization. This in turn relates to different historical legacies and the specific nature of industrial relations systems and practice in each country. As discussed in chapter 1, Hall and Soskice (2001) identified three different institutional frameworks for labour relations: liberal market economies such as Britain and America; coordinated market economies such as Sweden or Germany, where social considerations are integrated with market considerations; and Mediterranean economies such as Italy and Greece, where the state and political objectives are more influential. This leaves out of account the different versions of industrial relations in the countries of the Global South, which are still establishing themselves, and may or may not follow these patterns. Although the liberal market framework may predominate in the global economy, elements of other systems still come into play so that a single explanation will not cover every country (Frege 2006). As Blanchflower (2006: 4) pithily puts it in his analysis of union decline, 'one story clearly will not fit all'.

Indeed, union decline cannot be put down to the impact of globalization alone. It is certainly a long-term trend that has coincided with the spread of neo-liberal economics; but it also reflects the evolution of service-dominated economies in Western societies and changes in social values. In Britain, for example, commentators argued that, from the Thatcher era of the 1980s, an ideology of individualism and self-responsibility had replaced the old spirit of collectivism which had led people in the past to support unions (Smith and Morton 1993). Legal change is strongly implicated. Leigh (2005) argues that this was the reason for union decline in Australia, albeit instituted by conservative neo-liberal governments, which, during the 1990s and 2000s, enacted legislation designed to weaken union organization, including prohibiting compulsory unionism – the 'closed shop': in the 1980s more than half of union members were covered by closed shop agreements, but in the 1990s many workers chose to opt out. The same developments occurred in New Zealand a decade earlier, again initiated by governments following neo-liberal policies, leading to a rapid decline in union membership (Blanchflower 2006).

Sectoral change is another factor: large manufacturing enterprises and heavy industry, such as car plants and steel works, along with mines and transport services, formed the bedrock of unionism in most of the Global North. Deindustrialization saw employment shifting into sectors such as retail, finance and leisure, which were traditionally poorly unionized. As the service sector expanded, well-organized public-sector services tended to replace manufacturing as the most unionized area, but union membership in private services is very low in all countries (Blanchflower 2006); thus the global advance of privatization (linked to neo-liberalism) has further hastened union decline. In 2011, union density in the private sector was 14 per cent, compared to 57 per cent in the public sector. The figures are even starker in the US, where in 2005 just 8 per cent of private-sector employees and 36 per cent of public-sector employees were union members. In terms of occupations, union members had the highest representation in professional and related occupations (18 per cent), an interesting finding which shows how unions have changed since the old industrial days (Bronfenbrenner 2005).

The spread of mass unemployment and precarious employment has contributed to increasing inequality around the globe. Kaplinsky (2005) reports that the gap between the rich and poor countries, as measured by the Gini coefficient, has risen steadily from 1980, which he, like Visser (2006), considers to be when neo-liberal globalization really took off. The coefficient ranges from a theoretical state of perfect equality, measured as 0, to complete inequality, measured as 100. Between 1980 and 2005, if we use this measure, global inequality rose from 46 to 67. Many countries have also seen inequalities increasing internally. According to Kaplinsky (2005), out of seventy-three countries measured between the 1960s and 2000, fifty-four had experienced rising inequality, twelve had remained constant and only seven showed a diminution of inequality. These gaps between rich and poor will certainly have increased latterly since the onset of recession, as has been the case in Britain (see, for example, Resolution Foundation 2012).

The decline of the trade unions contributes to this increase in inequality, and explains why the income gap remains lower in Scandinavia where independent unionism, though recently declining, as shown in table 5.1, is still stronger than anywhere else. Studies in Britain, Canada and the USA have identified de-unionization as an important factor in the growth of inequality. In Australia, Jeff Borland has found that 30 per cent of the increase in earnings inequality among full-time males between 1986 and 1994 can be explained by declining unionization (Leigh 2005). Comparative studies clearly show that trade unions reduce earnings inequalities (Freeman 2005). Even the World Bank has confirmed that trade union membership improves conditions for workers: 'Workers who belong to trade unions earn higher wages, work fewer hours, receive more training and have longer job tenure on average than their non-unionized counterparts' (World Bank 2003 cited in Blanchflower 2006: 12).

There is little doubt, therefore, that the continuing decline of union membership and unions' loss of influence in countries dominated by globalization, neo-liberal policies and right-wing parties are a major problem for labour movements. Consequently, in the twenty-first century, unions have begun to recognize that new strategies, approaches and tactics are needed. The 'time–space compression' noted by Harvey (1989), meaning that it takes much less time to communicate around the world, also raises new opportunities for unions to share ideas and work together. It was these conditions that led to the formation of the ITUC, noted at the start of this chapter. If capital and (migrant) labour were both moving around the globe more rapidly, then unions must change their policies to confront this new economic paradigm.

Fairbrother (1989) has promoted the influential idea of union renewal, arguing that positive change in labour movements must come from below. A return to vigorous shopfloor and branch organization might regenerate enthusiasm and commitment to unions. Fairbrother believed that the modernization and bureaucratization of unions and the increasing distance between paid officers and members had created feelings of disillusion and disempowerment that needed to be reversed. Indeed, many union leaders would agree with Fairbrother. Unions in the USA and UK have championed the 'organizing union' model, with a focus on recruiting and mobilizing workers (Daniels 2009; Heery and Simms 2011). In the UK, the TUC's Organizing Academy trained a new generation of young officers to work on building membership at the grassroots level, using the principle that 'like recruits like' (Heery et al. 2003). It was based on a similar initiative in the USA which had met with considerable success in organizing employees, such as janitors, in previously unorganized sectors (Bronfenbrenner and Juravich 1998).

Throughout union history, involvement has tended to be confined to a core of activists. This does not mean that union leaders should abandon the attempt to mobilize their members. The rise of the precariat offers a chance to build upon the anger of many working people. As the Netherlands Trade Union Confederation declared, 'the trade union movement must reinvent itself in order to deal with the challenges of the 21st Century' (Kloosterboer 2007: 1). The globalization of work and employment requires unions to find new strategies to defend employees' rights. This may require them to mobilize on a more global basis, forming new alliances and collaborations, to address the increasingly globalized nature of major companies', especially MNCs', operations.

5.4 Fighting back: trade unions challenging globalization

The adverse consequences of globalization for trade unions around the world has, certainly, prompted renewed interest in how they can operate more effectively across national borders through a more vigorous labour internationalism. Attempts to develop international labour organization and trade unionism are not new, with the first formal international bodies emerging in the early 1900s (Croucher and Cotton 2009). Yet the history of international trade unionism during the twentieth century was dominated by the effects of pronounced differences, with Cold War divisions impeding efforts to build labour solidarity across national borders (Carew et al. 2000; Cohen 1991; McShane 1992). The main cleavage was ideological: the Western social-democratic-oriented ICFTU was formed in 1949 out of a split with the increasingly communist-dominated World Federation of Trade Unions (WFTU). The presence of a third international union organization – the WCL – which articulated a Christian religious identity, exacerbated divisions (Gumbrell-McCormick 2013).

Unions also organize internationally on a regional basis; the European Trade Union Confederation (ETUC), for example, was established in 1973 and represents eighty-five national union federations across thirty-six countries. Moreover, industry-based international union organizations have existed since the end of the nineteenth century – the International Trade Secretariats, which since 2002 have been called Global Union Federations (GUFs), of which there are ten. Some – the International Transport Workers' Federation, in particular – have been moderately successful in regulating pay and working conditions on an international basis (Munck 2002).

Over the years, the established international union confederations, particularly the ICFTU, attracted severe criticism. In particular, they were condemned for the part they played in advancing a 'Cold War political agenda', and upholding the colonial interests of the major world powers – the United States and the Soviet Union – in the Global South (Croucher and Cotton 2009: 33). More generally, international union organizations were viewed as weak instruments for promoting the interests of labour on a global basis. In the early 2000s, Waterman (2001) mounted a major attack on what he called the 'old' trade union internationalism. In particular, he castigated the ICFTU as being manifestly unfit to mobilize workers against the effects of neo-liberal globalization – for the following reasons:

- it operated within the framework of separate autonomous nation-states, and 'a world of such', rather than with a global mindset (2001: 313);
- its constituent national organizations (such as the British TUC and the US AFL–CIO) had historically been biased towards representing the interests of white male industrial workers;
- it was predicated on an idea of social partnership which belonged to the increasingly defunct tripartite corporatism, along with an anti-communist ideology reflected in the idea that it represented the unions of the 'free world';

- it was dominated by the powerful Northern nations and did not fully represent the needs of the Global South;
- it was hindered by internal political struggles between the leading unions and their officers;
- despite claiming to represent 150 million members, it was largely invisible, with a much lower media profile than the national union organizations such as the TUC or AFL–CIO.

In order to operate effectively under neo-liberal globalization, trade unions still need to work within their national contexts, but must also combine internationally to advance the interests of a global work-force at a transnational level (Frege 2006). This recognition was a key driver behind the formation of the ITUC in 2006; national union leaders acknowledged that they must collaborate more effectively to stop workers from different countries undercutting each other and facilitating a 'race to the bottom' in labour standards (see chapter 4). Moreover, the collapse of the Soviet Bloc in the 1980s meant that previous ideological divisions no longer posed such a major obstacle to collaboration.

Along with the development of the GUFs, the establishment of the ITUC portends a more effective international labour movement response to globalization. While acknowledging that it faces some profound challenges, Gumbrell-McCormick (2013: 19) welcomes the ITUC's greater 'openness', and its willingness to work alongside non-labour-movement bodies in pursuit of common objectives. Others, however, claim that the ITUC and the GUFs suffer from the same problems as their predecessors – in particular, an obsessive focus on formulating policy which distances them from actual workers: 'they produce a lot of (rather moderate) documents and statements, but they do not seem to be very eager to mobilize industrial actions or initiate solidarity movements' (Munck 2011: 299). Another problem which needs to be addressed is the absence from its membership of the largest national trade union federation in the world – the All-China Federation of Trade Unions (ACFTU).

The GUFs have played a key part in advancing IFAs with mul-tinationals. IFAs are accords negotiated between MNCs and GUFs which establish minimum employment standards, often based on the International Labour Organization's (ILO's) core labour stand-ards (discussed in chapter 4), in the firm's operations, and sometimes across its supply chain (Papadakis 2011; Riisgaard 2005; Stevis and Boswell 2007). While the first IFA was established in the French multi-national Danone during the 1980s, it is only since the early 2000s that their number has really grown. By 2012, some seventy-five IFAs had been established – perhaps a low number given how numerous MNCs are in the global economy (Niforou 2012); they were set up mainly in European multinationals, including the Swedish retailer H&M and the German car manufacturer Volkswagen (Croucher and Cotton 2009).

There is some evidence that the presence of an IFA can enhance the effectiveness of union organizing efforts, and produce improvements in labour standards (e.g. Wills 2002). Some see IFAs as having a strong potential to revitalize the international labour movement (e.g. Stevis and Boswell 2007). Yet their content is mainly concerned with workers' basic 'rights' (for example, to union representation and freedom from discrimination), rather than with substantive bargaining issues; this limits the extent to which they can actually deliver higher pay or better working conditions. The main problem with the rights-based approach which dominates IFAs is the emphasis placed on compliance with local labour laws, which, as discussed in the previous chapter, are often weak or poorly enforced (Croucher and Cotton 2009; Niforou 2012).

An alternative manifestation of how labour internationalism has developed under globalization concerns the linkages, forums and networks established by union representatives within MNCs themselves. This is particularly apparent within the motor vehicle industry, which is dominated by multinationals such as Ford, General Motors and Volkswagen. In such firms, union representatives have responded to the challenges posed by restructuring by using new transnational arrangements, such as European Works Councils (EWCs), as a means of forging cross-border collaboration and mobilization. Although the form of transnational labour activity varies markedly between firms, it has nonetheless helped to offset the difficulties caused by 'regime competition' (see chapter 3): 'In-firm labour transnationalism may not overcome competition, but it has introduced new principles of solidarity into the competitive environment of the international auto industry' (Greer and Hauptmeier 2008: 94).

While clearly not unwelcome, the main problem with this mode of labour transnationalism is that it is narrowly focused, and unhelpful for workers based outside major multinationals with their established union representative structures. The so-called 'new' labour internationalism involves extending the labour movement agenda to encompass a broader range of organizations and issues relating to improving people's working lives, particularly those whose interests have been neglected by unions in the past, such as workers in the informal economy. This, then, is a very different kind of labour internationalism from that developed by the international union organizations (Munck 2002, 2011). The concept of 'social movement unionism', something which originated in countries of the Global South such as South Africa and South Korea (see Moody 1997), is central to it. This refers to the operations of unions as part of a broader movement which pursues progressive social, economic and political changes beyond the workplace by building coalitions and alliances with other organizations. In some parts of Africa, for example, unions representing workers in the formal economy work with organizations of informal workers, albeit not without difficulties (Fletcher 2011; Lindell 2008).

Perhaps the main advocate of a 'social movement unionism' approach to revitalizing labour movements and unions on a transnational, global basis is Peter Waterman (2001), who sets out his vision of what a truly effective international union movement should look like. First, it should represent a much wider spectrum of interests, a key feature of social movement unionism; it should be concerned with the needs and rights of working people beyond the workplace; it should ally itself with other democratic movements seeking justice, and with people whose work has excluded them from union activity in the past, for example housewives, peasants, homeworkers and the self-employed. It would strive for democracy, against hierarchy, and promote education for working people.

Second, it should be truly international, not serving to favour the interests of workers in the Global North over those in the Global South. This would mean abandoning a patronizing attitude based on viewing the latter as recipients of 'aid', and working to achieve a true international solidarity. Waterman also suggests there should be much more activity based at grassroots level, rather than everything being managed hierarchically by officers, echoing Michels' views.

Waterman's vision may seem rather idealistic and will be slow to achieve. There are certainly many local initiatives which display the characteristics he recommends and which have been successful in promoting workers' rights. However, these are limited in scope and certainly do not constitute a coherent international movement. As mentioned before, one barrier to the kind of grassroots activism he advocates is the unwillingness of the mass of union members to become involved. Nonetheless, Waterman's ideas chime with the visions of a broader labour movement unity, which will be discussed in the next section. He also usefully highlights the importance of communication utilizing the new technologies of the internet. These make possible instant and more democratic conversations, as witnessed in the events of the 'Arab Spring' in 2011. Waterman advocates genuine dialogue between the various parties as a necessity if a fairer society is to be achieved.

Certainly he is right to highlight the problem of North/South conflicts of interest, which are magnified in a global arena by the increased mobility of labour and, especially, capital. As we have seen, corporations can – and do – move their operations to different countries to secure cheaper labour, bringing increased unemployment to parts of the Global North, while migrants into the more affluent societies are prepared to work for lower wages than native workers, which may exacerbate racial tensions. Trade unions often find these situations difficult to handle. Thus Johns (1998) has distinguished between accommodationist and transformatory types of solidarity. The former seeks to protect the privileged status of workers in the Global North as against those in the South, while the latter poses a more radical challenge to existing class relations and the international division of labour. It is easy for trade unions responding to their members' anxieties to fall into accommodationist positions, which undermine the kind of international alliance-building advocated by Waterman.

Box 5.3 Hands across the ocean: sharing issues about women and leadership

British academics Gill Kirton and Geraldine Healy worked with the Americans Sally Alvarez, Risa Lieberwitz and Mary Gatta in a novel collaboration to explore women's leadership in the UK and the United States: 20 women union leaders were involved in an exchange programme, visiting each other's countries to share experiences and attend conferences and discussion groups, along with a series of visits. The researchers also interviewed 119 women trade union leaders in the two countries, including some of the most senior union women. In both countries, women from both white- and blue-collar unions reported facing struggles in working within a male-dominated union context. Their efforts were often undermined and insulting remarks made about their abilities. The difficulties of leadership roles and the pressures of time were common themes. It was also suggested that many older male unionists favoured an authoritarian style of leadership, while women sought to be more democratic and inclusive.

There were national differences, however. The American visitors were impressed by the legislative rights and protection available in the UK, while the British women admired the American women's forceful and optimistic approach. Both groups felt they had learned from the other. The Americans acknowledged the value of establishing a more explicitly gendered approach within unions, and were enthused by the idea of developing an international agenda. The Britons liked the idea of the celebrations and awards with which US women unionists' achievements were recognized; they were also struck by the passionate commitment of the Americans to their local unions and saw the benefits of a more positive union culture. Both sides wanted to continue the linkages by setting up an e-network; individual exchange visits were arranged and many participants felt the effects of the experiment had been profound: 'This programme has been an inspirational and learning tool that I will share and carry with me forever. This should continue and lay the foundation for other programmes of this kind' (US participant).

Some discussed getting their unions to take up international issues and to extend solidarity to unionists beyond the countries of the Global North, around issues such as human trafficking, sex tourism or child labour, taking practical steps to globalize the local agenda for the first time: 'I was so impressed by the global view of women in union leadership roles in the UK that I have committed myself to developing a women's committee with a global perspective in our Local' (US participant).

Kirton et al. (2010: 6) concluded their findings with a statement of hope for the future, emphasizing the importance of getting women involved and promoting diversity if the unions are to prosper, in both a national or an international context:

> We argue that by focusing on women in union leadership we are also focusing on the survival of the movement. . . . For unions in most industrialized countries to thrive and more importantly to survive, they must recruit and retain women members and this means having an agenda that is fit for purpose – one that serves the needs of a diversity of workers. (Kirton et al. 2010: 6)

Thus they saw extending women's leadership capabilities as a 'vehicle for increasing unions' capacity to improve women's working lives globally' (Kirton et al. 2010: 8).

That said, many national unions in the Global North have built alliances with their counterparts in the South, through exchange visits, fact-finding missions and sponsorships. UNISON, for example, has developed strong links in Southern African countries, such as Botswana and Zambia, seeking to foster the development of effective public-sector unions in the area. It has campaigned on stopping the spread of HIV/AIDS, and in 2010 re-launched its International Development Fund to sponsor joint projects, for example capacity-building in Malawi, leadership schemes for women in Botswana and support for striking sugar-cane workers in Colombia. UNISON spells out its reasons for international activity on its website, in a statement that clearly recognizes its own location in a global network:

> Britain's economy and political system are interdependent with Europe and the rest of the world. In the current economic climate as we are all engaged in the struggle to protect our public services, it is vital that UNISON works with sister trade unions in other countries and through key international organizations to promote and protect members' interests and concerns. . . . Trade unionists in many other countries risk intimidation and even death for active membership in a union. Solidarity – joining together with others who share a common interest – is the very basis of trade unionism, and it shouldn't stop at national borders. (UNISON website)

Box 5.3 reports on a research project seeking to explore and facilitate women's leadership in trade unions through a programme of exchange. The authors highlight how crucial the promotion of women is for a regenerated international movement, which must be aware of the disadvantages faced by women in the Global South. An alliance with the international women's movement is thus a key element of 'social unionism'. The drive for gender equality is now a part of most major UK unions' platforms. This has particular salience in a global context where labour markets have been subject to increased feminization, both in the Global North where the decline in manufacturing has led to increased male unemployment and in countries such as China and India in the South, where women are often preferred because they are cheaper to employ. A strategy of union renewal has to take on board the fact that the 'typical' worker in the global economy is no longer a man with craft skills, but a female retail or care worker – see chapter 9. It is notable that the ITUC has been headed by a woman, Sharan Burrow, who stated in her acceptance speech on becoming its President:

> I am a warrior for woman and we still have work to ensure the inclusion of women in the workplace and in our unions. The struggles for women are multiple – too often within their families for independence, then in the workplace for rights and equal opportunity, in their unions for access and representation and then as union leaders. But the investment in and participation of women is not only a moral mandate, it is an investment in democracy and a bulwark against fundamentalism and oppression. Organizing women is and must continue to be a priority for the ITUC.

However, there remain obstacles to effective labour internationalism, as Ghigliani (2005) demonstrates in his case study of a meeting held in 2002 to promote international action against abusive labour practices at the notoriously anti-union McDonald's and its suppliers. The meeting was organized by, among others, the ICFTU, the international department of the Dutch Trade Union Confederation, and the GUF for the food industry, the IUF. Activities included a public demonstration outside a McDonald's restaurant in Brussels, and representation to the European Parliament. Organizations from eleven countries were involved. However, Ghigliani points to problems and tensions that arose over the course of the meeting. There were policy conflicts and differences of focus between the international and national bodies. For example, the IUF was less concerned with a global campaign to protect workers' rights than with representing its members, who did not see campaigning against McDonald's as a priority. While McDonald's was seen globally as a problem, it did not figure as such on most national union agendas. There were also conflicts between environmental and human rights organizations, who favoured radical forms of direct action, and the more conservative trade groups who focused on lobbying. Finally, the focus of the European bodies on utilizing EWCs as a means of organizing McDonald's annoyed unions from countries without such bodies. Ghigliani concludes that, even 'though many of the features of the allegedly new labour internationalism are present, they seem to be more a matter of form than substance' (2005: 359).

5.5 New social movements and community unionism

Waterman's vision of 'new social unionism', discussed in the previous section, is one of a package of approaches which academics and union activists have been advocating over the past decades, to enable the labour movement to recover some of its former political significance, lost because of membership decline, along with the demolition of the tripartite system and the threats posed by globalization. Canadian academic Carla Lipsig-Mumme (2003) lists some of these approaches: social movement unionism, labour internationalism, union renewal, global unionism and development of organizing cultures. These approaches have in common an attempt to embed unions in a broader movement of labour.

One of the most influential of these in the 1990s has been community unionism, which has been particularly advocated by unions in Canada and Australia. Canada, like the USA, has low union density and it may have been this which inspired activists to take this approach (Briskin and McDermott 1993). Lipsig-Mumme (2003) defines community unionism as 'a term to describe the several ways that trade unions work with communities and community groups'. 'Community' is a notoriously slippery term, and Lipsig-Mumme explains that it can have a number of meanings here: organized local community groups, communities of interest (for example gays and lesbians, ethnic minorities) or simply a loosely defined 'public' who may share unions' concern, for example, over job losses, welfare cuts or contested redevelopment schemes. However defined, the point is that union activists collaborate with such groupings on campaigns; this could be a short campaign on a single issue, such as a factory or hospital closure, or a long-lasting alliance to pursue a range of common interests. For example, in the USA in 1995, a number of organizations campaigned against the retail company Gap. A coalition was formed of trade unions, universities, consumer associations, church groups and others to compel the company to improve labour conditions within Mandarin, a subcontractor firm in El Salvador. Here, as in other Central American *maquiladoras* (see chapter 9), teenaged women worked for pitiful wages and were ill-treated by supervisors. Having formed their own union, SETMI, their grievances were picked up by the National Labor Campaign, a human and worker rights organization based in New York. Young activists calling themselves 'Gapatistas' picketed the shops and leafleted (Pattee 1996). The campaign was successful, although the alliance did not manage to extend this to other firms subcontracted by Gap (Cavanagh 1997).

Part of the idea behind community unionism, thus, is building alliances outside the confines of the trade union movement itself. This might be done at a very local and specific level, or it could be at a much more general level, with nationally based groupings. A major way of thinking about such alliances is through the idea of new social movements (NSMs).

This term was developed in the 1960s and 1970s (see Parkin 1968; Touraine 1971) to describe emergent protest movements which were viewed as increasingly influential: such movements include feminism, the peace movement, anti-racism and environmentalism. These movements seemed more appealing, especially to young people, than the 'old' class-based institutions of socialism and trade unionism. The implication was that unions would do well to learn from the methods of these movements – which appeared more lively and democratic than unions – to take on board their issues and to make common cause with them. A crucial point is that many NSMs were international in focus and ideology and so could respond more effectively to the context of globalization than the nationally based trade unions.

Theorists of NSMs (for example, Touraine 1971; Melucci 1980) suggested that they arose from post-industrialism and the decline of large-scale manufacture, which exposed trade union methods and concerns as somewhat outdated and irrelevant. Rather than being concerned with issues of production and distribution, NSM concerns focused on the sphere of reproduction, culture and consumption. It was suggested that, in these new social conditions (especially the affluence of the 1960s), people were less concerned with economic issues (such as income redistribution) and more concerned with rights and values. This was closely related to the idea of 'post-materialism' developed by Ronald Inglehart (1977). Young people in particular were said to hold post-material values, focusing on freedom, identity, culture and lifestyle rather than money. Inglehart did not see this as merely a lifecycle phenomenon, but argued that it represented a generational shift in values and ideas. Such concerns might include animal rights, vegetarianism, pacifism and multiculturalism.

Features of the NSMs which differentiated them from the old labour movements were that:

- they drew their membership more from middle-class people and marginalized groups, such as housewives and students, than from the working class;
- they often focused on a single issue;
- they avoided bureaucracy and hierarchy, preferring informal modes of organization and democracy; some of them even claimed to be 'leaderless organizations';
- they were anti-authoritarian and resisted incorporation into institutional levels;
- they had no exclusive relationship with any political party and were tolerant of a range of political views;
- they were more spontaneous and favoured a range of forms of direct action.

Critics of NSM theory pointed out that such movements were hardly new: pacifism, feminism and vegetarian movements had all formed in the nineteenth century. They also doubted whether the NSMs were as clear of traditional political involvements as was implied. Almost all could be seen as left-wing, there was considerable overlap of personnel, and many alliances on specific issues; for example, trade unions gave strong support to the feminist 'Our right to choose' campaign against limiting access to abortions. Nonetheless, it is clear that young people, especially students, have been drawn to these movements and are often put off by the bureaucratic formalism of trade unions and the dominance of white middle-aged men as leaders. There is a lesson for trade unionists here about style and organization. Although the NSMs may be more structured than at first appears, they have tended to eschew incorporation into the control mechanisms of the bureaucratic state.

Democracy and spontaneity have been features of emerging social and political movements in the twenty-first century, such as the Anti-Globalization Movement active since the 1980s, which holds protests at meetings of the G8 (the leading industrial nations) and holds Social Forums to counter the activities of the World Economic Forum and challenge the neo-liberal policies of current globalization; UK Uncut, which aims to highlight the tax misdemeanours of banks and MNCs; and the global Occupy movement, opposing the current patterns of distribution of wealth (see box 5.4). Trade unions have given support to these movements. New alliances continue to form between such groups and unions with their common objectives of resisting the worst impacts of neo-liberalism and of defending the rights of ordinary working people. Such alliances may provide the base of the 'new social unionism' advocated by Waterman.

Box 5.4 Occupy! A globalized NSM

The Occupy movement emerged in the summer of 2011 as a global response to the impact of recession in the Global North, the rise of poverty and unemployment and the growing gap between rich and poor. Protestors were inspired by the occupation of Tahrir Square in Cairo during the protests of the Arab Spring which led to the overthrow of the Egyptian dictator Hosni Mubarak, and by the 'Indignados' in Spain, young people who occupied the Plaza Mayor in Madrid protesting about massive unemployment (50 per cent among young people) and political corruption. Protestors in America issued a call to 'Occupy Wall Street', a rallying cry that was taken up across the country and spread to Europe. Encampments sprang up in well-known public spaces, including outside St Paul's Cathedral in London, and protestors declared they would stay there until a new political consciousness became widespread, recognizing the need for a fairer division of social resources. By the autumn, there were occupations in over 900 cities around the world, including 23 in Britain. Protestors were mainly aged below twenty-four, but came from all walks of life: students mingling with veterans of the wars in Iraq and Afghanistan, teachers and social workers side by side with the unemployed. At Occupy Bristol, an IT consultant explained the ideas behind the slogan 'we are the 99':

> I have three children and it is because of concerns for their future that I am here. . . The situation in the world is very serious and is the result of powerful interests in Wall Street, the money markets and other places manipulating our democracies in their own-self interest . . . We have a rising population, dangerous environmental

> degradation, climate change, loss of soil fertility and now the collapse of our economies and financial integrity. This amounts to a perfect storm and our political elites are unable or unwilling to confront it. Meanwhile the one per cent are steadily increasing their wealth and influence and driving us deeper into crisis. The majority need to come together, as we are doing here, to discuss a way forward that is in the interests of the many, not the few.
>
> This movement was firmly global in its range across continents; news of it spread via the internet, and groups communicated news to one another using Twitter and Facebook alongside their own websites; similar techniques, slogans and tactics spread between the groups. Its demands for economic reform, true democracy and care for the environment paralleled the concerns of the international labour movement and links were made with local unions and other campaigning groups. The global nature of Occupy! is summed up in this statement from Occupy London, issued in November 2011:
>
>> Our global system is unsustainable. It is undemocratic and unjust, driven by profit in the interest of the few. An economic system based on infinite growth, but which relies on finite resources, is leading humanity and the environment to destruction. As long as this system remains in place, people of the world continue to suffer from an increasingly unfair share of income and wealth. We seek a global system that is democratic, just and sustainable. The world's resources must not go to the military or corporate profit, but instead go towards caring for people's needs: water, food, housing, education, health, community. An international, global collaboration has started, and is working on a statement that will unite the Occupy movements across the world in their struggle for an alternative that is focused on and originates from people and their environment.

What might this future movement look like in its activities? Munck (2002) provides some ideas. He argues that international unionism must move beyond diplomatic visits and exchange of information to joint activities and protests. He emphasizes the important potential of internet technologies (mobile phones, wi-fi, Facebook, Twitter) in linking people together cheaply and quickly, as was apparent in the Arab Spring protest movements and the Occupy movement in 2011. In his words: 'The Internet does seem to have the potential to set up a countervailing "virtual" power (of the imagination) to that of the transnational corporations, cutting across traditional lines of hierarchy, divisions between national movements and distinctions between strategy, action and education' (2002: 157). This allows a more complex flow of information and dialogue than earlier technologies. He also suggests a repertoire of tactics drawing on some of those used by NSMs: media-staged events such as concerts and festivals, consumer boycotts, summit gatherings and e-petitions, which can be used in combination with older tactics such as strikes and demonstrations – see chapter 10. On a more formal level, labour movements need to fight for greater regulation of labour conditions: this might involve strengthening 'social clauses' in trade agreements, campaigning for international labour standards (see chapter 4), or engaging in a kind of 'benchmarking' parallel to that carried out by MNCs and other organizations: that is, identifying best practice and promoting it within an industry. While Munck acknowledges that all this will be hard to achieve, he emphasizes how crucial it is to attempt it.

5.6 Conclusion

> A fraternity of peoples is highly necessary for the cause of labour . . . not to allow our employers to play us off one against the other and so drag us down to the lowest possible condition.
> (British workers' plea to the French workers in 1863, cited in Munck 2002: 136)

Munck (2002) reminds us that trade unionism has had an international strand from early in its history, with the formation of the Workers' Internationals in the nineteenth century. The key principle of solidarity includes the idea of bonds across borders as well as within them, for both ethical (world unity, brotherhood and sisterhood) and practical reasons (to prevent undercutting and 'divide and rule'). The idea of international solidarity may have become rather tarnished in the Cold War period, when the ICFTU and the WFTU collaborated with their political masters to gain control of industrializing countries in the Global South. In a different political context, there may be real hope of a more altruistic espousal of internationalism.

This collaboration is needed because of the real threats posed to unions by globalization. There is no doubt it has helped speed the process of union decline. In the context of fierce and increasingly international competition, businesses committed to neo-liberalism see strong trade unions and protective legislation as obstacles to market success and flexibility (Cohen and Kennedy 2000; Rothstein 2012). Conservative governments and, increasingly, even social-democratic governments support them in this through legislative change. As this chapter has emphasized, however, there are considerable variations in the degree to which states implement neo-liberal policies, with some retaining stronger social-democratic or corporatist elements, and this affects the degree of union decline or recovery and the effectiveness with which unions can operate at the national level.

In a global economic climate dominated by MNCs, it remains hard for unions to replicate their national structures internationally, and to join hands across the various fault-lines – rich and poor nations, North/ South and East/West – but the blows inflicted by neo-liberal globalization pose challenges for union effectiveness which, as we have seen, may not be soluble at the national level alone. It is crucial that unions try to raise wages and improve working conditions in countries where workers are labouring under exploitative arrangements, and to organize the informal sector, reversing the current dynamic of the 'race to the bottom' mentioned in earlier chapters.

Most commentators agree on the necessity of international collaboration, although, of course, this should not mean the abandonment of national action. Indeed, the advice is to 'think locally, act globally', picking on local issues and attempting to build out from them. If the power of neo-liberal economics and ideology is to be challenged, and their worst effects reversed, unions need to position themselves as part of a wider dialogue and programme for change. The need for unions to avoid narrow sectionalism, and reintegrate firmly into a regenerated labour movement, based on the principles of social movement unionism, has hardly been greater.

Further reading and useful websites

Ronaldo Munck has written extensively on some of the issues covered in this chapter, including a notable book on the topic (2002), which is a highly readable and informative account of international labour movements. For a more recent analysis, see his chapter in Gall et al.'s edited book (2011). See Waterman (2001) for the prospects for a 'new' labour internationalism based around social movements. The most readable and up-to-date overview of the international trade union movement is Croucher and Cotton (2009).

For further information about the union organizations mentioned in this chapter, you can go to their respective websites:

ICTU – www.ituc-csi.org/
Global unions – www.global-unions.org/
ETUC – www.etuc.org/
TUC – www.tuc.org.uk/
AFL–CIO – www.aflcio.org
UNISON – www.unison.org
SEWA – www.sewa.org/
WIEGO – http://wiego.org/.

6 Work and the management of labour in 'global factories'

6.1 Introduction

In 2010 the National Labor Committee (NLC), a US organization that campaigns for improvements in workers' rights, published a report on working conditions in a Taiwanese-owned factory located in China that makes products for Microsoft and other global corporations. The report highlighted the extreme work pressures, gruelling hours, low pay, lack of legal protections and 'prison-like discipline' endured by the exhausted young workforce (NLC 2010). Also in 2010 a series of suicides in Chinese factories owned by the Taiwanese company Foxconn, which make iPods and other electronic products for multinationals such as Apple, drew attention to the highly alienating nature of work in such environments. Clearly, it is necessary to understand the nature of work and labour management issues in 'global factories' – plants sited in the Global South, especially in South-East Asia, which are involved in the high-volume production of items such as garments, toys and electronics goods for international markets (Grunwald and Flamm 1985). The increasingly important role of Chinese plants in global production networks (GPNs), particularly their contribution to globalization, has further stimulated interest in how global factories operate (Buckley 2009; Cantin 2008). We take a rather liberal view of what constitutes a 'factory', including data processing and call centres – sites for the production of information goods as well as those that make physical products.

Our approach is informed by labour process theory. This holds that there is an indeterminacy of labour power at the point of production. When hiring a worker to engage in productive effort, it is not possible for an employer to specify all of the duties and obligations that will be required during the course of their employment. Thus there is space for potential struggle over control of the terms of the employment relationship and the amount of effort to be expended. For employers, who have to ensure that latent labour power is realized in practice, managerial interventions to control labour and thus secure productive efficiency are keys to ensuring that the outcomes of this struggle benefit them. Management control is never absolute though; the indeterminacy of labour power means that workers always have some scope, however limited, to bargain over, or even challenge and resist, attempts to direct their labour. Thus a dialectic of management control and the potential for worker resistance lies at the heart of the labour process approach. We start by exploring the implications of globalization for the management of labour, before specifying the nature of managerial control regimes in global factories and examining issues relating to worker resistance and identity formation. In the final main section, we then consider the implications of globalization for understanding the labour process, including the nature of the transnational labour process.

6.2 Global factories and the new international division of labour

The distinctive feature of a global factory relates to its position within a production system which is organized on a transnational basis. In thinking about the 'global assembly line' (Cravey 2005; Ward 1990), then, we need to acknowledge that the division of labour extends across national borders, sometimes on a worldwide scale. As a result, it is imperative to develop an understanding of the nature of work, and how it is organized and experienced, in those factories which operate as hubs in global systems of production, making the products sold in world markets, particularly to consumers in the Global North.

Since the 1980s, parts of southern China have become dominated by large-scale factory production, with millions of largely female workers employed to make sports-shoes, toys, clothes and electronics goods for international markets (Cantin 2008; Lee 1998). The development of a new international division of labour since the 1960s is an integral feature of globalization, and one with profound implications for work and employment around the world. Multinationals from the Global North sought out low-cost manufacturing locations in the Global South where goods such as electronics products and clothing could be made cheaply for world markets by an emerging factory workforce (Froebel et al. 1980; Munck 1988). One of the most important effects of this dimension of globalization has been to draw into the factory workforce an enormous pool of hitherto non-industrial labour, the majority of whom previously worked in agriculture or undertook domestic tasks. In countries like Indonesia, a largely rural migrant labour force has increasingly been incorporated into factory work (Warouw 2008). Global factories in China, in particular, rely upon the labour of millions of migrant labourers who originate from the rural interior and are attracted to the factory jobs available in the coastal areas (Xue 2008).

Undoubtedly the most important characteristic of the new industrial workforce evident in the global factories concerns the dominance of women in production and assembly work. Factory managers exhibit a marked preference for female labour (Fernández-Kelly 1983); as a consequence, factory work in countries as diverse as Indonesia, Malaysia, Taiwan, Thailand and Mexico is dominated by the labour of women (Caraway 2007; Elias 2005; Gallin 1990; Pangsapa 2007;

Tiano 1990). The new international division of labour is highly gendered and involves a profound feminization of the workforce (Elson and Pearson 1981; Cravey 2005). As well as being dominated by female employment, global factories are generally marked by a highly gendered division of labour. Women's employment in export-sector production is generally organized as 'low wage, monotonous assembly line work in jobs structured in such a way that career progression is very limited and consequently women's employment is confined to low wage employment in a limited range of industries' (Elias 2004: 36).

Factory managers organize work and employment based on a set of gendered assumptions about the appropriateness of women for labour-intensive production – they are perceived as cheaper to employ, more malleable and compliant, and better suited to the intricate production tasks involved in making toys, clothing and electronics goods in comparison to men (Elson and Pearson 1981; Salzinger 2003). The docile nature and 'nimble fingers' of the women working in factories around the world are therefore viewed as essential features of manufacturing in a globalized production process (Elson and Pearson 1981; Fuentes and Ehrenreich 1983). As we see below, however, not only can women's participation in industrial work be an empowering process (Tiano 1994), but the assumption that women are inherently more compliant, and therefore particularly suitable for employment in global factories that demand a flexible, malleable and cheap labour force, is also highly questionable. We explore this gendering of work and employment more fully in chapter 9.

Not all production for international markets is undertaken in large-scale establishments though. The focus of the chapter is on 'global factories', but their size and nature vary considerably. On the one hand, massive enterprises like the Foxconn complex in southern China, which makes mass-market electronics goods such as the iPhone, employ hundreds of thousands of workers. On the other hand, products made for global markets often emanate from chains of subcontractor relationships, at the bottom of which are small-scale firms or small independently managed workshops, sometimes headed by women, with production often undertaken in workers' own homes. The importance of outsourced, subcontracted production arrangements is especially notable in Asia, where goods are often made or assembled in small family-based workshops – for example clothing products made in the Philippines for markets in the US and toys manufactured in Sri Lanka which are destined for Europe. Much of the industrialization of Taiwan was driven by manufacturing in household production units (Hsiung 1996). Clearly, the 'hidden assembly lines' of small-scale production in workshops and households are important elements of global supply chains (Balakrishnan 2002). For global capital, the system possesses a number of benefits. Outsourcing production in this way helps firms to enhance their flexibility; it enables them to alter output more readily by regulating the amount of work given to subcontractors. Small-scale workshop and household production arrangements have some advantages for workers: women are better able to accommodate childcare responsibilities, and undertake other domestic tasks, while still earning a living. However, the insecure production environment means that it is a very precarious form of employment. The availability of work is often uneven. Moreover, since it is often unclear where responsibility for upholding labour standards lies, the use of small-scale workshop and household production arrangements can lead to the erosion of working conditions and labour rights (Balakrishnan 2002).

6.3 Factory regimes in the global economy

During the 1970s the work of Braverman (1974) and others stimulated much interest in the nature of managerial control strategies in the workplace (e.g. Friedman 1977; Edwards 1979). For our purposes, though, the contribution made by Michael Burawoy (1985) with his concept of the 'factory regime' is central to understanding how globalization affects labour control within firms. His main insight is that managerial efforts to exercise control over labour formed part of a politics of production which not only incorporates the labour process at the point of production but is affected by broader political and ideological apparatuses beyond the workplace, notably by state policies. Burawoy (1985) distinguished between two broad types of factory regime under capitalism:

- despotic regimes, where the livelihood of workers is dependent upon the wages they receive from their employment, allowing employers to exercise coercive approaches to managing labour;
- hegemonic regimes, under which state intervention, in the form of welfare policies for example, means that workers are not reliant on wages alone, and that employers cannot rely entirely on coercion to secure control, but have to put more emphasis on winning worker consent, though not to the exclusion of coercion.

He suggested that the rise of state welfare provision during the twentieth century in the Global North had prompted a shift from broadly despotic to hegemonic regimes.

Yet Burawoy recognized that globalization posed a major challenge to established hegemonic regimes under advanced capitalism. Increasing capital mobility, the prospect of greater international competition and the threat of disinvestment and plant closures can be used by firms to extract concessions from workers in the Global North, weaken the bargaining power of unions and reinforce managerial control. This 'new despotism is founded on the basis of the hegemonic regime it is replacing. It is in fact a *hegemonic despotism*' (Burawoy 1985: 150).

Perhaps the main way in which Burawoy's insights have contributed to our understanding of globalization and work is in the use made of his concept of the factory regime, and the refinements that have been made to it, by scholars attempting to understand the nature of management control in global factories. Burawoy himself identified a number of specific variations on his two broad types of factory regime; as we see, however, globalization in general, and the rise of the global factory in particular, have stimulated further efforts to comprehend the nature of factory regimes and refine Burawoy's approach.

If we consider the internal dimensions of factory regimes, the management and organization of work in the factories in the Global South is marked by a strong emphasis on efforts to secure labour compliance (e.g. Pun 2005a). The nature of the labour process at the point of production and the operation of strict internal factory rules and disciplinary techniques for securing compliance are clearly key elements of the system of labour control in global factories. However, the factory regime concept means that we also need to consider the external imperatives, those that lie beyond the workplace, such as the nature of state policies which help to enable managers in global factories to effect control over labour.

Perhaps the most obvious mechanism for exercising managerial control relates to the organization of the labour process. Mass production environments, and the use of Taylorist forms of work organization, enable managers to operate methods of 'technical control' over labour, with workers required to yield to the pressures and demands of the assembly line production environment (Edwards 1979).

One contemporary description of the labour process in a Taiwanese-owned factory located in southern China, which makes sports-shoes for leading brands including Nike, Reebok and Adidas, attests to the resolutely Taylorist basis of work organization in the plant: 'On the cavernous factory floors of Yue Yuen, making sneakers is a science measured with stopwatches. A plastic sign in front of every station on the assembly line displays how many seconds a worker needs to complete a given task' (L. Chang 2009: 113). Needless to say, the way in which the labour process is organized leaves workers bored and alienated. One Chinese factory worker interviewed by Ngai Pun (2005a: 83) reflected on the tedious and mundane nature of her job: 'I don't need to use my mind anymore. I've been doing the same thing for two years. Things come and go, repeating every second and minute. I can do it with my eyes closed' (Pun 2005a: 83).

There has been much interest in the Global North in the extent to which the elaboration of new management techniques has rendered Taylorist methods of work organization obsolete. In particular, the high performance work system (HPWS) model posits a break with Taylorism, by holding that there are a range of preferred techniques for managing labour, for example teamworking arrangements, which help to deliver enhanced company performance by producing a more empowered and committed manufacturing workforce (Applebaum et al. 2000; Boxall and Macky 2009; Caspersz 2006).

There is some evidence that the HPWS model is appropriate not just in the manufacturing enterprises of the Global North, but also elsewhere in countries such as South Korea, India and Taiwan (Kim and Bae 2005; Som 2008; Tsai 2006). Overall, though, the global penetration of the commitment-based HPWS model has been rather limited. Global factories generally operate on the basis of a mass production paradigm, characterized by a narrow division of labour and a set of narrow, and highly standardized, Taylorized work tasks (e.g. Elias 2005; Xue 2008; Pun 2005a; Wilkinson et al. 2001).

Perhaps the most profound problem with the HPWS approach concerns its relevance in locations where managers tightly regulate working conditions. In his study of high-tech electronics production in the Philippines, Steven McKay (2006) found high levels of commitment, but in conditions where workers generally enjoyed little participation at work and were subject to strict control and discipline. Rather than seeing commitment as being of an affective kind, born out of loyalty to the organization, as do proponents of the HPWS, he contends that it is of a more 'alienative' nature, based on a lack of alternative employment.

In addition to the organization of the labour process, the mechanism of technical control evident in global factories is supplemented by highly regimented systems of rules, often in the form of elaborate factory codes, and the strict application of discipline – all of which are designed to shape workers' behaviour with the aim of driving improvements in productive efficiency (Warouw 2008). Rules govern such matters as appropriate clothing, talking and eating at work, penalties (generally fines) for lateness and absenteeism, among other things (Pun 2005a). The sheer number of factory regulations, and their elaborate detail, are designed to impose industrial discipline over labour, producing a strictly regimented workplace and cowed workers who submit more easily to the onerous demands of the production schedule. According to a female factory worker in Thailand: 'There are so many rules in my factory, I feel I am in a prison sometimes' (Theobald 2002: 143).

The exercise of discipline in global factories is marked by a decidedly punitive ethos: violations of rules often attract fines (Xue 2008), and sometimes worse. In her book *China's Workers under Assault*, Anita Chan (2001) points to the extensive use made of 'rigid systems of discipline' by factory managers in order to drive productive efficiency. In some cases, this even involved documented instances of corporal punishment and physical assaults on workers deemed to have transgressed factory rules. Managers of Korean-owned factories in China seem to be particularly fond of a belligerent approach to discipline, with workers being 'frequently subjected to the arbitrary applications of rules, physical violence, yelling, finger-pointing, unreasonable impatience and verbal harassment' (Won 2007: 317).

Discipline in global factories is not just a matter of rules, regulations and penalties for misbehaviour. The organization of work, manifest in the operation of highly regimented work schedules and timetables, also helps to create a highly disciplined environment and a subjugated workforce (Pun 2005a). Labour discipline in global factories is generally a highly gendered affair (Cantin 2008): largely male managers are responsible for supervising a predominantly female workforce. They often draw upon patriarchal assumptions about the presumed inferior status of women within society at large to help enforce control in the factory (Kaur 2000). Moreover, as we have already seen, one of the reasons why women are generally preferred for assembly line work, over men, is because factory managers assume that they are going to be more compliant (Kaur 2004b).

Why are such strict and regimented systems of discipline seen to be so necessary? The key thing to remember is that many of the workers employed in global factories are rural migrants and are therefore 'green' – in the sense of having little or no prior experience or knowledge of what it is like to work in an industrial factory environment, and the demands it imposes. Factory codes, strict rules and regulations, harsh penalties for misbehaviour and so on are therefore viewed as essential mechanisms for habituating and socializing inexperienced workers into industrial employment, inuring them to the rhythms and pressures of factory work (Warouw 2008). Such extensive measures to 'change the mindset of workers' (Won 2007) are necessary for the purpose of realizing productive efficiency.

6.4 Labour control regimes in global factories: the state and labour markets

While the focus of this section has, so far, been concerned with internal mechanisms for maintaining labour control in global factories, the despotic basis of managerial approaches is also conditioned by a complex mix of external factors, including supportive state policies, the nature of labour markets and the prevailing patriarchal assumptions about gender roles that characterize society in general (McKay 2006). Taking the role of the state to begin with, Burawoy (1985) emphasized how the rise of state intervention, particularly in the area of welfare provision, helped to promote the development of hegemonic factory regimes in the Global North during the twentieth century. Yet when we look at the nature of managerial control in global factories, the most striking observation about the role of the state concerns the ways in which its activities help to foster despotism. This is evident in five main respects.

First, countries in the Global South seek to attract and retain multinational investment by offering themselves as desirable locations for factory development. In chapter 4, we observed that, often, countries actually have quite rigorous labour laws on paper; however, governments are unwilling to enforce them for fear of discouraging multinational investment. In fact, some countries, particularly in Asia, have actively taken steps to reduce employment regulation, weakening established protections enjoyed by workers; thus, in relation to the management of global factories, the role of the state may be seen *not* as a regulator of employment rights and working conditions, but largely as a force for deregulation (D. Chang 2009: 176). Nowhere are this deregulatory approach and its consequences more evident than in the specially designated locations around the world, often called export processing zones (EPZs), where, in return for the investment they bring, firms are commonly exempted from swathes of local labour laws. In the Philippines, for example, labour compliance in EPZs is a product of the interactions between local elites, state officials and firms, based on a nexus of often informal and personalized relationships. These work together to create favourable environments for capital, for example by removing potentially troublesome union activists. This suppression of labour rights is a key element of the resulting 'local labour control regime' (Kelly 2001), whereby 'global capital's bidding is done on its behalf by various localized institutions which . . . have become convinced that what is good for global capital, in the form of industrial investors, is good for their locality' (Kelly 2001: 20).

Second, the pursuit of repressive, anti-union policies has been another way in which states have intervened to enable factory managers to effect despotic approaches to managing labour. States in those parts of the world where global factories predominate, like South-East Asia for example, are often marked by a preference for repression when it comes to dealing with organized labour (Deyo 1989). In order to offer desirable environments for multinational investment and factory development, states use a variety of measures to counter trade unions. Industrialization and factory development across a range of countries, including South Korea, the Philippines and Thailand, among others, have been accompanied by (not always successful) efforts to pursue political repression of free trade unions (Kim 1997; McKay 2006; Pangsapa 2007). One of the reasons why China is such an attractive location for establishing global factories is that independent trade unions are prohibited.

Third, some states, particularly those that have authoritarian political systems, operate residency rules that place restrictions on where workers can live. The *hukou* system of registration in China, for example, means that urban factory workers are theoretically prohibited from taking up long-term residence in the vicinity of the plants where they work, since they are registered for permanent residency purposes in their rural home towns and villages. This operates as a form of coercive labour control, and helps to maintain a despotic managerial approach by making workers more dependent upon their factory employment, in two main ways. First, it renders workers more compliant because if they lose their job they are liable to lose their temporary residency permit, and may have to return home, to the detriment of their livelihood. Second, the *hukou* system of registration also enables local governments to eschew any responsibility for housing and supporting factory workers, on the basis that they are not legitimate residents; instead, workers have to depend upon their employers for accommodation (often in the form of dormitories – see below) and welfare support (Chan 2001; Pun 2005a; Cantin 2008).

Fourth, in a global economy, where international migration has become increasingly commonplace, with factory work in the Global North often undertaken by migrant workers on a large scale, managers can exploit immigration laws in ways that render their migrant workforce more vulnerable. In her comparative study of plants making tortillas in the United States and Mexico, Bank Muñoz (2008) observed that, through their restrictive immigration laws, states influence the labour process, enabling a despotic managerial approach. The 'immigration regime' evident in the US factory was characterized by the employment of a pool of migrant workers who are rendered vulnerable, and thus more susceptible to coercive control by managers, because of their uncertain residency status.

Fifth, state initiatives in the area of welfare reform, and the erosion of welfare provision, also mean that workers come to be more dependent for their livelihoods on their jobs, leaving them more vulnerable to managerial coercion. In Nogales, Mexico, for example, the withdrawal of the state from providing healthcare, childcare and housing support meant that workers had either to pay for provision themselves or instead to rely upon their employers, part of a deliberate strategy designed to increase their vulnerability. It was evident that the local state's approach was 'geared toward providing transnational corporations with a dependent and relatively quiescent workforce by dismantling, deregulating, and privatizing social provision' (Cravey 2005: 114). Similarly, the exploitation of labour in Chinese factories has been facilitated by the absence of state welfare support, with the result that workers are overly dependent upon the wages from their employment, and thus more likely to be compliant (Merk 2008).

Clearly, states play a major role in influencing the management of the labour process, by intervening in ways that produce a more compliant workforce, thus enabling managers to operate coercive managerial approaches consistent with despotism. Yet while Burawoy's (1985) concept of the factory regime acknowledged that managerial control was rooted in influences beyond the workplace, his emphasis on the state meant that other aspects of a broader politics of production, particularly the influence of labour markets and contracts, were neglected (Lee 1998; Nichols et al. 2004). Evidently, though, these dimensions of employment have important implications for the nature of managerial control in global factories. Increasingly flexible labour markets have contributed to greater job insecurity in some parts of Asia, for example, with the result that workers become more vulnerable, come under greater pressure to demonstrate their value to the company, and are consequently more acquiescent to managerial imperatives (D. Chang 2009; Zhang 2008). Greater labour market flexibility, then, by generating a more casualized, insecure and vulnerable workforce, not only helps to foster coercive factory regimes marked by 'flexible despotism' (Chun 2001), but also undermines progress towards a more hegemonic approach based on winning workers' commitment (Nichols et al. 2004).

The key influence of the local labour market in helping to foster despotic management is evident from Ching Kwan Lee's (1998) study of a Hong Kong-owned electronics factory in Shenzhen, southern China. It was characterized by a highly regimented working environment, with a rigid disciplinary approach, including a set of factory regulations that carried on for ten pages! Working life was harsh and extremely onerous, with workers claiming that factory management didn't treat the workforce as human beings (Lee 1998: 115). In contrast, one of the company's other factories, which was located in Hong Kong itself, operated in a hegemonic fashion. The main reason for the differential treatment was not down to state policies; in the case of both plants, a lack of state intervention gave managers a largely free hand in dealing with their respective workforces. Rather, the different 'social organization of the labour market' in each case was the main source of variation. The Shenzhen plant was populated mainly by young, female, rural migrant workers, who were dependent on local networks for employment in a highly competitive labour market, and whose vulnerability was easily exploited by factory managers in a regime of 'local despotism'. The Hong Kong factory, however, was staffed largely by older, more experienced women with family responsibilities, for whom a more hegemonic regime, based on a degree of work autonomy – 'familial hegemony' – was the more effective managerial approach. Variations in the labour market, then, produce not only different types of female factory worker, but also different forms of management control (Lee 1998: 107).

In order to understand fully the dimensions of despotic management approaches in global factories, then, we need to consider not just state policies but also the nature of labour markets, which are often highly permeated by the influence of gender, and also race (see box 6.1). We have already observed that the workforce in global factories largely comprises women; for this reason, it is perhaps more appropriate to characterize approaches to organizing and managing the labour process within them not just as factory regimes, but more explicitly as gendered factory regimes (Lee 1998). Burawoy (1985: 156) himself acknowledged that gender is an important consideration in how factory regimes operate, and mused on how the organization of the labour process and the structure of the labour market reflected prevailing societal assumptions about respective gender roles. The highly gendered basis of the organization and management of the labour process in global factories is evident in a number of important respects.

Box 6.1 The 'apartheid workplace regime' in South Africa

Between the late 1940s and early 1990s, the South African government operated an apartheid regime, a system of state-sanctioned racial segregation under which those people deemed as 'non-white' were treated as inferior citizens, prohibited from living alongside 'whites' and not permitted to exercise civic rights, such as being able to vote. The system of apartheid supported and reinforced a highly unequal and racialized economic system, with prosperity concentrated among the minority white population. Apartheid had a major impact on work and employment in South African enterprises. The most obvious manifestation was a marked racialized division of labour, with workforces segregated on the basis of race. Whites were employed in managerial and supervisory positions, while Black workers generally filled lower-paid, low-skilled and blue-collar positions. Along with extensive levels of racial harassment and discrimination and the operation of segregated workplace facilities, this racialized division of labour contributed to an extremely coercive system of labour control, in the form of 'an apartheid workplace regime', within which the largely Black blue-collar workforce were managed in a highly despotic manner (von Holdt 2002).

Since the dismantling of apartheid, and the establishment of democratic government, many South African enterprises have tried to develop innovative techniques for managing labour, consistent with a high-performance approach. This includes the use of commitment-based human resource management interventions, such as quality circles and teamworking arrangements, as part of a broader concern with improving the competitiveness of South African firms. However, while apartheid no longer exists in a formal sense, the legacy of racial despotism it produced continues to exercise an important influence over the management of labour in South African workplaces. The persistence of racialized elements associated with the apartheid work regime, such as the reluctance of managers to engage in high-trust relations with their staff and their preference for coercive approaches to labour control, has hindered the take-up and effectiveness of new management techniques (Webster and Omar 2003).

For one thing, managers in global factories are often thought to prefer employing younger, female workers because they are presumed to be more malleable, compliant and docile than men, and also better suited to the intricate tasks frequently associated with assembly line production. Yet such a view overlooks the important ways in which managers themselves, through the use of highly gendered techniques relating to recruitment, labour utilization, work organization and supervision, actively attempt to produce a disciplined and subjugated female workforce. Factory managers do not recruit a cadre of acqui-escent female workers; rather, they actively engage in constructing docility themselves by operating gendered practices that treat women as if they are passive and compliant (Freeman 2000; Salzinger 2003).

In global factories, gendered ideologies and practices are often used as the dominant means of maintaining coercive managerial control. Managers draw upon relevant aspects of the local patriarchal culture, using and adapting them as appropriate to effect coercive means of labour control (Elias 2005; Kaur 2004b). At first glance, the largely female workforce in the tortilla plant in Baja California, Mexico, studied by Bank Muñoz (2008) appeared to benefit from a rela-tively lenient working environment, with managers seemingly taking a relaxed approach to enforcing discipline. However, this masked a more profound and extensive set of coercive managerial behaviours, in particular manifold incidents of sexual harassment. While male work-ers benefited from a hegemonic managerial approach, the women were subjected to a highly gendered form of despotism.

6.5 Identity and resistance in the global factory

Although the emphasis on managerial despotism in global factories is appropriate, there are different types of despotic regime, linked to the respective influences of state policies, labour markets and gender in particular. But there are clearly some circumstances where a more hegemonic approach is preferred by managers, linked to the labour market status of the workforce or their gender. Male workers in par-ticular often benefit from a factory regime based around hegemony (e.g. Bank Muñoz 2008). Yet in global factories operating high-tech production strategies, such as in the consumer electronics industry for example, the need for a stable workforce means that more hegemonic managerial approaches are increasingly preferred, based on securing workers' consent, though not to the exclusion of coercive techniques (McKay 2006).

A further critique of the stress on despotism is that it largely neglects interventions by workers themselves which are designed to challenge managerial control, and ignores the ways in which work in the global factories contributes to processes of identity formation. The assump-tion that women workers in global factories are inherently docile is profoundly mistaken. As we have seen, managers use gendered recruitment techniques and other interventions actively to produce an acquiescent and compliant workforce. But the labour process perspec-tive implies that we also should acknowledge the potential for workers to resist managerial control imperatives, something that may cast fur-ther doubt on the docility thesis. Moreover, while initially dominated by a focus on control and resistance, as the labour process tradition evolved it incorporated perspectives which put more emphasis on workers' subjectivity, including processes of identity formation. No account of work in global factories would be complete, then, without considering the implications for workers' identities.

Within global factories, efforts by workers to mobilize collectively in trade unions to challenge managerial control do occur, but they face considerable obstacles. In South Korea, for example, there was considerable labour militancy during the 1980s and 1990s linked to the demands for political change. Although strikes spread to the free trade zones, repressive behaviour by employers to suppress them stifled much of the resistance (Kim 1997). While the potential for collective resistance clearly exists, anti-union measures by firms and governments make it quite rare. Workers in global factories are understandably fearful of losing their jobs, given the relative ease with which global capital can respond to episodes of labour militancy by switching production elsewhere (Bank Muñoz 2008). Thus the insecure and vulnerable basis of employment in global factories creates an unpropitious environment for collective resistance to managerial imperatives.

That said, however, it is by no means out of the question. Pangsapa (2007), for example, compared two factories in Thailand, both of which were characterized by badly paid jobs undertaken by largely female workforces in poor working conditions. In neither case could the workers be said to be passive or docile. One of the factories staved off potential resistance by operating a paternalistic management style and creating an environment in which workers perceived themselves as subordinate to, and thus dependent upon, their employer. In the other factory, though, which made clothing products for global retail brands such as Nike and Gap, the women developed a specific collective identity in opposition to, and designed to challenge, the interests of their employer. As their activism developed and they formed a union, the women became more assertive and confident. In contrast to the other factory, where workers accommodated to, and thus became accepting of, their circumstances, the mobilizing efforts of a group of women activists proved critical to the development of a more militant consciousness.

If we adopt a broader conceptualization of resistance, one that does not just associate it with collective mobilization in the form of union militancy but rather incorporates a more varied set of behaviours which challenge managerial control, or hinder compliance with managerial expectations, then evidently it is widespread in global factories. In the 1970s, for example, production in some of the earliest Malaysian global factories was disrupted by outbreaks of 'mass hysteria', incidents of sabotage and – to the bemusement of Western managers – episodes of spirit possession. The largely female rural workforce drew on the stereotypical assumptions held by male managers about their supposed emotional instability in ways that disrupted the highly patriarchal labour control regime that governed their work and challenged the dislocation caused by rapid industrialization (Ong 1987).

Incidents of 'everyday resistance' (Kim 1997) to managerial control, in the form of covert actions to slow down production, unauthorized absences from the production line or arguments with managers, are commonplace in global factories (e.g. Tjandraningsih 2000; Theobald 2002). In the Chinese plants studied by Ngai Pun, workers often failed to comply with factory rules:

> Workers simply could not help but violate the regulations if they were to kill the boredom and the drowsiness. Individual defiance like deliberately not performing the job, speaking loudly, making fun of others, or leaving the work seat without waiting for a permit happened from time to time as well. Passing jokes on the line, some-times overtly, sometimes covertly, could be seen as resistance to the extreme work conditions and as a chance to refresh an empty mind.
> (Pun 2005a: 102)

But there is some ambiguity here. Behaviour that in some circum-stances can be classified as resistance might, in others, help to reinforce managerial control by helping workers to cope with onerous working conditions. It may also underline prevailing gendered assumptions about the subordinate status of women in paid employment. For example, in her study of Malaysian factories, Elias (2005) noted the occurrence of a considerable amount of 'everyday' forms of resistance to managerial control, including episodes of spirit possession and high absence rates. However, these behaviours actually served to reinforce the stereotypical assumptions held by male managers that, because women were more emotional and irrational than men, they were therefore unsuitable for anything other than low-status assembly-line work. Resistance by male workers tended to be rather more successful.

Regardless of how far work and employment in global factories are characterized by resistance to managerial control, an unambig-uous development has been the greater empowerment of women workers. Although factory managers draw upon patriarchal structures and ideologies found in the wider society to enforce labour control, involvement in paid employment has given many of the women work-ing within the factories a degree of freedom and autonomy they would never have enjoyed if restricted to domestic and household labour (e.g. Fernández-Kelly 1983; Tiano 1994). It has also had a marked effect on their social identity, through the formation of new gendered subjectiv-ities (Salzinger 2003). Material goods are not the only things produced in global factories; they are also responsible for generating a set of new gendered identities and subjects among the workers that populate them (Freeman 2000). See box 6.2 for the implications of professional identity construction among Indian call centre workers.

Perhaps the most striking example of this subjectivity concerns the formation of *Dagongmei* as a new social grouping in industrializing China. Understood as 'migrant working daughter', the concept of *Dagongmei* refers to a production of new subjects, marked by a dis-tinctive gendered social identity, among the largely young and female

Box 6.2 Professional identity formation in Indian call centres

The development of a particular sense of professional identity among call centre workers in India, explored in chapter 2, poses obstacles for effective trade union organization in the sector. During the 2000s, the Indian call centre sector, based around cities such as Mumbai and Bangalore, developed rapidly. India is an attractive location for Western firms looking to re-locate – or 'offshore' – some of their customer-facing and back office facilities. The cost of labour is cheaper than in their home territories, and there is a large pool of young, well-educated and English-speaking workers which they can draw upon to staff their operations. Work in the call centres is highly regimented. Strict performance targets, extensive monitoring arrangements and a systematic and punitive approach to enforcing workplace discipline all contribute to creation of a 'stringent' work system (Noronha and D'Cruz 2009). One would have thought that such a situation would offer the trade unions in India a good opportunity to organize the sector; and union activists have made efforts to build labour organization in call centres. However, a lack of support from call centre staff themselves has proved to be a significant obstacle to unionization; they view union membership and activity as being inconsistent with how they perceive their identity as professional employees. Unions were seen as institutions suitable for industrial workers who were being exploited in factories, not for 'professionals' employed in office-based locations who were dealing with international customers and clients. For the call centre employees, then, 'joining a union was seen as being inappropriate to the status of the international call centre employee and as rejecting professional values' (Noronha and D'Cruz 2009: 231). Through their work, they had developed, and internalized, a specific sense of professional identity, one which caused them to liken their labour to that undertaken by employees in skilled occupations, such as software engineers. The call centre staff maintained that 'intelligent, qualified, motivated, responsible and upwardly mobile professionals like themselves, whose jobs involved skill and challenge and provided good returns, whose work environments were modern and chic and whose employers looked after their well-being, were not in the same category as factory workers' (Noronha and D'Cruz 2009: 222).

Unionization would undermine their sense of professional identity and in their eyes put them on the same level as lower-status factory labour.

workforce who, as a result of their toil in China's global factories, have been exposed to capitalist employment relationships in a distinctive way (Pun 2004). While evidently a new social formation, viewing *Dagongmei* in terms of social class is problematic. Any incipient working-class consciousness has been stifled by the presence of a highly authoritarian state, the exigencies of global market forces and oppressive patriarchal family structures. Class, then, has been 'subsumed', or incorporated, within the emergent *Dagongmei* social formation, rather than taking primacy (Pun 2005a).

Viewed on its own terms, though, rather than simply through the lens of class, the *Dagongmei* phenomenon is highly suggestive. It captures how, on moving from domestic or agricultural work in rural areas to paid factory employment in urban areas, young female workers acquire a distinctive modern identity, manifest in greater interest in consumerism, for example. *Dagongmei* are sexualized subjects for whom consumption has become integral to being modern citizens. Workers share gossip, jokes and laughter about sex and romance. In the dormitories where they live, the women workers share 'with equal enthusiasm the satisfaction and frustration of shopping as well as work. Instead of keeping them separate, consumption bound them into a collectivity through their shared dreams and desires to become a new kind of gendered subject' (Pun 2004: 162–3).

Despite the oppressive environment in which they live and work, it is important to recognize that, although lacking any real power to contest their circumstances, *Dagongmei* are far from being simply passive or docile. Overt and covert efforts to subvert managerial control demonstrate that these workers are by no means inherently submissive, notwithstanding management efforts to delineate them as such (Pun 2004). See box 6.3 for some of the implications of dormitory accommodation for managing labour.

6.6 Globalization and the transnational labour process

The purpose of this section is to consider the implications of globalization for the labour process, drawing on insights taken from the experience of global factories that are part of transnational production systems. For our purposes, perhaps the key insight offered by the labour process perspective is the recognition that there is a connection to be made between behaviour in the workplace and developments in the broader political economy (Thompson and Smith 2009, 2010). This encompasses a concern with understanding the nature of, and the relationship between, the places where production happens and the spaces which multinationals inhabit (e.g. Elger and Smith 2005). It is not so much a case of evaluating the influence of globalization on work, as of recognizing that work in a globalized environment is structured and operates in different ways (Jones 2008). In examining the implications of globalization for the labour process and contemplating the main elements of a transnational labour process, we offer some key insights about how work and employment function in a globalized political economy.

Perhaps the most obvious feature of the labour process under globalization concerns the development of cross-border production networks and the implications of greater capital mobility. Clearly, they permit the exploitation of workers in global factories on a massive

Box 6.3 The dormitory labour regime in China

One of the most notable features of many large global factories in China is the provision of on-site, or adjacent, accommodation facilities in the form of workers' dormitories. They are not a new development (Pun and Smith 2007); nor are dormitories just confined to China. They also exist elsewhere, in Mexico for example (Cravey 1998). However, the use of dormitories on a large scale, and the development of a 'dormitory labour regime', has made an important contribution to the development of China as a major site for the production of low-cost, mass-produced goods (Pun and Yu 2008): 'In new global factories, the dormitory labour regime has been extended to the majority of production workers and is the norm. It is now more systemic and extensive' (Pun and Smith 2007: 32). Without the provision of dormitories, factories would find it difficult to access the migrant labour from rural areas on a large scale needed for production; since workers benefit from subsidized accommodation, the dormitory system also allows employers to keep wage levels under control (Pun and Smith 2007). Dormitories are also a key instrument of labour control. They enable factories to benefit from greater production flexibility, by lengthening the working day for example, and help to make workers more dependent upon their employers (Cantin 2008; Smith and Pun 2006; Pun 2007). Living conditions within dormitories are often highly regimented, sometimes akin to a military-style approach, encouraging workers to discipline themselves (Chan and Xiaoyang 2003; Pun and Smith 2007).

The dormitory labour regime can also be viewed as a specific kind of 'spatial production politics' (Pun and Smith 2007), in the sense that, by extending the reach of labour control beyond the immediate boundaries of the workplace, it helps to reconstitute production space. Moreover, it is also significant as a particular manifestation of the transnational labour process. The dormitory labour regime is embedded within, and helps to support, a system of low-cost, flexible production of goods for global markets on a mass scale. The transnational labour process involves 'work relations within a concrete or embedded production process, and one which is locked into transnational capital flows, labour flows, and work organization practices that are not only nationally bounded, but transnational and global in their structure' (Pun and Smith 2007: 42). Given how it regulates labour mobility, and renders capital mobility more effective, the dormitory labour regime exemplifies the transnational labour process in action.

scale, through coercive management techniques associated with despotism. Indeed, the very success of global capitalism demands the use of workforces which can be organized and managed in ways that support the process of capital accumulation on an international scale (Cantin 2008; Pun 2005a), while resulting in little obligation to promote their welfare, housing and livelihoods. Globalized production, then, involves the 'growing power of capital to organize and control labour on ever larger geographical scales while *ignoring* the social reproductive needs of labour' (Merk 2008: 80). Greater capital mobility, and the threat it poses to workers that, without their constant labours, work can be moved relatively easily to cheaper production sites with more compliant workforces, make workers more vulnerable and contribute to the despotic nature of labour management in many global factories (e.g. Pangsapa 2007). The coercive power of labour management in global factories is enhanced by the deregulatory policies pursued by states keen to use lax labour regulations to offer attractive investment locations to multinational capital (Kelly 2001). In all these ways, then, it is evident that the globalized political economy 'cannot be divorced from the internal production machinery of the factory' (Bank Muñoz 2008: 170).

Yet it is important not to exaggerate the extent of despotic management approaches. As factories in the Global South become responsible for the manufacture of a broader range of products, including increasingly technologically sophisticated electronic goods for example, then the need for stable production environments becomes more pressing, rendering simple coercion inappropriate. Efforts to build worker consent, and the elaboration of regimes based on hegemony, may become a more important dimension of labour management in global factories (McKay 2006). Moreover, in line with labour process theory, even in global factories marked by despotic managerial regimes, management control cannot be absolute. While worker resistance, on both an individual and a collective basis, is often easily suppressed, the indeterminacy of labour power means that its potential is ever present. Studies of Indian call centre locations indicate that even in highly regimented working environments, marked by coercion, the extent of management control over labour is moderated by the need to accommodate workers' concerns (Taylor 2010; Taylor and Bain 2005).

Moreover, the experience of global factories demonstrates that globalization not only is associated with greater worker exploitation, but also involves the production of new workforces. Factory employment has transformed the lives and prospects of largely female rural migrant workers across a range of countries in the Global South, including Mexico, Taiwan, South Korea, Malaysia and Indonesia, offering new opportunities for social advancement and empowerment (Fernández-Kelly 1983; Kung 1983; Kim 1987; Ong 1987; Wolf 1994). In China, for example, female factory workers are increasingly developing an urban lifestyle at odds with the character of the rural communities where they originated (L. Chang 2009). At the same time, though, the highly gendered nature of the labour process in global factories, allied to the articulation of a powerful patriarchal ideology, helps to constitute a distinctive form of coercive control, through the construction of an acquiescent female workforce: 'On myriad global shop floors, managers assess what is possible and acceptable in gendered terms, measuring efficiency and productivity with reference to, and sometimes in terms of, the global icon of productive femininity' (Salzinger 2003: 26).

It is often taken for granted that global capital scours the globe in search of cheap and acquiescent labour; in fact, the creation of new workforces with distinctive and varied identities has been central to the process of globalization (Cantin 2008). In Barbados, for example, women employed in the informatics sector, doing data processing work for international corporations, developed a new kind of gendered 'professional' identity, based around specific aspects of their demeanour, behaviour and appearance (Freeman 2000). Perhaps the most prominent example of how the construction of changing identities has been fostered by globalization is the case of the young female *Dagongmei* discussed in the previous section, a new type of feminine subject who has emerged at the 'intersection of global capitalism and the Chinese modernity project' (Pun 2005a: 12). Three related points are important here. First, the process of globalization, and its specific manifestation in the form of global factories, is not just associated with workforce exploitation and the exercise of coercive managerial control over workers; it also involves the creation of new subjects and new identities. Second, following on from this, global factories are involved in more than just the production of clothing, toys, electronic devices and other consumer goods; they 'are as much about the production of people and identities as they are about restructuring labor and capital' (Freeman 2000: 36). Third, the experience of work in global factories suggests that the subjectivity it produces is both liberating and constraining – liberating because the process of identity construction erodes and undermines traditional patriarchal values, and constraining because it upholds the operation of gendered forms of labour control based on the idea of productive femininity (Salzinger 2003).

It is sometimes assumed that under globalization the importance of specific places diminishes. This relates particularly to the location decisions of global capital which, because it is able to exploit space on a transnational basis, supposedly becomes less attached to, and dependent upon, particular settings. Paradoxically, though, the places where products are made or assembled become more important in the context of globalization; multinational capital, no matter how 'footloose' it aspires to be, has to materialize somewhere, for production to occur (McKay 2006). Recognizing how places matter, and the efforts undertaken by global capital to exploit, and take advantage of, the characteristics of specific places, in particular the type of workforce they can offer, is central to understanding the nature of the labour process in global factories and the dimensions of a new 'spatial politics of production' (Pun and Yu 2008: 110).

Places are important not only because capital is attracted to settings thought to be particularly suitable for the purpose of productive efficiency, but also because the characteristics of specific places in turn help to shape the practice of labour management within the factories themselves. Thus the labour process in global factories is not just a function of the relationship between global capital and local labour, but is also 'mediated' by the characteristics of specific places (Kelly 2001: 20). In the Philippines, for example, local and national actors, such as state officials, played an important part in reinforcing labour control by taking action to weaken labour unions and relaxing labour laws (Kelly 2001). The concept of the 'strategic localization of production' has been elaborated to capture the way in which firms do not simply take the characteristics of particular places for granted, or take advantage of locations that are already constituted in specific ways. Instead they engage in a process of actively drawing on, and reconstituting, the circumstances of the local environment. For example, the experience of electronics plants in the Philippines demonstrates how 'firms engage, manipulate, and try to reproduce local conditions and social relations to enhance production stability once investments are already sunk' (McKay 2006: 172–3). Their management strategy involved hiring young rural women workers who were considered particularly compliant and pliable. The key thing here is that firms' localization strategies vary according to the appropriateness of the setting (McKay 2006).

The interplay of, and the relationship between, the local and the global is therefore a key influence over the nature of the labour process in global factories (Lee 1998; Elias 2005). Given that capital has to manifest itself in particular places, studying how the 'localization of the global' (Freeman 2000) operates, and the way in which labour management in global factories draws upon, and is influenced by, the prevailing ideologies and practices of the local environment, is key to the analysis of globalization. This includes the constitutive role played by workers themselves in mediating global management practices in particular settings (Cravey 2005).

Clearly, the experience of global factories provides some important insights about the nature of the labour process under globalization; but what does it entail for understanding the transnational labour process? In other words, rather than just examine how globalization influences the labour process, we also need to be concerned with the distinctive features of the labour process at transnational level. Two key aspects need to be emphasized. First, evidently geographical concepts of space, place and scale are essential components of the transnational labour process. The rise of global factories is associated with development of 'new production spaces' (Elger and Smith 2005), or a new 'spatial politics of production' (Pun and Yu 2008), whereby global capital does not just exploit space, but actively reconstitutes it, to realize improvements in productive efficiency. However, as we have seen, it is not just space that is relevant, but also the nature of the places where global capital settles. Central to understanding of the transnational labour process is recognizing how the characteristics of specific places both influence, and help to reproduce, patterns of labour control and resistance (Kelly 2001). Moreover, the multi-scalar nature of globalization demands a focus 'not only on that which is explicitly global in scale but also on locally scaled practices and conditions that are articulated within global dynamics' (Sassen 2007: 18). The concept of the 'strategic localization of global production' (McKay 2006) demonstrates the relevance of geographical scale to understanding the nature of the transnational labour process. It describes the basis of the relationship between the policies of local and national states designed to attract global capital, and the behaviour of multinationals, which not only adapt their practices to suit local conditions, but also actively manipulate the characteristics of the local environment for the purposes of accumulation.

These insights into the nature of the transnational labour process need to be supplemented by an approach that acknowledges the influence of transnational flows of capital and labour. Adopting a flow perspective, then, adds to our understanding of the labour process in general, and the transnational labour process, in particular (Thompson and Smith 2009). As we have seen, the indeterminacy of labour power, whereby the amount of effort expended by a worker at the point of production cannot be specified in advance, is central to labour process theory. However, there is actually a double indeterminacy present. Labour power, or the capacity of workers to engage in productive activity, can be broken down into effort power and mobility power. In addition to the indeterminacy of effort power at the point of production, there is also the indeterminacy that arises from the decision of the worker about where to offer their labour power and the choice of an employer about where to site production. While the choice of workers about whether or not to take up employment with a particular firm creates uncertainty for employers, uncertainty for workers is generated by the capacity of employers to re-locate and thus no longer require their services (Smith 2006). The concept of the double indeterminacy enhances our understanding of the transnational labour process by highlighting the importance of mobility power. Under globalization, the 'external mobility of the employer is stronger than the mobility power of labour and is used to increase labour effort and control workers' (Smith 2010: 277). Firms can use the threat of re-location as a device for maintaining discipline over, and extracting greater productivity from, their workforces. The concept of mobility power also helps to explain the attractiveness as production locations of countries like China where, because of restrictions on workers' mobility among other things, 'the double indeterminacy of labour is more settled in favour of employers' (Smith 2006: 399).

6.7 Conclusion

One of the most important dimensions of globalization has been the rise to prominence of global factories, establishments located mainly in those countries in the Global South which manufacture and assemble the products destined for global markets. Our concern in this chapter has been to offer insights into the nature of work and labour management techniques in these global factories, highlighting the dominant, but by no means exclusive, use of coercive approaches. This is aided not just by state policies, but also by the nature of labour markets and the use of gendered ideologies and practices. Nevertheless, while workers in global factories generally labour in highly regimented and disciplined working environments, the potential for resistance to managerial control exists, even if it is often stifled by repressive policies. Moreover, globalization has stimulated the creation of new subjects and identities formulated among the largely female workforce of global factories. In a globalized political economy, moreover, it is possible to ascertain the features of an emergent transnational labour process. This is marked by a complex mix of geographical factors – namely place, space and scale – which help to constitute and reproduce patterns of labour control and resistance, and also by a flow perspective, recognizing the important influence of the respective mobility power of capital and labour.

Further reading

For an introduction to debates about labour process theory, see Thompson and Smith (2009). Burawoy (1985) draws a distinction between two broad types of factory regime – the despotic and the hegemonic. There is a wide range of good studies of the nature of work and labour management techniques in global factories; McKay (2006) on the Philippines is particularly insightful. Also highly recommended is Pun (2005a), which provides an in-depth investigation of work, labour and the process of identity formation in a Chinese global factory. Freeman (2000) and Salzinger (2003), who respectively focus on Barbados and Mexico, not only provide excellent insights about the importance of gendered ideologies and practices to the labour process in global factories, but also focus on the formation of new social identities. Finally, for the transnational labour process, and the concept of the double indeterminacy of labour power in particular, see the work of Chris Smith (2006, 2010).

7 Globalization and migrant labour

7.1 Introduction

It is important to stress at the outset of this chapter that migration is not a new or recent phenomenon. As Peter Stalker (2008: 10) notes, 'No nation on earth can claim always to have lived in the same place', thereby concluding that each contemporary nation-state is a 'product of multiple overlapping generations of immigrants'. Some scholars identify the era of mass migration as the period of European expansion and settlement of North America, namely 1870–1914. However, Castles and Miller (2009) describe the current era as the 'Age of Migration' because earlier migrations typically involved transatlantic routes, whereas recent decades have brought about the territorial 'globalization of migration' in a fuller sense.

The increased movement of labour – both *internally* within countries and *externally* between them – is seen as one of the defining features of contemporary global capitalism. Although the progress of capitalism has always involved the movement of landless people to work in cities, where they can earn a living that is not dependent on agriculture but on capitalist modes of production, the pace and frequency of such movements has accelerated significantly in recent decades. The total number of migrants has more than doubled since 1975, when it was 84 million. In 2010, the UN estimated that there were 213 million migrants – that is, people living outside the country in which they were born – in the world. Of these, 74 million moved from the Global South to Global North, 13 million from the Global North to Global South; 73 million moved from one country to another in the Global South, and 53 million moved within the Global North (UN 2012b). Thus, migrants from the Global South constitute the greatest numbers. It is estimated that women make up 49 per cent of international migrants.

The UN (1990) defines the term 'migrant worker' as 'a person who is engaged or has been engaged in a remunerated activity in a State of which he or she is not a national'. Whilst this may be a useful starting point for our discussion, it is limited, as it refers to one sort of movement: *international* or *external migration*. But, as we shall see, movement can also be within a nation-state, for example from remote rural areas to its 'global cities' (Sassen 1991; see chapter 8). Indeed, in countries with large populations, such as China, India and Brazil, rural to urban, *internal migration* exceeds external migration (Castles and Miller 2009; see box 7.1).

Box 7.1 Delhi's silent majority

In December 2011, a workshop was organized by UNESCO and UNICEF on 'Internal Migration and Human Development in India' in order to raise the profile of what they called 'India's neglected priority'. The 2001 Census revealed that a striking 309 million people in India were internal migrants and 70.7 per cent of these were women. The total figure comprises 30 per cent of the population. Moreover, Indian's urban population has increased from 285 million to 377 million between 2001 and 2011; this dramatic increase in rural–urban migration is having a profound effect on India's popular destination cities, particularly Delhi, Bangalore and Mumbai.

Batau, a thirty-year-old migrant from the state of Madhya Pradesh, left his village following crop failure. Interviewed for Delhi's *First City* magazine, his story resonates with those of millions of other internal migrants: 'Now I have come here to be a labourer. Soon my wife will come here and join me. We will do this for two–three months then return to our village to do farming again. I don't like the city, but who does? I don't want to stay here for long, only till I earn enough to go back and start again.'

Heavy rains, flooding and crop failure prompt the landless poor to leave their villages and seek jobs in cities, typically finding casual jobs in construction and domestic service. Yet in the city they can find themselves living in urban slums on a meagre 50–60 rupees a day, often facing threats of eviction, clearance and rent-seeking from government officials (UNESCO–UNICEF 2011). They become a 'floating population' in search of temporary and seasonal work, often moving between the city and home, yet losing access to social security and networks as a result.

The movement of people in search of jobs is described as economic migration. Economic migration is only one form of the broader phenomenon of migration, but it has always been an important aspect of peoples' movements around the globe. Much of this movement is voluntary, but it may be forced if people are ejected from their country or driven out by famine, warfare or political oppression. Stalker (2008: 10–12) introduces five main categories of international migrants:

- *settlers* (economic migrants and their families);
- *professionals* (employed by multinational and other global organizations);
- *temporary workers* who are allowed to live and work temporarily in a country to meet labour market shortages, for example in seasonal jobs;
- *refugees and asylum seekers* (fleeing from persecution and warfare in their home country);
- *unauthorized workers* without permission to enter or remain in

a country, who are often described as illegal or undocumented immigrants.

Yet in analysing the phenomenon of economic migration, as we aim to do here, it is worth noting that in practice these categories are often blurred. For example: Indian IT professionals in the USA can often be employed on temporary contracts; wives and husbands who join their professional spouses in a country of settlement are themselves often highly qualified; and many so-called 'labour migrants' who occupy unskilled jobs in a destination country may well be graduates, and are often over-qualified for the jobs they fill (see section 8.3).

In this chapter we introduce and explain the role of migrant labour in the global economy. In chapter 8 we go on to consider highly skilled migration specifically, and the emergence of distinct forms of 'elite' transnational mobility. Since economic migration is not a new phenomenon, we will begin by briefly considering some historical examples of labour migration to illustrate the different forms it has taken, before reviewing theories that address the question 'what makes people migrate', and contemporary migration systems (sections 7.3–7.4). The working conditions and working lives of migrants are considered here, as well as the reasons that cause them to travel long distances to get jobs that are often dirty, difficult and dangerous, the so-called '3–Ds' (Stalker 2008: 23).

7.2 A brief history of labour migration

From the beginnings of the civilizations that we know about, people have travelled around the world, in search of land, wealth and adventure, or to get away from oppressive rulers. The Greeks and Romans travelled extensively around Europe and Asia and set up colonies where many of them settled as farmers, officials or businessmen. They brought people back from these colonies to work as slaves, soldiers or craftsmen in their own cities. Muslim merchants, seamen and scholars formed trading networks that extended from the Persian Gulf to the Sea of Japan between the ninth and thirteenth centuries. These networks have been characterized as largely peaceful and mutually beneficial, fostering the exchange of knowledge and people as well as goods (Abu-Lughod 1989). In the Middle Ages, prior to the emergence of European colonial powers, the Normans settled in the British Isles, where their predecessors, Romans, Vikings and Anglo-Saxons, had already driven the original inhabitants, the Celts, Picts and Scots, into the further recesses of the islands. The British, as Rudyard Kipling's marvellous stories in *Puck of Pook's Hill* and *Rewards and Fairies* demonstrate, emerged as a 'mongrel nation'. Sociologists use the term 'social hybridity' to explain this mingling of ethnicities through the movements of colonialism (Young 2005).

From the sixteenth century, the British competed with the Spanish,

French, Dutch and Portuguese to gain new colonies in the remainder of the globe: the Americas, Africa, Australia, Malaysia, the Indian subcontinent and the islands of the South Pacific. The colonial adventurers sought gold, spices and other forms of wealth, as well as territorial expansion. They were often sponsored by kings and queens, and later by 'merchant venturers', groups of investors such as the East India Company, who can be seen as pioneers of capitalist techniques (Hobsbawm 1995). In the process of colonization, just as had happened in Britain, the original inhabitants – such as Australian aboriginals, New Zealand Maori, Native American 'Indians' or Amazon tribes – were killed by disease or dispossessed and driven to the margins of the territory, retreating to forests, mountains or deserts. As Karl Marx (1867) argued in *Das Kapital*, the wealth of the industrializing nations was built up on piracy, plunder and theft.

While the search for land and natural resources was the impetus behind colonial expansion, labour migration was also an integral part of it. As colonizers set up farms, plantations, mines and building processes in their new territories, they required labour for their enterprises. Colonialism thus triggered the more systematic movements of labour around the globe that are the ancestors of today's global flows. These large movements of citizens, constituting what we now know as *diasporas*, came from countries such as China and India that became major exporters of labour. These in turn led to processes of settlement in the 'host countries', which have created the patterns of ethnic diversity in contemporary societies, including America, Britain, France and Germany.

Khalid Koser (2007) suggests that migration typically occurs in 'waves', and gives a useful account of some of the most important ones in the past three centuries. The first wave was the forced migration of slaves from Africa to work in the plantations of America and the Caribbean. Britain was heavily involved in these movements through what has been termed the 'triangular trade' (Cohen 2006). Slaves from Africa endured the fearsome Atlantic crossing chained in the bowels of slave ships to work in the Caribbean or America growing sugar, rum, tobacco and cotton (although many died en route). These products were then shipped to Europe to be processed, and the proceeds were used to buy manufactured goods and taken to Africa to purchase more slaves. Following the abolition of slavery in the nineteenth century, some slaves stayed on plantations, but formerly 'free' indentured labourers were brought in to work in the fields from the Indian subcontinent and China. Indentured labourers replaced slaves, but were only 'free' in the sense that they could not be bought or sold (Cohen 2006: 40).

Koser's (2007) second wave describes the mass movement of people from Europe to the United States as the latter built itself into being the world's greatest economic power. The USA had a massive hunger for labour between the 1850s and the Great Depression of the 1930s.

Box 7.2 The Irish diaspora: from famine to prosperity?

Reporting on mass migration from Ireland in 1846, the *Liverpool Times* makes the distinction between 'emigrants of hope' and 'emigrants of despair', contrasting the experiences of farmers with some capital 'who go to seek means of improving their condition in Canada and the States', with those of migrants with barely the means to fund 'the trifle which is necessary to bring them over to this country' (cited in Davis 2000: 19). However, as Davis (2000) notes, migration from Ireland began much earlier, in 1815 following the Napoleonic wars, and continued throughout the twentieth century. Even before the famine years (1841–52), an estimated 50,000 people were leaving Ireland annually for Britain and North America because of increasing population pressure and a system of land use that left many labourers vulnerable to poor harvests and food shortages (Davis 2000: 19–20). Between 1840 and 1920, the second wave of migration to North America saw an exodus of 5 million Irish to the USA. Following 1921, Britain once again became the main destination for Irish migrants. Thus, Irish migration to Britain represents a special case due to the country's proximity to Ireland, as its nearest neighbour, and its role in furthering the spread of the Irish diaspora from its ports in Liverpool, Bristol and Plymouth to the rest of the English-speaking world. The Irish 'diaspora' includes people of Irish descent in Argentina, South Africa, Australia, New Zealand, Canada and the USA (Bielenberg 2000).

Much of the nineteenth-century Irish experience, as settlers, labourers and citizens, resonates with that of subsequent generations of migrants to Britain, North America and Northern Europe. Moreover, *where* migrants came from in Ireland shaped *where* they settled and the 'timing and subsequent persistence of their settlement' (Davis 2000: 22). The so-called 'Famine Irish', from the west of Ireland, were more likely to seek passage to North America, whereas Irish from the more advanced, industrialized north-east of the country were more likely to stay in Britain. The decline of the textile industry in the north of Ireland encouraged textile workers and weavers to seek work in Scotland, Yorkshire and Lancashire, whereas unskilled migrants from the south and west were more likely to head for the industrial cities of London, Liverpool, Manchester and Glasgow. For some, Britain was a stepping-stone to the rest of the English-speaking world, and learning English, acquiring skills and gaining political and trade union experience were invaluable to those who spent time in Britain before emigrating to North America (Harris 1994).

Yet, like subsequent generations of postcolonial and other migrants, the Irish faced discrimination, and their residential density in what were dubbed Irish 'colonies', 'ghettos' or even 'little Irelands' made them synonymous with the poor conditions of the early Victorian slums (Davis 2000: 24). They were resented for lowering wages and associated with a range of social, political and religious problems in nineteenth- and early twentieth-century Britain. They were depicted as 'savage and barbaric'. Sectarian conflicts – between Protestants and Catholics in Liverpool in the 1830s, and the Stockport Riots of 1852 – embedded anti-Irish sentiments whilst often neglecting the specific causes and conditions prompting the violence. Sweeping negative accounts published at the time tended to gloss over the diversity of the Irish experience in British cities. Both *where* they came from in Ireland, and *where* they ended up in terms of the specific constellation of employment, housing and political opportunities, framed the experience of migrants, and subsequent generations of British-born Irish.

Thousands migrated from Ireland to New York during the potato famine and were employed in factories and as domestic servants. Eastern Europeans were recruited to work in the slaughterhouses of Chicago, and Scandinavians headed further north to start small farms. According to Koser, 12 million of these migrants were processed through the immigration authorities on Ellis Island outside New York.

The third wave distinguished by Koser was during the period of reconstruction in Europe and elsewhere after the Second World War ended in 1945. Many nations had lost a lot of manpower in the fighting, and cities damaged by bombs needed to be rebuilt. In Britain the government promised to 'build homes fit for heroes' while the incoming Labour government under Clement Attlee heralded the expansion of the welfare state and, especially, the National Health Service, in which many migrants were to be employed.

Stalker (2008: 28–34) helpfully summarizes how economic cycles of expansion followed by contraction have shaped the demand for migrant labour globally. Generally, in earlier waves of migration, migrant workers were recruited to do jobs which the native population rejected or lacked the skills and training to do. In the postwar boom period until 1973, European countries – particularly Britain, France and Germany – had insufficient numbers of local workers to meet the demand for labour in manufacturing and public services – especially transport and health care – due to war-time losses. The British government recruited nurses and transport workers in the Caribbean, and employers recruited factory and textile workers in Pakistan and India. In France, North African migrants met the demand for labour in construction and manufacturing industries. Another type of migration trajectory is exemplified by the German *Gastarbeiter* scheme. On finding that migration from Southern Europe was insufficient, German employers recruited temporary workers from Turkey in the 1960s and 1970s to counter shortages. Following the oil crisis of 1973, demand for workers in these Northern European countries contracted in tandem with expansion of demand in the Gulf States. The construction of hotels, offices and retail parks initially drew workers from neighbouring Arab countries, before Asia became the major exporter of labour to the Gulf (see box 7.4). As demand for labour in the Gulf slackened in the 1990s, tighter immigration controls were imposed, and the Asian 'tiger' economies,

Singapore, Taiwan, South Korea and Hong Kong, became importers of labour.

We emphasize here the flow of labour from the poorer countries of the Global South to the Global North, but it is important to stress that such flows of labour were two-way movements. People from the less affluent sections of the middle classes were often attracted to work in the colonies, as civil servants, medical staff or officers in the police or armed forces. These jobs offered them an affluent lifestyle that might have been hard to achieve 'back home'. Opportunities and adventure also beckoned to skilled manual workers, farmers and professionals from Europe. Koser (2007) gives the example of the million or so 'Ten Pound Poms' who migrated to Australia as the government there encouraged new settlers by paying their passage over (by steamer) plus a grant of £10, which was worth a reasonable amount in the 1940s and 1950s. Many Greeks also settled in the cities of Australia. Some of these migrants from the industrial world subsequently returned home after the colonial period or were evicted after independence, but others settled for good in their new homes.

7.3 Theorizing migration: what makes people migrate?

The broad-brush distinction between 'emigrants of hope' and 'emigrants of despair' made in the *Liverpool Times*, 1846 (see box 7.2), resonates with the most common way of understanding and explaining migration – that is, by so-called 'push–pull theories'. *Push factors* are forces that drive people away from their countries of origin or that attract them to venture away from home. They include poverty, lack of jobs, wars, political oppression, famine and other natural disasters, while *pull factors* include job opportunities, higher standards of living, greater political freedoms and the attraction of individualistic Western culture with its consumer goods and lifestyles. For women, it may mean freedom from patriarchal controls within their families and homes. For some migrants, such as refugees and illegal immigrants, the move may be a desperate struggle for survival, for others a confident venture based on the calculation that they can use their skills to achieve a better life for themselves and their families (such as the Ten Pound Poms, Indian IT graduates in Silicon Valley, and Filipino nurses in Italy).

However, the problem with an emphasis on push and pull factors is that it assumes comprehensive knowledge about the destination country – relative to home – prior to a migrant's departure. The approach treats the prospective migrant as an individual rational actor who is able to evaluate potential options before making a calculated decision about whether and where to migrate. Castles and Miller (2009: 26) criticize push–pull theories for being simplistic and misleading because they neglect the familial and historical ties that often shape migration trajectories, and instead accentuate economic reasons. If push–pull theories were a reliable model for conceptualizing and predicting migration patterns, a migrant from one of the poorest countries in the world, such as Sierra Leone, on evaluating their options, may decide on the basis of income to migrate to Norway, yet this is not typically the case (Stalker 2008: 25–7). In addition, research shows that international migrants tend not to be the poorest of the poor, but rather people with the means and the impetus to migrate, who are typically in an *intermediate* situation in their society. Ballard (1994: 9–10) notes that migration is 'above all an entrepreneurial activity' that requires a significant initial investment in order to be successful. Thus, for the landless poor in South Asia, buying a railway ticket to Dhaka, Mumbai or Karachi is the only way out of their situation. Conversely, middle-income families who are not wealthy enough to be satisfied with their status at home, yet are able to afford a passport, visa and airfare, are more likely to migrate internationally.

In order to conceptualize migration adequately, the individual approach – which emphasizes the aspirations of the migrant – is typically used in tandem with structuralist approaches, which acknowledge the economic, political and social factors that shape the destinies and destinations of migrants. Castles and Miller's (2009) discussion of the main structuralist theories of migration helpfully captures their key features. One influential structuralist approach is the *dual* or *segmented labour market theory*. Advocates of dual labour market theory argue that post-industrial economies are characterized by a hierarchical dual economic structure requiring two or more tiers within the labour market that tend not to overlap: that is, a primary tier of highly educated, professional employees in specialized sectors of employment, and a secondary tier of unskilled workers in low-income routine jobs such as cleaning, catering, retail and factory-based production who, in effect, 'service' the professional classes (Sassen 1991). The former tend to be salaried whereas the latter are more likely to be engaged on temporary, casualized contracts and may well be undocumented migrants, thereby allowing employers to avoid paying the minimum wage or taxes, as discussed in chapter 1. Stalker notes that, previously, young people and women tended to fill poorly paid and unskilled jobs but, more recently, their rising credentials and expectations mean that they are less willing to do so. Labour markets are therefore increasingly dependent on migrants, who have limited bargaining power and are more willing to accept low-status, poorly paid jobs than their local counterparts. The characteristics of the two tiers are central to these approaches: male, ethnic-majority workers are more likely to hold 'primary tier' jobs, whereas women and ethnic minorities are more likely to occupy the secondary, subordinate-tier jobs (see Sassen 1991).

A second approach that combines structural (social and economic) factors in shaping migration trajectories is the so-called 'new economics of migration'. This approach acknowledges that migrants make decisions about whether and where to migrate not as individuals, but as groups. The decision to migrate for a family is a form of 'co-insurance' in countries where the welfare safety net is limited or non-existent, such that one child may enter higher education, whilst another seeks employment in the nearest big city and another goes to Dubai or Singapore to get work as domestic help (Stalker 2008: 22). This division of labour, geographically and in terms of sector, within a family is a form of income insurance that helps to secure their future prospects. 'Remittance' is the term used to describe the portion of income that migrants send to their families who remain in their home countries. This theory recognizes that the practice of sending remittances home has long been a feature of labour migration (see box 7.3). Contemporary studies of Indian construction workers in Dubai, Filipino care workers in Italy and, historically, the letters of Polish peasants in North America serve to underline this point (Zachariah et al. 2004; Zontini 2010; Thomas and Znaniecki 1958 – respectively).

Finally, a third approach which seeks to combine individual and structural considerations with the theorization of global capitalism and markets is world-systems theory. The leading proponent of the world-systems approach, Immanuel Wallerstein, contends that less-developed regions of the global economy are incorporated into a world system by the industrialized countries of the Global North. He states that the division of labour between states and regions is organized so that 'tasks requiring higher levels of skill and greater capitalization are reserved for higher-ranking areas' (Wallerstein 1974: 350). Wallerstein distinguishes between the 'core' rich, industrialized countries of the Global North with strong governments and national culture (such as Britain, France and the Netherlands); the semi-peripheral and moderately strong states, which are either emerging economies or core countries in decline (for example: Mediterranean countries, such as Spain and Portugal); and 'peripheral' countries that are poor, have weak states and are shaped by foreign direct investment (FDI), hence an 'invaded' culture (Eastern Europe and South America are cited as examples of these). In essence, labour flows in the opposite direction to capital, since FDI encourages rural–urban migration in peripheral regions, which – in turn – eventually promotes international migration (for example: from rural towns in Southern India to Bangalore to Silicon Valley). Since Wallerstein's theory sets out international relationships between states and regions, as opposed to globalizing trends, his perspective is sometimes cast as a precursor to more recent theories of globalization. Building on the insights of world-systems theory, more recent transnational network approaches attempt to analyse the intertwining of economic, political and social agendas, combining employers' demand and government immigration policies with individuals' and families' search for a better life. Theorists of transnationalism accentuate the simultaneous maintenance of social, political and economic ties across borders, albeit sometimes virtually, as integral to a way of life (Levitt and Glick Schiller 2004; see chapter 8).

Box 7.3 Building the future back home: Filipino migration and remittances

The Philippines is the world's foremost example of an institutionalized migratory state (Tyner 2009), with around 9 per cent of Filipinos living outside their country of birth. The Philippine state has struggled through economic crises for over forty years (Bello et al. 2005) and has relied upon contract labour migration to provide much-needed remittances, both for government coffers and to provide households with livelihoods. Powerful Philippines government agencies, such as the Philippines Overseas Employment Agency, co-operate with private manpower companies to ensure the continued spread of Filipino workers across the world. They work to market a global image of Filipinos as endlessly flexible and versatile at work: the overseas worker 'par excellence' (Tyner 2004: 30).

Initially, men constituted the majority of overseas Filipino workers, as seafarers and labourers in the Gulf States. Yet the proportion of female migrants from the Philippines currently exceeds the numbers of male migrants: women comprised 72 per cent of all Filipino migrant contract workers in 2006 (Tyner 2009: 38). Thus, the predominance of female migrants is seen as one of the defining features of Filipino migration. Given the feminization of labour and demand for workers in domestic, care and health sector jobs, Filipino women in particular filled a niche that emerged in post-industrial labour markets (Asis 2005). In addition, the education, qualifications and English-speaking skills of many Filipinos mean that they are a desirable category of immigrant in many immigrant-receiving countries. Popular destinations include Saudi Arabia, Hong Kong, Japan, UAE, the US, Canada, Singapore, Australia and Italy. The experience of Filipinos serves to illustrate human capital approaches to migration, since many understand it as an investment in the future for themselves and their families. Moreover, the practice of sending remittances home and retaining strong ties with their country of birth underlines the importance of transnational ties for understanding many Filipinos' experiences (Aguilar 2002). The Philippines government heavily encourages overseas Filipino workers to remain deeply involved with political and social initiatives back home, inviting them to send money for development and disaster relief. Unidirectional migration trajectories that involve permanent settlement in another country only represent about half of the Filipinos overseas. The other half are employed on temporary contracts, such that return or onward journeys are highly likely. The extensive scholarship about Filipino migrants has also shed light on the potentially painful emotional costs that migrants face when working abroad for long periods, focusing in particular upon women who, paradoxically, have to leave their children behind in order to provide for them (Salazar Parreñas 2001). Nonetheless, some Filipinos may cultivate a sense of belonging within their countries of residence, despite ill-treatment and the exclusionary conditions that they often face (see Jackson 2010).

Castles and Miller (2009: 30) conclude that 'No single cause is ever sufficient to explain why people decide to leave their country and settle in another.' Drawing on a range of perspectives and theories – as we have touched on here – is necessary to arrive at any meaningful description and understanding of labour migration. In summary, push–pull theories have been criticized for failing to capture historical and familial ties between regions that shape migration trajectories. Yet historical-structural approaches are thought to neglect the agency of migrants making their way in the world, the so-called 'human face' of globalization (Favell et al. 2006). Transnational approaches instead enable us to pay attention to how migrants and their families may actually live across borders, whilst also acknowledging the structures that facilitate their mobility. The next section explores regional migration systems that illustrate how patterns between regions vary depending on the sources of demand and supply of labour within the global economy.

7.4 Migration systems, routes and destinations in the global economy

By the middle of the twentieth century, it was possible to travel from 'any part of the planet to any other within 30 hours or so' (Waters 2001: 27). The *Times Atlas of World History* noted that the age of European dominance was over and remarked on the advent of 'an age of global civilization' (Barraclough 1978 cited in Waters 2001: 27–8). Nonetheless, established relationships between countries and regions continue to inform the patterns and movements of people within and between states. These patterns to some extent reflect Wallerstein's (1974) world-systems theory, since movements tend to be along routes between peripheral, semi-peripheral and core regions. Indeed, world-systems theorists argue that these migrations reinforce established hierarchies between core and peripheral states, since they continue to serve the interests of the core. Yet, given recent shifts in the balance of power between core and so-called 'peripheral' regions, and the globalization of migration, it is impossible to encapsulate recent migratory patterns – that is, migrants' routes, destinations or motivations – into a single overarching framework. Accordingly, many accounts of migration identify relationships between countries and regions that increase the likelihood of migration between them. International migrants tend to follow predictable paths. These may reflect colonial ties – for example, between Algeria and France – geographical proximity – as in the case of migration between Mexico and the USA – or established routes following a pioneering generation of migrant workers, as in the example of Turkish migration to Germany. These patterns have been described as 'migration systems' (Castles and Miller 2009: 27–30).

Massey et al. (2008) identify five distinct regional systems: the North American system, the European system, the Gulf system, the

Asia Pacific system and the South American system. In their analysis, they seek to bring reality (using data about migrant numbers) and theory together systematically, hence evaluating the validity of different theories in light of the available evidence. Acquiring parallel evidence that enables comparison across regions and countries is the first challenge to their analysis, since countries tend to deploy different systems for counting and recording their foreign-born populations. They note that, particularly within Europe, variation in the legal status of migrants in different countries limits the possibility of accurately recording and comparing the numbers of foreign-born residents (Massey et al. 2008: 110).

The North American system is the most significant in terms of numbers, since the USA is the world's principal destination for migrants. Virtually every immigrant-sending country in the world sends migrants to the USA and Canada. Moreover, since the 1960s there has been a remarkable shift in the sources of migrants to North America, since European countries are no longer the principal sending countries; instead, countries in Latin America, the Caribbean and Asia have risen to the fore. Massey et al. (2008: 64) note that, together, these three regions contribute a striking 85 per cent of migrants to the USA, and 67 per cent to Canada. This dramatic shift has been brought about by a change in the implicitly racist US immigration policy of the 1960s that favoured European migrants. The countries in these regions that provide the largest numbers of migrants tend to be those that have strong economic, political and military links with the USA (for example Haiti, Cuba, Dominican Republic, Japan, Korea and the Philippines). Some of these countries house US bases, whereas others comprise its principal combatants. Thus, as Massey et al. (2008: 67) note: 'In no small way, then, the North American migration system is a *political* economy that reflects the interests of the super power at its core.' Unsurprisingly, given their proximity and shared border, Mexico is the principal source of migrants to the USA. Yet, notably, emergent routes between Japan, Korea, the Philippines, China and North America have transformed many American and Canadian cities into the multi-ethnic metropolises that they are today.

The European system is a relative late-comer to the migration statistics. Although migration between European countries has long characterized the continent, and transformed the populations of its states, it was only after the end of the Second World War that Europe began to receive significant numbers of migrants from beyond its borders. Cohen notes that, paradoxically, 'The emigration imperialists failed to anticipate the extent to which industrialization in the core countries of nineteenth-century Europe (France, England and Prussia/Germany) would require the importation of labourers from the surrounding areas, and from abroad, in order to fuel their own growing manufacturing bases' (Cohen 2006: 45).

Postwar migration to Europe is typically described with reference to two distinct phases: the era of industrial expansion from 1950 up to the oil crisis of 1973, followed by an era when increasingly restrictive immigration legislation meant that family reunification and political asylum became the primary (legal) reasons for immigration. In the first phase, Northern European countries – particularly, Belgium, France, Germany and Switzerland – recruited initially from Southern European countries – Italy, Greece, Spain and Portugal; yet when labour supply was insufficient to meet demand in these countries, recruits were found further afield in Turkey and North Africa. In the second phase, these Southern immigrant-sending countries became recipients of migrants – from North Africa, the Middle East, the Philippines, Thailand and troubled states such as Iran and Somalia. To give one striking example, 'centuries-old patterns of Italian emigration suddenly reversed itself in the 1970s', with the number of immigrants to Italy exceeding the number of emigrants for the first time in the country's history (Massey et al. 2008: 115). Another trend increasing the foreign-born population of Southern Europe has been the marked increase in the numbers of 'lifestyle migrants' from Northern European countries – especially Britain, Germany and Scandinavia – seeking better weather and a higher quality of life in the Mediterranean (Benson and O'Reilly 2009).

Zlotnik (1992) describes the countries of Western Europe as a single migration system because of parallels in their immigration systems, close economic and political ties and their geographical proximity. In addition, they have witnessed the transition from being countries of emigration to countries of immigration in recent history. However, she identifies Britain and Scandinavia as outliers from this system: Britain because the number of migrants from its former colonies and Commonwealth countries far exceeded the number of arrivals from within Europe; and Scandinavia because migration from Finland constituted a third of migrants to Sweden, and subsequent migrations to Norway and Sweden from the Balkans, Iran, Turkey, Chile and sub-Saharan Africa exceeded the limited number of migrants from within Europe in the second phase of European immigration.

The Gulf system contrasts with North American and European migration systems in which migrants transitioned from being sojourners to settlers in the latter decades of the twentieth century. Instead, the laws and policies governing migration in Gulf States are significantly stricter than those in North America and Europe. Firstly, residence permits are only given to people with jobs and, secondly, these tend to inhibit family reunification. Moreover, whereas industrialization attracted labour migrants that, in turn, created wealth in North America and Northern Europe, in the Gulf States the large oil reserves on which they sit created wealth that, in turn, required labour migration in order to industrialize (Massey et al. 2008: 134–42). The countries of Saudi Arabia, Kuwait, Bahrain, Qatar, Oman and the United Arab Emirates are formally connected in the Gulf Cooperation

Council (GCC) and they have a common policy of restricting labour migration, inhibiting settlement and making naturalization virtually impossible. Political and social incorporation of migrants into Gulf States, in tandem with settling, is thereby prohibited for all categories of migrants. The Gulf system encompasses the GCC countries, other countries in the region – Egypt, Sudan, Jordan, Palestine, Lebanon and Syria – and, increasingly, a number of Asian countries as sources of migrants.

In 1973, the declaration of an oil embargo by members of the Arab oil-producing countries (OAPEC) triggered a dramatic increase in oil prices and increased demand for labour in the region. This demand was met initially by countries neighbouring the GCC, but intra-region migration was soon superseded by migration from Asia, especially India, Pakistan, Sri Lanka, Korea and the Philippines. Notably, migration to the Gulf from India began in the 1930s, when British and American oil companies deployed Indian labour, yet has increased significantly since the 1980s. The GCC countries are extraordinarily dependent on migrant labour: foreign-born workers comprise 'only' 51 per cent of the workers in Bahrain, 70 per cent in Oman and more than 80 per cent in Saudi Arabia and the United Arab Emirates (Massey et al. 2008: 137–8). Moreover, Asian workers have explicitly been preferred to migrants from neighbouring countries because of their cultural, phenotypical and linguistic differences from the local population, which thereby inhibit social mixing or settlement. The dependence of the indigenous population, and their respective governments, on migrant workers has been labelled 'demographic imbalance theory', since large sectors of the economy effectively rest in foreign hands (Zachariah et al. 2004). In order to rectify this 'imbalance' and prevent UAE nationals from being marginalized, tight restrictions are imposed on so-called 'contract migrants', including mandatory employer sponsorship and enforced departure on the completion of contract. Moreover, the conditions facing workers in all Gulf States are characterized by stark divisions, depending on their country of origin (see box 7.4).

Massey et al. (2008: 142) question: 'Will the GCC countries succeed in preventing permanent settlement where European and North American governments have failed?' They conclude, succinctly: 'Only time will tell.' Either way, international migration has become an integral feature of economic and social life in Gulf States, regardless of whether individual migrants decide to leave or stay.

The Asia Pacific migration system is characterized by its distinctiveness in comparison to the North American, European and Gulf systems, and its relative newness. As we have discussed, migrant routes developed between the Asia Pacific region, North America and the Gulf in the 1970s and 1980s, which transformed the ethnic composition of these countries and their labour forces, particularly in the case of the latter. In tandem with these developments, migration within the Asia Pacific region has transformed in recent decades due to the

Box 7.4 The dark side of Dubai

'Dubai's skyscrapers are stained by the blood of migrant workers' (*The Guardian*, 27 May 2011).

In May 2011, an Indian migrant worker jumped from the highest skyscraper in Dubai, Burj Khalifa. He was a cleaner who had allegedly been denied holiday time. The *Guardian* journalist notes that his death was not atypical and was casually described by one observer as 'inaugurating' the building. In the same week, another Indian man had jumped from Jumeira Lake Towers. The Indian Consulate in Dubai reports that there are on average two suicides a week; most of these are skilled or semi-skilled, blue-collar workers. This 'dark underbelly' of Dubai's prosperity rests on its treatment of certain expatriate workers. European and North American expatriates working in multinationals enjoy tax-free incomes and few restrictions on their 'Western' hedonistic lifestyles, whereas Pakistanis and Indians, working as construction workers and in transport and services, find their pay and holidays restricted and realize they cannot afford to return home or send their planned remittances, in a situation which parallels that of nineteenth-century indentured labourers.

Pakistanis and Indians comprise almost two-thirds of migrant workers in the United Arab Emirates (878,000 persons – Ministry of Interior 1995 estimate). Pakistani and Indian workers migrate for jobs with a view to earning a living and sending remittances to their families at home. These workers, especially those in unskilled jobs, are particularly susceptible to exploitation by their employers. Many single male migrants live in 'worker camps' on the peripheries of Abu Dhabi, Dubai and Sharjah in crowded conditions (on average four to eight to a room) and are transported daily to the construction sites, and other locations where they work. Wages, non-wage benefits, return airfare home and accommodation are stipulated in the terms of migrant workers' contracts. However, breaches of these contracts are rife. Terms – such as non-wage benefits, accommodation and provision of return airfare, in particular – are often violated. One particularly insidious practice is that of employers retaining the passports of contract migrant workers. The employer is thereby given control over the movements of migrants and can refuse to release passports in cases of wage disputes or when workers wish to return home (Zachariah et al. 2004).

repeal of the controversial Australian 'whites only' immigration policy in 1965, and also due to a shift in patterns of migration to Japan away from its reliance on Korea, its historical source of migrants, to include other Asian countries. Troubles in Vietnam, Laos and Cambodia displaced thousands in the late 1970s and 1980s, and whilst many of these ended up in the US as refugees, others sought asylum within the region in Japan, Hong Kong, Taiwan and, especially, Australia (Massey et al. 2008: 160–70). Conversely, New Zealand ceased to be a country of net in-migration in 1976 following Britain's entry into the

European Union, and its subsequent loss of its privileged access to the British market. Since the 1990s, the so-called 'Asian tiger' economies – Singapore, Taiwan, South Korea and Hong Kong – have become net receivers of migrants. Malaysia and Thailand are both senders and receivers of migrants, whereas the significant sending countries in the region are Bangladesh, Burma, Cambodia, China, India, Laos, Pakistan, the Philippines, Sri Lanka and Vietnam.

Finally, the fifth migration system outlined by Massey et al. (2008) is the South American system; their account of it excludes Mexico and the Caribbean which are included in the North American system. The significant era of European migration to South America was from 1880 to 1930, although Italian, Spanish and Portuguese colonial exploits in the region began much earlier. Argentina, Brazil and Uruguay industrialized in the latter decades of the nineteenth century and early twentieth century, and these countries thereby formed 'the core of a well-defined international migration system' (Massey et al. 2008: 196). After the Second World War, numbers of migrants from Europe steadily declined due to return emigration or, given the age-profile of this population, death, whilst the numbers from other countries in South America increased. Rural-to-urban migration – within and across national borders – increased dramatically in this period, and transformed the cities of Buenos Aires, Saõ Paulo and Montevideo. Rural-to-rural migration has also been a prominent feature of the South American migration system, as seasonal workers – particularly from the neigbouring countries of Chile, Paraguay and Bolivia – entered Argentina temporarily for agricultural work. Argentina is described as the core of the South American system; it has strong economic ties with Brazil, Paraguay, Uruguay and Venezuela that were formalized in the 1991 MERCOSUR free trade agreement.

From our survey of these regional migration systems, it is clear that labour migration is a critical feature of the global economy, yet, despite many countries being reliant on migrants to fill crucial roles and gaps in their own labour forces, migrants are often stigmatized and ill-treated in the societies that they arrive in. In the following section, we discuss racism and discrimination and consider whether these are unavoidable consequences of labour migration.

7.5 Racism, discrimination and 'destatusing'

Violence targeted at foreigners, such as neo-Nazi and skinhead attacks on migrant workers in Germany and elsewhere in Europe, are blatant forms of racism that affect the lives of migrants. Yet, alongside these phenomena, migrants and their children encounter 'countless expressions of everyday racism which reduce the life chances of ethnic minorities' (Castles 2000: 163). It is this type of racism in the labour market that we focus on in this section.

After the scientific rejection of the biological concept of 'race' to describe phenotypic differences between peoples, scholars have questioned the enduring relevance of the term 'racism'. Cohen (2006: 92) argues that, since 'races' are 'artificial social constructs anyway', people can be treated as racially different without the existence of race. He concludes: 'In short, we can have "racism" without "race".' In the example of the Irish workers in British cities in the nineteenth century, we can see that the language used to describe the Irish cast them as dirty, immoral and slovenly, distinguishing them from British workers in explicit and racialized ways, even though they could not be defined as a distinct race (see box 7.2; Walters 2010). Moreover, since prejudice on racial grounds continues to affect the reception of migrants in many destination countries, the salience of the concept of racism remains, albeit in a redefined form.

Since migrants leave their countries of birth in search of a better life elsewhere, for themselves and their children, it is important to consider whether they fulfil their aspirations, or whether the stress of migration, followed by the discrimination and loss of status that they encounter in destination countries, ultimately undermines their ambitions. Heath and McMahon's (1997) analysis of the employment outcomes of migrants and their children in Britain provides a useful model for conceptualizing and measuring what they call the 'ethnic penalty'. This penalty is defined as the disadvantage experienced by ethnic minorities and migrants in the labour market relative to their white British counterparts. Notably, ethnic diversity in Britain is framed and measured with reference to ethnic, national and colour differences between peoples, due to the extent of migration from its former colonies in the postwar period. Heath and McMahon contend that migration is likely to involve 'destatusing' of migrants on arrival in a new country for a number of reasons, including not being native-language users, having foreign qualifications and the time taken adjusting to a new context. They hypothesize that, for the children of migrants, all things being equal, being born, socialized and educated in their country of residence – in this case Britain – should mean that their prospects are significantly higher than their migrant parents'. However, their analysis of 1991 Census data suggests otherwise. They conclude that inter-generational patterns of 'ethnic' disadvantage continue to affect the prospects of the next generation (Heath and McMahon 1997).

Moreover, Heath and Cheung's (2006) more recent analysis of UK labour force survey data indicates that British-born Indian, Pakistani and Caribbean residents continue to encounter difficulties securing employment compared with their 'white' counterparts, albeit to a slightly lesser extent than the migrant generation. In contrast, the children of Irish migrants do not experience ethnic penalties and may even benefit from 'ethnic premiums' (Heath 2007: 651). Heath and Cheung (2006) note that statistical evidence of ethnic penalties cannot be equated directly with discrimination. They conclude, nonetheless, that there is considerable evidence to suggest that 'unequal treatment on grounds of race or colour is likely to be a major factor underlying the pattern of ethnic penalties' (Heath and Cheung 2006: 2).

Anthony Heath (2007) has replicated this approach to analyse the employment of the children of European and non-European migrants to destination countries: Australia, Canada and the USA and, in Europe, Austria, Belgium, Britain, France, Germany and the Netherlands. Notwithstanding the technical difficulties involved in achieving this comparison, he finds that (controlling for educational attainment) so-called 'visible' minorities from non-European countries often experience ethnic penalties in terms of both their access to employment and occupational attainment. For example, Mexicans and Puerto Ricans in the USA and Moroccans and Turks in Belgium and the Netherlands are more likely to be unemployed than their 'white' counterparts. Conversely, the next generation of Europeans – including Irish, Italians, Greeks and Poles – tend not to experience significant differences from the established populations, and may even benefit from 'ethnic premiums'. Interestingly, Italians do as well as, or better than, the established populations of Canada and Australia, but experience slight penalties in Belgium and Germany.

Field experiments have been conducted to measure discrimination in different countries by analysing employers' responses to job applications from different ethnic groups. One such study by the Commission for Racial Equality in Britain shows that white applicants were three times more likely than Asian applicants and five times more likely than Black applicants to be invited to interview (cited in Heath and Cheung 2006). Heath (2007: 676) notes that in every country where such experiments have been carried out – including Austria, Belgium, Britain, the Netherlands and the USA – evidence of substantial discrimination against 'visible' minorities has been found. These findings appear to confirm Ballard's observation that 'colour acts as an inescapable social marker' (Ballard 1994: 2).

Segmented labour market theories – as well as world-systems theories, to an extent – tend to support the idea that migrant workers provide a reserve army of labour for jobs that indigenous residents are unwilling to do. These jobs are typically characterized by poor working conditions, insecurity and low wages. If the jobs that migrants fill tend to be low-status, and they are more willing to take these jobs than established citizens, economic reason rather than prejudice may inform the segmentation of labour markets. Nonetheless, these patterns could perpetuate racialized perceptions (and prospects) of ethnic 'others', even beyond the migrant generation. Despite the introduction of anti-discrimination legislation in Britain and the US – following the civil rights movement of the 1960s – racial prejudice persists in reducing the employment prospects of migrants and their children, even in states adopting multicultural policies. Castles (2000: 179) contends that de-industrialization and economic crises in the industrialized countries of the Global North have provoked 'new racisms'. Globalization, he argues, gives rise to new forms of racism that are characterized by 'increased prevalence and intensity'. The increased mobility of capital and labour can bring about cultural openness and enriching diversity but, as Castles concludes: 'All these changes are ambivalent: they offer new horizons and possibilities of emancipation, but they can also lead to social and psychological insecurity, and threaten feelings of identity and community' (Castles 2000: 180). The activities of Australia's One Nation party, neo-Nazi movements such as Golden Dawn in Greece, and the English Defence League serve to illustrate how certain members of non-migrant populations react to the challenges that international migrants – in their view – pose to their societies.

7.6 The feminization of migrant labour?

Theories of migration have been criticized by some analysts for conveying a gender-neutral account of migration when in fact they focus upon male migrants' experiences in the labour market (Kofman et al. 2000). It is clear that migration trajectories have long been gendered, and the migration of men and women in the 'age of migration' confirms these distinctive trends. Marks' (1990) research on Irish women in domestic service in nineteenth- and twentieth-century England provides an early example of the distinctive experiences of female migrants in employment. Irish women undertook piecemeal home-based work, sewing and washing, and domestic service in private households (cited in Walters 2010).

The period of postwar reconstruction in Europe, the 'third wave' within Koser's framework, is associated initially with the arrival of men from Southern Europe, and former colonies in North Africa, South Asia and the Caribbean, in France, Belgium, the Netherlands and Britain, to meet labour shortages in factories and transport. Accordingly, the arrival of women migrants since the 1970s has been linked to family reunification, the transition from 'sojourner to settler' and the establishment of ethnic-minority communities (Ballard 1994). These women were associated with family, culture and community, and to an extent their economic and political participation in society was neglected analytically. Moreover, perceptions of migrant women as docile and unskilled meant that those who did enter the labour market often faced loss of status and poor working conditions.

However, recently a number of researchers have sought to redress this imbalance. Women and men migrate for a range of reasons including the pursuit of a better life, and the flight from rural poverty and joblessness, as well as more acute circumstances such as conflict, persecution and famine. Yet, whatever the impetus driving migration, the ways in which men and women encounter new settings and countries are always gendered. Kofman et al. (2000) contend that non-economic factors play a greater role in prompting the migration of women. They cite marital discord, violence and the impossibility of divorce, as well as social constraints, that are usually more restrictive of women's behaviour than men's in their home societies, as alternative factors. In one early study, Morokvasic argues that, in the Global North, migrant women

> represent a ready-made supply which is, at once, the most vulnerable, the most flexible and, at least in the beginning, the least demanding work force. They have been incorporated into sexually segregated labour markets at the lowest stratum in high technology industries or at the 'cheapest' sectors in those industries which are labour intensive and employ the cheapest labour to remain competitive. (Morokvasic 1984: 886)

Since many female migrants work in domestic jobs and textiles, which are considered part of the informal sector, they tend to lack adequate government regulation and protection. Minimum wages and working hours' restrictions are often ignored and piece-rates (payment per item rather than per unit of time worked) are sometimes also implemented. Moreover, in tandem with the feminization of the labour market, there has been a resurgence in demand for migrant women in domestic work – often involving poor working conditions – as 'local' middle-class women take up full-time jobs in professional sectors and seek to 'outsource' household tasks. Thus, since the 1990s, the shift from industrial to post-industrial society in the economies of the Global North has led to the so-called 'feminization of migration', caused by the increasing demand for jobs that are regarded as 'typically female' in domestic work, catering, hotels, assembly lines and entertainment (Castles 2000: 105). Moreover, whereas in previous generations family reunification was the primary reason for female migration, increasingly women migrate *independently* of their families in search of opportunities (for example Favell 2008). Indeed, sociologists have recently moved away from assumptions that women labour migrants experience their time working abroad as solely exploitative and alienating.

Nonetheless, women migrants do continue to be particularly vulnerable to sexual and other forms of exploitation (see chapter 9 for a fuller discussion of this).

7.7 Conclusion

Human beings have always travelled long distances – for survival, in the pursuit of wealth and adventure and, simply, in search of better lives. Yet, as we have discussed in this chapter, the extent of labour migration has increased dramatically since the early 1970s. Labour migration has not only transformed the lives and employment prospects of individual migrants and their families, it has transformed societies – as the economic demand for labour has resulted in often-unforeseen political and social consequences in destination countries. Progressively tighter immigration legislation has been introduced in North American, European and Gulf States in order to control and restrict the flow of migrants and, no doubt, to respond to nationalist hostility against migrants amongst their established populations. Nonetheless, these measures are unlikely to stem global flows. As *internal* rural–urban migration often acts as a precursor to secondary *external* migration, the dramatic increases we have seen in the numbers of internal migrants suggest that international numbers are set to continue increasing (see chapter 11). New destinations and routes will emerge in response to labour demand in emerging sectors and regions of the global economy, as previous eras have shown us. Thus, the poor living and working conditions which migrants often encounter in cities and countries, on arrival, are unlikely to diminish over time – although new categories of migrant may come forward to fill these positions. The feminization of labour migration we have seen in recent decades poses serious questions about the costs of migration – professionally, given the lower-skilled jobs that women often accept and, personally, due to women's separation from their families and children for long periods.

Another question arising from this chapter relates to how temporary and circular migrations – undertaken by highly skilled professionals and low-skilled seasonal workers alike – affect both the prospects of these migrants, and the countries to which they return. The exchange of ideas, culture and capital that they bring about is likely to be a defining feature of sending and receiving countries in the future.

Further reading

For very good, short introductions to international migration see Stalker (2008) and Koser (2007). They introduce key concepts and explain how economic, political and social conditions in both sending and receiving countries affect the routes and prospects of migrants. Castles and Miller (2009) lucidly introduce the different theories of migration and raise prescient questions regarding the effect of migration on development. The challenges migration scholars face in finding and comparing reliable cross-national data on migrant numbers are touched on by Stalker (2008), and explained in detail in Massey et al.'s comprehensive analysis of the field. The scope of Massey et al. (2008) – in terms of both the migration systems covered and the depth of their analysis – exceeds many more generalized accounts.

8 Globalization and transnational mobility

8.1 Introduction

Against the backdrop of mass labour migration of the twentieth century, discussed in the previous chapter, highly skilled migration has historically been a somewhat neglected field. Nonetheless, the migration of substantial numbers of highly skilled and qualified professionals in the fields of medicine, health, engineering, IT, telecommunications and advanced services has made a significant contribution to the late capitalist economies of the Global North in recent decades. Take, for example, Indian doctors in the National Health Service in Britain, British bankers and financiers in South-East Asia, Filipino nurses in the Middle East, and Indian software engineers in North America, and we can begin to see how particular fields have been shaped both by local and regional skills shortages and by the arrival of migrants from different countries with the relevant expertise to fill these 'gaps' in advanced sectors. Moreover, since the rise of India and China as powerhouses of economic growth – in tandem with declining production and employment in the post-industrialized economies of the West – the direction of movement between regions is being reversed in certain sectors. This is creating distinct types of mobility and migrants through the outsourcing of business processes to Asia and other so-called 'emerging markets'.

Thus, while inter-war and postcolonial migration occurred in distinct phases that culminated in the settlement of migrants into 'host' societies for both professionals and labour migrants, recent decades have witnessed the rise of transnational mobility whereby economic, social and political ties are maintained *simultaneously* across borders (Levitt and Glick Schiller 2004; Vertovec 2009). Migration trajectories are therefore no longer presumed to be linear and one-way. Indeed, transnational labour markets may be better conceptualized as 'circuits' around which corporate executives and professionals move, often for time-delimited projects (Bozkurt 2006). The term 'transnational' is used to refer to people, organizations and institutions that routinely cross borders, whose agendas and loyalties do not derive from affiliation to a single state (Sklair 2001). Indeed, Sklair explicitly identifies the 'transnational capitalist class' as people who see their own interests and those of their social group as best served by identifying with the capitalist global system. What is distinctive about the condition of transnationality, therefore, is that integration into a single destination country is not necessarily an outcome of it. Instead, capital mobility lends itself to the emergence of transnational actors and organizations that transcend place and thrive on their ability to do so. Donnatella, an Italian data analyst living in London interviewed for Favell's study of European mobility, aptly sums up this situation as follows: 'I see myself as an expatriate. Not a migrant, not at all. It depends on your perspective. If your perspective is global, then you are not a migrant. You are a mover, your mobility is much higher' (Favell 2008: 4). Notably, her understanding of the word 'migrant' as a derogatory term is informed by her experience as a southern Italian migrant in Milan, and the associated decline in status she encountered there, prior to her move to London.

Many theorists of globalization engage with it analytically at a distance – accentuating the 'flows' of capital and information – yet neglecting the activities and people that facilitate these transactions (Ley 2004). To some extent, scholars in sociology, anthropology and human geography have stepped in to bridge the empirical gap between 'objective' globalizing processes and the ways in which they affect specific people and places. In this chapter, we draw on this literature to consider the consequences of transnational employment for those engaged in it. We consider how economic globalization affects people's lives and the places that they live; and question whether established hierarchies continue to inform access to privileged positions in international labour markets or not.

8.2 Is there a transnational capitalist class?

As discussed in chapter 6, the consequences of heightened capital mobility are far from positive for employees in global factories – neither for workers in the advanced industrial countries of the West, with formerly protected conditions of employment, nor in the export processing zones of southern China, South Korea and Mexico where despotic labour regimes prevail. Invariably, capital mobility serves to disempower labour that is *fixed* geographically within specific regions and countries. Conversely, the actors and organizations that transcend specific localities and regions are thought actively to drive – hence benefit from – globalizing processes. In Sklair's (2001: 4) terms, the 'transnational capitalist class' comprises four overlapping fractions:

- corporate executives
- globalizing bureaucrats and politicians
- globalizing professionals
- consumer elites.

Corporate executives are the most influential category since they own or control transnational corporations. The latter three categories are typically employed by international or inter-governmental agencies, governments, professional organizations and transnational corporations. They advocate and sustain the values and political conditions that enable the market expansion of transnational corporations, and promote the consumerist ideologies (and specific global brands) that foster demand. Although Sklair acknowledges that there is considerable overlap between these categories in practice, they represent an important analytical distinction for him.

Sklair's global systems theory is an attempt to provide an account of the forces driving economic globalization, namely the multinational companies (MNCs), and the actors and ideologies that underpin capital mobility and facilitate the continued expansion of markets. Global systems theory – like any social theory – accentuates certain features of the social world and de-emphasizes others in order to present a model that captures abstract yet material realities in simplified form. In this case, Sklair challenges what he calls 'impersonal' interpretations of globalization by introducing specific categories of actors as central to his theorization. Yet, paradoxically, he does not engage analytically with these employees' lives, characteristics or values. For him, the analysis of 'subjective' and cultural aspects of globalization, for example what Giddens (1990) calls 'planetary consciousness', represents a distraction from theorizing the 'objective' economic and political globalizing forces at work (Sklair 2002: 2–3).

Sklair's account is contested by those who question whether a transnational capitalist class exists. That is, does inherited and inter-generational privilege form the basis of belonging to this category of transnational actors? And is membership of that class determined by established global hierarchies, based on nationality, ethnicity and gender, for example? Thus, analytically, we must distinguish between hierarchies that influence access to transnational employment opportunities, and are informed by country of origin, gender, immigration status, education and skills, for example, and class as a source of inter-generational advantage (although there is clearly a correlation between access to higher education and class advantage). Chakravartty's (2006) study poignantly reveals that Indian IT professionals who have been privately educated before attending elite technology institutes benefit from class, and implicitly upper-caste, privileges in India *and* North America, whereas many Indian workers have entered the sector via less privileged routes, typically attending technology colleges before securing offshore 'body shop' employment in cities like Bangalore (see box 8.1). The latter may encounter exploitative working conditions in the US. Thus class differences within the category of Indian IT workers continue to shape their access to, and experience of, professional opportunities in US firms.

It is important to note that the privilege and mobility enjoyed by some, typically Western, expatriates contrasts with others whose conditions of employment and immigration status provide the basis for

Box 8.1 Symbolic analysts or indentured servants?

The somewhat crude distinction between 'symbolic analysts' and 'indentured servants' has been used to characterize, and expose, some of the exploitative conditions of employment that numbers of highly skilled Indian workers face in the high-tech centres of Silicon Valley, New Jersey and Chicago. Critical US commentators highlight their poor pay and low-quality jobs as posing a threat to US workers, in particular, and the pay and conditions of local white-collar employees more generally.

Indeed, Chakravartty's (2006) study of Indian computer programmers with H-1B visas in the USA presents a challenge to the notion that highly skilled migrants – in the fields of IT, telecommunications and engineering – necessarily occupy elite positions on their arrival in destination countries. The H-1B visa programme enables employers to recruit workers with theoretical or technical expertise in these specialized fields for temporary periods of between 3 and 6 years (see box 8.2). Through her analysis of the pay and conditions of Indian computer programmers, Chakravartty demonstrates how these temporary visas, which are linked to a specific employer and contract, can underpin exploitative conditions of employment. As one young female Indian programmer comments: 'Although personally, I've had no problems, there are restrictions on H-1B holders. We have to work more. Everyone leaves around 3:30 or 4:00, working 7 to 8–hour days, but H-1Bs stay for 10 to 11 hours' (Chakravartty 2006: 175). Chakravartty's interview-based study sheds light on this category of highly skilled migrant, to illustrate that these workers can benefit from access to transnational networks and professional experience despite the potentially exploitative conditions that they endure. She therefore concludes that, despite the challenges many H-1B workers face, the benefits they accrue in terms of symbolic capital are often worth it. Moreover, since a high proportion of H-1B migrants secure Green Cards (that is, permanent residence) after their initial contract, the longer-term benefits are clear.

exploitation. Although whiteness, or at least having certain Western credentials, continues to influence who is defined as 'expatriate', in sociological research as well as common parlance (Beaverstock 2002; Leonard 2010a), defining highly skilled migrants in these terms tends to overlook the experience of many expatriates with roots in India, China and elsewhere (Ley 2004; Chakravartty 2006; Yeoh and Willis 2005).

Highly skilled migration raises further questions about the consequences of transnational employment for these employees and their families. Ethnographic studies have addressed some of these themes, drawing on fieldwork in expatriate 'communities' to examine how transnational employment affects professionals' identities and social networks following re-location (Amit 2007; Butcher 2009; Walsh 2006). Yet, hitherto, disciplinary interests and methodological preferences have limited the ways in which transnational employment has been studied, hence theorized. Thus, paradoxically, much of this research neglects employment itself, and instead conceptualizes expatriates as archetypal 'ethnic' communities who – despite occupying trans-national social fields both in and outside employment – can be neatly categorized and hence studied in keeping with the ethnographic tradition (Amit 2007). More specifically, questions of ethnicity, integration and identity have preoccupied scholars over and above analysis of the repercussions of these movements for work. In *The Human Face of Global Mobility*, Favell et al. (2006) instead propose a research agenda that captures the intersections between macro-economic, globalizing processes, meso-institutional settings, and micro-individual ethnographies of people and places. They argue that research into professional mobility is a means to examine and identify the 'persisting limitations' on global labour mobility and challenge certain assumptions that require interrogation. In doing so, they set out a number of assumptions that are widely promulgated yet fail to capture the experiences of many highly skilled and professional migrants. First, they challenge the contention that labour migrants are polarized, that is they consist of either highly skilled elites or unskilled labourers. They argue instead that significant numbers of migrants are 'ordinary' people whose backgrounds and biographies are somewhere in between the extremes of labour migrants and privileged 'elites': 'so-called "elites", who have opted to move internationally under present conditions of globalization, are not at all from elite backgrounds, but provincial, career-frustrated "spiralists", who have gambled with dramatic spatial mobility in their education and careers abroad to improve social mobility opportunities that are otherwise blocked at home' (Favell et al. 2006: 8–9).

Since elites tend to benefit from established privileges and opportunities in their countries of origin, moving becomes an alternative route for those whose opportunities might otherwise be 'blocked' at home (see also Favell 2008). We use the term 'highly skilled migrants' here, therefore – instead of 'transnational class' or 'elite' – in order to acknowledge that, although these migrants are often professional and well qualified, they do not necessarily benefit from elite backgrounds or distinct class privileges.

Second, Favell et al. challenge the brain-drain hypothesis. The metaphor of the brain drain is one of the most widely propagated ideas used to conceptualize the movements of highly skilled migrants from the Global South to the Global North in recent decades. So, as in the era of colonialism, does the Global North benefit disproportionately from the fruits of the labours of people from the Global South? Instead, Favell et al. contend that transnational corporations and networks, through the phenomenon of outsourcing, contribute to migrants' countries of origin as well as to their 'receiving' countries. Indeed, they put forward the alternative metaphor, 'brain circulation', as a better way of conceptualizing these phenomena in recent times: 'the zero-sum game assumption underlying "the brain gain/drain" debate is that this formulation ignores, or at best, understates the frequent back and forth movement of migrants, ideas, knowledge and skill sets, that is now a routine part of contemporary transnationalism' (Favell et al. 2006: 12). And, third, they debunk the notion of highly skilled mobility being somehow unfettered by the particularities of place or indeed border controls (see section 8.3).

Thus, what we have called the 'stickiness' of labour has consequences for highly skilled employees and professionals, as well as factory workers. Casting these transnational agents as the unequivocal beneficiaries of globalization bypasses concerns regarding compliance, exploitation and the employment relationship that analyses of factory work provoke.

Research in the field of international human resource management finds that expatriate assignees often struggle with the consequences of re-locating to unfamiliar countries and cultures; and that this leads to the premature return of many (Okpara and Kabongo 2011). Other qualitative studies demonstrate that professional mobility often entails costs as well as benefits (see box 8.3). For example, Ley (2004: 151) concludes that, despite 'the expansive reach and mastery imputed to global subjects, their flight from the particular and the partisan, their dominance and freedom from vulnerability, are far from complete'. Based on his interviews with businessmen and professionals operating in Canada and South-East Asia, he found that transnational arrangements often involved men living apart from their so-called 'astronaut' families who were established in Canada, as they engage in the 'Pacific shuttle' between sites. These arrangements, unsurprisingly, exact a 'heavy social burden'; as one businessman put it: 'I travelled back and forth, coming to Vancouver four times a year for 2–3 weeks. At first you try not to remember but then the intimate feeling is lost. Living apart is very difficult and divorce obvious. I really regret it and advise others against being an astronaut family' (Ley 2004: 158).

8.3 Defining and measuring highly skilled migration

The Global Commission on International Migration (United Nations 2005b) describes mobility of highly skilled labour – in tandem with that of capital and goods – as essential for global economic growth. Yet, although highly skilled migration is increasingly acknowledged as a field that warrants investigation and analysis, scholars and policy makers face a number of challenges in documenting what 'highly skilled' actually entails. The UN's Population Division estimates that there are over 200 million migrants living outside their country of origin (UN 2005a), of whom about three-quarters are of working age and at least one-eighth are defined as highly skilled, that is, about 23 million people (Dumont et al. 2010). Moreover, it states that the likelihood of emigrating from one's country of birth is much greater for highly skilled people from all regions (Dumont et al. 2010). Skill levels are measured by the level of tertiary education in this data. However, delineating the highly skilled from other types of labour migrant is not as clear cut as we might assume. Koser and Salt (1997: 286) explain that this ambiguity is due to uncertainty about both 'who is highly skilled and what constitutes a migration'. The reasons for this are two-fold: firstly, the increasing frequency of short-term movements between countries by corporate executives, entrepreneurs and professionals does not – at least in conventional accounts – constitute 'a migration'. Secondly, what is highly skilled is subject to different definitions depending on the occupation and its categories, experience, qualifications, national standards and transnational accreditation agreements (where they exist).

A study based in the Swedish city of Malmo illustrates this point. The study found that 44 per cent of taxi drivers of foreign origin in the city had graduate degrees. Clearly, being a graduate *in itself* does not ensure migrants' access to the opportunities or sectors for which they are qualified (cited in UN 2005b). Indeed, although some models use tertiary education as a proxy for skill levels, the validity of this measure is questionable since many entrepreneurs, executives and knowledge workers have gained their skills through practice rather than study (Koser and Salt 1997). One business analyst who began working in London's financial sector, aged sixteen, in Beaverstock's study describes himself as a 'typical barrow boy from Brentwood, Essex, come good' (2005: 256). Indeed, the potential for mismatch between the skill levels and employment of migrants is well documented. Moreover, there has – in Reitz's (2001) terms – been an 'upgrading of immigrant selection' based on 'human capital criteria' in Canada and other significant destination countries, including Australia, Britain, Germany and the USA, in recent years. Highly skilled migration is assumed to be demand-led, hence driven by 'pull' rather than 'push' factors (Allsop et al. 2009). Yet even in Canada, where the points-based immigration system is long established, and points are allocated on the basis of qualifications and demand for specific skills, the underemployment of skilled migrants is marked (Reitz 2001). Thus, if skills are quantified in order to gain entry to a country, yet they do not facilitate access to professional jobs, can migrants still be defined as highly skilled?

Koser and Salt (1997) put forward three conceptual bases for defining highly skilled migration: the migrant, the state and the employer. These bases inform the way in which highly skilled migrants are defined. The emphasis on the *migrant* accentuates the aspirations and ambitions of individuals or groups seeking opportunities and advancement elsewhere. Thus, highly skilled migrants are presumed to exercise agency to a greater degree than others (Leonard 2010a: 1). Nonetheless, as Koser and Salt point out, 'Some highly skilled people may move, however, for reasons unrelated to expertise' (1997: 287). They cite Jewish migration from Russia as an example. From the perspective of the *state*, the receiving country, in-coming workers are framed in terms of their capacity to benefit the national economy; and, since highly skilled migrants are admitted on the basis of their employability and mobility, they are presented as unlikely to become a drain on local resources. The state may establish quotas and identify particular occupations that are especially desirable. For example, the recently established British points-based immigration system lists migrants with exceptional talent, entrepreneurs, investors, business persons and highly skilled migrants in their Tier 1 'high value' category (Home Office 2011). The final base, the *employer*, accentuates requirements – especially for MNCs – to be able to determine the skills and expertise they need, hence, to an extent, the people they employ in different countries. Corporate executives and other types of knowledge workers facilitate the transfer of capital and information between sites within MNCs (Bozkurt 2006). Moreover, since the costs of relocation packages for these 'international assignees' is extremely high – estimated at three times the cost of hiring a local worker – typically, only senior executives and professionals with established credentials and considerable 'know-how' are considered for expatriate assignments (Beaverstock 2002).

Box 8.2 Immigration law and points systems

As discussed, there are three main drivers of highly skilled mobility, depending on the impetus and agency sustaining it: individuals, organizations and states (Koser and Salt 1997). Although these subcategories are not mutually exclusive, they serve to highlight the crucial difference between

- individuals (and their families) for whom the decision to migrate is informed by the lure of opportunities in employment and education rather than a specific job or employer;
- employment that is tied to an employing organization which is effectively the 'sponsor' for a foreign national's right to enter and remain in another country, and which may well be delimited by fixed parameters and conditions.

Moreover, since the late 1960s and the progressive tightening of immigration laws in many formerly attractive destination countries of Northern Europe and North America, prospective highly skilled migrants are increasingly required to fill smaller and more specific gaps in these labour markets and comply with complex points systems governing their access to work permits for time-delimited periods.

Two-thirds of all highly skilled migrants from countries in the Global South emigrate to the USA (Batalova and Lowell 2006). Its lure as a destination country became significant during the nineteenth century, to the extent that restrictive conditions on immigration were implemented as early as the 1920s (Massey et al. 2008). The current architecture of US immigration policy is based on the 1965 Immigration Act, which was amended and updated in 1990 to allow greater fluidity with respect to highly skilled migrants' temporary access to the country, as well as the potential for renewals and transitions to permanent visas (Batalova and Lowell 2006). Freeman and Hill (2006) note that US immigration is a highly politicized field with influential groups lobbying both to promote and to restrict immigration, depending on their broader political and economic agenda.

Two of the main categories of migrant to the US are based on family reunion or employment. That is, they require a settled family member to act as a sponsor, or sponsorship by an employer. The alphabetized system of temporary visas for highly skilled employment is detailed in table 8.1. Since there are sixty types of US visa in total, we do not include all of them here, but confine our description to the main types affecting highly skilled migrants.

Table 8.1 US visa categories for temporary (non-immigrant) workers

Visa	Category	Length of stay permitted
B1	Business visitors	6 months – 1 year
H-1B	'Speciality occupations' with at least a bachelor's degree (including but not limited to science, engineering, education and healthcare)	Up to 6 years
H-2B	Non-professional specialist workers (typically in science or engineering)	Up to 1 year
L-1	Intra-corporate transfers: executives, managers or specialist knowledge workers	3–7 years
O-1A	Professionals with extraordinary abilities in science, education, business or athletic fields (excluding the arts, film and television industries)	Up to 3 years
O-1B	Professionals with extraordinary abilities in the arts, film or television industries	Up to 3 years
P-1A	Internationally recognized athletes	Up to 10 years
P-1B	Internationally recognized entertainers	Up to 1 year
TN	Professional workers who are citizens of Canada or Mexico in accordance with the NAFTA agreement	Up to 3 years

Source: US Citizenship and Immigration Services (2013).

8.4 Expatriate lifestyles, whiteness and diversity in transnational workspaces

Sklair contends that the success and dominance of global capitalism is intimately bound up with the legacy of nineteenth-century British imperialism and the emergence of the USA as the leading international power of the twentieth century. Accordingly, the 'ruling classes' of these two countries continue to provide many members of the contemporary transnational elite (Sklair 2001). Indeed, research into the experiences of expatriates demonstrates the continued legacy of colonialism and salience of whiteness in the emerging markets of the non-Western world. As Hannerz (2006: 107) surmises: 'the transnational and the territorial cultures of the world are entangled with one another in manifold ways . . . Most of them are in different ways extensions or transformations of the cultures of western Europe and North America.'

He thereby concludes that the transnational workspaces of this world 'tend to be organized so as to make people from western Europe and North America feel as much at home as possible (by using their languages, for one thing)' (Hannerz 2006: 107). Indeed, further ballast to this argument is provided by evidence that shows that transnational elites from non-Western countries, including the emergent BRIC economies, often acquire their credentials by attending prestigious European and North American business schools, in order to consolidate their positions in transnational corporations (Devadason and Fenton 2013; Iredale 2001), thereby reinforcing the status of 'First World' education and professional characteristics, albeit in an ethnically diversified workforce.

Leonard (2010a) notes that the term 'expatriate' is baggage-laden due to its association with middle-class professional privilege and whiteness. She cites the hedonistic lifestyles and locally scandalous behaviour of expatriates in Dubai and elsewhere as evidence of the disjuncture between this privileged global elite and local cultures. In her study of British expatriates in Hong Kong, Leonard (2010b) notes that British employees continue to occupy influential positions in corporations and organizations in the city, despite their inability to speak Chinese and consequent lack of relevant local knowledge. Leonard also describes how the privileges these expatriates enjoy produce ambivalence, because their advantaged status is no longer legitimately grounded in the postcolonial order of the global economy. Moreover, in order to consolidate their positions in the so-called 'emerging economies' of the Global South, MNCs are increasingly recruiting from a more diverse labour pool, such that the conventional understanding of expatriation from the countries of Global North to the Global South is becoming somewhat outdated, or at least it provides only one side of an increasingly complex and diverse picture with respect to who constitutes an expatriate and who does not.

Many MNCs now regard recruiting and managing a globally diverse workforce as a business priority (Nishii and Özbilgin 2007). For European- and North American-headquartered MNCs, in particular, seeking to expand their markets, where markets *are* expanding, a homogenous workforce is neither desirable nor practical. Corporations that used to pride themselves on their national workforces and production sites could not sustain their competitive edge in global markets should they continue to do so (Jack and Lorbiecki 2007). Accordingly, the movement of expatriates from the BRIC economies of the Global South to the Global North characterizes much highly skilled mobility in the contemporary era.

Box 8.3 Diversity in a multinational corporation

Devadason's study of transnational mobility and its consequences for staff in global organizations suggests these transnational actors experience and interpret the process of 'going international' in their careers quite differently, depending on their status and citizenship at these organizations' European headquarters (Devadason 2012; Devadason and Fenton, 2013). Cartwrights global bank is centred on an Anglo-American core and is headquartered in London. It has established regional centres in Western Europe and North America, as well as the emerging markets of countries in Africa, South Asia and Russia. Territorial hierarchies between these corporate nodes are expressed in executives' biographies and in the ways that they talk about their jobs. British corporate executives perceive 'going international' as a natural 'stepping stone' in their careers, which they assume will bolster their progression, whereas for executives from the Global South this transition is often experienced as socially transformative. Since the latter encounter setbacks and uneven corporate power dynamics en route to progression, they develop strategies to circumvent these hurdles, which they relate in their accounts. The following biographies of James and Adeyemo serve to illustrate how established global hierarchies shape executives' careers, choices and power within a corporation.*

James, forty-five, is a British senior executive at Cartwrights. He joined the organization in 2005, having completed his degree in banking and finance and established what he describes as a 'UK-centric' career in financial services. Having progressed to a senior level in the organization, he accepted a two-year international assignment in Dubai for the company. His decision to 'go international' is framed in pragmatic and instrumental terms as follows: 'It was a promotion and I viewed it as an opportunity to add value to my career to date. The opportunities outweighed the downside of the actual location which was not somewhere I would otherwise have wanted to live and work.'

The job facilitates a lifestyle that he and his wife could not afford at home in London. They live in a large house in a Dubai suburb designed especially for expatriates, with swimming pools and other leisure facilities. Nonetheless, James reflects in detail on the personal costs of the intensive work-travel regime he undertakes, which included forty long-haul international flights in the preceding year. It is clearly 'detrimental' to any work–life balance he would aspire to and reinforces a traditional division of labour within the household since his wife looks after their two young children full-time. He pragmatically accepts these conditions as a 'fact of life' for senior management in the corporation, stating: 'one hopes that the pecuniary rewards and the career satisfaction, whatever turns you on, is worth it. None of us signed up for [the] 9 to 5 so that's fine.' Whereas acquiring international experience is a natural stepping stone in James' career, for ambitious graduates from the Global South it is perceived as critical for securing their positions at home and abroad. Adeyemo, thirty-one, an executive from Zimbabwe, is based at Cartwrights in London yet has undertaken a number of short-term international assignments to different-country business units for his job. He was recruited following an international MBA at a prestigious European business school. From the outset of his career, a sense of insecurity has seemed to drive his ambition to secure his position in the world.

> I always sat back and thought to myself it's all well and good that I'm doing well here [Zimbabwe], but if I travelled and lived in another country would I do as well in another country as I'm doing here? Or am I always going to live under the insecurity that somebody who has travelled or has worked in another country would always be able to come and take my job away?

Having done well in his own country, on re-locating he describes 'regressing professionally' due to 'the first world not having the same appreciation for my aptitude that the third world had'. He continues: 'I found this quite frustrating and subsequently went to study at one of the world's best and most expensive business schools so that people could acknowledge that I had cut the grade amongst their own. That worked.'

Both James and Adeyemo are acutely aware of uncertainty in the global economy, and resultant shifts in Cartwrights' organizational design to which they are vulnerable. Their accounts underline how, despite being influential transnational executives, their control and power are limited. Yet, notably, Adeyemo and other executives from the Global South require work permits, hence the sponsorship of the organization, before they are able to work at the headquarters of the MNC in London. Thus, additional credentials in the form of MBAs and tacit requirements pose further hurdles to progression.

For Adeyemo, internationalization is a learning curve that equips him with the know-how to deal with hierarchies in the organization and operate comfortably in the boardroom. Yet for British executives, including James, their ability to engage in these everyday social aspects of transnational working are taken for granted (Devadason and Fenton 2013).

*Pseudonyms are used here to protect the identities of individuals and the organization.

Hannerz (2006) suggests that global corporate cultures tend not to require European and North American employees to adapt their behaviour to operate in the emerging markets of the Global South. Beaverstock's study of the British lawyers, accountants and bankers in Singapore implies that their whiteness signifies internationalization in the city, and the kudos associated with it, whereas 'Asian' employees and clients are defined as 'local', despite also being outsiders from China, Korea and Japan. The enduring salience of *whiteness* for expatriate professionals in non-Western settings does not, however, confirm that inter-generational class privilege forms the basis of access to transnational employment (see section 8.1). Nonetheless, Beaverstock's (2002) emphasis on the tacit knowledge or 'know-how' of expatriates in Singapore, in addition to their practical knowledge and credentials, suggests that cultural capital and social networks curry favour in the era of 'soft capitalism' (Thrift 1997) in which connections are formed on the golf-course and in other exclusive social settings. Thus, established patterns of class advantage are likely to be influential across borders, as demonstrated in studies of expatriate clubs across Asia (Beaverstock 2011; Hannerz 2006). Devadason and Fenton (2013) find that being 'comfortable in the boardroom' is described as a skill to be acquired by executives who do not possess the quintessential expatriate characteristics of being middle-class, British and male in British-headquartered MNCs (see box 8.3).

High incomes and generous re-location packages offered by MNCs allow corporate executives to access elite lifestyles, including residence in exclusive neighbourhoods, private-school fees for their children and membership of expatriate clubs (Beaverstock 2011). The tastes and lifestyles of the transnational class are thereby thought to exemplify and advance the patterns of global consumerism which they promote (both directly and indirectly).

8.5 Transnational employment in global cities

In light of the de-industrialization of advanced capitalist economies and technological advances that limit the need for face-to-face transactions, some accounts of globalization accentuate the declining significance of place in the global economy. However, Sassen (1994: 2) contends that 'it is precisely the combination of the global dispersal of economic activities *and* global integration' that contributes to the rising importance of specific 'global cities'. She defines London, New York and Tokyo as archetypes in this respect (Sassen 1991). These cities act as 'hubs' in the global economy due to the concentration of advanced and specialist services that multinational businesses require – namely, accountants, bankers, lawyers and other professional and technical services – and the *intensity of transactions* they facilitate. These cities are thereby characterized by their strategic locations and the transport infrastructure which connects them – via road, rail and international airports – to other global cities and production sites around the world. They act as 'strategic nodes' in the global economy, facilitating the transfers of finance, capital and information with other strategic locations that fuel economic growth (Sassen 1994). As 'hubs', they are attractive destinations for migrant workers (from within and beyond their countries) seeking opportunities that they would not find at home. Notably, the image of the global city is most definitely multi-ethnic, but opportunities are clearly not evenly distributed within them. Sassen (1994) contends that the labour markets of global cities are essentially polarized, since post-industrial economies promote the existence of an elite working in specialized niches of employment, such as advanced services, finance, IT, engineering, media and communications, whilst individuals who are unable or ill equipped to exploit these highly skilled niches fill the increasing numbers of low-waged jobs, such as jobs in catering, cleaning, call centres and retail (see also Bauman 1998b). Accordingly, in her account, the 'working poor' – typically women and ethnic minorities – may be employed in high-tech, booming sectors yet in low-waged, 'dead-end jobs' (Sassen 1994: 99).

The strategic location and concentration of multinational head-quarters, international organizations and regional bases facilitate face-to-face contact and exchanges to take place between corporate executives, professionals and politicians, typically in financial districts, such as New York's Wall Street and the City of London (Beaverstock 2005). It is worth highlighting, therefore, that heightened capital mobility promotes the often very embedded socio-spatial practices of expatriates living and working in global cities (Beaverstock 2002, 2005). An emergent literature addresses the ways in which particular neighbourhoods not only meet the tastes and lifestyles of transnational elites but also provide the 'tightly bound spaces' within cities that facilitate the social, economic and political transactions which sustain capital mobility (Beaverstock 2002). Executives and professionals are often clustered residentially in particular exclusive neighbourhoods that suit the lifestyles of this 'globally connected gentry' (Butler and Lees 2006). Butler's (2003) study of middle-class residents in Islington underlines this point. Islington somehow functions as a 'bubble' sheltered from many of the risks presented by the global city, through its exclusive, upper-middle-class milieu. Nonetheless, he contends, minorities and others who are marginalized within the city act as 'a kind of social wallpaper' that white, middle-class residents appreciate but do not interact with (Butler 2003: 2484). Rofe (2003) cites art galleries, bars, ethnic restaurants and delis as key features of gentrified neighbourhoods in globalizing cities. The advantages of these spatial concentrations are two-fold: they enable the interactions outside work that in turn consolidate into influential networks and provide leisure-oriented social spaces that are somehow sheltered from the risks presented by the global city, no doubt in part due to escalating real-estate prices (Beaverstock 2002; Castells 2000). Thus, another defining and troubling feature of global cities is the marked geographies of inequality they sustain.

One policy development arising from what Sassen (1994: 4) calls these 'new geographies of centrality' is the increasing importance of place branding in response to competition between cities. Cities are marketed as being attractive locations for highly skilled professionals to live and work, as well as providing the strategic locations and infrastructure, to attract foreign direct investment, multinational headquarters, international organizations, conventions and tourism. The quality of living index ranks cities globally based on a number of factors, including culture and an attractive urban milieu, that appear to be as important as infrastructure – if not more so – in certain cases. In an article in the *Financial Times* entitled 'Liveable v Loveable' the author comments that cities – such as Vancouver, Vienna and Zurich – that rank highly on *Mercers' Quality of Living* index are less popular destinations than the more chaotic and dynamic metropolises, New York, Los Angeles or London (6 May 2011). The apparent sacrifice in terms of quality of life that many Italian, French, Swedish and Australian young adults make when migrating to London underlines this point (Favell 2008).

Box 8.4 London: the global Eurocity

Favell (2008: 37) suggests that the 'cultural caché' of London is unprecedented within Europe, and even globally, as Philippe, an executive working for Unilever, describes: 'I remember well, I think in 2000, the fact that England, London was the place to be, probably in the world. It was thriving, booming, exploding. It was all over the place. And we were really really happy that the position we were offered was in the UK' (Favell 2008: 34).

Global cities are often characterized as much by their connectedness to the rest of the world as by their local distinctiveness (Massey 1993). Thus, in many ways, London epitomizes Sassen's account of the 'global city'. Moreover, as the executive hints in the above quotation, migrants re-locate to London for more than work. In *Eurostars and Eurocities*, Favell (2008) draws on his comparison with Amsterdam and Brussels to conclude that the allure of London for young Europeans rests on both the ease by which foreigners can access the labour market and an apparent inclusivity that stems from being the most internationalized city in Europe. At the time of the 2011 Census, 37 per cent of the population of London were born outside the UK (ONS 2012). Migration between European regions and cities is distinctive because it is a particularly European phenomenon that allows unprecedented freedom of movement within the European Union. Similar agreements between neighbouring countries in NAFTA (the North American Free Trade Agreement) and ASEAN (the Association of South East Asian Nations) do not allow the same level of undocumented movement or indeed encompass the right to work without seeking permission. Favell et al. (2006: 15) conclude: 'Only in Europe has a genuine freedom of movement of persons been legally institutionalized alongside the freedom of movement of goods and capital.' Moreover, this lack of regulation is especially pronounced in London. Since the British state does not require registration with local authorities, much of this movement remains statistically untracked (Favell 2008).

Moreover, London 'offers the "outsider" freedom of not belonging yet feeling at home, a place of comfortable anonymity' (2008: 36). Favell (2008) thereby contends that the capital provides a 'rite of passage' for many young Europeans who want to escape from provincial and parochial lives and opportunities, yet remain within easy travelling distance of their families, regions and health-care systems. Employers are well placed to benefit from this well-educated, middle-class and enthusiastic young workforce. Favell cites the London-based chain Pret à Manger as one company that explicitly tailors its recruitment policy towards European new arrivals in the capital, and benefits accordingly. For Favell, the economic benefits of English-speaking, well-educated European migrants seeking employment in London underline the unique place of London as the unofficial capital of Europe; it was the invisible boost to the British economy that enabled it to coast through the recession of the early 1990s relatively unscathed.

However, there are personal costs involved. For example, the high cost of housing in London precludes many from settling, but returning home is not an option for those who have left provincial towns and villages in Southern Italy or France. Moreover, the social distance between these new European Londoners and their friends and peers back home expands over time, as the latter settle into conventional family-oriented lifestyles. Moving to the suburbs of Greater London is not perceived as an option for those who have moved to escape provincial and suburban settings. Low-income migrants, even well-educated ones, have effectively been priced out of desirable locations such as Islington, Kensington and West Hampstead in recent years. Savage et al. (2004) suggest that gentrification in an era of globalization contributes to the displacement of urban residents who did not choose to live where they do, namely the 'working poor'. Notably, in the case of London, British Bangladeshis and other residents who do not benefit from middle-class credentials express a lower sense of belonging to the city than other more recent, yet advantaged, European migrants who describe themselves as 'Londoners' (Devadason 2010; Favell 2008). For many young well-educated Europeans, the city functions as a stepping stone to the rest of the world; as Donnatella puts it: 'I can easily move to another country, and get a very good job easily . . . Maybe Hong Kong, Singapore, New York . . .' (Favell 2008: 44).

8.6 The personal consequences of transnational employment

Transnational employment requires not only workers who possess the skills, qualifications and expertise that can cross borders but also people who exhibit the personal qualities and characteristics to take such movements in their stride. Beaverstock notes that 'expatriates' may be less dislocated by mobility between global cities than people whose biographies, families and networks are embedded in particular locations. Thus, some scholars have ascribed 'frequent travellers' with cosmopolitan characteristics and qualities that distinguish them from locals. In his influential essay on this topic, Hannerz (1990) conceptualizes the personal consequences of transnational employment in terms of the 'cosmopolitan' disposition and qualities it fosters. For him, 'genuine cosmopolitanism' is a competence that entails a 'personal ability to make one's way in other cultures, through listening, looking, intuiting and reflecting' (Hannerz 1990: 239). He contrasts this with Paul Theroux's (1986: 133) concept of 'home plus' that, instead, reflects a lack of openness to the 'somewhat unpredictable variety of experiences' (Hannerz 2006: 104) one may encounter following migration. Thus, for many British migrants, Spain for example is 'home plus sun' whereas India may be perceived as 'home plus servants'. These alternative modes of adapting and reacting to geographical mobility illustrate that the 'cosmopolitan' qualities required to engage with cultural differences represent a *savoir-faire* that cannot easily be taught (despite the attempts of HR executives in multinational corporations to create effective cultural training programmes). Moreover, certain types of highly skilled mobility may not require employees to transcend or transgress their 'normal' ways of being.

The phrase 'openness towards difference' emerges in the accounts of scholars, HR executives and, most notably, highly skilled migrants themselves, to encapsulate the somewhat indefinable quality that enables them to pursue a transnational career (Devadason and Fenton 2013). Yet, given the complexity and varied conditions that highly skilled migrants encounter – in terms of entry requirements, visa arrangements, length of stay, motivations and occupations – which, in many cases, constrain their mobility, the ideal of 'genuine cosmopolitanism' may be irrelevant for many who occupy transnational niches in the global economy. Indeed, since developments in IT have opened channels between the Global South and post-industrialized economies in recent decades, in particular between India and the US, it is worth noting that the technical expertise of these jobs requires English, yet does not necessarily encourage attention to cultural differences or dialogue in the workplace (Iredale 2001). The longer working hours H-1B workers encounter, relative to their American counterparts, is a case in point (see box 8.1). Similarly, many studies of expatriates in global cities describe the reproduction of ethnically based networks in distant locations rather than significant encounters across groups (Fechter 2007; Beaverstock 2002). Thus, the question of whether transnational mobility actually encourages an open disposition towards difference or – due to prejudice, discrimination and hierarchical conditions of employment distinguishing between 'locals', privileged expatriates and other types of highly skilled migrant – it encourages segmentation and segregation along ethnic lines remains a pertinent one.

These dynamics can sometimes become more apparent in social settings than in the workplace. For example, in her study of European expatriates in Jakarta, Fechter (2007) describes how certain German wives are reluctant to admit the Asian wives of expatriate professionals into their social gatherings. Fechter's use of the metaphor 'living in the bubble' illustrates what she sees as some of its key characteristics:

> life in the 'expat bubble' is sheltered, glittering, but also fragile; an existence that never quite touches the ground, but hovers above it; to some extent an artificial world that can become suffocating . . . The membranes of the bubble are not hermetically sealed, but permeable; the Outside is seeping into the bubble, as much as expatriates make attempts to extend or transcend its boundaries, while avoiding bursting it altogether. (Fechter 2007: 167)

Others describe the identity work of expatriates as they cultivate different ways of being to adapt to different cultures that they encounter in and outside work (Butcher 2009). Butcher's analysis resonates with Hannerz's (2006: 103) distinction between two modes of cosmopolitanism: one that selectively appropriates aspects of a culture 'to construct [a] unique personal perspective out of an idiosyncratic collection of experiences' and another mode that does not make 'invidious distinctions' between the particular elements of the foreign culture but 'accepts it as a package deal'. However, as discussed in section 8.4, the transnational social spaces associated with corporate transfers – namely, expatriate clubs, exclusive neighbourhoods, hotels and leisure pursuits – often do not require engagement with cultural difference by North American and European expatriates who are comfortable within their 'bubble'(Fechter 2007; see box 8.3).

8.7 Conclusion

In Sklair's account of the *Transnational Capitalist Class*, corporate executives are cast as the drivers and beneficiaries of economic globalization. Yet his account glosses over the diversity within corporations, and the ways that actors are differentially placed within them, depending on their identities, placements and power within the global economy. In this chapter, we have considered the human consequences of transnational working for executives and professionals employed by MNCs and other global organizations. Since MNCs drive the mobility of capital, information and people across the world, their employees are often represented as 'elites' who benefit from advancing the globalizing project, in Amoore's sense (see chapter 1). Yet they themselves are vulnerable to some of the insecurities and transience that are typically associated with unskilled work, albeit with much higher incomes that help to offset some of these challenges.

Moreover, it is clear that globalization is not experienced evenly by different categories of highly skilled migrant. In recognizing the ambiguity surrounding what constitutes a migration and what being highly skilled means, we demonstrate how categories – highly skilled versus unskilled, temporary versus permanent, transient versus settler – are often blurred (section 8.3). Thus, migration provides opportunities for upwardly mobile 'spiralists' that would not exist in their home country, yet for others it involves losing status by moving into less prestigious jobs in their field relative to their local counterparts. The direction of movement clearly plays a role here, since highly skilled migrants from the Global North typically re-locate for high-status executive positions that often encompass generous re-location packages, whereas those from the Global South moving northwards may find themselves working their way up career ladders for the second time in their working lives (Devadason and Fenton 2013). Moreover, the entry criteria for highly skilled migrant programmes in many popular destination countries – including the US, Canada, Britain, Australia and New Zealand – often involve organizational sponsorship and thereby limit the length of stay and autonomy of the individual migrant. H-1B workers in the US provide a specific example that illustrates the complicating of the relationship between class, professional qualifications and status.

Transience and heightened mobility have some consequences that cannot be offset by higher incomes as we see in the case of Ley's study of East Asian 'astronaut' families in Canada and Devadason and Fenton's analysis of the intertwining of the personal and the professional in corporate executives' biographies and careers. Despite shifts in the balance of power between the Global South and the Global North in recent decades, alongside postcolonial and other migrations that have disrupted established relationships between 'race' and region, whiteness continues to privilege some American and European expatriates in certain transnational workplaces. However, professionals from Africa, Asia and South America, through gaining qualifications at prestigious European and North American institutions, are disrupting unequivocal relationships between whiteness and privilege.

Further reading

For an excellent overview of key debates relating to highly skilled migration that draws empirical and theoretical accounts together, see Smith and Favell (2006); the introductory chapter by Favell et al., and chapters by Bozkurt, Chakravartty and Favell, provide a valuable counter to generalized accounts of transnational mobility. Beaverstock's (2002, 2005) and Leonard's (2010a and b) work addresses important questions about how knowledge is embodied and privilege maintained by certain expatriate elites, and Hannerz' (2006) ethnographic account weaves together nuanced theoretical and empirical observations.

9 Work, gender and intersectional inequalities

9.1 Introduction

> Fast communications, the compression of time and space and the global reach of corporations do not necessarily create a homogeneous world, and certainly not a harmonious one, but rather increasing diversity and conflict.
>
> (Ray 2007: xiv)

This chapter will focus on the diversity and conflict referred to in this quotation from Larry Ray. Previous chapters have shown how globalization in its neo-liberal form has impacted on the workforce, mostly with adverse effects on the lives of employees. Multinational companies (MNCs) are able to 'play the globalization game', utilizing threatened or actual closures or re-locations to cheapen labour costs and weaken labour resistance and trade unions, as we saw in chapter 5. While some professionals with valued or scarce skills (in ICT, the creative industries or international sport, for example) benefit from entrance to the global labour market, the majority of working people remain trapped in national or local labour markets with more limited options. Moreover, in many societies, the impact of recession and the 'credit crunch' have led national governments to cut public and state employment. This has led to increased unemployment and the development of a 'precariat' of employees in insecure jobs, often suffering from work overload, stress and anxiety.

Inevitably such developments impact upon existing patterns of inequality. Most societies have witnessed a class polarization, with the corporate elite becoming ever richer and the development of a low-paid or benefit-dependent sector of the working class. Ackroyd (2012) has highlighted a notable product of globalization, the rise of a tiny but highly powerful group, the super-rich, an international grouping which lives 'offshore' but plunders wealth around the world, for example investing in property as absentee landlords in London, thereby driving up rents and distorting the housing market. Down at the other end of the social continuum, the competition for jobs is intense even for 'dead-end jobs', with migrants from the rural areas (in the Global South) and international migrants (in Europe) often undercutting the urban poor.

Alongside this class polarization, the development of a new international division of labour, plus the increase in migration of different types (chapters 7 and 8), has had important impacts on gender and ethnic relations around the globe, which are the subject of this chapter. Its chief aim is to explore how globalization has affected the sexual division of labour in employment and in the home. The changing roles of men and women in the labour market are discussed, looking at the occupational locations in which women are working. Particular forms of gendered work apparently encouraged by globalization are explored: migrant domestic labour, the sex industry and new types of female enterprise. The chapter considers the reorganization of care in the contemporary world, alongside the apparent persistence of the traditional domestic division of labour. Finally it questions whether the cultural and social dimensions of globalization can offer challenges to gender inequalities and oppression around the globe. Although the complexities of multidimensional inequality cannot be fully explored in a single chapter, we will advocate an intersectional approach, which notes how the sexual and ethnic divisions in the labour market are influenced by class and age.

9.2 Globalization, inequalities and intersectionality

The term 'intersectionality' is attributed to the Harvard legal theorist Kimberlé Crenshaw (1991), who used it to highlight the particular position of Black women in terms of their quest for social justice. It was then developed by Patricia Hill Collins (2000). It refers to the way in which the position of particular categories of individuals is determined by the interplay of different forms of division and discrimination. Thus, Black women are affected both by their ethnic position, and the racism that attends it, and by their gender, and the sexual discrimination which that provokes. However, this is not a question of simply adding the disadvantages of race and of gender together: the interplay of race and gender creates very distinct positionings which cannot be reduced to either. An example is the way that women of African descent are stereotyped as unsuitable to fill management roles, because of their often straight-talking and big-hearted behavioural style; this does not apply to either white women or Black men (Bradley and Healy 2008). Similarly, this group of women has a distinct family position, with a higher proportion of lone-mother-headed families than other ethnic groups. The situation is complicated further by the intersection of ethnicity and gender with other sources of social differentiation: in Collins' words, 'systems of race, social class, gender, sexuality, ethnicity, nation, and age form mutually constructing features of social organization, which shape Black women's experiences and, in turn, are shaped by Black women' (2000: 299).

The framework of intersectionality has become increasingly popular in the study of divisions and inequalities. Its theoretical implications are still being explored and elaborated (Brah and Phoenix 2004; McCall 2005). One problem is that it is very difficult to conduct an analysis if all these various dimensions of inequality have to be considered at once; a related difficulty is where to start! The strategy employed in this chapter is to take gender as the starting point, and to examine issues of ethnicity, class, age and so forth where they seem particularly significant in relation to the inequalities between men and women in the workplace.

In virtually every known society, women and men carry out different social tasks and fill different positions in the occupational structure (Bradley 1996). Indeed, in the richer countries, similar designations of certain jobs as 'men's work' or 'women's work', a process known as sex-typing, can be observed. Characteristically, mining, construction, skilled industrial crafts, engineering and military posts are seen as jobs suited for men, while women are found working as secretaries, nurses, hairdressers, cleaners and childminders. Some occupations may be seen as 'gender neutral' in that both sexes are found working together in them: clerical work is a good example, as increasingly are the once male-dominated professions of medicine, law and accountancy. However, even in these occupations, women often occupy what Crompton and Sanderson (1990) have labelled 'gendered niches'. For example, in medicine men are surgeons, women are paediatricians and GPs; in law, men dominate in corporate specialisms, women in family law.

These designations are not universal, however, and in the Global South there may be more variation, determined sometimes by local custom and religious belief. For example, in Pakistan, nursing is seen as a male occupation for reasons of religious propriety, while in India women can be found working on construction sites. The processes of globalization may reinforce or challenge these established patterns of sex-typing. Thus, in Europe, office cleaning has been seen historically as women's work, but increasingly is also carried out by migrant men from Islamic societies, such as Pakistan, Somalia and Indonesia, where the proportion of women who work outside the home is much lower.

Whatever the precise gender allocation of tasks and occupations, every nation has a pattern of gender segregation. Two kinds of segregation can be observed (Hakim 1979): horizontal segregation, the clustering of women and men into different jobs which we have just discussed, and vertical segregation, the domination by men of the top posts in any employment pyramid, while women are concentrated in the lower tiers. This is a reflection of men's greater social power, and is also manifested in the 'gender pay gap'. Although paying women less than men when they work in the same jobs was made illegal in most of the Global North during the second half of the twentieth century, vertical segregation ensures that men continue to earn higher salaries than women (in the UK in 2012, after thirty-six years of equal pay legislation, the gap was 18 per cent – see box 9.1).

In most of the Global South no such protective legislation exists – and, indeed, since the onset of the 2007 recession, business interests

Box 9.1 The gender pay gap

The gender pay gap (GPG) shows the difference between men's and women's earnings, by expressing the average hourly earnings of women as a percentage of men's average earnings. Hourly earnings are taken as the fairest measure, as men habitually work more hours in the week, often including overtime. Thus, if women earn 80 per cent of men's average hourly earnings, the GPG is 20 per cent. The GPG is an important measure of the way that women's work is less valued than men's and it is also indicative of gendered occupational segregation. The chart (figure 9.1) shows gender pay gaps in the EU in 2008, highlighting variations between nations. The GPG is highest in Estonia, the Czech Republic and Austria, lowest in Slovenia, Italy and Malta, with the UK towards the higher end at around 20 per cent.

Eurostat data show that there are differences not just between countries, but also between age groups. In virtually every country, the GPG is lower among the young age groups. For example, in the UK the gap is 7 per cent among those aged 25–34, and 22 per cent among 55- to 64-year-olds. This may reflect the improved qualifications of younger women but also the impact of maternity on women's promotion chances over a lifetime. In a couple of countries – Slovenia and Luxembourg – the GPG is reversed among the younger age groups, with men earning less than women. This may offer a hopeful prospect for women's earnings in the future.

The GPG also varies by occupational sector, and in general is greater in the private than the public sector. This reflects the prevalence of equal opportunities policies in state-owned industries, and may well be a result of the higher levels of unionization in the public sector (see chapter 5). Unions have taken up the call for equal pay in recent decades and, for example in the UK, have pushed for equal pay audits. Thus neo-liberal austerity cuts in public-sector employment are likely to have a negative impact on gender pay equality.

Source: Eurostat (2013).

Fig. 9.1 The gender pay gap in Europe

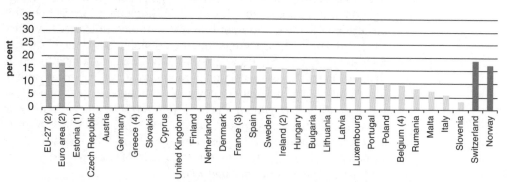

(1) Enterprises employing 10 or more employees. NACE Rev 2 B to S [– O]. (2) Provisional. (3) 2007 data and NACE Rev. 1.1, sections C to O [– L]. (4) 2008. Source: Eurostat (tsdsc340)

in the Global North have called for the removal of equality legislation, stating that it impedes the operation of free markets and makes the richer nations less able to compete with the poorer. The riposte to this neo-liberal dogma would be that the introduction transnationally of legislation to stop the exploitation of women and other vulnerable workers would make for more balanced terms of trade, as well as attacking poverty. Thus, the United Nations strongly supports the equalization of pay, through its programme of gender targets known as the Beijing Platform.

The UN has been a major player in promoting gender equalization in the Global South since its inception. In 1979 it drew up CEDAW, the Convention for the Elimination of All Forms of Discrimination Against Women. Countries are invited to ratify CEDAW – that is, sign up to its objectives. A Committee of twenty-three oversees the convention and reports regularly on progress. The UN also sponsors world conferences on women, attended by non-governmental organizations (NGOs) and advocates of women's rights. Particularly notable was the Beijing Conference of 1995 which drew up the Platform for Action, which has since been regularly reviewed. It is based on the principle that gender equality is a fundamental human right.

Particular attention is paid in the Beijing Platform to the trafficking of women and children; the welfare of girls and their access to education; poverty, especially in female-headed families (an estimated four out of ten worldwide, with highest proportions in Southern Africa and the Caribbean); sexual and reproductive health (including AIDS); violence to women and the impact of armed conflict – all of which are issues of particular concern to women of the Global South. Gray et al. (2006), in a careful quantitative investigation, found that countries which ratified CEDAW scored higher than those that did not on four measures: female life expectancy, levels of female literacy, women's labour market participation, and their inclusion in parliamentary bodies. However, the disparities between women and men are still marked in the latter two measures.

Gender pay gaps and the lack of women in top posts are often explained in terms of the disadvantage women suffer within the labour market because of their domestic responsibilities when they have children. Glucksmann (1995) argues that women, as a result, enter the labour market on different and less favourable terms than men. However, while motherhood definitely acts as an impediment to women climbing up career ladders (Bradley 1999; Crompton 1997), even single women working in the professions find themselves being paid less than men. Women professors have been shown to earn less than their male counterparts in most Western societies, though many in the past chose career rather than children, and most have passed the age at which their work is limited by childcare responsibilities.

How, then, are women faring in the context of globalization? Are the established structures of segregation being challenged? Are particular groups of women benefiting, while others see their opportunities diminishing? What is the role of migration, and does globalization create new forms of work for women and for men? These are the questions we shall explore in the next sections of this chapter.

9.3 Men and women in globalized labour markets

Araghi has argued that the second half of the twentieth century witnessed a 'global depeasantization' (1995). Between 1950 and 2000, the proportion of the world population living in urban areas increased from 29 to 50 per cent. Momsen (2009) reports that, from the onset of the 1980s, the proportion of the labour force employed in agriculture fell everywhere around the world, except in some of the transition societies of Eastern Europe, where the break-up of Soviet-era collective farms led to the re-establishing of smaller family farms. The rise of agribusiness has made the lives of small farmers harder, so that peasant families have felt the need to send family members to towns to subsidize farm income. This in turn impacts on gender relations, though in complex ways. Where men go off to search for work in the towns, or even migrate in search of better opportunities, women may be freed from the patriarchal control typical of many countries of the Global South, meaning that they gain greater social standing in their communities (Ray 2007). On the other hand, it may also increase the burden of household work for women struggling to provide for family needs (Perrons 2004). In contrast, the strategy of some agrarian families is to send young women to the towns to work in the factories of MNCs such as Nike and Foxconn (manufacturers for Microsoft and Apple), where they are a preferred source of labour because of their cheapness and perceived 'docility' and 'nimble fingers'. Grossman (1979) noted the abuse of young women in Malaysia and elsewhere in microelectronics assembly work. Young women were housed in dormitories, virtual prisoners of the corporations, working long hours with their work closely supervised. Many of the young women had to wear glasses because the work of microchip assembly using large magnifying glasses was so damaging to their eyesight. Though in their twenties, they were referred to as 'grannies'.

An International Labour Organization (ILO) report on global trends took a pessimistic view of such developments, pointing out that, of the 550 million people estimated to be part of the 'working poor', 60 per cent (330 million) were women, and that women were more likely than men to be employed in the informal and unregulated economy (ILO 2003). The report also highlighted that when women enter the labour market, they still remain responsible for childcare and domestic work, as will be discussed later in this chapter. Since the jobs they characteristically enter are of low quality and ill-paid, the report denies that these developments have led to women's empowerment, a point we will return to later.

Another important trend associated with globalization is the continued development of tourism, including opening up new areas and resorts in the Global South (Momsen 2009). Cheaper airflights and desire for adventurous long-haul travel experiences have created new opportunities for employment in the industry. Tourism creates jobs for women in retail, in the production of souvenirs, especially in traditional craft work. Women in Mexico paint bowls in bright colours to sell in hotels and Turkish girls thread beads and shells to make bracelets and necklaces. Apart from these jobs in the informal and small-enterprise sectors, the main employment opportunities for women are in the hotel and accommodation industry, as maids, domestics and waitresses. These jobs are low-paid and hard graft but they do offer reasonably secure employment outside the home for women, both young and old, and the chance for tips from foreign tourists to prop up the family resources. Moreover, contact with female tourists, along with holiday romances, may open up new perspectives for workers in the industry, both women and men, and help to challenge established patriarchal gender norms.

The dark side of the industry is sex tourism, which has been particularly associated with Thailand. Girls, often little beyond puberty, are enticed to Bangkok with promises of bar work or modelling, and then find themselves working as prostitutes. Some are even sold to the pimps by poverty-stricken parents. Prostitution, of course, occurs everywhere around the world, but the growth of international travel and increased level of migration, legal and illegal, have led to a boom in the trafficking of young women and girls across nations, especially from Africa and the 'transition countries' of the former Soviet bloc, the only part of the world witnessing a decline in employment for women during the 1990s. India's federal police said in 2009 that they believed around 1.2 million children in India to be involved in prostitution, and Thailand's Health System Research Institute reported that children in prostitution make up 40 per cent of prostitutes in Thailand (see box 9.2).

Sectoral changes of the kinds noted above brought a worldwide rise in women's employment between 1980 and 2000, although there are great national and regional variations. Diane Perrons (2004) provides very useful statistics. Figure 9.2, reproduced from her study, shows ILO figures for male and female labour force participation at two time periods, first the 1950s to 1960s, before the onset of the present phase of globalization in the 1980s, and then the late 1990s. The figure shows the participation rates by world region. It demonstrates an overall fall in men's participation and, in most parts of the world, an increase in women's participation, though the variations can be seen. It should be noted that these regional statistics themselves hide national variations. For example, female participation in the Rest of Europe region is much higher in the Nordic countries and lowest in the Mediterranean countries. There are also variations between women from different ethnic backgrounds: for example, African-Caribbean women in Britain

Box 9.2 The global sex industry: intersections of gender, class and ethnicity

While prostitution has been described as 'the oldest profession', the period of globalization has witnessed a boom in the worldwide sex industry, fostered by migration, cheaper air travel and new practices such as telephone sex and internet pornography, which make sexual services more easily available to everyone. This is a massive industry. Millions of women and children are involved. In Thailand the sex industry is worth $35 billion, in Japan $27 billion. The pornography industry has larger revenues than Microsoft, Google, Amazon, eBay, Yahoo!, Apple and Netflix combined. In 2006, revenues from the industry reached $97.06 billion.

The industry has been boosted by an increase in the trafficking of women and children, said to be the fastest-rising form of international crime, bigger than drugs or weapons. To try and counter this, the UN set up a protocol which was signed in Palermo in 2000 by over eighty countries: the Protocol to Suppress, Prevent and Punish Trafficking in Persons, Especially Women and Children (Momsen 2009). Trafficking is defined as:

> the recruitment, transportation, transfer or receipt of persons, by means of the threat or use of other forms of coercion, of abduction, of fraud, of deception, of the abuse of power or of a position of vulnerability or of the giving and receiving of benefits to achieve the consent of a person having control over another person, for the purpose of exploitation. Exploitation shall include, at a minimum, the exploitation of the prostitution of others or other forms of sexual exploitation, forced labour or services, slavery or practices similar to slavery.

Despite the legislation, the UN estimates that at any given time some 2.5 million people are in forced labour, including prostitution. The bulk are in Asia, but an estimated 11 per cent are in the industrialized countries (United Nations Global Initiative to Fight Human Trafficking – see www. unodc.org/pdf/gift%20brochure.pdf).

Prostitution is the branch of the sex industry which has been most researched and it provides an interesting case for intersectional analysis. There is a hierarchy in the industry, from high-class 'call girls' down to 'common prostitutes' or street-workers. One of the former wrote a blog under the title of Belle du Jour: she was in fact a scientific researcher, Dr Brooke Magnanti, who had worked for an escort agency, being paid £300 an hour. Dr Magnanti claimed to have enjoyed the work and has become an advocate for prostitutes. There have been a string of other cases reported of middle-class students becoming sex-workers to pay for their studies. As well as working through agencies, some prostitutes act as a self-employed business, working from home and employing a maid (O'Connell Davidson 1998).

However, the majority of prostitutes come from poor backgrounds and many are trafficked or illegal migrants. An estimated 2 out of 3 in the industrialized nations come from Eastern Europe; thousands of Mexican girls are smuggled into the USA; in India, many prostitutes are brought in from Pakistan, associated with the nation's Muslim minority population. It is this position of inferiority in class or ethnic terms which makes them so vulnerable to being beaten and raped by clients and pimps: the murder rate for prostitutes in America is 204 in every 100,000 making it the nation's most dangerous occupation.

Statistics provided by British lobbying group, Object, tell a very different story from that of Belle du Jour: 74 per cent of women cite poverty as the primary motivator for entering prostitution. According to Home Office reports, up to 70 per cent of women in prostitution have spent time in care, 45 per cent report sexual abuse and 85 per cent physical abuse within their families, while 95 per cent are problematic drug users, addicted to heroin or crack cocaine. Prostitution and drugs are mutually reinforcing; the money is needed to finance the habit, but the drug takes the edge off the unpleasantness of the work.

Prostitution is a controversial issue and society struggles to deal with it. Some researchers see it as a free choice, a viable career which is better-paid than alternative jobs available to women. High-class prostitutes can earn £1,000 a day, and many hope to retire and take up another trade. Other researchers see it as a constrained rather than voluntary option, a form of exploitation of particularly vulnerable women, especially illegal migrants. Nordic countries have tried to deal with it by decriminalizing the prostitutes themselves, but criminalizing the users, as a way to discourage prostitution. However, the demand from men is such that change is unlikely to happen unless the majority of ill-paid women's jobs become better rewarded, opening up better options for desperate women.

and in Latin America have higher participation rates than Caucasian women, illustrating the need for intersectional exploration.

Figure 9.2 shows that, at the worldwide level, we can legitimately talk of a feminization of the labour force as a result of globalization, interpreted by some as a move towards gender equality. However, in every region a higher proportion of men are in the labour force, and, in the regions dominated by Islam, women's participation is still very low. In these countries patriarchal tradition, legitimated by religious observance, forbids the free movement of women into the public sphere. In Saudi Arabia in 2012, in response to the demand for employment by highly educated women (there is a separate women's university), the government declared it would set up an industrial 'woman's city' in Hofuf, to maintain strict work segregation. In addition, women's participation fell in West Africa and South Asia, possibly as a result of the spread of Islam in these regions, though it could also be due to warfare and social disruption. In both periods, the highest female participation was in the Soviet bloc, the result of policies of the communist regimes. These comparisons are important, as they show that female

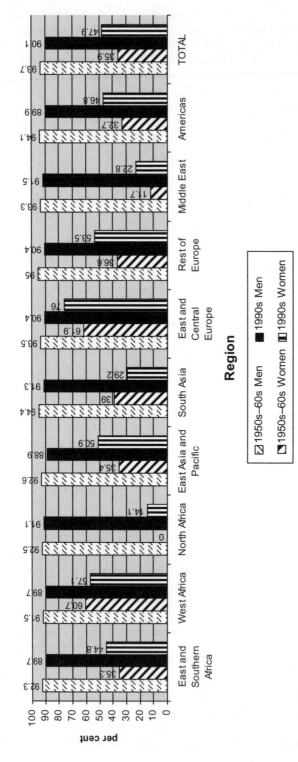

Fig. 9.2 Labour force participation rates by region and sex, for people aged 20–59

Source: data from Perrons (2004: 82).

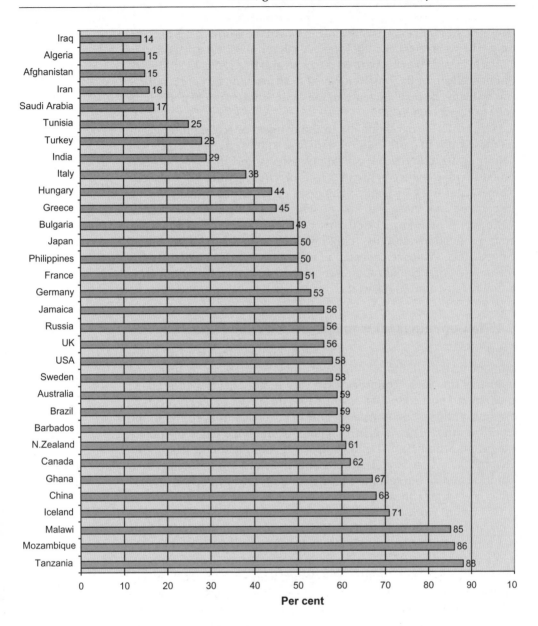

Fig. 9.3
Percentage
of women in
employment,
selected countries
2011

participation is not just determined by processes of economic development, but also heavily influenced by cultural and political factors.

Figure 9.3 shows current female participation rates within a range of
countries, using data from the World Bank, demonstrating wide variations at this level. Lowest participation continues to be in the Muslim
countries, with sub-Saharan African countries displaying the highest
rates, and Europe and the Anglo-Saxon world in the middle.

The slight decline in the world female participation rate since 2005,
from 52.5 per cent to 51 per cent, might be linked to world recession.

However, it is influenced by decline in two of the world's largest economies: between 2000 and 2011, female labour market participation in China fell from 70 per cent to 68 per cent, and from 2005 to 2011 it fell dramatically in India from 35 per cent to 29 per cent. By contrast there was a steady, if small, increase in the Arab world, from 20 per cent in 2002 to 22 per cent in 2011.

Perrons (2004) rightly points to the dangers of relying too heavily on these kinds of cross-cultural statistical studies, given that different countries use different classification systems and that classification processes may change between census or survey points. For example, women who work in family businesses or on family farms may not be counted, and those who take on what used to be seen in Britain as 'little jobs' of an informal kind carried out from home (such as baking, craft production, laundry, childminding) may also be excluded. Nonetheless, evidence collected in different ways generally confirms the premise that globalization has involved feminization, although at different rates around the world.

9.4 New openings for women?

Some of this increase in women's working reflects the trend of development in the Global South, away from agrarianism to increased industrialism. Some countries have very quickly developed a highly modernized post-industrial sector based on services and IT. A classic example of this is the transfer of customer service work from Europe to call centres in the modern suburbs of the huge cities of India – Bangalore, Mumbai and Delhi – employing young graduate labour (see chapter 2). As discussed elsewhere, both men and women are utilized, but in a country where female participation is low, this opens up new areas of work for educated middle-class young women.

Call centre work can be seen as paradigmatic of both globalized work and the feminization of work associated with globalization. This is a form of work which arose precisely because of the way time and space can be reconfigured by the use of new technologies and business processes. Thus locating call centre workers in India is a way of drawing on the cheaper labour of the Global South without the political inconvenience and conflict surrounding processes of mass migration (see chapter 7). It also draws upon the legacy of British imperialism in the subcontinent, which offered a young middle-class workforce produced by a private education system, who had grown up with English as a familiar second language. But this means that time has to be reconfigured for the call centre employees, who must work night shifts to accommodate calls to and from the other side of the globe. Call centre outsourcing can link together two people who are half a world away from each other in different time zones. As Reena Patel points out, this has striking implications for the nature of work as it involves not only reorganizing employees' identities, as discussed in chapter 2, but also adjusting the conventional nine-to-five routine (Patel 2010).

Call centre work is viewed as 'pink-collar work', suitable for middle-class women because it is clean, indoors, often monotonous (women are stereotyped as tolerating boredom better than men) and involves customer service skills. However, Patel's (2010) study of women's call centre work in India highlights the complexities of this within a patriarchal culture. She interviewed seventy-two workers in a variety of call centres in Mumbai, Bangalore and Ahmedabad, most of them women. In the call centres she visited, women constituted 30 to 50 per cent of the workforces. The gender ratio will vary according to the nature of the task – for example, men are employed as credit chasers, because it demands a more aggressive approach to the customer, while women deal with airline reservations, which require conventional skills of pleasing the customer: jobs involving 'emotional labour' may be allocated to women.

The great attraction of the call centres is the high wages they pay, higher than the young recruits could find elsewhere. Commentators have suggested that these are excellent jobs for women, as they pay more than much 'women's work' and allow women to escape from the home and from family control, offering the hope of independent living. However, Patel points out the difficulties that arise for women because of the necessity of working at night: not only are urban streets in India unsafe for women after dark (New Delhi is known as the rape capital of India and the police are heavily implicated in sexual crimes against women), but also working at night is seen as improper for women, with its association with prostitution and bar work. The father of one of Patel's respondents told his daughter that 'call centre girl equals call girl'. Even though most companies provide shuttle transport for their employees, this causes anxiety for the women and their families. Moreover, waiting for the shuttle, which drops off many workers, can add up to two hours to the working day. In addition, Patel states that call centre work does not have high social standing, and the idea that it could be a launch-pad for a professional career is somewhat illusory.

Call centre work is designed for middle-class recruits (the reason it pays well?) because of the necessary language skills. Here we see the intersection of class and gender; a more common aspect of feminization is the employment of young working-class women in factories and sweat shops in various locations in the Global South, such as China and Malaysia. Young women, typically aged between eighteen and twenty-four, are drawn by the lure of city life and regular wages, but may find themselves working in unhygienic conditions for very low pay. A classic example is the *maquiladora* system in Mexico, also known as the Border Industrialization Programme (BIP), which was developed in the 1960s and has expanded massively. A *maquiladora* is an export assembly plant, making goods largely for the USA. The system was established to stop the flow of migrants from Central

America, legal and illegal, into the USA. In 2004, over a million Mexican workers were employed at some 3,000 such plants near the United States – Mexico border. The majority were women, seen as suitable for low-skilled assembly work – especially of electrical and electronic goods – and for textile and garment work. They are a preferred source of labour because of their perceived docility and dexterity. Initially, young single women were chosen because they lacked experience of working in better conditions and had no domestic constraints, but with high turnover among them employers switched to employing mothers, whose need for money prevented them quitting (Kalm 2001). Sarah Kalm interviewed women in Tijuana, and found that their earnings were vital for their families, helping to pay schooling costs.

The *maquiladora* workers typify the situation of many women in the Global South. We should not forget, however, the continued role of women in agriculture. As mentioned before, this is often invisible and does not figure in statistics, but women's farming work is vital for social and family survival. Twice as many women as men work in agriculture in the Global South, and between 1950 and 2000 the proportion of these women rose from 39 per cent to 44 per cent (Momsen 2009). Boserup (1970) argued that the modernization of agriculture benefited men at women's expense: they took the higher-paid jobs handling machinery, such as tractors and harvesters. Nonetheless, women continue to do the bulk of monotonous, back-breaking field-work, such as planting, weeding and picking, especially in Asia and sub-Saharan Africa. The growth of agribusinesses providing luxury foods for people in the Global North also created new jobs for women: Momsen cites rose-growing in Ecuador for the US market (70 per cent women workers) and cashew nut processing in Brazil and Sri Lanka. Both are unpleasant jobs: the rose workers report headaches, nausea, blurred vision and exhaustion, and higher than average rates of miscarriage, as a result of exposure to harmful pesticides and high-speed work handling the flowers, while cashew processing involves removing the poisonous husk and is harmful to the skin (Momsen 2009).

Finally, a rise in female entrepreneurship can be linked to the dynamic of neo-liberal globalization. Paradoxically, the steady growth and dominance of giant MNCs (see chapter 3) has been combined with government encouragement for the growth of small businesses, in the production of both goods and services. This has been accompanied in the Global North by attacks on public services and loss of jobs within them which were filled by women; privatization is the name of the game. These processes have encouraged the rise of a class of small businesses run by women, often known as micro-businesses. In the Global South, these tend to be sponsored by NGOs working to support and empower women; they help them to set up village industries, often based on co-operative principles. In the Global North, such women have been referred to as 'mumpreneurs' as their work is often linked to a commercialized baby industry, for example selling baby clothes, providing playgroups or childminding services, running children's parties or offering massage for babies and tired mothers. Although insecure and not highly profitable, the work is compatible with motherhood and draws upon networks established through nurseries and schools. Also popular is craftwork (jewellery, glassware, clothing, jams and cakes), built on hobbies and domestic skills and sold through local fairs and markets. Although it may do little more than supplement husbands' income, this 'cupcake economy' serves to link women into their community and to develop skills of marketing, which can be used in later employment. It also helps lighten the isolation of domestic work, discussed in the next section.

9.4 The work of reproduction and caring: 'women's work is never done!'

> When we Home are come
> Alas! We find our Work but just begun;
> So many Things to our Attendance call
> Had we ten Hands we could employ them all.
> Our Children put to Bed, with greatest Care
> We all things for your coming Home prepare.
> You sup, and go to Bed without delay
> And rest yourselves till the ensuing Day
> While we alas! But little Sleep can have
> Because our froward Children cry and rave;
> Yet, without fail, soon as Day-light doth spring,
> We in the Field again our Work begin.
>
> (Mary Collier, washerwoman and poet,
> *The Woman's Labour*, 1739)

When social scientists talk of 'work' nowadays, they normally mean waged work. That is the paramount meaning of work in the context of capitalism. Thus, when the UK government talks of getting single parents 'back into work', it implies that work is equivalent to earning. But if we take a broader social definition of work, as being productive activity necessary to maintain and develop society, then we acknowledge the vital role of other forms of labour: the care of children and elders, the maintenance of homes, the provision of support in communities. Though some of this is carried out as paid work (by nannies, cleaners, charity employees), the bulk is performed as domestic and voluntary labour by unpaid women.

One reason why this work is often ignored or downgraded is that, historically, caring and domesticity have been seen as 'natural' for women because of their reproductive role, though there is no necessity for childbearing and child rearing to be carried out by the same person. This view of women as naturally caring was central to the functionalists' account of the family division of labour under industrial capitalism. They argued that the roles of homemaker and wage-earner demanded fundamentally different personality structures: the wage-earner must be tough, competitive and ruthless, the homeworker soft, kindly and nurturing. These ideas have become deeply embedded in many cultures around the world and are reflected in the fact that, when women enter employment, it is often in caring and domestic occupations, such as nursing, teaching, childminding, beauty therapy, counselling or social work. Arlie Hochschild (1983) has highlighted women's involvement with what she called 'emotional labour' – that is, ensuring the well-being and comfort of clients and customers. The classic example she used was that of airline hostesses. Carol Wolkowitz (2006) has also explored the role of women in 'body work', jobs involving intimate physical contact with clients, ranging from massage to elder care. Such work can be viewed as an extension of the physical care women perform in the home for children and other family members.

Women's responsibility for childcare and housework is a worldwide constant; surveys indicate they carry out two-thirds or more of work in the home. Combined with their increased labour market participation, this has created problems for women who struggle with the 'double burden' or 'second shift', as Hochschild (1989) has called it, competing in increasingly demanding occupational cultures as well as retaining the major household responsibilities. Indeed, Hochschild identified a 'third shift': sustaining the emotional and mental well-being of the family, what one might term 'domestic emotional labour'. The role of mothers in many societies goes beyond the work of physical reproduction of children (feeding, cleaning, clothing) to responsibility for the child's emotional and intellectual development. What has been termed 'intensive motherhood' seems to have originated in the USA (Hays 1996) but has spread to other countries. Chinese mothers in migrant communities, for example, expend great effort in putting their young children through what Lareau (2003) has called 'concerted cultivation', a punishing regime of music lessons, sporting activities, tutoring, acting, dance classes and so forth, designed to equip children for success in their adult occupational lives. This form of mothering is class-specific (see box 9.3), but it adds to the burden of work for the more privileged women in the Global North. In intersectional perspective, the nature of domestic labour is varied by class, nationality and level of development of the society, but its assignation to women is virtually universal.

In 2010–11 Bradley, Atkinson and Sales carried out a study of 28 households from different class backgrounds in Bristol. One of the topics under scrutiny was the way the households managed the business of bringing up their children, as shown in box 9.3.

The busy lives of professional middle-class women in the context of globalization have created an interesting new phenomenon, known as 'global care chains'. Again the first usage of this term is credited to Hochschild, who provided the following definition:

Box 9.3 A tale of three households: intersections of gender and class

Louisa was the wife of a barrister who lived in a large detached house in a wealthy area of Bristol. The family had five children, all girls. The couple had a good income and standard of living, with several glamorous holidays a year. The girls, whose ages ranged between sixteen and five, were bright and lively, doing well at their school. Yet the burden of care for them fell heavily on Louisa, since her husband worked very long hours and had to travel away from home as part of his job. Louisa had a student *au pair* lodging in the house, like many upper-middle-class families. Despite the fact that this gave her help with tasks such as washing up and getting the children to bed, Louisa still had responsibility for cooking the family meals (often at different times owing to the complex timetabling requirements of the children), shopping and planning for the family. She was constantly driving the children to their many out-of-school activities: swimming and music lessons, dancing and acting classes, tennis, 'play-dates' for the little ones. She appeared anxious and tired, with little time to cultivate her own interests, especially as she was supplementing the family income with a part-time job and running her own micro-business in childcare provision.

Celia, a teacher, and her husband, with one child, had a much more modest lifestyle. They lived in a small house in a formerly working-class part of the city which had recently been gentrified. Celia's husband was a freelance web designer. Both had formerly been full-time employees, but because they experienced stress and ill health they had decided to 'downsize' and work reduced hours. Celia's income was the steadier and provided the basis for the family finances; in contrast to Louisa and her husband, this couple shared domestic tasks – for example cooking and shopping. Nonetheless, Celia felt that the pressure for the household maintenance fell upon her, as she had to plan the meals, make the shopping list and coordinate activities. While her husband spent a lot of time with their son, she viewed them as like two boys playing together: the serious work of raising her boy she felt fell upon her.

Finally, Karen was a single mother of two girls living in a rented property in a poorer though still pleasant area. Her former husband had let her down by wasting away their shared income, accruing debts from gambling and drinking. He had subsequently remarried. Previously, Karen had a job as a nursery nurse, which she loved, but after her husband left her she had to give it up as it conflicted with the demands of looking after her children: she could not afford any childcare. She now had a job she disliked, working part-time in a supermarket during school hours, which was compatible with claiming income support. Karen struggled on her income to maintain her family: at the end of the month she had barely enough to pay the household bills. The family subsisted on a modest diet, and towards the end of the month Karen's own meals sometimes consisted of toast and jam. There were no expensive extra-curricular activities for her children: all their leisure activities had to be free, and Karen herself had no money for trips or outings. Her life was defined by hard work, worries about the budget and lack of hope for a better future.

These three families – upper-middle-, middle- and working-class, respectively – lived very different lives, shaped by class advantage and disadvantage. Yet in all three cases women bore the major responsibility for domestic work and all felt that the men had the better part of the deal. Even where the nature of the couples' jobs allowed for more sharing, Celia felt that her husband did not fully pull his weight. In very different ways and circumstances, all three women were taking the role of domestic managers, shouldering responsibility for family well-being.

> A series of global links between people across the globe based on the paid or unpaid work of caring. Usually women make up these chains though it's possible that some chains are made up of both women and men, or, in rare cases, made up just of men. . . . One common form of such a chain is 1) an older daughter from a poor family who cares for her siblings while 2) her mother works as a nanny caring for the children of a migrating nanny who, in turn, 3) cares for the child of a family in a rich country. (Hochschild 2000: 131)

Thus, the work of caring is displaced down the chain from the rich to the poorer nations. As Perrons (2004) points out, these chains often involve racialized hierarchies. Women of particular ethnicities provide cheap forms of labour in the rich world, for example Filipinas in Britain, Cap Verdeans in France and Mexicans in the USA. As the work of cleaning and childminding is lowly valued and rewarded, majority women are unwilling to do it if other jobs are available. In the nineteenth century, middle-class women in industrializing nations employed white working-class women as domestic servants, but as jobs in factories and shops became available they turned their back on work seen as tiring, endless and demeaning. Global care chains display the interaction of class, gender and ethnicity constructing forms of work: they allow middle-class women to work in professional jobs marked by increasingly long hours of work, while at the other end of the chain people too poor to employ substitute labour utilize help from within the family network, often unpaid.

Yeates (2005), in a critical examination of the literature on global care chains, has argued that the concept should be extended to cover relationships outside nuclear family arrangements. For example, she points out that such migrant women are not necessarily married or mothers, though they may still be connected to the extended family back home. She notes that these arrangements also operate outside the family situation in institutional provision of care. Private care homes for the elderly are often highly dependent on migrant labour: 'The current emphasis on care workers in individualized domestic/ household settings needs to be widened to also include those in institutionalized settings (hospitals, schools, etc.), distinguishing between state and non-state care work environments' (Yeates 2005: 12).

Yeates uses the example of nursing to illustrate this. There is a tradition of nurses migrating to England from Ireland, where there is a supply of nurses with trained specialisms: they can secure better pay and promotion chances if they move to places with shortages of nurses. However, this leaves a gap in Ireland, which is filled by migrant Filipina nurses, who in turn experience higher rewards and better opportunities than 'back home'. Thus another type of global care chain is established (Yeates 2005). This points to the way that patterns of uneven development around the world, in combination with the increased migration associated with globalization (Perrons 2004), promote these hierarchical structures of labour deployment.

Yeates also points out that not all those who migrate as care workers from sending countries, such as Mexico or the Philippines, are necessarily from poor families. Uneven industrial development also means that educated women from poorer countries may choose lower-status, but nonetheless more financially rewarding, work in the Global North in order to, for example, send their children to college, and provide a better lifestyle for their families:

> Furthermore, as a measure of their social status, the sending families are often able to afford to employ more than one domestic worker of their own. This latter point in particular emphasizes the importance of examining the class position of families in the sending countries, which is key to understanding whether care needs are met by buying in care labour or by outsourcing to other members of the extended family. (Yeates 2005: 114)

Because of the invisibility and isolated nature of domestic care work within the household, workers of this type are particularly vulnerable to exploitation, having to work long hours, in poor conditions and open to abuse. If they are migrant workers, they commonly lack information about their rights and support to attain them. Things are even worse, obviously, for illegal migrants. This is explored in *Doing the Dirty Work?*, a powerful study by Bridget Anderson (2000) – see box 9.4.

The positive side of this, however, is that some of these migrant women do manage to escape into more favourable forms of employment in the host countries. It is also a source of support for families living in very poor circumstances, since the migrating women can send remittances home. On the downside, this is clearly disruptive to family relations, as women are parted from their own children, which brings sadness for both parties. Nonetheless, as with other emergent practices of globalization, such changes can challenge relations of patriarchy in some countries of the Global South.

Box 9.4 *Doing the Dirty Work?* Migrant domestic workers in the global cities

Bridget Anderson carried out a pioneering in-depth study of migrant women working as domestics in five major European cities: Athens, Barcelona, Berlin, Bologna and Paris. Working with the UK-based organization Kalaayan, which helps support such workers, she interviewed migrants from many countries, including the Philippines, Ethiopia and Peru. Her argument was that their experiences and treatment varied according to their immigrant status (legal or illegal, short- or long-term contracts) and whether they were 'live-in' servants or daily employees. Her interviews with her participants revealed stories of terrible treatment, and she concluded that live-in domestic work actually constituted a modern form of slavery. If women had come into the countries with a contract allowing them only to work for one particular employer, they were trapped in total dependence and had to accept all sorts of abuse or face deportation.

Women told stories of vicious behaviour by employers: of being made to sleep on the floor or in cupboards, being forced to clean up dog mess, being perpetually on call, being beaten, being locked up, being sexually persecuted by male family members, and so forth. A particular focus of the study is on the relation between the mistress or 'madam' (ironically the same name as that of the female brothel-keeper) and her domestic worker. Anderson challenges the romantic stance of some feminist notions of 'sisterhood', by demonstrating how the middle-class women used their wealth and power to exploit and humiliate the domestics. Thus, Anderson argues, certain categories of women oppress other women: the mistress/domestic relation appeared to be one in which some rich women treated the domestics as though they were their personal possessions. Anderson points out that what is purchased is not the 'labour power' of the servant – in Marxist terms, the capacity to work – which is the normal situation in the contractual employment relationship. Rather, the employers were actually buying the whole person and body of the domestic, a process which is very close indeed to the practice of slavery (Anderson 2000).

9.5 Global cultures and the spread of feminism

> We expect to find a considerably mixed picture: some women will benefit from globalization and some will be hurt: the status of women will improve in some respects but not others. Nevertheless, we advance the hypothesis that, on balance and over time, increasing cross-national exchange and communication lead to improvements in women's status and equality.
>
> (Gray et al. 2006: 293–4)

Throughout this chapter, we have highlighted both negative and positive effects of globalization, in terms both of the opportunities facing individual women and of the promotion of more egalitarian gender relations. As the quotation indicates, different groups of women –

from different classes, ethnicities, nations, religions – experience the impacts differently. This is precisely what we would expect to be revealed by an intersectional analysis.

However, we can still attempt to make a few generalizations. As we have seen, there is considerable evidence to suggest that the recent phase of neo-liberal globalization has promoted a worldwide process of feminization, opening up, for some at least, new opportunities and new types of jobs. Some women – especially, though not exclusively, if they are middle-class and from majority populations – can take advantage of this to gain career chances and financial independence. Others, especially in rural parts of the Global South, will at least find new sources of income, for example in tourism or micro-businesses, to aid them in the task of supporting their families.

However, many of these new jobs, deemed suitable as 'women's work', are low-paid, health-threatening, with little chance of upward mobility. The massive profitability of the sex industry on a global scale threatens the well-being of thousands of young women and children who are sucked into it, whether wittingly or not. Women, especially migrant women, are still confined to the lowest tiers of the occupational structure, and gender segregation obstinately persists. There are also indications that, in the context of recession and austerity programmes in the Global North, women will suffer job losses, especially in public services where they are concentrated, so that female unemployment and underemployment will rise.

On balance, then, it is hard to say whether the economic impact of globalization is positive or negative in terms of prospects for gender and ethnic equality, but our view would incline somewhat to the negative. However, many individual women may be winners, just as others become losers. For many, the situation seems still to hang in the balance, as in the case of the call centre night-shift workers of Patel's study.

There is, however, a non-economic side to all this, as Gray et al. (2006) point out. That is the challenge to gender norms and ideologies, and to ideas of racial superiority and inferiority, promoted by patterns of migration and by the interchange of cultures and information linked to globalization and its attendant technologies. Women from national elites – politicians, academics, creative artists, sports stars, lawyers – can travel as part of their work or as tourists, and observe patterns of greater gender equality, taking new values back with them. Global patterns of communication – television and the internet particularly – encourage dialogue and discussion between women from different cultures. This is not a one- way dialogue: while women of the South assimilate ideas of gender egalitarianism, women of the North may learn to question the consumerism, sexualization and individualism of their societies.

An interesting example of cultural influence was the 2012 Olympic Games in London, where, for the first time, women athletes were fielded by every competing nation. Jacques Rogge, President of the Olympic Committee, referred to this in his opening speech as a 'boost for gender equality', a statement roundly applauded by the audience. Saudi Arabia's Sarah Attar became the first woman athlete from her country to take part in the Games, competing in the 800 metre heats, and running in hijab. Although she came last, the crowd cheered her wildly, realizing the significance of this for Saudi Arabian women. Attar, who holds Saudi Arabian and American dual nationality, told a BBC interviewer that she competed 'to make a difference' and hoped to 'spark something amazing'. Events such as the Games, watched by millions of viewers around the world, give women in overtly patriarchal societies hope of opening opportunities to share life as full citizens. They also give the lie to stereotypes of women as frail, weak and uncompetitive, as we see images of the female judokas and boxers, and witness the ferocious energy of women's handball or hockey. Since these events are watched around the world, they have the potential to raise questions about women's purported unsuitability for certain types of employment and to inspire new impulses to feminist activism (see box 9.5). In many places, groups of young educated women come into contact with new ideas, leading some to seek change and fight for gender equality, while CEDAW and the Beijing Platform provide a formal framework for pro-woman politicians and NGOs.

9.6 Conclusion

In this chapter we have argued that the effects of globalization on existing relations of gender and ethnicity are complex and sometimes contradictory. It would be wrong to say that the effects are all negative, though current globalizing practices in their neo-liberal form, combined with the world recession of the 2000s, have made life harder for many women, for example in afflicted parts of the Eurozone, such as Greece and Spain.

This chapter has emphasized the value of an intersectional approach, showing how the impact of globalization on women's working lives is highly contingent upon class, ethnicity and, indeed, age. Women of the privileged classes can take advantage of global career openings, and use their wealth to buy help to relieve them of some of the burden of reproductive and domestic work. Such work is characteristically carried out by working-class women and by women of colour, based on stereotypes about differential capacities. Poor women with children continue to sacrifice their health and leisure to work in unpleasant ill-paid jobs to support their families, while older women in patriarchal societies may find it difficult to accept challenges to customary norms and ideas. To understand fully the gender effects of globalization, we need to look at different groups of women through an intersectional lens.

However, as Sassen argues, while women from the Global South may be confined to relatively disempowering and low-paid jobs in the emergent global economy, employment outside the home gives access

Box 9.5 Women's activism in the transition countries

While women were making news winning medals at the 2012 Olympics, very different types of female activities were going on in other places. Women from the Ukrainian protest group, Femen, were arrested outside London's City Hall, where they had stripped off their tops in a demonstration deploring the inclusion of countries with patriarchal and tyrannous regimes (such as Syria, Afghanistan and Iran) in the Olympic Games. Femen are notorious for their topless protests against the ill-treatment of women.

At the same time in Moscow, three young women from feminist punk pop group Pussy Riot were on trial inside a glass cage on charges of hooliganism and inciting religious hatred. Their crime had been to read out a prayer in the Cathedral of Christ the Saviour, calling for the removal of President Vladimir Putin. The show trial of these three young women, who were subsequently sentenced to two years in prison, was seen by political commentators as a deterrent to the growing opposition to Putin's increasingly dictatorial grip on the Russian Federation.

The extremist tactics employed by these young women from the former Soviet bloc were explicitly influenced by the American group Riot Grrrls, who practised similar tactics in New York. The influence of Western feminist movements and ideals on these young women is shown by the manifesto which Femen put on their website:

> We unite young women based on the principles of social awareness and activism, intellectual and cultural development. We recognize the European values of freedom, equality and comprehensive development of a person irrespective of the gender. We build up a national image of femininity, maternity and beauty based on the Euro-Atlantic Women's Movements' experience. We set up brand new standards of the civil movement in Ukraine. We have worked out our own unique form of a civil self-expression based on courage, creativity, efficiency and shock. We demonstrate that the civil movements can influence the public opinion and lobby the interests of a target group. We plan to become the biggest and the most influential feminist movement in Europe.

Their campaign, 'Ukraine is not a brothel', was targeted at sex tourism in the country and they have also campaigned against its sex and pornography industry.

to independent income and higher social status, and thus challenges existing gender hierarchies and conventions. As she puts it, 'Women . . . gain more control over budgeting and other domestic decisions and greater leverage in requesting help from men in domestic chores. There is a second important outcome – their greater participation in the public sphere and their possible emergence as public actors' (Sassen 1996: 26–7).

Further reading and useful websites

Janet Momsen (2009) gives a comprehensive and engaging account of women's lives in the Global South. Diane Perrons (2004) contains useful material on gender issues. Three very accessible and readable studies of particular areas of work and employment are Patel (2010), Anderson (2000) and Ehrenreich and Hochschild (2003). Gray et al. (2006) is a quite demanding quantitative piece but gives a comprehensive overview of the economic impacts of globalization on women, and Yeates (2005) on global care chains is a classic piece.

The World Bank website, http://data.worldbank.org/data-catalog/global-development-finance, has comprehensive data on women's labour market participation, and details about CEDAW can be found on the United Nations' Womenwatch website: www.un.org/women-watch/daw/cedaw/cedaw.htm.

10 Globalization and labour conflict

10.1 Introduction

Prominent instances of labour conflict have been evident in many parts of the world since the late 2000s. Workers in a number of European countries, including Spain, Portugal, France and Greece, have participated in mass strikes to protest against austerity measures imposed by their governments as a result of the economic crisis. During the summer of 2012 thousands of coal miners based in the region of Asturias in Northern Spain went on strike against government austerity measures which threatened the future of their pits. Their action, which included protests, demonstrations and a march on the country's capital, Madrid, attracted attention from around the world. Strikes and labour conflict are not just a European phenomenon. In 2010 there was a massive three-week public-sector strike in South Africa which involved nearly a million and a half workers taking action in pursuit of a pay rise. China is seeing growing levels of strikes and labour conflict. In June 2010 the multinational automobile firms Honda and Toyota were forced to suspend production in several of their Chinese plants after workers walked out in pursuit of higher pay and better working conditions. Just over two years later, in October 2012, some 4,000 workers at Foxconn's Zhengzhou plant, who make the latest version of the Apple iPhone, walked out in a dispute over work pressures and restrictions on holiday entitlements. These might seem rather puzzling developments. This is because it is often assumed that workers are reluctant to pursue contention, not least because globalization has shifted bargaining power so much in favour of capital that strikes and other manifestations of labour conflict are to be regarded not just as futile, but even as aberrant (Godard 2011). As we will see in this chapter though, not only is labour conflict a notable feature of a globalizing world, but also it has been influenced in some important ways by globalization.

We use the term 'labour conflict' to refer to actions by working people, their representatives and their allies that challenge the dominant interests of capital, represented by employers and governments, and which derive from, are informed by or relate to work and employment. The chapter is organized in three main sections. First, we focus on strike activity, assessing the impact of globalization on strike levels around the world. It is often assumed that strikes, indeed labour conflict in general, are becoming a thing of the past, particularly in an increasingly globalized world which is dominated by the power of capital. While it is evident that globalization has contributed to falling strike levels around the world, its effects are more complex than is often supposed. As we show in the next section, moreover, in some important respects globalization is actually associated with a greater propensity for strikes and labour conflict. The experience of China, in particular, where labour unrest has reached endemic proportions, offers some notable insights. Finally, we also need to be aware of how globalization has affected the nature of labour conflict. For good reasons, much attention tends to be directed at examining strike activity. Yet strikes are by no means the only manifestation of labour conflict. Under globalizing conditions, a variety of other modes of contention have come to the fore, and these are examined in the following section.

10.2 Globalization and strikes

Strikes involve workers collectively withdrawing their labour for a temporary period, in order to express a grievance or to enforce a demand (see Hyman 1977) and are the most extensively scrutinized manifestation of labour conflict. They 'are regarded as being relatively more open, visible and important, in turn, making them more worthy of measurement and more measurable' (Gall and Hebdon 2008: 597). Moreover, if we conceive of the relationship between an employer and a worker as a 'structured antagonism' (Edwards 1986), meaning that it is inherently exploitative, then the potential for conflict to arise is present in all circumstances where employers direct the labour of workers. A further consequence is that strikes, and other manifestations of labour conflict, are rational forms of behaviour. They are undertaken with a particular purpose in mind – to protest against, or to try and prevent, redundancies, for example, or as a means of trying to secure improvements in pay and conditions (Hyman 1977; Gall and Hebdon 2008).

Strikes are generally organized by trade unions, on the basis that when workers mobilize on a collective basis they will enjoy greater bargaining leverage over employers and governments as a result. Without the presence of a union, which can mobilize workers, organize the action and coordinate responses to the counter-mobilization efforts of employers and governments, strike action is difficult to uphold (Hyman 1989). A distinction can be made between 'economic' strikes and 'political' strikes (Gall and Hebdon 2008). The former are directed mainly at employers and concern issues such as pay, benefits and working conditions, matters which have economic consequences for the firms and workers involved. Political strikes, though, are generally targeted at governments, and concern broader policy issues. Recent strikes by European workers over pension changes are an example.

During the 1960s and 1970s, rapid increases in the level of strike activity in many countries meant that the question of labour conflict attracted a considerable amount of interest from academics and policy makers (Aligisakis 1997). 'In policy circles, industrial conflict and worker resistance were major – if not dominant – concerns, fuelled in large part by increasing strike activity and fears of widespread industrial instability' (Godard 2011: 282). Since the 1980s, however, there has been a large decline in the level of recorded strike activity around the world, reflecting a supposedly more pacified and quiescent workforce. As a consequence, strikes, and labour conflict in general, are somewhat neglected topics these days. They have received little attention in conventional accounts of globalization.

While the 'withering away' of strikes has – erroneously, it turns out – been predicted in the past (Ross and Hartman 1960; Van der Velden 2007), records of strike statistics do certainly point to a dramatic decline in the level of strike activity during the 1980s, which then continued into the 1990s and 2000s (Aligisakis 1997; Wallace and O'Sullivan 2006).

First, though, a caveat – we need to be extremely cautious about how much weight we attach to strike statistics, given the 'notoriously flawed' reliability of the data (Godard 2011: 284). Official statistics markedly understate the genuine level of labour conflict in a country (Gall 1999; Lyddon 2007; Wallace and O'Sullivan 2006). The data only document strikes (and employer lockouts in some countries), and disregard other manifestations of labour conflict, such as overtime bans or work-to-rules (Gall and Hebdon 2008). Moreover, there are marked differences in the eligibility criteria used to record the number of strikes; the United States, for example, only registers disputes involving more than 1,000 workers, meaning that many simply go unregistered. Even when we take into account the unreliability of the data, though, the scale of the decline in the level of strike activity between the 1970s and the 2000s is marked.

Table 10.1 provides details of strike trends for a selection of countries from the Global North, based on annual averages of days not worked per 1,000 employees for successive ten-year periods between 1972 and 2001, and the seven-year period from 2002 to 2008. The use of this measure, rather than simply the frequency (overall number) of strikes or the aggregate number of days not worked because of strike action, helps to control for differences in the size of the labour force between countries, thus facilitating comparative analysis. The right-hand column shows the percentage change in the average number of days not worked per 1,000 employees between 1972–81 and 2002–8. Even in those countries which are marked by generally high levels of strike activity – Spain, Italy and Canada, for example – there was a substantial decline over the whole period. Interestingly, while the absolute decline in strike activity is quite pronounced, the relative position of each country is largely unchanged. Countries which had relatively

Table 10.1 Working days not worked per 1,000 employees in the Global North (annual averages), 1972–1981 to 2002–2008

	1972–81	1982–91	1992–2001	2002–8	% change 1972–81 to 2002–8
Australia	675	250	88	28	−96
Austria		<8	2	1	
Canada	945	425	183	163	−83
Denmark	295	147	169	38†	−87
Finland	548	355	114	61	−89
France	191	65	85	27#	−86
Germany*	23	30	9	6	−74
Italy	1,218	500	117	103††	−92
Japan	149	<8	2	0#	−100
Spain	629	585	282	141	−78
Sweden	138	100	30	34†	−78
Switzerland		<5	2	3	
UK	531	278	22	29	−95
US	428	95	48	15†	−96

* West Germany before 1992–2001; # incomplete data; †2002–6 only; ††2002–7 only
Sources: Bird (1992); *Employment Gazette* (1983); Monger (2003); Hale (2008); and the International Labour Organization http://laborsta.ilo.org/.

high strike levels in the 1970s still did so in the 2000s. The same applies to countries at the other end of the scale. In the twenty-first century, Germany has one of the lowest strike rates in the Global North, just like in the 1970s.

The initial fall in strike levels during the 1980s prompted one commentator to ponder on the extent to which growing pacification reflected a period of 'labour quiescence' (Shalev 1992). Further decline in the 1990s and 2000s suggests that a 'new level of quiescence' may have been reached, as workers and their unions have become increasingly unwilling to use the strike weapon to challenge employers and governments (Vandaele 2011: 8). The diminution in the level of strike activity is not something restricted to the countries of the Global North, but is also apparent elsewhere (Wallace and O'Sullivan 2006). Table 10.2 shows the marked fall in the average annual frequency of recorded strikes in a selection of countries in the Global South for which data are available.

Such a broad trend of declining strike activity, affecting a wide range of different countries, in both the Global North and the Global South, suggests that we should look for the explanation at an international level, with globalization seemingly the key factor (Wallace and O'Sullivan 2006). How, then, is it supposed to have contrib-

Globalization and labour conflict   217

Table 10.2 Strike frequencies in selected Global South countries (annual averages), 1980–1989 to 2000–2008

	1980–9	1990–9	2000–8	% change 1980–9 to 2000–8
Brazil	1,132	854	359	−68
India	2,175	1,411	528	−76
Malaysia	23	14	8†	−65
Mexico	587	96	38	−94
Philippines	268	114	28	−90
South Africa	592	708	62	−90
South Korea	827	153	249	−70
Turkey	129#	138	28	−78

incomplete data; †2000–3 only
Source: International Labour Organization http://laborsta.ilo.org/.

uted to diminishing strike levels? One aspect concerns compositional change: global capitalist restructuring is linked to the rise of service-based economies, especially in the Global North. Since strikes tend to predominate in production industries, the growing proportion of employment in services would seem to have had a moderating effect on strike levels (Wallace and O'Sullivan 2006). Across the Global South, the expansion of the informal economy, where workers are largely unorganized, may also have helped to curb strike activity (RoyChowdhury 2010). Yet the compositional approach fails to appreciate the capacity of workers in services to mobilize and challenge their employers; in Europe, for example, public-sector workers have demonstrated an increased readiness to take strike action. Even private firms are not immune from strikes. The giant US retailer Walmart, which does not recognize unions, had been strike-free for half a century. Yet 2012 saw growing incidents of strike activity over labour standards by workers in some of its stores, culminating in a coordinated day of action in November that year, involving some 1,000 walk-outs and protests across the country. Furthermore, using the rise of service-based economies to account for the decline of strike activity neglects the importance of production industries to countries such as China, where they are often associated with major labour unrest (see section 10.3).

The contribution of globalization to declining strike levels is more likely to be related to its impact in reducing the bargaining power of workers relative to that of employers. Increased competitive pressures associated with globalization mean that employers have a greater incentive to avoid potentially disruptive strikes (Piazza 2005). The elaboration of high performance work systems (see chapter 6) is designed to foster a more co-operative climate of labour relations. The declining levels of union density discussed in chapter 5 have weakened the capacity of organized labour to challenge the policies of governments and employers (Godard 2011; Piazza 2005). Increasingly mobile global capital can use the threat of re-location to intimidate labour, for example, helping to engender a more 'disciplined' and thus quiescent workforce (Vandaele 2011). All this has contributed to a climate in which strikes are now viewed not just as unnecessary or undesirable, but as an almost abnormal social phenomenon (Godard 2011).

Also crucial are the efforts undertaken by national governments to repress labour. Global competitive pressures mean that maintaining stable investment environments in order to attract foreign capital is privileged over the rights of workers to take strike action, as in the Philippines for example (McKay 2006). The case of Turkey is instructive in this respect. During the 1970s the country was the site of major labour struggles. Since the 1980s, however, Turkey has instituted a series of reforms with the effect that 'labour rights deemed as impediments to the implementation of neo-liberal economic policies were curtailed and trade unions, particularly militant ones, were suppressed' (Yildirim and Calis 2008: 216). A set of highly restrictive legal statutes inhibits the capacity of Turkish unions to organize strike action – for example, around a quarter of the unionized workforce are employed in sectors where strikes are prohibited by law. As mentioned in chapter 5, in Australia, the right-wing government led by John Howard from 1996 to 2007 enacted a series of changes in the law designed to restrict the capacity of unions to organize strikes. As a result of these neo-liberal reforms, by the latter half of the 2000s collective labour conflicts 'had been all but killed off' (Cooper and Ellem 2008: 544). These examples demonstrate the important influence of national government policies on strike levels, in particular the way in which states use the greater competitive pressures associated with globalization as leverage to suppress organized labour and stifle strikes.

Perhaps it is not inappropriate to contemplate the prospect of labour quiescence on a global scale (Wallace and O'Sullivan 2006). However, there are a number of problems with the assumptions, first, that falling strike activity is a global phenomenon; second, that it is the expression of a compliant, quiescent workforce; and third, that it reflects the profound influence of globalization. For one thing, using the incidence of strikes as a proxy for labour power can be problematic. Union movements can achieve their objectives without necessarily having to resort to strikes (Kelly 2011). In Latin America, for example, in a form of 'partisan politics', unions often exert their influence formally through their institutional connections with sympathetic political parties (Murillo 2001). The generally very low levels of strike activity in Austria can be explained with reference to the influence unions have traditionally exercised through corporatist arrangements, restricting their bargaining freedom in exchange for institutionalized participation in the state's policy-making apparatus (Vandaele 2011).

This leads to a second point, which is that while the influence of globalization seems to have prompted a degree of convergence towards low levels of strike activity (Scheuer 2006), as tables 10.1 and 10.2 demonstrate, marked cross-national variations nonetheless prevail. Scholars have long been concerned with analysing the factors that explain strike rates within individual countries. Economists have tended to focus on the influence of the business cycle, with low unemployment associated with higher levels of strike activity, for example (Ashenfelter and Johnson 1969). Sociologists and political scientists, however, tend to place more emphasis on the role of institutions (e.g. Brandl and Traxler 2010) and the mobilizing capacity of workers – their preparedness, willingness and capacity to engage in strikes – in the context of particular institutional arrangements (e.g. Shorter and Tilly 1974).

In order to explain strike levels, then, we need to be concerned with the structure of collective bargaining, the nature of the political system (to what extent does it allow workers through their unions to influence social and economic policies?) and the legal framework. In many areas of the world, including Russia, Turkey and much of South-East Asia, unions are hampered by restrictive laws when trying to organize strikes. Unsurprisingly, strike levels in these countries are relatively low. The high level of strike activity evident in Spain can be explained with reference to a combination of relevant institutional factors (see box 10.1).

Box 10.1 Explaining the high level of strike activity in Spain

As can be seen from table 10.1, Spain has quite a high level of strike activity relative to other countries, which is rather puzzling given that union membership levels are not particularly high. What explains Spain's high strike levels? Five factors seem to be relevant. First, collective bargaining at industry-sector level produces disputes which, while rather short-lived, also involve a large number of workers. Second, the traditional weakness of political institutions means that Spanish unions tend to lack effective influence over policy outcomes, something which produces quite a large number of mass general strikes over matters of public policy. Third, in some sectors, such as on the railways, enterprise restructuring has been a source of contention. Fourth, despite the not especially pronounced level of trade union membership, unions have been quite effective at mobilizing workers in general to pursue demands. This may reflect the presence of a solidaristic culture which, in addition to being embedded in families and neighbourhoods, also permeates the workplace. Fifth, related to this, enterprise-level works committees – the presence of which reflects, and helps to contribute to, this culture of solidarity – also have the power to call strike action (Rigby and Aledo 2001).

To analyse the implications of globalization for strikes, then, we need to recognize the important influence of national-level institutions, with the implication that, because institutional arrangements vary considerably from country to country, global economic pressures will have a differential impact depending on the country concerned. For example, Piazza (2005) demonstrates that, although in general globalization is associated with a diminution of strike activity, the decline is more marked in countries which have low levels of trade union membership.

A third problem concerns the assumption that under globalization the level of strike activity is in secular decline, official statistics notwithstanding. There is growing evidence from around the world indicating that this is palpably not the case, exemplified by the experience of Egypt (see box 10.2). In Russia, moreover, the number and intensity of strikes has risen since the mid-2000s, dispelling the myth that the country's workers have faced their circumstances with passivity. While the disputes of the 1990s about unpaid wages were a largely defensive product of Russian workers' desperation, the strike wave which developed during the second half of the 2000s, and affected automobile, oil and gas plants among others, had a more offensive character, as workers used their growing bargaining power to press for wage increases (Greene and Robertson 2010). While the official trade unions remain cautious about engaging in conflict, alternative unions have been at the apex of a wave of labour unrest in sectors where economic growth has helped to raise workers' expectations (Ashwin 2011).

For similar reasons, the late 2000s also saw rising strike levels in the major Latin American economies of Argentina and Brazil. Economic growth and governments run by parties sympathetic to labour have enhanced the bargaining power of the organized working class, which their unions have used to mobilize support for strikes in pursuit of higher wages (Boito and Marcelino 2011; Etchemendy and Collier 2007; Senén González and Medwid 2009).

The economic recession of the late 2000s, and the austerity policies devised by many governments in response, generated increases in strike activity, particularly in emerging Latin American economies, including Argentina, Brazil and Chile (ILO 2010, 2011). Europe has also been affected by an upsurge in labour unrest linked to the unfavourable economic climate. In 2010, for example, mass strikes occurred in France, Greece, Italy, Spain and Portugal, as workers took to the streets to protest against government austerity measures (Vandaele 2011). All this suggests it is wrong to assume that strikes are bound to wither away under globalization. Much depends on the extent to which the prevailing economic conditions provide workers with the incentive to engage in strike action, and on their capacity to mobilize to pursue their interests (Kelly 1998).

Finally, a fourth issue concerns the nature of strikes as a manifestation of labour conflict. It is not so much that strikes have become

Box 10.2 The strike wave in Egypt

Between 2005 and 2010, Egypt was affected by a major wave of strikes. Initially concentrated in the textiles sector, the strikes spread throughout much of the economy. In 2006, over 2,000 instances of labour conflict were recorded in Egypt, including strikes and worker demonstrations (Beinin 2008). Despite strikes and labour protests technically being illegal, a feature of the period was 'the dominance of forms of protest which have brought large numbers of workers together in mass meetings, static demonstrations and sit-ins' (Alexander 2010: 250). The mobilization of Egyptian workers has to be seen in the context of a severely deteriorating economic climate and worsening labour market conditions. Neo-liberal economic policies helped to drive up food prices, increase poverty and raise the level of inequality; young people, in particular, found it increasingly difficult to find employment. Young men with university degrees had to work as taxi drivers in tourist resorts, for example. But contention was also sustained by the development of an emergent democratic trade union movement which, unlike the official trade union federation, is independent from the state. During this period, Egyptian workers became increasingly prepared to organize and participate in labour protests, something that has helped to inform the development of democratic trade unions (Alexander 2010). This also influenced the movement for broader political change in Egypt, in particular the protests and demonstrations which caused the February 2011 collapse of President Hosni Mubarak's regime.

unimportant, rather that they have changed. For example, there is a trend towards the use of strikes to achieve political, rather than economic, goals (Kelly 2011). This is evident in the increased frequency of general strikes, those involving workers from more than one industry who withdraw their labour on a mass scale in protest against governmental economic, political or social policies. In Europe in the first nine months of 2010 alone there were eleven such episodes: 'The data on general strikes suggests that union movements in many parts of Western Europe have demonstrated a remarkable capacity and willingness to mobilize people in protest against these reforms and to seek concessions from governments' (Kelly 2011: 25).

Worker discontent may increasingly come to inform, and be subsumed within, broader political struggles (Godard 2011), rather than be displayed in organized, temporary withdrawals of labour as in the past. If globalization has ushered in a period of labour quiescence, it may only apply to one type of labour conflict, the use of economic strikes as a bargaining tool. Given the broader forms that labour conflict can take, it would be mistaken to assume that labour has been pacified (Gall and Hebdon 2008). Moreover, while capitalist globalization may have helped to stifle strike activity in the Global North, elsewhere it seems to have been responsible for generating contention. It is to this issue that we turn next.

10.3 Globalizing labour conflict

As Harvey (2011: 66) notes, the potential for labour conflict under capitalism never goes away: 'unrest can well up as a serious problem, at any time and in any place'. Globalization has, indeed, been responsible for stimulating labour conflict around the world, particularly in parts of the Global South. Two examples illustrate the linkages between globalization and labour conflict. The first of these concerns the emirate of Dubai in the Middle East, a city state which, during the 2000s, served to epitomize the process of globalizing capitalism. Scores of new hotel complexes, luxury apartments and retail malls were erected to serve booming global leisure and tourist markets (see Krane 2009). However, few of the benefits of globalization reached the massive construction workforce, comprised mainly of migrant labourers from India, Pakistan and Bangladesh. These worked in oppressive conditions on low wages and were restricted to living in barrack-style accommodation in compounds. Even though strikes are illegal in Dubai, during 2006 and 2007 major labour unrest was reported among migrant construction workers as they protested against low and unpaid wages, sub-standard accommodation and poor working conditions. The second example concerns Egypt where, in the latter half of the 2000s, there were rising levels of labour unrest linked to the adverse effects of neo-liberal globalization on working people, particularly growing poverty, inequality and increasing levels of unemployment (Paciello 2011).

There are a number of reasons why globalization is associated with a rise in levels of labour unrest. For one thing, labour conflicts form part of a broader protest movement contesting neo-liberal policies associated with globalization, particularly in Latin America (Almeida 2007). In Bolivia, for example, during the early 2000s, labour struggles were part of the broad-based movement, made up of organizations of workers, peasant farmers, indigenous people and the urban poor, which developed to oppose the extensive neo-liberal policies of market reforms and privatization imposed upon the country by international financial institutions. The established class-based union federations had been severely weakened by the neo-liberal reforms. Resistance in Bolivia was spearheaded by a coalition of unions and other bodies, often mobilized on a territorial basis, rather than based in workplaces, who organized street protests, demonstrations and blockades, as well as strikes (Kohl and Farthing 2006).

The case of Argentina is also instructive. During the 1990s it had vigorously pursued neo-liberal economic policies, the effects of which were rises in levels of unemployment, poverty and inequality, before defaulting on its debt in 2001, something which set the basis for a gradual recovery. Compromised by its close relationship with the ruling Peronist party, the official union confederation failed to mount an effective challenge to neo-liberalism in Argentina. Instead, much of the resistance came from grassroots movements of unemployed and under-employed workers in the informal sector which developed in Argentina during the late 1990s and early 2000s. They mobilized, often within local communities, and with the support of left-wing activists, to challenge reductions in social welfare benefits and resist workplace closures (Garay 2007). Conflict took the form of worker occupations, demonstrations, street protests and blockades, rather than strikes (Patroni 2008). During this time, many of the 'routines of daily life in urban Argentina were peppered by constant protests, the occupation of land by the dispossessed, workplace takeovers, and road stoppages by myriad marginalized groups demanding better living conditions and social change' (Vieta 2010: 300).

Box 10.3 FDI and labour conflict in Zambia

Africa has become an increasingly important recipient of Chinese FDI. In 1997, for example, a Zambian textile factory was re-opened under Chinese ownership. The influence of Chinese capital had important consequences for work and employment in the factory. Greater casualization occurred; and the new management tightened managerial control over the workforce, instituting a harsher, more oppressive disciplinary regime, under which workers' movements were much more closely restricted. Understandably, the indigenous Zambian workforce became increasingly dissatisfied with working life in the factory. Although rising levels of discontent prompted a number of strikes, these tended to be rather isolated and intermittent affairs, which had little impact on the factory's operation. However, in 2006, this changed when labour conflict broke out on a much larger scale than witnessed before, closing the factory. Although low wages and exploitative working conditions were in part responsible for causing the strike, the changing political context in Zambia, with some politicians promoting anti-Chinese sentiment for crude populist purposes, was the main reason why it occurred at this particular time. The strike was quite a violent affair, as workers blockaded the road outside the factory, built barricades and clashed with the police. Although the dispute was seemingly resolved, and the factory re-opened, after the workers received appropriate payments, the Chinese owners continued with their efforts to lower wages and maintain strict control. Further labour protests ensued, before the factory closed permanently in December 2006. Higher wage levels had made it uncompetitive in the eyes of its Chinese owners, with the extensive levels of labour conflict evidently an additional motive for the closure (Brooks 2010).

The second reason for the connection between globalization and labour conflict concerns the role of foreign direct investment (FDI), particularly in rapidly industrializing countries in the Global South such as Vietnam and Sri Lanka (Chan 2011; Teitelbaum 2007). In China, for example, the rapid rise in labour disputes (see below) seems to be directly connected with FDI: foreign-owned enterprises, particularly those under the ownership of Korean and Taiwanese capital, tend to operate highly regimented work environments marked by oppressive working conditions which stimulate worker unrest (Gallagher 2005). See box 10.3 for a case of labour conflict in a Chinese-owned enterprise in Africa.

What explains the linkage between FDI and labour conflict, particularly since foreign investment is generally linked with higher income? Three main factors seem to be relevant (Robertson and Teitelbaum 2011). First, FDI seems to encourage a degree of 'social dislocation', upsetting established social norms and practices in the arena of work and generating conflict. Second, multinational employers are more likely than indigenous firms to be cautious about using repressive tactics to subordinate labour, for reputational reasons. Third, the structure of multinationals, particularly their reliance on complex supply chains and production networks, renders them particularly susceptible to labour disputes, giving workers greater leverage as a result. It also allows workers in one country to compare their circumstances with workers performing similar jobs, for better pay and conditions, in other countries, creating the possibility of international 'injustice frames' as a catalyst for mobilization. For these reasons, then, FDI is associated with a higher incidence of labour unrest, particularly in authoritarian political regimes; however, the effect appears to dwindle when countries become more democratic, as institutional mechanisms to channel workers' discontent become established, such as free collective bargaining through trade unions (Robertson and Teitelbaum 2011).

We must also see labour unrest as integral to the very process of globalizing capital itself. Instead of being in secular decline, strikes and other manifestations of labour conflict have been 'displaced' to other parts of the world (Godard 2011; Wallace and O'Sullivan 2006). This argument is one of the main claims made by Beverly Silver in her book *Forces of Labor* (Silver 2003). Drawing on a world-systems theory approach to understanding the development of capitalism, Silver explains how structural changes in the global economy, namely the re-location of production industries, have exported labour militancy around the world. While labour unions have been 'weakened in the locations from which productive capital emigrated, new working classes have been created and strengthened in the favoured new sites of investment' (Silver 2003: 5), contributing to increasing levels of worker militancy in the Global South.

Focusing on the automobile industry, Silver (2003) examines changes in the spatial distribution of labour unrest over time. During the 1960s and 1970s, for example, the rise of an organized working class and of combative labour unions was a feature of the development of the automobile industry in Spain, Italy and Argentina; this process was replicated during the 1980s in South Korea, Mexico, Brazil and South Africa as production sites were established in these countries. The experience of the latter two countries was marked by the emergence of a specific form of 'social movement unionism' (see chapter 5). This was based on the integration of broader political and social demands, for example over income redistribution, with workplace struggles under authoritarian regimes (Seidman 1994). We often think of how multinationals scour the globe in search of low-waged, compliant and quiescent workforces when seeking to organize their production activities. However, the experience of the automobile industry suggests a more complex picture, since the continuing process of spatial re-location of production generates the conditions for working-class consciousness, assertive trade unions and labour militancy in new settings (Silver 2003: 64).

The experiences of two Asian countries, South Korea and Indonesia, demonstrate how economic change under capitalist globalization, in particular the process of industrialization, produced an emergent working class which was increasingly conscious of its own specific interests. The 1980s, for example, saw the rapid development of an independent labour movement in Korea, which increasingly used strikes to advance the interests of workers. Oppressive working conditions and labour subordination in the factories generated numerous grievances and strong feelings of injustice which, given the authoritarian nature of the political regime in the country at that time, had no obvious channel for resolution. The rapid rise in the number of labour strikes in Korea as a result, and the efforts of the government to repress them, not only helped to stimulate the development of an independent workers' movement, but also informed the momentum for political change and democratic reform (Kim 1997; Kim 2011; Koo 2001). Similarly, in authoritarian Indonesia during the 1990s growing levels of overseas investment and rapid industrialization, linked to the country's integration into the global economy, helped to create the conditions for greater worker militancy and an increasingly combative labour movement. Labour conflict was particularly evident within export-oriented industries producing for multinationals, and strikes contributed to the 1998 collapse of the Suharto regime (La Botz 2001; Silver 2003).

China is a powerful example of this. Since the mid-1990s there has been a rapid growth in the level of labour unrest, which has accompanied the country's integration into the global economic order, exemplified by its membership of the World Trade Organization (WTO) in 2001, the growing multinational presence and its role as the world's 'global factory' (see chapter 6). The re-location of production to China, while on a larger scale than seen before, represents the most recent stage in the spatial restructuring of capitalism on a global basis. Based on the past experiences of other countries, the development of an increasingly class-conscious, independent and combative labour movement, willing to engage in conflict, should therefore be expected in China (Silver 2003).

The evidence would seem to bear out Silver's (2003: 106) claim that the 'importance of the Chinese industrial working class to the future of world labour unrest would appear to be incontrovertible'. Recent labour unrest in China has been endemic, and its incidence has risen markedly. Economic reforms, in particular the development of capitalist market relations, have been responsible for generating widespread conflicts, over matters such as unpaid wages, for example, and employer violations of labour regulations (see Chan 2010; Cooke 2008; Friedman and Lee 2010; Lee 2007), many of them in the foreign-owned sector (Gallagher 2005). While labour disputes in China generally concern an individual worker's employment circumstances, there has been a marked rise in the number of collective labour disputes (Shen 2007), including strikes, indicating that workers may be developing a shared awareness of the exploitative conditions under which they labour.

Chinese government statistics indicate a major rise in the level of labour conflict between 1994 – when the country established a formal system of resolving disputes based on mediation, arbitration and, ultimately, the court system – and 2007: from 19,000 to over 500,000 recorded disputes (Friedman and Lee 2010). That said, it is difficult to gauge the true level of labour unrest in China. Since strikes have in theory been illegal since 1982, the Chinese government often lets them go unrecorded. When instances of collective workers' action are documented, they tend to be subsumed under the broad label of 'mass incidents', applied to general incidents of social unrest in the country. Official data, then, may 'reveal only the tip of the iceberg of the true level of labour discontent in China' (Cooke 2008: 113).

The two principal factors responsible for rising levels of worker unrest in China relate to the commodification and casualization of labour (Friedman and Lee 2010). Commodification refers to the way in which workers in many Chinese enterprises are treated as factors of production, enjoying few rights or protections, with extensive violations of labour standards evident. One of the key reasons for the rise in the number of labour disputes concerns the absence of effective labour regulations and the preference of employers to exercise arbitrary power over their workforces (Shen 2007). Casualization is manifest in the profound insecurity that marks the lives of many workers in China, especially those whose factories are under threat of closure or re-structuring, as employers seek to realize efficiency savings and become more competitive in global markets.

Two broad types of labour protest can be distinguished – 'rustbelt' and 'sunbelt' actions (Lee 2007). Rustbelt labour protests predominate in the established industrial heartlands of China, in the north-east of the country in particular, and are centred on state-owned enterprises (SOEs), whose workforces were once regarded as the aristocracy of the Chinese working class. They are 'protests of desperation', sparked by the threat to workers' jobs and conditions posed by privatization, plant closures and the prospect of redundancies (Lee 2007). Workers mobilize out of a sense of injustice and unfairness; their actions, which include strikes, protests and factory occupations, are motivated by the principle of defending their erstwhile privileges (Chen 2006). In so doing, they draw 'on the concepts and ideology of Maoism in defence of their suddenly impinged-upon livelihoods' (Friedman and Lee 2010: 518).

Sunbelt labour protests, by contrast, are 'protests against discrimination'. These are localized, spontaneous and 'cellular', in the sense of being largely isolated and disconnected from one another. For example, there are protests by migrant workers employed in the foreign-owned factories that predominate in parts of the southern and coastal areas of China. Workers raise disputes about their treatment as second-class citizens – the absence of legal protections in particular – and are largely motivated by a desire to be treated equally under the law and have their rights respected (Lee 2007). Whatever their objectives, it is evident that migrant factory workers have developed a greater preparedness to engage in labour unrest (Friedman and Lee 2010). Interestingly, there is a suggestion that the Chinese authorities may be somewhat relaxed about labour protests by migrant factory workers, especially when they are directed at foreign owners, since it helps to invoke support for nationalist ideology, rather than feeding into a class-based movement with the potential to undermine the regime (Gallagher 2005).

Amidst concerns about the threat to social stability posed by labour unrest, the Chinese state has invested a considerable amount of resources in the development of legal and administrative arrangements for the purpose of resolving labour disputes outside the workplace. Anxious not to discourage foreign firms from investing in China, who might be put off by the disruptive consequences of too much labour conflict, the government has developed a system of mediation, arbitration and courts of law for dealing with instances of labour conflict (Gallagher 2005). Arbitration and litigation have become progressively more important processes for resolving labour disputes, and have often been the preferred method used by workers wanting to assert their rights at work, rather than forming independent trade unions, engaging in collective bargaining and taking conventional strike action (Shen 2007). China's government, then, has prioritized the development of legal and administrative systems for channelling and stifling workers' grievances (Friedman and Lee 2010); the 'goal is to demobilize worker discontent through the institutionalized legal and bureaucratic systems' (Chan et al. 2010: 46). Related to this is the development of a 'legal aid movement' in China, encompassing non-governmental organizations (NGOs) concerned with helping workers to exercise their legal rights (Chan 2011; Friedman and Lee 2010). A key consequence is that, generally, Chinese workers mobilize to protect or assert their 'rights', such as the right to be paid the minimum wage, or to have their job security respected, through the deployment of legal and administrative mechanisms, rather than seeking to advance their interests – by demanding better pay and conditions, for example – through independent unions and collective bargaining (Chan 2011).

That said, however, workers are frequently let down by an administrative and legal system which favours the interests of capital; local state institutions and officials, for example, are often more concerned with maintaining a favourable investment climate than with ensuring that workers have their rights upheld. As a result, 'workers' rights often end at the courtroom door' (Chan et al. 2010: 59). The consequences can be seen in the activities undertaken by workers when grievances are not addressed to their satisfaction – including strikes, petitions, road blockades, street protests and demonstrations, which often meet with a violent response from the state (see Chan 2009; Chan 2011; Leung and Pun 2009): 'Where official channels are perceived to be ineffective and beyond the level of tolerance, workers tend to mobilize other mechanisms to express their discontent and demand for solution. Typically, they turn to the street to seek justice, although this is often illegal and highly damaging to themselves, both politically and physically' (Cooke 2008: 127–8).

For some commentators, labour conflict in China has been dominated by a narrow concern on the part of workers with enforcing their existing legal rights, rather than mobilizing to promote their interests in the employment relationship. This tendency has been fostered by the authorities' promotion of legal and administrative arrangements as a mechanism for resolving disputes (Friedman and Lee 2010). As a consequence, 'China has been heading in a direction that is becoming increasingly litigious, interrupted sporadically by industrial violence' (Chan 2011: 47), when the legal route is seen to have failed workers. That said, however, the 2010 wave of strikes affecting automobile and electronics plants in China suggests that a new interest-based form of labour disputes may be emerging, one that involves the formation of independent unions and a willingness to use, or threaten, strike action in pursuit of bargaining goals (Larsen 2011). Striking workers at Honda won pay rises of between 20 and 30 per cent as a result of their action. Given the growing realization that legal and bureaucratic arrangements are weak mechanisms for tackling their grievances and satisfying their interests, workers seem likely to engage in more solidaristic activities, and to mobilize to take collective action, in pursuit of their goals as workers (Chan 2011; Chan et al. 2010; Leung and Pun 2009).

While the experience of China demonstrates that labour conflict has the potential to thrive under globalizing conditions, it also suggests that there are some problems with the proposition that the rising level of labour unrest in the country is largely a product of capitalist economic restructuring on a global scale, which has exported contention to newly industrializing parts of the world (see Silver 2003). For one thing, it is evident that a more complex set of factors underlies both the extent and the nature of labour protests in China – the role of state interventions, for example, such as the elaboration of legal and bureaucratic mechanisms for handling disputes, and the subjective experiences and identities of the workers themselves (Lee 2007). Moreover, the rise of interest-based struggles signifies the development of a new kind of working-class solidarity in China, marked by contestation generated from below, through the forging of labour solidarity, rather than being the expression of abstract economic forces at a global level (Umney 2011). Labour conflict, then, is a product of the capacity of workers to mobilize in pursuit of their goals, in opposition to the interests of capital, in specific contexts (Kelly 1998). While the development of global capitalism provides the opportunity, around the world, in countries as diverse as Egypt, Argentina, China and Thailand, it is workers themselves, through the expression of a shared consciousness and sense of solidarity, who join to challenge dominant interests in ways that produce labour conflict (see Alexander 2010; Atzeni 2010; Leung and Pun 2009; Pangsapa 2007).

10.4 Globalization and the transformation of labour conflict

Perhaps the most remarkable feature of labour conflict under globalization relates to how its forms have changed, with new modes of contestation developing as workers collectively mobilize to challenge neo-liberal policies. How, then, has labour conflict been transformed in a globalizing world?

To begin with, perhaps the most notable effect of globalization on labour conflict concerns the greater potential it creates for multi-scalar contention, especially evident in highly internationalized sectors such as the shipping industry (e.g. Lillie 2006). The development of a transnational dimension to labour conflict is often remarked upon. In the global ports industry, for example, solidarity action across borders has helped to mobilize effective union opposition to proposed liberalization (Turnbull 2006). Transnational solidarity action seems to be a particularly important means of supporting striking workers in countries with authoritarian or repressive policies towards labour. Cross-border campaigns, involving international union federations and sympathetic NGOs, can put pressure on multinational companies (MNCs), by exposing them to adverse publicity for example, helping to settle disputes in favour of the workers (e.g. Gunawardana 2007; Wad 2007). See box 10.4 for a case of how transnational solidarity action contributed to the successful outcome of a strike in Turkey. Moreover, support from international union groups has been an important factor encouraging recent strike activity in Russia (Ashwin 2011). There is often a role also for non-labour movement solidarity networks in supporting workers involved in local disputes. In Colombia, for example, labour struggles in defence of public services benefited from the

Box 10.4 Transnational solidarity and labour conflict in Turkey

The contribution made by transnational labour activism to supporting strike action is evident from the experience of a dispute which affected the Novamed factory in Turkey. A subsidiary of a German multinational, Novamed provides medical products and services. Motivated by dissatisfaction over their pay and working conditions (the use of the toilet was strictly regulated, for example), in 2004 some workers started a campaign to establish a trade union in the factory and get it recognized by management. Negotiations proved fruitless, however, and so in September 2006 the workers organized a strike in pursuit of their recognition claim. Although the prospects of victory initially seemed low, there were two main reasons why the largely female workforce was eventually successful in winning union recognition. For one thing, the strike attracted considerable support from non-labour activists and social movement organizations, particularly from women's groups in Turkey. The second main reason concerns the support provided by workers and unions from other countries, particularly solidarity actions pursued by foreign trade unions. In the case of transnational production sites like Novamed, national labour struggles on their own are likely to be insufficient for success; international solidarity actions can help to ensure more positive outcomes to labour conflicts for workers and unions (Fougner and Kurtoğlu 2011).

lobbying and campaigning interventions of international human rights organizations (see also examples in chapter 5).

A further way in which labour conflict is changing under globalization concerns the use of distinctive 'repertoires of contention' (Tilly 1995; Tarrow 1998) as alternatives to conventional strikes. Direct action is more common in some circumstances. In 1990s Argentina, for example, the adverse effects of neo-liberal economic policies prompted a spate of factory occupations in the car industry, as workers acted to defend their interests, and protect their livelihoods, in the face of an indifferent formal union hierarchy (Atzeni 2010). Later, during the 2000s, grassroots mobilization against the dire economic and social consequences of neo-liberal reform prompted alternative modes of contention, including street protests, blockades and workplace occupations. Many of these actions were undertaken by unemployed and under-employed workers, for whom going on strike was clearly not an appropriate form of protest (Garay 2007; Vieta 2010).

In France, direct action is sometimes manifested in the form of 'bossnapping', whereby senior managers of MNCs are held captive temporarily by workers as a protest against proposals to close factories or shed jobs. Between 2008 and 2010, there were a number of such incidents. For example, the French head of office equipment firm 3M, Luc Rousselet, was released following two days and nights of captivity after the company agreed to re-negotiate redundancy terms for its staff, to the disgust of many workers who felt that more concessions could have been extracted. The bossnapping phenomenon is not new to France. However, factory closures, exacerbated by the economic recession, prompted a spate of such incidents. They were widely seen to be a legitimate response from workers fighting against the adverse effects of neo-liberal economic globalization (Parsons 2013).

Labour conflict, then, does not just take the form of strike activity, but can encompass a range of other modes of contention. Although many strikes go unreported in Eastern Europe, and are thus absent from official statistics, workers are far from quiescent: 'public dem-onstrations, political lobbying, warning strikes and stoppages are also more frequent than official strikes, which are subject to strict procedural regulations' (Meardi 2007: 517). We have already men-tioned how government austerity measures, devised in response to the economic crisis of the late 2000s, caused a wave of strike activity. They also prompted broader social and labour unrest (ILO 2010, 2011). In Lithuania, for example, opposition to austerity and deteriorating labour conditions provoked major public demonstrations and street protests rather than conventional strikes (Woolfson 2010).

Alternatives to conventional strikes are also evident in the strug-gles of largely unorganized workers employed in service occupations. The rise of service-based economies is sometimes associated with the diminution of labour conflict, since workers supposedly enjoy fewer opportunities to engage in collective solidarity (Wallace and O'Sullivan 2006). However, different repertoires of contention may be used by unorganized workers in the service and informal sec-tors. In the United States, for example, campaigns to improve the wages of poorly paid service-sector workers, such as contract cleaners, have tended not to involve strikes, largely because these workers can be relatively easily replaced and therefore lack sufficient bargaining power. Instead, initiatives designed to give them 'justice' and 'dignity', or to ensure that they are paid a 'living wage', have relied upon civic campaigns, street protests, petitions and demonstrations to mobilize public opinion (see Erickson et al. 2002; Silver 2003: 109–10; Waldinger et al. 1998). Moreover, immigrant worker centres in the US sometimes use direct action, including holding demonstrations outside employ-ers' premises, in order to raise support and put pressure on employers to change their practices (Fine 2006). Although the rise of the service economy may have reduced the effectiveness of conventional forms of labour conflict, particularly strikes, it has also been responsible for generating alternative repertoires of contention.

Under globalization, the concept of labour conflict can be broad-ened to encompass campaigns against corporations, putting pressure on firms to alter their practices, often with the involvement of broader social movements (Juravich 2007). These can encompass consumer boycotts, promoting shareholder activism and adverse publicity campaigns, directed at enhancing the leverage of labour in its dealings with capital, especially where conventional industrial action may be less effective or in countries where unions are weak (Dixon and Fiorito 2009), or at a transnational level. Corporate campaigns are designed to raise awareness of the effects of multinationals' actions and make them more accountable to workers and citizens in the countries where they operate. One of the best-known examples is the campaign mounted against Coca-Cola, which has been targeted because of its alleged involvement with violent anti-union repression in Colombia. Unions, though, are often wary about being involved in corporate campaigns. Boycotts, for example, can have counterproductive effects, for example if they lead to a company deciding to scale back its investment, jeopardizing the jobs and livelihoods of the workers (Snell 2007).

The question of corporate campaigns draws attention to the important role often played by broader social movements in such contentious activity, as discussed in chapter 5. Struggles against neo-liberal globalization and its consequences often comprise a range of social actors, as well as organized labour, especially in parts of Latin America and Asia. In Bolivia, for example, indigenous movements, peasant farmers and organizations of the urban poor were at the forefront of the fight against neo-liberal economic policies (Kohl and Farthing 2006). Social movements have offered the principal source of resistance to neo-liberal policies in Argentina, especially organizations of unemployed and precarious workers, with unions often playing only a 'secondary' role (Atzeni and Ghigliani 2011). The factory occupation movement in Argentina was strongly influenced by the experience of grassroots social movements (Vieta 2010). In Colombia, efforts to protect public services saw the main union involved mobilize on a social movement basis, through the development of alliances with community organizations (Novelli 2007). One of the most notable examples of social movement mobilization concerns developments in South Korea. Here, labour rights and anti-globalization organizations have helped to mobilize temporary workers, whose interests have largely been ignored by the official trade union movement, resulting in grassroots labour struggles – including strikes – against the effects of neo-liberal policies (Shin 2010).

Mobilization against capital comes not just, perhaps not even primarily, from workers organized collectively in unions, but from a broad coalition of actors and movements of which organized labour is but a part. What Mason (2012: 61) terms the 'new global unrest' involves mobilization by three broad groups of actors: increasingly politicized students anxious about the diminution of their career prospects, unemployed and under-employed urban youths, as well as established organized labour movements.

In Europe and North America, effective challenges to corporate interests increasingly come from broad-based protests and campaigns, exemplified by the global rise of the 'Occupy' movement which, from its origins in New York (Occupy Wall Street), spread throughout much of the world during the autumn of 2011 (see chapter 5). These movements coalesce around issues of inequality and social and economic justice, attacking the privileged treatment accorded to globalized capital, especially financial corporations (Van Gelder 2011). While campaigns such as Occupy Wall Street have served to act as a catalyst and inspiration to union protests, notwithstanding initial caution from organized labour, they also pose something of a challenge to them (Gupta 2012). In a globalizing world, labour conflict becomes less the province of workers organized in unions, though this remains important. It becomes a more diffuse phenomenon, involving a broad range of actors whose objectives and activities are supportive of working people in general.

Our final point relating to how globalization has transformed labour conflict relates to the spatial dimension. Traditional forms of contention, namely the strike, and other forms of industrial action organized by trade unions, tended to be rooted in specific workplaces. One of the most notable features of labour conflict under globalization concerns the development of new spaces for action. There is 'a growing tendency for workers to take action outside the workplace and against targets that are not their direct employers' (Mason 2012: 71).

Social movement struggles concerned with labour issues are often organized on a territorial basis, founded on mobilization within specific communities (Kohl and Farthing 2006). Rather than engaging in strike action, which may be of limited effectiveness given their lack of bargaining power, workers often prefer more public forms of protest. This is exemplified by the predilection of French and of Chinese workers to take to the streets and demonstrate when looking for their grievances to be addressed. For unemployed and under-employed workers, controlling public space – by instituting road blockades, for example – is evidently a more rational form of behaviour than strikes (Patroni 2008). In some countries, such as Colombia and Indonesia, there has been a trend for workers to occupy notable civic buildings (Juliawan 2011; Novelli 2007). The occupation of television towers also seems to have become a more popular tactic (e.g. Shin 2010).

There are several reasons for this emphasis on taking control of space as a repertoire of labour contention. For one thing, the potentially highly disruptive and visible effects of street protests and demonstrations put pressure on government authorities, who are often the target of such actions, to reach a settlement (Juliawan 2011). Second, such tactics are designed to garner support from sympathetic citizens, helping to increase the impact of the action. Third, perhaps most importantly, taking to the streets, seizing control of public spaces and occupying prominent buildings enhance workers' visibility, and also that of their goals (e.g. Novelli 2007). These actions do not just attract publicity for workers' grievances – they also help to foster more effective collective support and thus constitute a power resource.

Indonesia, for example, saw a proliferation of street protests during the 2000s.

> The act of taking to the streets itself bears a symbolic significance that goes far beyond the possible material gains. Having been deprived of a collective identity for decades, workers assert their existence by congregating in large numbers, then disrupting the traffic or occupying government buildings. Such actions force authorities to deal with them as a group and to recognize their collective power, while persuading the general public to pay attention to the hardships that they endure. (Juliawan 2011: 363)

Effective labour protest, then, increasingly seems to involve attempts to seize prominent public spaces, something which gives participants more leverage than they would have enjoyed by organizing a conventional strike.

10.5 Conclusion

Clearly labour conflict has not been unaffected by globalization. However, the idea that labour around the world is somehow characterized by an unparalleled level of quiescence is not borne out by the evidence. The pacification thesis is largely derived from strike data, particularly taken from the countries of the Global North. Relying on strike statistics as a proxy for labour conflict is highly unsatisfactory given the extensive under-reporting that exists, let alone the assumption that labour conflict is synonymous with strikes; and anyway there is some evidence that for many countries the incidence of strikes may have increased again during the late 2000s. Moreover, while there are some problems with the notion that, linked to the process of capitalist restructuring, globalization has displaced labour conflict from one group of countries to another, it is evident that such conditions have both helped to produce, and influenced the nature of, labour protests around the world, particularly in an emerging major economy like China. However, perhaps the most remarkable feature of labour conflict under globalization relates to how it has changed, with new modes of contention coming to the fore as workers mobilize collectively to contest the effects of neo-liberal policies. Workers' struggles are increasingly informed by, and evident in, broader social and political contention, alongside sympathetic social movements for example, and in many parts of the world are manifest through efforts to secure the control of public space, rather than being restricted to the workplace. Expressions of labour conflict, while clearly influenced by globalizing conditions, are often evident in behaviours which reflect distinctive national or local traditions, as the example of 'bossnapping' in France demonstrates. Efforts to ascertain the nature, extent and consequences of labour conflict under globalization, then, need to extend beyond both the confines of the workplace and the boundaries of the employment relationship, to explore the broader social, political and spatial dimensions of contention.

Further reading

For an overview of the main issues and debates relating to labour conflict see the book chapter by Gall and Hebdon (2008). The article by John Godard on strikes (Godard 2011) raises some interesting and pertinent questions regarding the significance of labour conflict and how to interpret it. There is a paucity of good, up-to-date texts dealing with labour conflict from a global perspective. The book chapter by Wallace and O'Sullivan (2006) contains some insights, but is rather narrowly restricted to strikes in a way that does insufficient justice to the topic of labour conflict in general. See Vandaele (2011) for an overview of strike trends in Europe. Silver (2003) is a stimulating read, though you should be aware that her emphasis on the implications of global capitalist restructuring for the displacement of labour conflict around the world has come in for some criticism. For understanding labour conflict in China, the best short piece is Friedman and Lee (2010). However, Lee (2007) is currently the definitive work. Finally, for a fascinating study of the changing spatial dynamic of labour conflicts, see Juliawan (2011) on street protests in Indonesia.

11 Conclusion

The purpose of this concluding chapter is three-fold: first, to review the main contribution this book makes to understanding globalization and work; second, to consider the key current challenges and future prospects for work and employment under globalization; and third, to outline some of our ideas relating to how globalization can operate in ways that better serve the interests of working people around the world.

11.1 Reviewing globalization and work

Perhaps the most important contribution of this book concerns the spotlight it places on the relevance of work and employment to globalization. Clearly work and employment are affected by globalization in some important ways – for example the decline of traditional labour movement organizations in the Global North. Moreover, there are several key aspects – the cross-border diffusion of working practices by multinationals, international labour migration and the international division of labour – that highlight the notable extent to which changing patterns of work and employment are integral to the process of globalization. The book also indicates how work and employment in a globalizing world are marked by a transnational dimension, one that transcends the borders of nation-states. Among other things, this is evident in: supra-national efforts to regulate labour standards; efforts by unions to build cross-border networks and alliances; and the development of a transnational labour process apparent in global factories.

The book also attests to the adverse consequences of the neo-liberal globalization project for work and employment around the world. The manifold power of global capital is manifest in a number of ways: the race to the bottom in labour standards, union repression and exacerbated gender and ethnic inequalities. But our material also points to a more complex and multifaceted pattern of change. The management of labour in multinationals, for example, is influenced by a range of dynamic and relational processes of interaction between different actors. It is too simplistic to view executives working for multinationals simply as an 'elite', who are unambiguous beneficiaries of globalization. As chapter 8 shows, while they may enjoy a high income, they are also affected by feelings of vulnerability and insecurity. Although there is plenty of evidence that neo-liberal globalization has aggravated gender and ethnic divisions and inequalities, in chapter 9 we demonstrate that the implications for existing relations of gender are actually rather complex and sometimes contradictory.

A further contribution of the book concerns the emphasis given to recognizing how workers and other social actors produce globalization – it is not just something that happens to them. This is particularly evident from the material on consumption and identity in chapter 2, where a focus on the experiences of workers highlights how the process of globalization is resisted through the reclaiming and consumption of national identities by workers in the Global South. In addition, chapter 6 focuses on the way in which globalization has stimulated the creation of new subjects and identities among the largely female workforce of global factories. This points to the contribution made by taking a grounded perspective on globalization and work, one which recognizes the continuing importance of specific places – like the global cities explored in chapter 8 – in not just mediating the impact of global processes, but also producing and reproducing them.

Following from this, the book also considers the important extent to which the project of neo-liberal globalization is subject to challenges by other actors, including unions, transnational activist organizations and working people in general. Indeed, the process of globalization itself embodies challenges to the dominance of global capital: for example, working people and their allies contest the neo-liberal globalization project through attempts to develop more effective transnational arrangements for regulating labour standards. Moreover, as chapter 10 shows, labour conflict is not just something that has been stimulated by globalization, but instead has to be viewed as an integral feature of work and employment in a globalizing world. Thus challenges to the project of neo-liberal globalization can be seen as inherent in the overall process of globalization.

11.2 Globalization and work: current challenges and future prospects

Despite the rather dismal record sociology has when it comes to making predictions (something it shares with all other social sciences, and most human beings), we think it is important at this point to look at some of the current challenges and future trends in globalization and work. Predicting future events may be foolish, but it is sensible to consider the trajectory that work is taking in a globalizing world, and to make some extrapolations from this.

But first, we do need to add a caveat. This is a book about globalization and work and, whilst we have considered a range of wider social issues – economic and political change, social and community action, environmental change, to name a few – we have focused on work and employment and considered these in context. We have been unable to do full justice to some of the wider, interconnected aspects of a globalizing world. Again, it is worthwhile considering the poor record of sociology in this respect; accounts of globalization by sociologists tend to focus too closely on particular aspects, such as culture. We should remind ourselves of the interconnectedness of global social, cultural, economic and political processes when considering current circumstances and future possibilities, and be wary of presenting trends and trajectories in isolation.

In contemplating future prospects for work and employment in a globalizing world, a primary consideration is the state of global labour markets. Two related trends are particularly relevant. The first is the rise in size of the global labour force. Between 1980 and 2010, it grew from 43 to 47 per cent of the world's population (UNCTAD 2011). Yet the enduring economic crisis and reduced levels of economic growth mean that the global economy is not in a very strong position to create jobs. Urgent action by policy makers is needed to mitigate the effects of this jobs deficit, particularly measures that tackle unemployment (ILO 2012b).

Second, related to this deficit is the growth of urbanization – the large-scale movement of people from rural to urban environments, largely as a result of changes in agricultural practices and the re-location of production facilities from the Global North to the countries of the Global South. A significant landmark in human history took place in 2005 when the urban population of the world outnumbered the rural population for the first time (Davis 2004: 5). Table 11.1 shows that the world population increased from 3.7 billion in 1970 to around seven billion in 2011, and is projected to reach over 9 billion in 2050. But the really striking feature of the data in this table concerns the change in the ratio between urban and rural areas. The world's rural population is expected to decline slightly between 2011 and 2050; in the same period the urban population is projected to increase by nearly 3 billion, with the result that some 70 per cent of the world's population will live in cities.

Most of the increase in the world's urban population is projected to come in Africa and Asia. The five fastest-growing 'megacities' (those with more than 10 million people) are all in Asia – Dhaka, Delhi, Karachi, Istanbul and Mumbai (Birch and Wachter 2011). Clearly, a key issue is going to be finding jobs for the rapidly expanding populations of cities. In countries like India, it is beyond the capacity of the formal

Table 11.1 Global urban and rural population trends

Estimates and projections (billions)	1970	2011	2030	2050
World population total	3.70	6.97	8.32	9.31
Urban population total	1.35	3.63	4.98	6.25
Rural population total	2.34	3.34	3.34	3.05

Source: United Nations (2012a).

sector to provide a sufficient number of employment opportunities for the rising number of urban dwellers, meaning that the informal economy is likely to play a key role in providing opportunities for paid work. Since this trend is not going to go away, and may actually increase in importance, measures are needed to protect and advance the interests of workers in the informal sector (Bairagya 2012). Moreover, it is not just a question of jobs: cities also face the challenge of providing housing, transport, welfare and other services for their rapidly expanding populations (Birch and Wachter 2011).

The global financial and economic crisis, triggered in 2007 by the collapse of the sub-prime mortgage market in the United States, and followed by the collapse of a number of major banks and investment firms in the Global North, has made it much harder to generate jobs on a sufficient scale for a growing, and increasingly urbanized, global labour force. As of 2013, employment around the world had yet to recover from the global economic recession caused by the crisis. Some countries, like the UK, have yet to emerge from a prolonged economic downturn. The economic stability of Europe was disrupted by the imbalance between the economies sharing a common currency within the Eurozone; the richer countries, led by Germany, imposed fierce austerity policies on countries like Greece and Spain. Unemployment and underemployment, especially among young people, rocketed in these countries. The pace of job creation has generally been weak throughout the Global North (OECD 2012b). Nevertheless, some countries have performed relatively well. Australia, for example, has benefited from continuing high demand for its natural resources and its close economic ties with South-East Asia, where the impact of the crisis was less acute.

The International Labour Organization (ILO) highlights the seriousness of the jobs challenge. It estimates that the financial and economic crisis has created a global unemployment backlog of 200 million people. Since some 400 million new jobs will need to be created over the ten-year period from 2012 to 2022 just to prevent unemployment increasing any further, this means that a total of 600 million new jobs are necessary by 2022 (ILO 2012a). As mentioned, levels of youth unemployment are a particular concern (ILO 2012a; OECD 2012b). The task of job creation is all the more insuperable given the predominance of growth-destroying austerity policies, which means there is little prospect of a major economic recovery throughout much of the Global North (see later in this section).

The global jobs challenge is not just a matter of quantity, but also one of ensuring that work is of a decent quality. One of the main features of employment in most countries in the Global North is the growing proportion of workers who are employed on a part-time and/or temporary basis because they cannot find full-time, permanent jobs (ILO 2012b). Involuntary part-time and temporary employment arrangements, marked by a low level of job security, are indicators of precarious work (see chapter 1). There is evidence from countries like the United States that the incidence of such precarious work has increased (Kalleberg 2011). Migrant workers are often concentrated in jobs that are of a precarious nature (McDowell et al. 2012). The global economic downturn seems to have generated an increase in precarious working arrangements (ILO 2012b). But even those in relatively secure employment may have seen the quality of their jobs decline as a result of work intensification, tightened surveillance and punitive performance management regimes. Kalleberg (2011) suggests that the proportion of good jobs has diminished sharply, with only a small elite enjoying the kind of autonomy and job satisfaction associated in the past with middle-level occupations, for example in health, education and the civil service.

Precarious work is particularly commonplace in the Global South. The ILO (2012b) estimates that some 40 per cent of jobs in countries from which data are available are in the informal economy. As we have seen already, the rapid growth of the urban population means that informal employment is likely to continue to be a major source of jobs in many parts of Asia, Africa and Latin America. Moreover, it is becoming increasingly evident that work and employment in some parts of the Global South have been subject to a process of 'informalization'. Workers ostensibly employed in the formal sector of the economy – including those working for large manufacturing enterprises – have seen their job security diminish as, for efficiency reasons, firms adopt more flexible employment arrangements. In China, for example, there has been a notable increase in the number of temporary agency workers (Kuruvilla et al. 2011). Given that informal and precarious employment is unlikely to wane in importance, the emphasis should be on developing effective regulatory approaches which can help to promote decent work. There is growing recognition that well-designed employment regulation can: help to share the risks of employment (e.g. job loss) between workers and employers on a more equitable basis; operate to the benefit of employers (through increased productivity, for example); and further progress towards desirable social goals, such as greater gender equality (Lee and McCann 2011).

However desirable such employment regulation is in principle, though, the deregulatory thrust of the neo-liberal globalization project makes it difficult to put into practice. The global financial and economic crisis was very much a crisis of the neo-liberal capitalist free market order which had hitherto been predominant, and initially seemed to herald its demise (Mason 2009). Yet massive state intervention, including government-sponsored rescues of failed banks, has been deployed to salvage it (Milne 2012). Moreover, since the late 2000s, much of the Global North has been dominated by austerity programmes involving drastic reductions in budget deficits designed to stabilize banking institutions and reassure global financial markets. There has also been a pronounced emphasis on labour market deregulation, based on the neo-liberal canard that greater employment flexibility – a euphemism for making it easier for employers to fire workers – is a key precondition for economic growth.

These policies not only have failed to alleviate the impact of the recession on work and employment, but also have evidently made it worse (ILO 2012b). Greece, for example, fell into a deep economic depression as the result of enacting extreme austerity measures – including massive spending cuts, pension reductions and tax rises for low-income households – imposed by the so-called 'Troika' of the IMF, European Central Bank and the European Union. Six years of economic recession will have caused the economy to contract by an extraordinary 25 per cent between 2008 and 2014. In January 2013, 27 per cent of the workforce was unemployed; the youth unemployment rate was a staggering 57 per cent. Not to be discouraged, the Troika insisted that Greece impose a widespread programme of labour reforms designed to promote greater labour market flexibility, including the tearing up of national collective bargaining agreements with trade unions. Similar processes have afflicted the workforce in Spain. The ILO has forthrightly condemned such policies, claiming that they have simply prolonged the economic crisis. 'In countries that have pursued austerity and deregulation to the greatest extent, principally those in Southern Europe, economic and employment growth have continued to deteriorate . . . [moreover] the weakening of collective bargaining is likely to provoke a downward spiral of wages, thereby delaying recovery further' (ILO 2012b: viii).

What accounts for the attachment of international agencies and some governments to neo-liberal policies of austerity and deregulation, given their adverse consequences for economic growth and jobs? Naomi Klein's insights in *The Shock Doctrine* (Klein 2008) are useful here. She explains that, notwithstanding the rhetoric about promoting growth and competitiveness, in reality neo-liberal reforms form an ideological project designed to benefit the interests of global capital by subordinating and repressing the interests of labour. Klein illustrates these shock tactics by drawing on the examples of Pinochet's regime in Chile, Thatcher's policies following the Falklands war, and Russia in the post-Cold War era. She points to the way in which political, economic and environmental crises are used by capital to justify 'shock therapy', in the form of economic and labour market reforms that in normal circumstances would be viewed as repellent. Clearly, global capital and its agents have not been shy of turning a crisis of neo-liberal globalization into an opportunity to advance market-friendly policies and structural reforms. Large-scale public-sector cuts and resultant job losses across Europe have been justified and legitimated by the need to tackle budgetary deficits. However, these economic arguments are a cloak for a highly ideological commitment to the pursuit of greater privatization and the dismantling of state provision.

That said, though, by no means does neo-liberalism command a consensus; moreover, there are increasing signs that it may be becoming more vulnerable (Shahrokhi 2011). On one level, there are growing calls for an alternative, more interventionist approach to promote economic recovery which focuses on tackling the global jobs crisis rather than providing reassurance to financial markets. The ILO (2012a and b), for example, has called for a greater emphasis on economic stimulus measures, designed to raise employment levels, and for more effective regulation of international labour standards, part of an alternative approach to generating economic growth through productivity improvements.

Challenges to the neo-liberal globalization project are also evident in workplaces, in communities and on the streets, around the world. In chapters 5 and 10, we highlighted the role of labour unions and social movements in challenging global capital. As this chapter is being completed (February 2013), workers in Greece are holding another general strike in protest against the austerity programme imposed on their country, the twenty-first such strike in three years. A renewed global challenge to neo-liberal globalization, and the austerity measures associated with it, has been inspired by the 2011 'Arab Spring'. This is most evident in the rise of the various Occupy movements around the world, discussed in chapter 5. Resistance to austerity has emerged, first in Europe and then, more surprisingly, in the United States, where the Occupy Wall Street movement has upended many political preconceptions. Such initiatives demonstrate 'how the power of ideas, when pushed forward by an active protest movement, can be amplified by the power of modern communications technology' (Quiggan 2012: 237, 238).

Perhaps the most striking challenge to neo-liberal globalization is evident from the recent experience of Latin America, a part of the world where neo-liberal policies were imposed with devastating social and economic effects in the 1980s and 1990s. Since the late 1990s, however, there has been a political shift to the left in many countries, exemplified by the electoral success of the populist president Hugo Chavez in Venezuela (Milne 2012; Nilsson 2012). The case of Bolivia is instructive (see box 11.1). While not wishing to downplay the persistence of massive economic inequalities and social problems, it is evident that, generally, Latin America has coped with the global financial and economic crisis rather better than the United States and most of Europe (Nilsson and Gustafsson 2012). Countries such as Argentina have pursued alternatives to neo-liberal economic policies, largely in the form of a more interventionist role for the state (Bernal-Meza and Fryba-Christensen 2012), and have been able to recover from the crisis more quickly as a result.

The experience of Latin America highlights a major shift in the structure of global capitalism, namely the growing influence of the major economies of the Global South, which seem to have weathered the global economic and financial crisis rather better than their

Box 11.1 Contesting neo-liberal globalization in Bolivia

The election in 2005 of Evo Morales, the first indigenous president of Bolivia, marked a historic break in that country's history of foreign domination and oppressive government. Morales, in his first speech as president, hailed the 'end of the colonial and neoliberal era' (Artaraz 2012: 13). As we saw in chapter 1, Bolivia had experienced years of neo-liberalism-inspired *laissez-faire* capitalism that promoted the primacy of the market over democracy, and resulted in hyperinflation, and a forced 'structural adjustment' regime that consisted of all-out privatization and fiscal austerity (Artaraz 2012: 179). Yet Bolivians voted for a president and a constitution that would bring about decentralization, re-establish the social protection role of the state, integrate excluded minorities and regain for the state a dominant role in steering the economy; denounced imperialism; and proposed a plurality of forms of economic practice and property ownership. As Artaraz (2012: 180) puts it, Bolivia is on course for a post-neo-liberal paradigm; given the general 'turn to the left' in Latin America, it is plausible to suggest that other nations may follow suit.

counterparts in the Global North. Table 11.2 provides data on economic growth (as measured by the annual changes in Gross Domestic Product – GDP) for selected countries and regions for the period 2009–13. While economic recovery in the Global North has been sluggish at best – indeed some countries have struggled to promote growth at all – since 2010 the economies of countries like China and India have continued to grow, albeit at a slower pace than before. In China the impact of the global financial and economic crisis resulted in some 36 million job losses in 2008–9; however, there is recent evidence of a renewed demand for labour (Giles et al. 2012).

Yet unrestrained economic growth will have some undesirable consequences. Increasing warnings from the scientific community of dramatic, even catastrophic, climate change are not being met with much action at any level – local, regional, national, continental or global. Economic growth, in the context of capitalism, relies on increasing consumption, and increasing consumption requires more resources to be processed and consumed, a process that can only be achieved through increasing energy use. The global scientific community has shown that increasing greenhouse gases that are producing climate change are coming from human activities – chiefly energy and food production; the prediction that more growth is coming can only spell trouble for the global environment. Short-term increases in, for example, job security through improved economic growth may be matched by long-term job insecurity as global warming produces environmental catastrophes and requires substantial adaptations by human populations (Giddens 2011; Stern 2008). While conservative regimes have been sceptical about scientific claims about climate

Table 11.2 GDP growth (%), selected countries and regions 2009–2013

	2009	2010	2011	2012*	2013*
Europe	−4.0	2.2	2.0	0.1	0.8
'Advanced' Europe	−4.1	1.8	1.4	−0.3	0.4
'Emerging' Europe (e.g. Eastern Europe, Turkey)	−3.6	4.5	5.3	2.0	2.6
UK	−4.9	1.4	0.8	−0.4	1.1
Germany	−4.7	3.6	3.1	0.9	0.9
France	−3.5	1.4	1.7	0.1	0.4
Spain	−3.7	−0.1	0.4	−1.5	−1.3
Italy	−5.0	1.3	0.4	−2.3	−0.7
United States	−3.2	3.0	1.8	2.2	2.1
Japan	−5.2	4.0	0.8	2.2	1.2
Australia	1.2	2.7	2.1	3.3	3.0
Asia	3.6	8.2	5.8	5.4	5.8
China	9.1	10.3	9.2	7.8	8.2
India	5.7	10.1	6.8	4.9	6.0
South America	−0.2	6.6	4.8	2.9	4.0
Argentina	0.9	9.2	8.9	2.6	3.1
Brazil	−0.2	6.6	4.8	1.5	4.0

*Projections

Sources: IMF *World Economic Outlook Reports* 2010–12.

change, the increases in extreme weather events – tsunamis, hurricanes, heavy flooding and earthquakes – along with the rapid melting of glaciers and polar ice caps is making even the sceptics think again.

It is likely that we will see the development of a multi-polar world, marked by a more evenly shared distribution of global economic power between the major economies of the Global North and the Global South. The World Bank predicts that by 2025 six major emerging economies – Brazil, China, India, Indonesia, South Korea and Russia – will account for more than half of all global growth. Perhaps the dominance of the US dollar in global finance will be long past by that date (World Bank 2011). The consequences of these global shifts are very difficult to predict. It could be that Global South countries and regions will be the beneficiaries of this shift, with more direct investment, and a much higher level of production, thereby ushering in new regional finance centres that will in turn direct global economic power away from the Global North. However, the trend in this direction could be curtailed by increased protectionism by the countries and regions of the Global North, and by attempts by current MNCs to hold on to their power and expand their existing production facilities.

One trend that is evident is that MNCs originating from the Global South are exercising more influence around the world, as we mentioned in chapter 3. Unfortunately, in some ways there is little to distinguish their behaviour from that of their counterparts originating in the Global North, with cross-border investment decisions and the promotion of regime competition creating some adverse consequences for work and employment. The largest steel company in the world, ArcelorMittal, was founded in 2006 following the takeover of the European Arcelor by the India-based Mittal Steel. In October 2012, it announced its intention to close permanently two blast furnaces at the firm's Florange site, in North-East France, with the loss of over 600 jobs. There is some evidence that MNCs originating in the Global South, especially Chinese and East Asian firms, operate a characteristically harsh approach to managing work and employment issues, particularly in their African sites. Although working conditions in Chinese companies in Africa differ across countries and sectors, there are some common trends, such as tense labour relations, hostile attitudes by Chinese employers towards trade unions, violations of workers' rights, poor working conditions and unfair labour practices (Baah and Jauch 2009: 13).

Regardless of predictions about future multipolarity, and the shift of economic power away from the Global North, we should not write off the influence of established MNCs on work and employment around the world. For one thing, it remains highly likely that they will try to maintain and improve their position in global markets through further foreign direct investment (FDI) in areas of the Global South. The iniquitous role of multinationals sometimes comes to the surface when there are instances of industrial strife. Nowhere was this more evident than in South Africa during 2012 when the mining industry there, which is dominated by global multinationals such as Lonmin, Anglo-American Platinum and AngloGold Ashanti, was the site of widespread labour unrest involving over 100,000 miners. Working conditions in the industry are poor, and the work itself is very dangerous; the miners themselves often live in sub-standard dormitory accommodation. Sparked initially by demands from Lonmin workers for a substantial wage rise, the strikes were marked by a considerable amount of violence, including the shooting dead of thirty-four striking workers by the police.

Attempts to create larger, and hence more powerful, global conglomerations through merger and acquisition activity also demonstrate the continued relevance of multinationals from the Global North. Efforts made in 2012 to create a merger between two of the largest arms manufacturers in the world, BAE Systems and EADS, provide a glimpse of likely trends in this direction. The proposed merger would have created a massive corporation with powerful military and civilian production able to rival, and surpass, US multinational rivals such as Boeing. Indeed, the merger would have been very similar to Boeing's takeover of McDonnell Douglas in 1997. There is an almost inexorable logic in MNCs combining with one another, a trend towards monopoly first identified in the context of capitalist production by Karl Marx over a century ago. Yet it is possible to discern some novel and distinctive features of contemporary global capitalism, most notably the increasing influence of financial capital. As Bieler and Lindberg (2011: 7) note, firms 'are more and more owned by big institutional capital investors . . . who are not involved in the direct running of companies on a day-to-day basis'. The process of financialization, discussed in chapter 1, means that takeover bids are increasingly made by investors who only want to take on the profitable elements of an organization and then jettison the remainder, invariably leading to job losses. This asset-stripping is even starting to occur in the university sectors of the USA and the UK, as private interests step in, encouraged by governments with neo-liberal values. Given that it is difficult to identify the source of actual decision-making, this poses a considerable challenge for trade unions and other actors wanting to influence the policies and practices of multinationals. A consequence of this insidious process is that work and employment in a world which is continuing to globalize are likely to be characterized by further turbulence and instability.

11.3 A different vision of globalization and work

> After 27 years in the Inland Revenue, following the introduction of lean [production], I am now deskilled, de-motivated and stressed out, most days, afraid to be sick, feel unappreciated, provide a poor service for customers, am not allowed to voice my opinion. Looking forward to the day I can leave for good.
>
> (Taylor 2012)

This quotation, from a disillusioned UK government employee, is typical of comments made by workers about the impact of restructuring and loss of rights in their organizations, which have been fostered by the neo-liberal macro-economic policies discussed in the previous section. It is hard not to arrive at a rather gloomy estimation of the impact of globalization on work and employment relations.

However, the message of this book has been that we must not confuse the *process* of globalization with *its practice*. Globalization is not in itself a negative force – indeed, in this book we have pointed to some of its advantages: improved communications technologies, cultural exchanges between nations which may promote democracy, challenges to gender and ethnic stereotyping, the opening up for young people of opportunities to travel and work outside their native countries, cultural enrichment of our daily lives. The problem afflicting work and employment relations is that this latest phase of globalization has largely developed under the auspices of governments favouring neo-liberal ideas and policies, who privilege the needs of capital and the free market, allowing MNCs to dominate the world economy largely unchecked. This alliance of conservative or oppressive governments and big business has pursued deregulation, to the detriment of employee and worker rights, and is unconcerned by the growth of inequality. This agenda has allowed the rich to flourish, while the poor languish. Moreover, we increasingly seem to witness the proletarianization of middle-level occupations, as foretold in the labour process theory of Harry Braverman (1974) – albeit somewhat later than he predicted.

A common mantra is 'there is no alternative'. However, we would contest this. As we have noted in the previous section, the process of globalization *from below* has seen the gradual development world-wide of an opposition to neo-liberalism, which maintains that 'It doesn't have to be this way.' While this movement may as yet be rather incoherent and in its infancy, we have also the example of a group of countries which has continued to reject the premises of unchecked capitalism and offer an actually existing alternative: the 'Scandinavian model', as practised by Norway, Sweden, Finland and Denmark. These Nordic countries continue, even in the context of the recession, to cling on to ideals of fairness and egalitarianism. In Scandinavia, where employees are treated with more respect and the dignity of labour more widely acknowledged, there has evolved a rather different arrangement between the worker and the state.

The Scandinavian model is based around the notion of active citizenship, whereby all adults, including women, are expected to work towards holding a job. In return, the state seeks to enable this activity through the provision of free higher and vocational education, by providing comprehensive pre-school childcare, and by funding parental leave. In addition, a decent level of support is offered to those who, for whatever reason, cannot find employment, in order to prevent the kind of personal and community degeneration long-term unemployment commonly causes in most other countries of the Global North. Although union density has fallen in these countries, as elsewhere, it remains relatively high and the trade unions continue to wield a much greater social influence and to fight more effectively to protect their members' pay and conditions than in much of the Global North.

It has often been stated that these are the most woman-friendly countries in the world. We have seen in chapter 9 that their female employment rates are relatively high. Women's participation is helped by the nursery provision which enables them to return to their jobs, although they also have generous parental leave arrangements, which allow mothers and fathers to share the responsibility of childcare. Indeed, the introduction of compulsory 'Daddy weeks' in Norway, whereby men are obliged to stay at home and take their turn as domestic workers and child-minders, has led to a much more marked conception of parenting as something to be shared. Norway is also noted for its requirement that company boards have a female quota of 40 per cent. In all the Nordic countries in 2012, including Iceland, women constituted over 40 per cent of Members of Parliament, except for Denmark – at 39 per cent! For comparison, the figures for the UK and USA were 22 per cent and 17 per cent, respectively (Interparliamentary

Union website). Women, therefore, in these countries, are much more integrated into the world of work and into public life.

We should not, however, think of these countries as Utopian paradises. Although their record on gender equality is strong, they are much less impressive on racial equality. Migrant workers, such as Somalians and Pakistanis, remain clustered in the least desirable jobs, such as cleaners or refuse collectors, and have made limited inroads into the professions. They are far more likely to be unemployed than the native populations. Moreover, despite higher participation rates, gender segregation in employment is still marked. Nonetheless, the example of Scandinavia shows that, where there is political will, we can do things differently.

We mentioned earlier in the chapter that Australia was doing better than other countries in handling the recession. Although in chapters 5 and 10 we highlighted the impact of repressive legislation on unions, since then Australia has sought to establish a new social contract. It has developed a 'Fair Work Programme' (the name is indicative) which tries to achieve a balance between the needs of employers, employees and trade unions and promote a harmonious communication among them. The Fair Work Act of 2009 promised a 'safety net for workers', laying down minimum labour standards. Among these is a minimum hourly wage of $15.96 (£10.51), set considerably higher than the British £6.19 (2012 figures). Other arrangements include a special low-paid bargaining stream, intended to help workers who have missed out on the benefits of bargaining in the past, another reason for the disparity between pay for men's and women's work. These include workers in areas like childcare, elderly care, community services, security and cleaning. There are provisions designed to promote a balance between work and family life, such as provision for the making of individual flexibility arrangements, allowing for genuine flexibility for both employees and employers, and an increased amount of unpaid parental leave available to parents.

As a result, Australia appears to fare well on the measures of well-being monitored by the Organization for Economic Co-operation and Development (OECD) which concern the economy:

> In Australia, the average person earns USD 26,927 a year, more than the OECD average of 22,387 USD a year. In terms of employment, over 72% of people aged 15 to 64 in Australia have a paid job, above the OECD employment average. Some 79% of men are in paid work, compared with 66% of women. People in Australia work 1,686 hours a year, less than most people in the OECD who work 1,749 hours. (OECD Better Living Index website)

Again, we do not claim that Australia is a paradise: there is a major gap between the rich and the poor, as in all the OECD countries; men do better than women; too many people have to work very long hours and suffer poverty and social exclusion. However, the Fair Work

Programme does seem designed to promote a more egalitarian working climate.

These examples show there is more than one way to manage a market society, with the state in these countries seeking to balance the needs of capital and labour, rather than privileging capital at the expense of labour. Thus we suggest it is possible to set down principles for a new phase of globalization, which would involve a new contract between the state and its citizens, building from these examples of Scandinavia and Australia, in order to create a climate in which work and employment relations were of better quality and social wealth was more equitably distributed. Such principles might include:

- the implementation around the globe of international labour standards, as discussed in chapter 4, overseen by the ILO and the UN;
- a reversal of the trend of employment deregulation in the Global North, with the restoration of employment protection legislation which is properly enforced when infringed;
- the extension of employment legislation to cover the informal sector;
- the enforcement in the Global South of the principles of CEDAW and the Beijing Platform to promote a better life for girls and women, monitored and controlled by the UN;
- the establishment in every country of a minimum wage for workers appropriate to the standard of living, to counter the 'race to the bottom';
- the provision by states in the Global North of high-quality affordable childcare as in the Scandinavian model, to enable women and men to combine parenthood with employment more effectively;
- the revival of tripartite arrangements for negotiation between governments, employers and trade unions, and an end to the demonization of trade unions as enemies of the state;
- the development in countries such as China and Russia of independent and legally recognized trade unions, which can bargain freely with employers and protect their members' interests;
- the establishment or re-establishment of the principle of the safety net in welfare provision, for those excluded from employment;
- welfare and childcare provisions to be financed by progressive tax regimes and international collaboration to prevent tax evasion by wealthy individuals and by MNCs such as Google, Starbucks and Apple;
- implementing programmes to stimulate growth, following the example of the New Deal which lifted America out of the Great Depression of the 1930s.

While such policies may take a long time to achieve, nevertheless we believe that this is the kind of programme catering for the well-being of all sections of society which should be pursued by the growing opposition movement discussed earlier in the chapter, and by progressive political parties and governments wishing to promote a better deal for what government ministers in the UK like to call 'hard-working families'. It is also important that pressure groups work hard to encourage the international organizations in a position to influence processes of globalization – such as the United Nations, ITUC, ILO, UNESCO, the IMF, the World Bank, the EU and the OECD, among others – to adopt these policies.

In his useful book on globalization, Larry Ray (2007) concludes:

> Globalization is inescapable, but it is a complex multifaceted process with highly uneven effects and consequences for human welfare . . . It is not one thing and cannot be judged 'good' or 'bad' in itself. In some ways it has become a metaphor for multiple and often unsettling changes that impact on everyday lives. But at the same time multiple resistances to globalization themselves produce 'the global' both as an object of loathing and a space within which co-operation and action take place. (2007: 206)

We endorse Ray's conclusions, and in this book with its focus on work and employment we have sought to reveal some of those facets and complexities. Our focus on globalization *from below* has insisted that as human agents we have the potential to work together to produce better outcomes. While opposition to neo-liberalism globalization is still in its infancy, it is growing. We hope our thinking in this book, especially in this concluding chapter, will assist all those who labour in different ways to promote the well-being of working men and women and to give contemporary work relations a more human and humane face.

Bibliography

Abu-Lughod, J. 1989: *Before European Hegemony: the World System A.D. 1250–1350.* New York and Oxford: Oxford University Press.

Ackroyd, S. 2012: 'Economy, class, ideology and the transformation of the organisational field in Britain and the USA: a neo-Marxian view'. Paper presented to the British Sociological Association Annual Conference, Leeds University.

Adam, K. 2011: 'Occupy Wall Street protests go global'. *Washington Post,* 15 October, www.washingtonpost.com/world/europe/occupy-wall-street-protests-go-global/2011/10/15/gIQAp7kimL_story.html.

Adams, M. and Raisborough, J. 2010: 'Making a difference: ethical consumption and the everyday'. *British Journal of Sociology,* 61, 2, 256–74.

Adams, M. and Raisborough, J. 2011: 'Encountering the Fairtrade farmer: solidarity, stereotypes and the self-control ethos'. *Papers on Social Representation,* 20, 1, 8–21.

Aguiar, L. and Herod, A. (eds.) 2006: *The Dirty Work of Neoliberalism: Cleaners in the Global Economy.* Oxford: Blackwell Publishing.

Aguilar Jr, F. V. (ed.) 2002: *Filipinos in Global Migration: At Home in the World?* Quezon City: Philippine Social Science Council.

Albin, E. and Mantouvalou, V. 2012: 'The ILO Convention on Domestic Workers: from the shadows to the light'. *Industrial Law Journal,* 41, 1, 67–78.

Alden, C. 2007: *China in Africa.* London: Zed Books.

Alexander, A. 2010: 'Leadership and collective action in the Egyptian trade unions'. *Work, Employment and Society,* 24, 2, 241–59.

Aligisakis, M. 1997: 'Labour disputes in western Europe: typology and tendencies'. *International Labour Review,* 131, 1, 73–94.

Almeida, P. 2007: 'Defensive mobilization: popular movements against economic adjustment policies in Latin America'. *Latin American Perspectives,* 34, 3, 123–39.

Almond, P. and Ferner, A. (eds.) 2006: *American Multinationals in Europe.* Oxford: Oxford University Press.

Allsop, J., Bourgeault, I., Evetts, J., Le Bianic, T., Jones, K. and Wrede, S. 2009: 'Encountering globalization: professional groups in an international context'. *Current Sociology,* 57, 4, 487–510.

Alston, P. 2004: '"Core labour standards" and the transformation of the international labour rights regime'. *European Journal of International Law,* 15, 3, 457–521.

Amable, B. 2003: *The Diversity of Modern Capitalism.* Oxford: Oxford University Press.

Amin, S. 2008: 'Foreword', in A. Beiler, I. Lindberg and D. Pillay (eds.), *Labour and the Challenges of Globalization.* London: Pluto, xiv–xxii.

Amit, V. 2007: *Going First Class? New Approaches Towards Privileged Travel and Movement.* London and New York: Berghahn Press.

Amoore, L. 2002: *Globalisation Contested.* Manchester: Manchester University Press.

Anderson, B. 2000: *Doing the Dirty Work? The Global Politics of Domestic Labour.* London: Zed Books.

Anderson, B. 2010: 'Migration, immigration controls and the fashioning of precarious workers'. *Work, Employment and Society*, 24, 2, 300–17.

Anner, M., Greer, I., Hauptmeier, M., Lillie, N. and Winchester, N. 2006: 'The industrial determinants of transnational solidarity: global interunion politics in three sectors'. *European Journal of Industrial Relations*, 12, 7, 7–27.

Applebaum, E., Bailey, T., Berg, P. and Kalleberg, A. 2000: *Manufacturing Advantage: Why High-Performance Work Systems Pay Off*. Ithaca NY: Cornell University Press.

Araghi, F. 1995: 'Global depeasantization 1945–1990'. *Sociological Quarterly*, 36, 2, 337–68.

Arnold, D. and Shih, T.-H. 2010: 'A fair model of globalization? Labour and global production in Cambodia'. *Journal of Contemporary Asia*, 40, 3, 401–24.

Artaraz, K. 2012: *Bolivia: Refounding the Nation*. London: Pluto Press.

Arthurs, H. 2002: 'Private ordering and workers' rights in the global economy: corporate codes of conduct as a regime of labour market regulation', in J. Conaghan, R. Fischl and K. Klare (eds.), *Labour Law in an Era of Globalization*. Oxford: Oxford University Press, 471–88.

Ashenfelter, O. and Johnson, G. 1969: 'Bargaining theory, trade unions and industrial strike activity'. *American Economic Review*, 59, 1, 35–49.

Ashwin, S. 2011: 'Russian unions after communism: a study in subordination', in G. Gall, A. Wilkinson and R. Hurd (eds.), *The International Handbook of Labour Unions: Responses to Neo-Liberalism*. Cheltenham: Edward Elgar, 187–206.

Asis, M. 2005: 'Caring for the world: Filipino domestic workers gone global', in S. Huang, B. Yeoh and N. Abdul Rahman (eds.), *Asian Women as Transnational Domestic Migrants*. Singapore: Marshall Cavendish.

Atzeni, M. 2010: *Workplace Conflict*. Basingstoke: Palgrave Macmillan.

Atzeni, M. and Ghigliani, P. 2011: 'Pragmatism, ideology or politics? Unions' and workers' responses to the imposition of neo-liberalism in Argentina', in G. Gall, A. Wilkinson and R. Hurd (eds.), *The International Handbook of Labour Unions: Responses to Neo-Liberalism*. Cheltenham: Edward Elgar, 44–61.

Baah, A. Y. and Jauch, H. (eds.) 2009: *Chinese Investments in Africa: A Labour Perspective*. Accra: African Labour Research Network.

Baccaro, L. and Howell, C. 2011: 'A common neoliberal trajectory: the transformation of industrial relations in advanced capitalism'. *Politics and Society*, 39, 4, 521–63.

Bach, S. and Bordogna, L. 2011: 'Varieties of new public management or alternative models? The reform of public service employment relations in industrialized democracies'. *International Journal of Human Resource Management*, 22, 11, 2281–94.

Bairagya, I. 2012: 'Employment in India's informal sector: size, patterns, growth and determinants'. *Journal of the Asia Pacific Economy*, 17, 4, 593–615.

Balakrishnan, R. (ed.) 2002: *The Hidden Assembly Line: Gender Dynamics of Subcontracted Work in a Global Economy*. Bloomfield CT: Kumarian Press.

Baldamus, W. 1961: *Efficiency and Effort: An Analysis of Industrial Administration*. London: Tavistock Publications.

Ballard, R. 1994: *Desh Pardesh: the South Asian Presence in Britain*. London: Hurst & Co.

Bank Muñoz, C. 2008: *Transnational Tortillas: Race, Gender, and Shop-Floor Politics in Mexico and the United States*. Ithaca NY: ILR Press.

Barnard, C. 2012: 'The financial crisis and the Euro Plus Pact: a labour lawyer's perspective'. *Industrial Law Journal*, 41, 1, 98–114.

Barraclough, G (ed.) 1978: *The Times Atlas of World History*. London: Times Books.

Barrientos, S. 2008: 'Contract labour: the "Achilles Heel" of corporate codes in commercial value chains'. *Development and Change*, 39, 6, 977–90.

Barrientos, S. and Kritzinger, A. 2004: 'Squaring the circle: global production and the informalization of work in South African fruit exports'. *Journal of International Development*, 16, 81–92.

Barrientos, S., Kritzinger, A., Opondo, M. and Smith, S. 2005: 'Gender, work and vulnerability in African horticulture'. *IDS Bulletin – Institute of Development Studies*, 36, 2, 74–9.

Barrientos, S., Mayer, F., Pickles, J. and Posthuma, A. 2011: 'Decent work in global production networks: framing the policy debate'. *International Labour Review*, 150, 3–4, 299–317.

Barrientos, S. and Smith, S. 2007: 'Do workers benefit from ethical trade? Assessing codes of labour practice in global production systems'. *Third World Quarterly*, 28, 4, 713–29.

Bartlett, C. and Ghoshal, S. 1989: *Managing Across Borders: The Transnational Solution*. Boston: Harvard Business School Press.

Bartley, T. 2003: 'Certifying forests and factories: states, social movements, and the rise of private regulation in the apparel and forest products fields'. *Politics and Society*, 31, 3, 433–64.

Bartley, T. 2007: 'Institutional emergence in an era of globalization: the rise of transnational private regulation of labor and environmental conditions'. *American Journal of Sociology*, 113, 2, 297–351.

Bassett, T. 2010: 'Slim pickings: fairtrade cotton in West Africa'. *Geoforum*, 41, 1, 44–55.

Batalova, J. and Lowell, B. 2006: '"The best and the brightest": immigrant professionals in the U.S.', in M. Smith and A. Favell (eds.), *The Human Face of Global Mobility: International Highly Skilled Migration in Europe, North America and the Asia-Pacific*. New Brunswick NJ: Transaction Press, 81–101.

Bauman, Z. 1998a: *Globalization: The Human Consequences*. Cambridge: Polity.

Bauman, Z. 1998b: *Work, Consumerism and the New Poor*. Cambridge: Polity.

Bauman, Z. 2007: *Consuming Life*. Cambridge: Polity.

BBC News Online 2011: 'Bodies found as Mexicans march against drug violence', 7 April, www.bbc.co.uk/news/world-latin-america-12992664.

Beaverstock, J. 2002: 'Transnational elites in global cities: British expatriates in Singapore's financial district'. *Geoforum*, 33, 4, 525–38.

Beaverstock, J. 2005: 'Transnational elites in the city: British highly skilled inter-company transferees in New York City's financial district'. *Journal of Ethnic and Migration Studies*, 31, 2, 245–68.

Beaverstock, J. 2011: 'Servicing British expatriate "talent" in Singapore: exploring ordinary transnationalism and the role of the expatriate club'. *Journal of Ethnic and Migration Studies*, 37, 5, 709–28.

Beck, U. 2000: *The Brave New World of Work*. Cambridge: Polity.

Beinin, J. 2008: 'Underbelly of Egypt's neoliberal agenda'. Middle East Research and Information Project, 5 April, www.merip.org/mero/mero040508.

Bello, W., Docena, H., de Guzman, M. and Malig, M. 2005: *The Anti-Development State: The Political Economy of Permanent Crisis in the Philippines*. New York: Zed Books.

Benson, M. and O'Reilly, K. 2009: *Lifestyle Migration*. Farnham: Ashgate.

Bercusson, B. and Estlund, C. 2008: 'Regulating labour in the wake of globalisation: new challenges, new institutions', in B. Bercusson and C. Estlund (eds.), *Regulating Labour in the Wake of Globalisation*. Oxford: Hart Publishing, 1–18.

Bergh, A. and Nilsson, T. 2010: 'Do liberalization and globalization increase income inequality?' *European Journal of Political Economy*, 26, 4, 488–505.

Bernal-Meza, R. and Fryba-Christensen, S. 2012: 'Latin America's political and economic responses to the process of globalization', in M. Nilsson and J.

Gustafsson (eds.), *Latin American Responses to Globalization in the 21st Century*. Basingstoke: Palgrave Macmillan, 16–35.

Bhabha, H. 1994: *The Location of Culture*. London: Routledge.

Bhagwati, J. 2004: *In Defense of Globalization*. Oxford: Oxford University Press.

Bielenberg, A. (ed.) 2000: *The Irish Diaspora*. London: Pearson Education.

Bieler, A. and Lindberg, I. 2011: 'Globalization and the new challenges for transnational solidarity: an introduction', in A. Bieler and I. Lindberg (eds.), *Global Restructuring, Labour and the Challenges for Transnational Solidarity*. Abingdon: Routledge, 3–15.

Bieler, A., Lindberg, I. and Pillay, D. (eds.) 2008: *Labour and the Challenges of Globalization*. London: Pluto.

Biles, J. 2009: 'Informal work in Latin America: competing perspectives and recent debates'. *Geography Compass*, 3, 1, 214–36.

Birch, E. and Wachter, S. 2011: 'World urbanization: the critical issue of the twenty-first century', in E. Birch and S. Wachter (eds.), *Global Urbanization*. Philadelphia: University of Pennsylvania Press, 3–23.

Bird, D. 1992: 'International comparisons of industrial disputes in 1991'. *Employment Gazette*, December, 609–14.

Blanchflower, D. 2006: *A Cross-Country Study of Union Membership*. Bonn: Institute for the Study of Labour.

Blinder, A. 2006: 'Offshoring: the next industrial revolution?' *Foreign Affairs*, 85, 2, 113–28.

Blowfield, M. 1999: 'Ethical trade: a review of developments and issues'. *Third World Quarterly*, 20, 4, 753–70.

Blowfield, M. 2002: 'The ETI: a multistakeholder approach', in R. Jenkins, R. Pearson and G. Seyfang (eds.), *Corporate Responsibility and Labour Rights: Codes of Conduct in the Global Economy*. London: Earthscan, 184–95.

Boito, A. and Marcelino, P. 2011: 'Decline in unionism? An analysis of the new wave of strikes in Brazil'. *Latin American Perspectives*, 38, 5, 62–73.

Boserup, E. 1970: *Women's Role in Economic Development*. New York: St Martin's Press.

Boxall, P. and Macky, K. 2009: 'Research and theory on high-performance work systems: progressing the high-involvement stream'. *Human Resource Management Journal*, 19, 1, 3–23.

Boyer, R. 2005: 'How and why capitalisms differ'. *Economy and Society*, 34, 4, 509–57.

Bozkurt, O. 2006: 'Wired for work: highly skilled employment and global mobility in mobile telecommunications multinationals', in M. Smith and A. Favell (eds.), *The Human Face of Global Mobility*. New Brunswick NJ: Transaction Press, 211–46.

BP 2009: *Annual Review*, www.bp.com/assets/bp_internet/globalbp/globalbp_uk_english/set_branch/STAGING/common_assets/downloads/pdf/BP_Annual_Review_2009.pdf.

Bradley, H. 1996: *Men's Work, Women's Work*. Cambridge: Polity.

Bradley, H. 1999: *Gender and Power in the Workplace*. London: Macmillan.

Bradley, H., Erickson, M., Stephenson, C. and Williams, S. 2000: *Myths at Work*. Cambridge: Polity.

Bradley, H. and Healy, G. 2008: *Ethnicity and Gender at Work*. Basingstoke: Palgrave Macmillan.

Brah, A. and Phoenix, A. 2004: 'Ain't I a woman? Revisiting intersectionality'. *Journal of International Women's Studies*, 5, 3, 75–86.

Brandl, B. and Traxler, F. 2010: 'Labour conflicts: a cross-national analysis of economic and institutional determinants, 1971–2002'. *European Sociological Review*, 26, 5, 519–40.

Brandt, W. 1980: *North–South: A Program for Survival*. Cambridge MA: MIT Press.

Braverman, H. 1974: *Labor and Monopoly Capital: The Degradation of Work in the Twentieth Century.* New York: Monthly Review Press.

Breining-Kaufman, C. 2007: *Globalization and Labour Rights.* Oxford: Hart Publishing.

Brewster, C. and Wood, G. 2007: 'Introduction: comprehending industrial relations in Africa', in G. Wood and C. Brewster (eds.), *Industrial Relations in Africa.* Basingstoke: Palgrave Macmillan, 1–14.

Briskin, L. and McDermott, P. 1993: *Women Challenging Unions.* Toronto: Toronto University Press.

Brodzinsky, S. 2003: 'Coca-Cola boycott called after killings at Colombian plants'. *The Guardian*, 24 July, www.guardian.co.uk/media/2003/jul/24/marketingan-dpr.colombia.

Bronfenbrenner, K. 2005: 'Organizing women: the nature and process of union organizing efforts among US women workers since the mid-1990s'. *Work and Occupations*, 32, 4, 441–63.

Bronfenbrenner, K. and Juravich, T. 1998: 'It takes more than house calls: organizing to win with a comprehensive union-building strategy', in K. Bronfenbrenner, S. Friedman, R. Hurd, R. Oswald and R. Seeber (eds.), *Organizing to Win: New Research on Union Strategies.* Ithaca NY: ILR Press, 19–36.

Brooks, A. 2010: 'Spinning and weaving discontent: labour relations and the production of meaning at Zambia–China Mulungushi Textiles'. *Journal of Southern African Studies*, 36, 1, 113–32.

Brown, D. 2001: 'Labor standards: where do they belong on the international trade agenda?' *Journal of Economic Perspectives*, 15, 3, 89–112.

Buckley, P. 2009: 'The impact of the global factory on economic development'. *Journal of World Business*, 44, 131–43.

Buckley, P. and Casson, M. 1976: *The Future of the Multinational Enterprise.* London: Macmillan.

Bulut, T. and Lane, C. 2011: 'The private regulation of labour standards and rights in the global clothing industry: an evaluation of its effectiveness in two developing countries'. *New Political Economy*, 16, 1, 41–71.

Burawoy, M. 1985: *The Politics of Production.* London: Verso.

Burawoy, M. 2001: 'Manufacturing the global'. *Ethnography*, 2, 2, 147–59.

Burawoy, M., Blum, J., George, S., et al. 2000: *Global Ethnography.* Berkeley and Los Angeles CA: University of California Press.

Butcher, D. 2009: 'Ties that bind: the strategic use of transnational relationships in demarcating identity and managing difference'. *Journal of Ethnic and Migration Studies*, 35, 8, 1353–71.

Butler, S. 2012: 'Cambodian workers hold "people's tribunal" to look at factory conditions'. *The Guardian*, 2 February, www.guardian.co.uk/world/2012/feb/02/cambodian-workers-peoples-tribunal-factory?newsfeed=true.

Butler, T. 2003: 'Living in the bubble: gentrification and its "others" in North London'. *Urban Studies*, 40, 12, 2469–86.

Butler, T. and Lees, L. 2006: 'Super-gentrification in Barnsbury, London: globalization and gentrifying global elites at the neighbourhood level'. *Transactions of the Instiute of British Geographers*, NS 31, 467–87.

Cantin, É. 2008: 'Making the "workshop of the world": China and the international division of labour', in M. Taylor (ed.), *Global Economy Contested: Power and Conflict across the International Division of Labour.* Abingdon: Routledge, 51–76.

Caraway, T. 2007: *Assembling Women: The Feminization of Global Manufacturing.* Ithaca NY: Cornell University Press.

Caraway, T. 2009: 'Labor rights in East Asia: progress or regress?' *Journal of East Asian Studies*, 9, 2, 153–86.

Carew, A., Van Goethem, G., Gumbrell-McCormick, R. and van der Linden, M. 2000: *The International Confederation of Free Trade Unions: A History of the Organization and its Precursors.* Bern: Peter Lang.

Casanova, L. 2009: *Global Latinas: Latin America's Emerging Multinationals.* Basingstoke: Palgrave Macmillan.

Casey, C. 1995: *Work, Self and Society: After Industrialism.* London: Routledge.

Cashore, B. 2002: 'Legitimacy and the privatization of environmental governance: how non-state market-driven (NSMD) governance systems gain rule-making authority'. *Governance*, 15, 4, 503–29.

Caspersz, D. 2006: 'The "talk" versus the "walk": high performance work systems, labour market flexibility and lessons from Asian workers'. *Asia Pacific Business Review*, 12, 2, 149–61.

Castells, M. 2000: *The Rise of the Network Society: The Information Age, Economy, Society and Culture*, Volume I. Hoboken, NJ: John Wiley & Sons (2nd edition).

Castells, M. 2001: *The Internet Galaxy.* Oxford: Oxford University Press.

Castles, S. 2000: *Ethnicity and Globalization.* London: SAGE.

Castles, S. and Miller, M. 2009: *The Age of Migration.* London: Routledge (4th edition).

Cavanagh, J. 1997: 'The global resistance to sweatshops', in A. Ross (ed.), *No Sweat*. London: Verso, 39–50.

Chakravartty, P. 2006: 'White collar nationalisms'. *Social Semiotics*, 16, 1, 29–55.

Chan, A. 2001: *China's Workers under Assault.* Armonk NY: M. E. Sharpe.

Chan, A. 2011: 'Strikes in China's export industries in comparative perspective'. *The China Journal*, 65, 27–51.

Chan, A. and Xiaoyang, Z. 2003: 'Disciplinary labor regimes in Chinese factories'. *Critical Asian Studies*, 35, 4, 559–84.

Chan, C. K. C. 2009: 'Strike and changing workplace relations in a Chinese global factory'. *Industrial Relations Journal*, 40, 1, 60–77.

Chan, C. K. C. 2010: *The Challenge of Labour in China: Strikes and the Changing Labour Regime in Global Factories.* Abingdon: Routledge.

Chan, C. K. C., Pun, N. and Chan, J. 2010: 'The role of the state, labour policy and migrant workers' struggles in globalized China', in P. Bowles and J. Harriss (eds.), *Globalization and Labour in China and India: Impacts and Responses.* Basingstoke: Palgrave Macmillan, 45–63.

Chang, D. 2009: 'Informalising labour in Asia's global factory'. *Journal of Contemporary Asia*, 39, 2, 161–79.

Chang, L. 2009: *Factory Girls: Voices from the Heart of Modern China.* London: Picador.

Chen, F. 2006: 'Privatization and its discontents in Chinese factories'. *The China Quarterly*, 185, 42–60.

Christopherson, S. 2007: 'Barriers to "US-style" lean retailing – the case of Wal-Mart's failure in Germany'. *Journal of Economic Geography*, 7, 4, 451–69.

Chun, J. 2001: 'Flexible despotism: the intensification of insecurity and uncertainty in the lives of Silicon Valley's high-tech assembly workers', in R. Baldoz, C. Koeber and P. Kraft (eds.), *The Critical Study of Work: Labor, Technology and Global Production.* Philadelphia: Temple University Press, 127–54.

CIA 2012: *CIA World Factbook*, https://www.cia.gov/library/publications/the-world-factbook/.

Clean Clothes Campaign 2009: *Full Package Approach to Labour Codes of Conduct.* Amsterdam: Clean Clothes Campaign.

Cleveland, S. 2003: 'Why international labor standards?' in R. Flanagan and W. Gould IV (eds.), *International Labor Standards: Globalization, Trade, and Public Policy.* Stanford CA: Stanford University Press, 129–78.

Coates, D. 2000: *Models of Capitalism: Growth and Stagnation in the Modern Era.* Cambridge: Polity.

Coe, N. 2012: 'Geographies of production II: global production networks A–Z'. *Progress in Human Geography,* 36, 3, 389–402.

Coe, N. 2013: 'Geographies of production III: making space for labour'. *Progress in Human Geography,* 37, 2, 271–84.

Coe, N., Dicken, P. and Hess, M. 2008: 'Global production networks: realizing the potential'. *Journal of Economic Geography,* 8, 3, 271–90.

Cohen, R. 1991: *Contested Domains.* London: Zed Books.

Cohen, R. 2006: *Migration and its Enemies: Global Capital, Migrant Labour and the Nation State.* Aldershot: Ashgate.

Cohen, R. and Kennedy, P. 2000: *Global Sociology.* London: Macmillan.

Collins, J. 2003: *Threads: Gender, Labor, and Power in the Global Apparel Industry.* Chicago: University of Chicago Press.

Collins Hill, P. 2000: *Black Feminist Thought: Knowledge, Consciousness and the Politics of Empowerment.* London: Routledge.

Compa, L. 2001: 'Free trade, fair trade and the battle for labor rights', in L. Turner, H. Katz and R. Hurd (eds.), *Rekindling the Movement: Labor's Quest for Relevance in the Twenty-First Century.* Ithaca NY: Cornell University Press, 314–38.

Compa, L. and Diamond, S. (eds.) 2003: *Human Rights, Labor Rights and International Trade.* Philadelphia PA: University of Pennsylvania Press.

Cooke, F. L. (2008). 'The changing dynamics of employment relations in China: an evaluation of the rising level of labour disputes'. *Journal of Industrial Relations,* 50, 1, 111–38.

Cooper, R. and Ellem, B. 2008: 'Annual review article 2007: the neoliberal state, trade unions and collective bargaining in Australia'. *British Journal of Industrial Relations,* 46, 3, 532–54.

Cravey, A. 1998: *Women and Work in Mexico's Maquiladoras.* Lanham MD: Rowman & Littlefield.

Cravey, A. 2004: 'Students and the anti-sweatshop movement'. *Antipode,* 36, 2, 203–8.

Cravey, A. 2005: 'Working on the global assembly line', in L. Nelson and J. Seager (eds.), *A Companion to Feminist Geography.* Oxford: Blackwell Publishing, 109–22.

Crenshaw, K. 1991: 'Mapping the margins: intersectionality, identity politics, and violence against women of colour'. *Stanford Law Review,* 43, 6, 1241–99.

Crompton, R. 1997: *Women's Work in Modern Britain.* Oxford: Oxford University Press.

Crompton, R. and Sanderson, K. 1990: *Gendered Jobs and Social Change.* London: Unwin Hyman.

Crouch, C. 2005: *Capitalist Diversity and Change.* Oxford: Oxford University Press.

Crouch, C. 2011: *The Strange Non-Death of Neoliberalism.* Cambridge: Polity.

Croucher, R. and Cotton, E. 2009: *Global Unions, Global Business.* Hendon: Middlesex University Press.

Dahrendorf, R. 1959: *Class and Class Conflict in Industrial Society.* London: Routledge.

Daniels, G. 2009: 'In the field: a decade of organizing', in G. Daniels and J. McIlroy (eds.), *Trade Unions in a Neo Liberal World: British Trade Unions under New Labour.* Abingdon: Routledge, 254–82.

Das, D., Dharwadkar, R. and Brandes, P. 2008: 'The importance of being "Indian": identity centrality and work outcomes in an off-shored call center in India'. *Human Relations,* 61, 11, 1499–530.

Davis, G. 2000: 'The Irish in Britain', in A. Bielenberg (ed.), *The Irish Diaspora.* London: Pearson Education, 19–36.

Davis, M. 2004: 'Planet of slums: urban involution and the informal proletariat'. *New Left Review*, 26, 5–34.

Deacon, B. 2007: *Global Social Policy and Governance*. London: SAGE.

Deardoff, A. and Stern, R. 2002: 'What you should know about globalization and the World Trade Organization'. *Review of International Economics*, 10, 3, 404–23.

Deere, C. 2005: *The Feminization of Agriculture? Economic Restructuring in Rural Latin America*. Geneva: United Nations Research Institute for Social Development.

Delbridge, R., Hauptmeier, M. and Sengupta, S. 2011: 'Beyond the enterprise: broadening the horizons of international HRM'. *Human Relations*, 64, 4, 483–505.

Devadason, R. 2010: 'Cosmopolitanism, geographical imaginaries and belonging in North London'. *Urban Studies*, 47, 14, 2945–63.

Devadason, R. 2012: *Humanitarians without Borders: Work, Mobility and Wellbeing in UNHCR*. UNHCR Policy and Evaluation Service paper series, no. 237, available at www.unhcr.org/4fbf50549.html.

Devadason, R. and Fenton, S. 2013: 'Power, reflexivity and difference in a multinational corporation'. *Ethnicities*, 13, 4, 475–93.

Deyo, F. 1989: *Beneath the Miracle: Labor Subordination in the New Asian Industrialism*. Berkeley CA: University of California Press.

Diallo, Y., Hagemann, F., Etienne, A., Garbuzer, Y. and Mehran, F. 2010: *Global Child Labour Developments: Measuring Trends from 2004 to 2008*. Geneva: ILO.

Dicken, P. 2007: *Global Shift: Mapping the Contours of the World Economy*. London: SAGE (5th edition).

Dixon, M. and Fiorito, J. 2009: 'Can unions rebound? Decline and renewal in the US labour movement', in G. Gall (ed.), *Union Revitalisation in Advanced Economies: Assessing the Contribution of Union Organising*. Basingstoke: Palgrave Macmillan, 154–74.

Doogan, K. 2009: *New Capitalism?* Cambridge: Polity.

Dore, R. 1973: *British Factory – Japanese Factory*. Berkeley CA: University of California Press.

Dörrenbächer, C. and Geppert, M. (eds.) 2011: *Politics and Power in the Multinational Corporation*. Cambridge: Cambridge University Press.

du Gay, P. 1996: *Consumption and Identity at Work*. London: SAGE.

Dumont, J.-C., Spielvogel, G. and Widmaier, S. 2010: *International Migrants in Developed, Emerging and Developing Countries: An Extended Profile*. OECD Social, Employment and Migration Working Papers No.114, www.oecd.org/els/workingpapers.

Dunning, J. 1997: *Alliance Capitalism and Global Business*. London: Routledge.

Dunning, J. 2000: 'The eclectic paradigm as an envelope for economic and business theories of MNE activity'. *International Business Review*, 9, 2, 163–90.

Dunning, J. 2001: 'The eclectic (OLI) paradigm of international production: past, present and future'. *International Journal of the Economics of Business*, 8, 2, 173–90.

Dunning, J. and Lundan, S. 2008: *Multinational Companies and the Global Economy*. Cheltenham: Edward Elgar (2nd edition).

The Economist 2012: 'Caught in the net', 28 January, 37–8.

Edwards, P. 1986: *Conflict at Work*. Oxford: Basil Blackwell.

Edwards, P. and Wajcman, J. 2005: *The Politics of Working Life*. Oxford: Oxford University Press.

Edwards, R. 1979: *Contested Terrain: The Transformation of the Workplace in the Twentieth Century*. London: Heinemann.

Edwards, T. 2011: 'The transfer of employment practices across borders in multinational companies', in A.-W. Harzing and A. Pinnington (eds.), *International Human Resource Management*. London: SAGE, 267–90 (3rd edition).

Edwards, T., Colling, T. and Ferner, A. 2007: 'Conceptual approaches to the transfer of employment practices in multinational companies: an integrated approach'. *Human Resource Management Journal*, 17, 3, 201–17.

Edwards, T. and Ferner, A. 2002: 'The renewed "American challenge": a review of employment practice in US multinationals'. *Industrial Relations Journal*, 33, 2, 94–111.

Egels-Zandén, N. 2007: 'Suppliers' compliance with MNCs' codes of conduct: behind the scenes at Chinese toy suppliers'. *Journal of Business Ethics*, 75, 45–62.

Ehrenreich, B. and Hochschild, A. 2003: *Global Woman: Nannies, Maids and Sex Workers in the New Economy*. London: Granta.

Elger, T. and Smith, C. 2005: *Assembling Work*. Oxford: Oxford University Press.

Elias, J. 2004: *Fashioning Inequality: The Multinational Company and Gendered Employment in a Globalizing World*. Aldershot: Ashgate.

Elias, J. 2005: 'The gendered political economy of control and resistance on the shop floor of the multinational firm: a case-study from Malaysia'. *New Political Economy*, 10, 2, 203–22.

Elliott, K. and Freeman, R. 2003: *Can Labor Standards Improve under Globalization?* Washington DC: Institute for International Economics.

Elson, D. and Pearson, R. 1981: '"Nimble fingers make cheap workers": an analysis of women's employment in third world export manufacturing'. *Feminist Review*, Spring, 87–107.

Employment Gazette 1983: 'International comparisons of stoppages'. *Employment Gazette*, March, 105–14.

Erickson, M., Bradley, H., Stephenson, C. and Williams, S. 2009: *Business in Society*. Cambridge: Polity.

Erickson, C., Fisk, C., Milkman, R., Mitchell, D. and Wong, K. 2002: 'Justice for Janitors in Los Angeles: lessons from three rounds of negotiation'. *British Journal of Industrial Relations*, 40, 3, 543–67.

Esbenshade, J. 2004: *Monitoring Sweatshops: Workers, Consumers and the Global Apparel Industry*. Philadelphia PA: Temple University Press.

Esping-Andersen, G. 1990: *The Three Worlds of Welfare Capitalism*. Cambridge: Polity.

Etchemendy, S. and Collier, R. 2007: 'Down but not out: union resurgence and segmented neocorporatism in Argentina (2003–2007)'. *Politics and Society*, 35, 3, 363–401.

Eurostat 2013: *Gender Pay Gap Statistics*, http://epp.eurostat.ec.europa.eu/statistics_explained/index.php/Gender_pay_gap_statistics.

Everett, J., Neu, D. and Martinez, D. 2007: 'Multi-stakeholder labour monitoring organizations: egoists, instrumentalists, or moralists?' *Journal of Business Ethics*, 81, 117–42.

Fairbrother, P. 1989: *Workplace Unionism in the 1980s: A Process of Renewal*. London: Workers Educational Association.

Fanon, F. 1967: *Black Skin White Masks*. New York: Grove Press.

Farndale, E., Scullion, H. and Sparrow, P. 2010: 'The role of the corporate HR function in global talent management'. *Journal of World Business*, 45, 161–8.

Favell, A. 2008: *Eurostars and Eurocities: Free Movement and Mobility in an Integrating Europe*. Oxford: Blackwell.

Favell, A., Feldblum, M. and Smith, M. 2006: 'The human face of global mobility: a research agenda', in M. Smith and A. Favell (eds.), *The Human Face of Global Mobility*. New Brunswick NJ: Transaction Books, 1–25.

Featherstone, L. and United Students Against Sweatshops 2002: *Students Against Sweatshops*. London: Verso.

Fechter, A.-M. 2007: *Transnational Lives: Expatriates in Indonesia*. Farnham: Ashgate.

Fernández-Kelly, M. 1983: *For We are Sold, I and My People: Women and Industry in Mexico's Frontier*. Albany NY: State University of New York Press.

Ferner, A. 2010: 'HRM in multinational companies', in A. Wilkinson, N. Bacon, T. Redman and S. Snell (eds.), *The SAGE Handbook of Human Resource Management*. London: SAGE, 541–60.

Ferner, A., Almond, P. and Colling, T. 2005: 'Institutional theory and the cross-national transfer of employment policy: the case of "workforce diversity" in US multinationals'. *Journal of International Business Studies*, 36, 304–21.

Ferner, A. and Edwards, P. 1995: 'Power and the diffusion of organizational change within multinational corporations'. *European Journal of Industrial Relations*, 1, 2, 229–57.

Ferner, A., Edwards, T. and Tempel, A. 2012: 'Power, institutions and the cross-national transfer of employment practices in multinationals'. *Human Relations*, 65, 2, 163–87.

Fields, G. 2003: 'International labor standards and decent work: perspectives from the developing world', in R. Flanagan and W. Gould IV (eds.), *International Labor Standards: Globalization, Trade, and Public Policy*. Stanford CA: Stanford University Press, 61–79.

Fine, J. 2006: *Worker Centers: Organizing Communities at the Edge of the Dream*. Ithaca NY: Cornell University Press.

Fishman, C. 2007: *The Wal-mart Effect*. New York: Penguin.

Flanagan, R. 2003: 'Labor standards and international competitive advantage', in R. Flanagan and W. Gould IV (eds.), *International Labor Standards: Globalization, Trade, and Public Policy*. Stanford CA: Stanford University Press, 15–59.

Flanagan, R. 2006: *Globalization and Labor Conditions: Working Conditions and Worker Rights in a Global Economy*. New York: Oxford University Press.

Fletcher, B. 2011: 'Interaction between labour unions and social movements', in G. Gall, A. Wilkinson and R. Hurd (eds.), *The International Handbook of Labour Unions: Responses to Neo-Liberalism*. Cheltenham: Edward Elgar, 270–90.

Fougner, T. and Kurtoğlu, A. 2011: 'Transnational labour solidarity and social movement unionism: insights from and beyond a women workers' strike in Turkey'. *British Journal of Industrial Relations*, 49, S2, s353–75.

Freeman, C. 2000: *High Tech and High Heels in the Global Economy*. Durham NC: Duke University Press.

Freeman, G. and Hill, D. 2006: 'Disaggregating immigration policy: the politics of skilled labor recruitment in the US', in M. Smith and A. Favell (eds.), *The Human Face of Global Mobility: International Highly Skilled Migration in Europe, North America and the Asia-Pacific*. New Brunswick NJ: Transaction Press, 103–30.

Freeman, R. 2005: *Labour Market Institutions without Blinders: The Debate over Flexibility and Labour Market Performance*. NBER Working Paper No.11286.

Frege, C. 2006: 'International trends in unionization', in M. Morley, P. Gunnigle and D. Collins (eds.), *Global Industrial Relations*. London: Routledge, 221–38.

Frenkel, S. 2001: 'Globalization, athletic footwear commodity chains and employment relations in China'. *Organization Studies*, 22, 4, 531–62.

Frenkel, S. 2006: 'Towards a theory of dominant interests, globalization, and work', in M. Korczynski, R. Hodson and P. Edwards (eds.), *Social Theory at Work*. Oxford: Oxford University Press, 388–423.

Frenkel, S. and Kim, S. 2004: 'Corporate codes of labour practice and employment relations in sports shoe contractor factories in South Korea'. *Asia Pacific Journal of Human Resources*, 42, 1, 6–31.

Frenkel, S. and Scott, D. 2002: 'Compliance, collaboration, and codes of labor practice: the Adidas connection'. *California Management Review*, 45, 1, 29–49.

Friedman, A. 1977: *Industry and Labour: Class Struggle at Work and Monopoly Capitalism.* London: Macmillan.

Friedman, E. and Lee, C. K. 2010: 'Remaking the world of Chinese labour: a 30-year retrospective'. *British Journal of Industrial Relations*, 48, 3, 507–33.

Friedman, T. 2006: *The World is Flat: The Globalized World in the Twenty-First Century.* London: Penguin (new edition).

Froebel, F., Heinrichs, J. and Kreye, O. 1980: *The New International Division of Labour.* Cambridge: Cambridge University Press.

Froud, J., Haslam, C., Johal, S. and Williams, K. 2000: 'Shareholder value and financialization: consultancy promises, management moves'. *Economy and Society*, 29, 1, 80–110.

Fuentes, A. and Ehrenreich, B. 1983: *Women in the Global Factory.* Boston: South End Press.

Gabel, M. and Bruner, H. 2003: *Global Inc: An Atlas of the Multinational Corporation.* New York: New Press.

Gall, G. 1999: 'A review of strike activity in Western Europe at the end of the second millennium'. *Employee Relations*, 21, 4, 357–77.

Gall, G. and Hebdon, R. 2008: 'Conflict at work', in P. Blyton, N. Bacon, J. Fiorito and E. Heery (eds.), *The SAGE Handbook of Industrial Relations.* London: SAGE, 588–605.

Gall, G., Hurd, R. and Wilkinson, A. 2011: 'Labour unionism and neo-liberalism', in G. Gall, A. Wilkinson and R. Hurd (eds.), *The International Handbook of Labour Unions: Responses to Neo-Liberalism.* Cheltenham: Edward Elgar, 1–12.

Gallagher, M. 2005: *Contagious Capitalism: Globalization and the Politics of Labor in China.* Princeton NJ: Princeton University Press.

Gallie, D. 1978: *In Search of the New Working Class.* Cambridge: Cambridge University Press.

Gallie, D. (ed.) 2007: *Employment Regimes and the Quality of Work.* Oxford: Oxford University Press.

Gallin, D. 2001: 'Propositions on trade unions and informal employment in times of globalization'. *Antipode*, 3, 3, 531–49.

Gallin, S. 1990: 'Women and the export industry in Taiwan: the muting of class consciousness', in K. Ward (ed.), *Women Workers and Global Restructuring.* Ithaca NY: ILR Press, 179–92.

Gamble, J. 2006: 'Introducing Western-style HRM practices to China: shopfloor perceptions in a British multinational'. *Journal of World Business*, 41, 328–43.

Gamble, J. 2011: *Multinational Retailers and Consumers in China: Transferring Organizational Practices from the United Kingdom and Japan.* Basingstoke: Palgrave Macmillan.

Garay, C. 2007: 'Social policy and collective action: unemployed workers, community associations and protest in Argentina'. *Politics and Society*, 35, 2, 301–28.

Geiger-Oneto, S. and Arnould, E. 2011: 'Alternative trade organization and subjective quality of life: the case of Latin American coffee producers'. *Journal of Macromarketing*, 31, 3, 276–90.

Gereffi, G., Humphrey, J. and Sturgeon, T. 2005: 'The governance of global value chains'. *International Review of Political Economy*, 12, 1, 78–104.

Ghigliani, P. 2005: 'International trade unionism in a globalizing world: a case study of new labour internationalism'. *Economic and Industrial Democracy*, 26, 3, 359–81.

Giddens, A. 1990: *The Consequences of Modernity.* Cambridge: Polity.

Giddens, A. 2011: *The Politics of Climate Change.* Cambridge: Polity.

Giles, J., Park, A., Cui. F. and Du, Yang 2012: *Weathering the Storm: Survey-based Perspectives on Employment in China in the Aftermath of the Global Financial Crisis.* World Bank Policy Research Working Paper No. WPS 5984.

Glucksmann, M. 1995: 'Why "work"? Gender and the "total social organization of labour"'. *Gender, Work and* Organization 2, 2, 63–75.

Godard, J. 2011: 'What has happened to strikes?' *British Journal of Industrial Relations*, 49, 2, 282–305.

Goldthorpe, J. 1984: *Order and Conflict in Contemporary Capitalism.* Oxford: Clarendon.

Goldthorpe, J., Bechofer, F., Lockwood, D. and Platt, J. 1968: *The Affluent Worker: Industrial Attitudes and Behaviour.* Cambridge: Cambridge University Press.

Goldthorpe, J., Bechofer, F., Lockwood, D. and Platt, J. 1969: *The Affluent Worker in the Class Structure.* Cambridge: Cambridge University Press.

Gould IV, W. 2003: 'Labor law for a global economy: the uneasy case for international labor standards', in R. Flanagan and W. Gould IV (eds.), *International Labor Standards: Globalization, Trade, and Public Policy.* Stanford CA: Stanford University Press, 81–128.

Government of India 2012: *Economic Survey 2010–11.* Chandigarh: Government of India.

Gray, M., Kittilson, M. and Sandholtz, W. 2006: 'Women and globalization: a study of 180 countries, 1975–2000'. *International Organization*, 60, 293–333.

Greene, S. and Robertson, G. 2010: 'Politics, justice and the new Russian strike'. *Communist and Post-Communist Studies*, 43, 73–95.

Greer, I. and Hauptmeier, M. 2008: 'Political entrepreneurs and co-managers: labour transnationalism at four multinational auto companies'. *British Journal of Industrial Relations*, 46, 1, 76–97.

Gross, J. 2003: 'A long overdue beginning: the promotion and protection of workers' rights as human rights', in J. Gross (ed.), *Workers' Rights as Human Rights.* Ithaca NY: Cornell University Press, 1–22.

Gross, J. 2009: 'Takin' it to the man: human rights at the American workplace', in J. Gross and L. Compa (eds.), *Human Rights in Labor and Employment Relations: International and Comparative Perspectives.* Champaign IL: Labor and Employment Relations Association, 13–41.

Gross, J. and Compa, L. 2009: 'Introduction', in J. Gross and L. Compa (eds.), *Human Rights in Labor and Employment Relations: International and Comparative Perspectives.* Champaign IL: Labor and Employment Relations Association, 1–11.

Grossman, R. 1979: 'Women's place in the integrated circuit'. *South East Asia Chronicle – Pacific Research*, 66, 9, 2–17.

Grunwald, J. and Flamm, K. 1985: *The Global Factory: Foreign Assembly in International Trade.* Washington DC: The Brookings Institution.

Gumbrell-McCormick, R. 2013: 'The International Trade Union Confederation: from two (or more?) identities to one'. *British Journal of Industrial Relations*, 51, 2, 240–63.

Gunawardana, S. 2007: 'Struggle, perseverance and organization in Sri Lanka's export processing zones', in K. Bronfenbrenner (ed.), *Global Unions: Challenging Transnational Capital through Cross-Border Campaigns.* Ithaca NY: Cornell University Press, 78–98.

Gupta, A. 2012: 'What Occupy taught the unions'. *Salon.com*, 2 February, www.salon.com/2012/02/02/occupys_challenge_to_big_labor/.

Hakim, C. 1979: *Occupational Segregation by Sex.* Department of Employment Research Paper No. 9. London: Department of Employment.

Hale, A. and Wills, J. (eds.) 2005: *Threads of Labour: Garment Industry Supply Chains from the Workers' Perspective.* Oxford: Blackwell.

Hale, D. 2008: 'International comparisons of labour disputes in 2006'. *Economic and Labour Market Review*, 2, 4, 32–9.

Halkier, B. 2010: *Consumption Challenged*. Farnham: Ashgate.

Hall, J. and Leeson, P. 2007: 'Good for the goose, bad for the gander: international labor standards and comparative development'. *Journal of Labor Research*, 28, 658–76.

Hall, P. and Soskice, D. 2001: 'An introduction to varieties of capitalism', in P. Hall and D. Soskice (eds.), *Varieties of Capitalism: The Institutional Foundations of Comparative Advantage*. Oxford: Oxford University Press, 1–68.

Hamann, K. and Kelly, J. 2008: 'Varieties of capitalism and industrial relations', in P. Blyton, N. Bacon, J. Fiorito and E. Heery (eds.), *The SAGE Handbook of Industrial Relations*. London: SAGE, 129–48.

Hancké, B. (ed.) 2009: *Debating Varieties of Capitalism*. Oxford: Oxford University Press.

Hancké, B., Rhodes, M. and Thatcher, M. (eds.) 2007: *Beyond Varieties of Capitalism: Conflict, Contradictions and Complementarities in the European Economy*. Oxford: Oxford University Press.

Hannerz, U. 1990: 'Cosmopolitans and locals in a world culture', in M. Featherstone (ed.), *Global Culture: Nationalism, Globalization and Modernity*. London: SAGE, 237–51.

Hannerz, U. 2006: *Transnational Connections*. London and New York: Routledge.

Harris, R.-A. 1994: *The Nearest Place that Wasn't Ireland: Early Nineteenth-Century Labor Migration*. Ames: Iowa State University Press.

Harvey, D. 1982: *The Limits to Capital*. Oxford: Blackwell.

Harvey, D. 1989: *The Condition of Postmodernity*. Oxford: Blackwell.

Harvey, D. 2005: *A Brief History of Neoliberalism*. Oxford: Oxford University Press.

Harvey, D. 2011: *The Enigma of Capital*. London: Profile Books.

Hassel, A. 2008: 'The evolution of a global labor governance regime'. *Governance*, 21, 2, 231–51.

Hays, S. 1996: *The Cultural Contradictions of Motherhood*. New Haven CT: Yale University Press.

Hayter, S. and Weinberg, B. 2011: 'Mind the gap: collective bargaining and wage inequality', in S. Hayter (ed.), *The Role of Collective Bargaining in the Global Economy: Negotiating for Social Justice*. Cheltenham: Edward Elgar, 136–86.

Heath, A. 2007: 'Cross-national patterns and processes of ethnic disadvantage'. *Proceedings of the British Academy*, 137, 639–95.

Heath, A. and Cheung, S. Y. 2006: *Ethnic Penalties in the Labour Market: Employers and Discrimination*. Department for Work and Pensions Research Report No. 237. Leeds: Department for Work and Pensions.

Heath, A. and McMahon, D. 1997: 'Education and occupational attainments: the impact of ethnic origins', in V. Karn (ed.), *Ethnicity in the 1991 Census*. TSO: London, 91–113.

Heery, E. and Simms, M. 2011: 'Seizing an opportunity? Union organizing campaigns in Britain, 1998–2004'. *Labor History*, 52, 1, 23–47.

Heery, E., Simms, M. and Delbridge, R. 2003: *The Organizing Academy – Five Years On*. Cardiff: New Unionism Research Unit at Cardiff Business School.

Held, D. 1995: *Reinventing the Global Order: From the Modern State to Cosmopolitan Governance*. Cambridge: Polity.

Held, D. and McGrew, A. 2007: *Globalization/Anti-Globalization*. Cambridge: Polity.

Held, D., McGrew, A., Goldblatt, D. and Perraton, J. 1999: *Global Transformations*. Cambridge: Polity.

Hepple, B. 2005: *Labour Laws and Global Trade*. Oxford: Hart Publishing.

Herod, A., Rainnie, A. and McGrath-Champ, S. 2007: 'Working space: why incorporating the geographical is central to theorizing work and employment practices'. *Work, Employment and Society*, 21, 2, 247–64.

Hill, E. 2009: 'The Indian industrial relations system: struggling to address the dynamics of a globalizing economy'. *Journal of Industrial Relations*, 51, 3, 395–410.

Hirst, P., Thompson, G. and Bromley, S. 2009: *Globalization in Question*. Cambridge: Polity (3rd edition).

Hobsbawm, E. 1995: *The Age of Empire*. London: Weidenfeld & Nicolson (2nd edition).

Hochschild, A. R. 1983: *The Managed Heart*. Berkeley CA: University of California Press.

Hochschild, A. R. 1989: *The Second Shift*. London: Piatkus.

Hochschild, A. R. 2000: 'Global care chains and emotional surplus value', in W. Hutton and A. Giddens (eds.), *On the Edge: Living with Global Capitalism*. London: Jonathan Cape, 130–46.

Hochschild, A. R. 2003: *The Commercialization of Intimate Life*. San Francisco and Los Angeles CA: University of California Press.

Hofstede, G. 2001: *Culture's Consequences*. Thousand Oaks CA: SAGE (2nd edition).

Home Office 2011: 'High value migrants', www.ukba.homeoffice.gov.uk/visas-immigration/working/tier1/.

Hsiung, P. C. 1996: *Living Rooms as Factories: Class, Gender and the Satellite Factory System in Taiwan*. Philadelphia PA: Temple University Press.

Hudson, R. 2001: *Producing Places*. New York: Guilford Press.

Hutton, W. 2002: *The World We're In*. London: Little, Brown.

Hyman, R. 1977: *Strikes*. Glasgow: Fontana/Collins (2nd edition).

Hyman, R. 1989: *The Political Economy of Industrial Relations*. Basingstoke: Macmillan.

Hyman, R. 2001: *Understanding European Trade Unionism: Between Market, Class and Society*. London: SAGE.

Hymer, S. 1976: *The International Operations of National Firms: A Study of Direct Foreign Investment*. Cambridge MA: MIT Press.

(ILO) International Labour Organization 2002: *Decent Work and the Informal Economy*. Geneva: ILO.

(ILO) International Labour Organization 2003: *Global Employment Trends Model*. Geneva: ILO.

(ILO) International Labour Organization 2004: *A Fair Globalisation: The Role of the ILO*. Geneva: ILO.

(ILO) International Labour Organization 2009: *Rules of the Game: A Brief Introduction to International Labour Standards*. Geneva: ILO (revised edition).

(ILO) International Labour Organization 2010: *World of Work Report 2010: From One Crisis to the Next?* Geneva: ILO, International Institute for Labour Studies.

(ILO) International Labour Organization 2011: *World of Work Report 2011: Making Markets Work for Jobs*. Geneva: ILO, International Institute for Labour Studies.

(ILO) International Labour Organization 2012a: *Global Employment Trends 2012*. Geneva: ILO.

(ILO) International Labour Organization 2012b: *World of Work Report 2012: Better Jobs for a Better Economy*. Geneva: ILO, International Institute for Labour Studies.

Inglehart, R. 1977: *The Silent Revolution: Changing Values and Political Styles among Western Publics*. Princeton NJ: Princeton University Press.

Iredale, R. 2001: 'The migration of professionals: theories and typologies'. *International Migration*, 39, 5, 7–26.

(ITUC) International Trade Union Confederation 2012: *Annual Survey of Violations of Trade Union Rights 2012*, http://survey.ituc-csi.org/.

Jack, G. and Lorbiecki, A. 2007: 'National identity, globalization and the discursive reconstruction of organizational identity'. *British Journal of Management*, 18, S79–94.

Jackson, V. 2010: 'Belonging against the national odds: globalization, political insecurity and Philippine migrant workers in Israel'. *Global Society*, 25, 1, 49–71.

Jenkins, J. and Turnbull, P. 2011: 'Can workers of the world unite? Globalization and the employment relationship', in P. Blyton, E. Heery and P. Turnbull (eds.), *Reassessing the Employment Relationship*. Basingstoke: Palgrave Macmillan, 195–224.

Jenkins, R., Pearson, R. and Seyfang, G. 2002: 'Introduction' in R. Jenkins, R. Pearson and G. Seyfang (eds.), *Corporate Responsibility and Labour Rights: Codes of Conduct in the Global Economy*. London: Earthscan, 1–10.

Jenkins, S., Delbridge, R. and Roberts, A. 2010: 'Emotional management in a mass customised call centre: examining skill and knowledgeability in interactive service work'. *Work, Employment & Society*, 24, 3, 546–64.

Johannessen, S. and Wilhite, H. 2010: 'Who really benefits from fair-trade? An analysis of value distribution in fair-trade coffee'. *Globalizations*, 7, 4, 525–44.

Johns, R. 1998: 'Bridging the gap between class and space: US worker solidarity with Guatemala'. *Economic Geography*, 74, 3, 252–72.

Jones, A. 2008: 'The rise of global work'. *Transactions of the Institute of British Geographers*, 33, 12–26.

Jones, G. 2005: *Multinationals and Global Capitalism: From the Nineteenth to the Twenty-First Century*. Oxford: Oxford University Press.

Juravich, T. 2007: 'Beating global capital: a framework and method for union strategic corporate research and campaigns', in K. Bronfenbrenner (ed.), *Global Unions: Challenging Transnational Capital through Cross-Border Campaigns*. Ithaca NY: Cornell University Press, 16–39.

Juliawan, B. 2011: 'Street-level politics: labour protests in post-authoritarian Indonesia'. *Journal of Contemporary Asia*, 41, 3, 349–70.

Kalleberg, A. 2009: 'Precarious work, insecure workers: employment relations in transition'. *American Sociological Review*, 74, 1, 1–22.

Kalleberg, A. 2011: *Good Jobs, Bad Jobs: The Rise of Polarized and Precarious Employment Systems in the United States, 1970s to 2000s*. New York: Russell Sage Foundation.

Kalm, S. 2001: 'Emancipation or exploitation? A study of women workers in Mexico's maquiladora industry'. *Statsvetenskaplig Tidskrift*, 104, 3, 224–58.

Kaplinsky, R. 2005: *Globalization, Poverty and Inequalities*. Cambridge: Polity.

Katz, H. and Darbishire, O. 2000: *Converging Divergences: Worldwide Changes in Employment Systems*. Ithaca NY: Cornell University Press.

Kaufman, B. 2004: *The Global Evolution of Industrial Relations*. Geneva: ILO.

Kaur, A. 2000: 'Working on the global conveyor belt: women workers in industrialising Malaysia'. *Asian Studies Review*, 24, 2, 213–30.

Kaur, A. 2004a: 'Economic globalisation, trade liberalisation and labour-intensive export manufactures: an Asian perspective', in A. Kaur (ed.), *Women Workers in Industrialising Asia: Costed, Not Valued*. Basingstoke: Palgrave Macmillan, 17–34.

Kaur, A. 2004b: 'The global factory: cross-border production networks and women workers in Asia', in A. Kaur (ed.), *Women Workers in Industrialising Asia: Costed, Not Valued*. Basingstoke: Palgrave Macmillan, 99–127.

Keck, M. and Sikkink, K. 1998: *Activists Beyond Borders: Advocacy Networks in International Politics*. Ithaca NY: Cornell University Press.

Kelly, J. 1998: *Rethinking Industrial Relations*. London: Routledge.

Kelly, J. 2011: 'Theories of collective action and union power', in G. Gall, A. Wilkinson and R. Hurd (eds.), *The International Handbook of Labour Unions: Responses to Neo-Liberalism*. Cheltenham: Edward Elgar, 13–28.

Kelly, P. 2001: 'The political economy of local labour control in the Philippines'. *Economic Geography*, 77, 1, 1–22.

Kerr, C., Dunlop, J., Harbison, F. and Myers, C. 1962: *Industrialism and Industrial Man*. London: Heinemann.

Kim, D. O. and Bae, J. 2005: 'Workplace innovation, employment relations and HRM: two electronics companies in South Korea'. *International Journal of Human Resource Management*, 17, 7, 1277–302.

Kim, M. 2011: 'Gender, work and resistance: South Korean textile industry in the 1970s'. *Journal of Contemporary Asia*, 41, 3, 411–30.

Kim, S. K. 1997: *Class Struggle or Family Struggle? The Lives of Women Factory Workers in South Korea*. Cambridge: Cambridge University Press.

Kingma, M. 2006: *Nurses on the Move: Migration and the Global Health Care Economy*. Ithaca NY: Cornell University Press.

Kingsnorth, P. 2003: *One No, Many Yeses*. London: Free Press.

Kirton, G., Healy, G., Alvarez, S., Leibewitz, R. and Gatta, M. 2010: *Women as Union Leaders in the UK and USA*. Report for the Leverhulme Foundation. London: Queen Mary University of London.

Klein, N. 2000: *No Logo*. London: Flamingo.

Klein, N. 2008: *The Shock Doctrine*. London: Penguin Books.

Kloosterboer, D. 2007: *Innovative Trade Union Strategies*. Utrecht: FNV.

Kofman, E., Phizacklea, A., Raghuram, P. and Sales, R. 2000: *Gender and International Migration*. London and New York: Routledge.

Kohl, B. and Farthing, L. 2006: *Impasse in Bolivia*. London: Zed Books.

Kondo, D. 1990: *Crafting Selves: Power, Gender and Discourses of Identity in a Japanese Workplace*. Chicago: University of Chicago Press.

Koo, H. 2001: *Korean Workers: The Culture and Politics of Class Formation*. Ithaca NY: Cornell University Press.

Koser, K. 2007: *International Migration: A Very Short History*. Oxford: Oxford University Press.

Koser, K. and Salt, J. 1997: 'The geography of highly skilled international migration'. *International Journal of Population Geography*, 3, 285–303.

Krane, J. 2009: *Dubai: The Story of the World's Fastest City*. London: Atlantic Books.

Krauss, C. 2005: 'Wal-Mart battle puts Quebec on edge'. *International Herald Tribune*, 11 March, www.iht.com/articles/2005/03/10/business.walmart.php.

Kung, L. 1983: *Factory Women in Taiwan*. Ann Arbor MI: UMI Research Press.

Kuruvilla, S., Lee, C. K. and Gallagher, M. (eds.) 2011: *From Iron Rice Bowl to Informalization: Markets, Workers and the State in a Changing China*. Ithaca NY: Cornell University Press.

Kuruvilla, S. and Verma, A. 2006: 'International labor standards, soft regulation, and national government roles'. *Journal of Industrial Relations*, 48, 1, 41–58.

La Botz, D. 2001: *Made in Indonesia: Indonesian Workers since Suharto*. Cambridge MA: South End Press.

Lankshear, G., Cook, P., Mason, D., Coates, S. and Button, G. 2001: 'Call centre employees' responses to electronic monitoring: some research findings'. *Work, Employment and Society*, 15, 3, 595–605.

Lapavitsas, C. 2011: 'Theorizing financialization'. *Work, Employment and Society*, 25, 4, 611–26.

Lareau, A. 2003: *Unequal Childhoods: Class, Race and Family Life*. Berkeley CA: University of California Press.

Larsen, J. 2011: 'Recent labour unrest in China'. *Transfer*, 17, 1, 91–3.

Lawrence, F. 2011: 'Spain's salad growers are modern day slaves, say charities'.

The Guardian online, 7 February, www.guardian.co.uk/business/2011/feb/07/spain-salad-growers-slaves-charities.

Leary, V. 2003: '"Form follows function": formulations of international labor standards – treaties, codes, soft law, trade agreements', in R. Flanagan and W. Gould IV (eds.), *International Labor Standards: Globalization, Trade, and Public Policy.* Stanford CA: Stanford University Press, 179–205.

Lee, C. K. 1998: *Gender and the South China Miracle.* Berkeley CA: University of California Press.

Lee, C. K. 2007: *Against the Law: Labor Protests in China's Rustbelt and Sunbelt.* Berkeley CA: University of California Press.

Lee, E. 1997: 'Globalization and labour standards: a review of the issues'. *International Labour Review*, 136, 2, 173–89.

Lee, S. and McCann, D. (eds.) 2011: *Regulating for Decent Work: New Directions in Labour Market Regulation.* Basingstoke: Palgrave Macmillan.

Leidner, R. 1993: *Fast Food, Fast Talk: Service Work and the Routinization of Everyday Life.* Berkeley CA: University of California Press.

Leigh, A. 2005: 'Decline of an institution'. *Australian Financial Review*, 7 March, 21.

Leonard, P. 2010a: *Expatriate Identities in Postcolonial Organizations – Working Whiteness.* London: Ashgate.

Leonard, P. 2010b: 'British expatriates in Hong Kong'. *Gender, Work and Organization*, 17, 3, 340–58.

Leung, P. N. and Pun, N. 2009: 'The radicalisation of the new Chinese working class: a case study of collective action in the gemstone industry'. *Third World Quarterly*, 30, 3, 551–65.

Levitt, P. and Glick Schiller, N. 2004: 'Conceptualising simultaneity: a transnational social field perspective on society'. *International Migration Review*, 38, 3, 1002–39.

Levy, D. 2008: 'Political contestation in global production networks'. *Academy of Management Review*, 33, 4, 943–63.

Ley, D. 2004: 'Transnational spaces and everyday lives'. *Transactions of the Institute of British Geographers*, 29, 151–64.

Lillie, N. 2006: *A Global Union for Global Workers.* Abingdon: Routledge.

Lindell, I. 2008: 'Building alliances between formal and informal workers: experiences from Africa', in A. Bieler, I. Lindberg and D. Pillay (eds.), *Labour and the Challenges of Globalization: What Prospects for Transnational Solidarity?* London: Pluto Press, 217–30.

Lipsig-Mumme, C. 2003: *Forms of Solidarity: Trade Unions and Community Unionism.* Melbourne: Australian Confederation of Trade Unions.

Lloyd, C. and Payne, J. 2009: 'Full of sound and fury, signifying nothing'. *Work, Employment and Society*, 23, 4, 617–34.

Locke, R., Amengual, M., and Mangla, A. 2009: 'Virtue out of necessity? Compliance, commitment, and the improvement of labor conditions in global supply chains'. *Politics and Society*, 37, 3, 319–51.

Locke, R., Kochan, T., Romis, M. and Qin, F. 2007: 'Beyond corporate codes of conduct: work organization and labour standards at Nike's suppliers'. *International Labour Review*, 146, 1/2, 21–40.

Locke, R., Rissing, A. and Pal, T. 2012: 'Complements or substitutes? Private codes, state regulation and the enforcement of labour standards in global supply chains'. *British Journal of Industrial Relations*, early view, http://onlinelibrary.wiley.com/doi/10.1111/bjir.12003/abstract.

Locke, R. and Romis, M. 2010: 'The promise and perils of private voluntary regulation: labor standards and work organization in two Mexican garment factories'. *Review of International Political Economy*, 17, 1, 45–74.

Lukose, Ritty A. 2009: *Liberalization's Children: Gender, Youth, and Consumer Citizenship in Globalizing India*. Durham NC: Duke University Press.

Lury, C. 2011: *Consumer Culture*. Cambridge: Polity (2nd edition).

Lyddon, D. 2007: 'Strike statistics and the problems of international comparison', in S. Van der Velden, H. Dribbusch, D. Lyddon and K. Vandaele (eds.), *Strikes around the World, 1968–2005*. Amsterdam: Askant Academic Publishing, 24–39.

Lyon, S., Aranda Bezaury, J. and Mutersbaugh, T. 2010: 'Gender equity in fair-trade–organic coffee producer organizations: Cases from Mesoamerica'. *Geoforum*, 41, 1, 93–103.

Mamic, I. 2004: *Implementing Codes of Conduct: How Businesses Manage Social Performance in Global Supply Chains*. Geneva: International Labour Organization.

Mandel, E. 1998: *Late Capitalism*. London: Verso.

Marginson, P. and Meardi, G. 2009: *Multinational Companies and Collective Bargaining*. Dublin: European Foundation for the Improvement of Living and Working Conditions, www.eurofound.europa.eu/docs/eiro/tn0904049s/tn0904049s.pdf.

Marginson, P. and Meardi, G. 2010: 'Multinational companies: transforming national industrial relations?' in T. Colling and M. Terry (eds.), *Industrial Relations: Theory and Practice*. Chichester: John Wiley, 207–30 (3rd edition).

Marginson, P. and Sisson, K. 1994: 'The structure of transnational capital in Europe: the emerging Euro-company and its implications for industrial relations', in R. Hyman and A. Ferner (eds.), *New Frontiers in European Industrial Relations*. Oxford: Blackwell, 15–51.

Marginson, P. and Sisson, K. 2004: *European Integration and Industrial Relations: Multi-Level Governance in the Making*. Basingstoke: Palgrave Macmillan.

Marks, L. 1990: *Working Lives and Working Mothers: A Comparative Study of Irish and East European Married Women's Work and Motherhood in East London 1870–1914*. London: University of North London Press.

Martell, L. 2010: *The Sociology of Globalization*. Cambridge: Polity.

Marx, K. 1975: *Early Writings*. Harmondsworth: Penguin.

Mason, P. 2009: *Meltdown: The End of the Age of Greed*. London: Verso.

Mason, P. 2012: *Why It's Kicking Off Everywhere: The New Global Revolutions*. London: Verso.

Massey, D. 1993: 'Power geometry and a progressive sense of place', in J. Bird, B. Curtis and T. Putnam (eds.), *Mapping the Futures: Local Cultures, Global Change*. London: Routledge, 59–69.

Massey, D., Arango, J, Hugo, G., Kouaouci, A., Pellegrino, A. and Taylor, J. 2008: *Worlds in Motion: Understanding International Migration at the end of the Millennium*. Oxford: Clarendon (2nd edition).

Mathias, P. 1983: *The First Industrial Nation*. London: Methuen & Co.

Maurice, M., Sellier, F. and Silvestre, J.-J. 1986: *The Social Foundations of Industrial Power: A Comparison of France and Germany*. Cambridge MA: MIT Press.

McCall, L. 2005: 'The complexity of intersectionality'. *Signs*, 30, 3, 1771–82.

McDowell, L., Batnitzky, A. and Dyer, S. 2008: 'Internationalization and the spaces of temporary labour: the global assembly of a local workforce'. *British Journal of Industrial Relations*, 46, 4, 750–70.

McDowell, L., Batnitzky, A. and Dyer, S. 2012: 'Global flows and local labour markets: precarious employment and migrant workers in the UK', in J. Scott, S. Dex and A. Pagnol (eds.), *Gendered Lives: Gender Inequalities in Production and Reproduction*. Cheltenham: Edward Elgar, 123–51.

McKay, S. 2006: *Satanic Mills or Silicon Islands? The Politics of High-Tech Production in the Philippines*. Ithaca NY: Cornell University Press.

McKenna, S., Richardson, J., Singh, P. and Xu, J. J. 2010: 'Negotiating, accepting and resisting HRM: a Chinese case study'. *International Journal of Human Resource Management*, 21, 6, 851–72.

McKinlay, A. and Starkey, K. (eds.) 1998: *Foucault, Management and Organization Theory: From Panopticon to Technologies of the Self*. London: SAGE.

McShane, D. 1992: *International Labour and the Origins of the Cold War*. Oxford: Clarendon.

Meardi, G. 2007: 'More voice after more exit? Unstable industrial relations in Central Eastern Europe'. *Industrial Relations Journal*, 38, 6, 503–23.

Meardi, G. 2012: *Social Failures of EU Enlargement: A Case of Workers Voting with their Feet*. Abingdon: Routledge.

Meardi, G., Marginson, P., Fichter, M., Frybes, M., Stanojevi , M. and Tóth, A. 2009: 'Varieties of multinationals: adapting employment practices in Central Eastern Europe'. *Industrial Relations*, 48, 3, 489–511.

Melucci, A. 1980: 'New social movements: a theoretical approach'. *Social Science Information*, 19, 2, 199–216.

Mendoza, C. 2003: *Labour Immigration in Southern Europe: African Employment in Iberian Labour Markets*. Aldershot: Ashgate.

Merk, J. 2008: 'Restructuring and conflict in the global athletic footwear industry: Nike, Yue Yuen and labour codes of conduct', in M. Taylor (ed.), *Global Economy Contested: Power and Conflict across the International Division of Labour*. Abingdon: Routledge, 79–97.

Merk, J. 2009: 'Jumping scale and bridging space in the era of corporate social responsibility: cross-border labour struggles in the global garment industry'. *Third World Quarterly*, 30, 3, 599–615.

Micheletti, M. 2010: *Political Virtue and Shopping: Individuals, Consumerism, and Collective Action*. New York and Basingstoke: Palgrave Macmillan.

Micheletti, M. and Stolle, D. 2007: 'Motivating consumers to take responsibility for global justice'. *Annals of the American Academy of Political and Social Science*, 611, 1, 157–75.

Michels, R. 1911: *Political Parties*. New York: Free Press.

Milanovic, B. 2005: *Global Income Inequality: What It Is and Why It Matters*. Washington DC: World Bank.

Mills, C. W. 1948: *The New Men of Power: America's Labor Leaders*. New York: Harcourt Brace.

Milne, S. 2012: *The Revenge of History: The Battle for the 21st Century*. London: Verso.

Momsen, J. H. 2009: *Gender and Development*. London: Routledge.

Monger, J. 2003: 'International comparisons of labour disputes in 2001'. *Labour Market Trends*, April, 181–9.

Moody, K. 1997: *Workers in a Lean World*. London: Verso.

Moore, F. 2005: *Transnational Business Culture: Life and Work in a Multinational Corporation*. Aldershot: Ashgate.

Moore, F. 2006: 'Strategy, power and negotiation: social control and expatriate managers in a German multinational corporation'. *International Journal of Human Resource Management*, 17, 3, 399–413.

Morokvasic, M. 1984: 'Birds of passage are also women'. *International Migration Review*, 18, 4, 886–907.

Morris, M. and Barnes, J. 2009: *Globalization, the Changed Dynamics of the Clothing and Textile Chains and the Impact on Sub-Saharan Africa*. Vienna: United Nations Industrial Development Organization.

Mort, F. 1997: 'Paths to mass consumption: Britain and the USA since 1945', in M. Nava, A. Blake, I. MacRury and B. Richards (eds.), *Buy this Book: Studies in Advertising and Consumption*. London: Routledge, 15–33.

Mosley, L. 2011: *Labor Rights and Multinational Corporations*. New York: Cambridge University Press.

Mosoetsa, S. and Williams, M. 2012: 'Challenges and alternatives for workers in the Global South', in S. Mosoetsa and M. Williams (eds.), *Labour in the Global South*. Geneva: International Labour Organization, 1–15.

Mueller, F. and Purcell, J. 1992: 'The Europeanization of manufacturing and the decentralization of bargaining: multinational management strategies in the European automobile industry'. *International Journal of Human Resource Management*, 3, 1, 15–24.

Müller-Jentsch, W. 1985: 'Trade unions as intermediary organizations'. *Economic and Industrial Democracy*, 6, 1, 3–33.

Munck, R. 1988: *The New International Labour Studies: An Introduction*. London: Zed Books.

Munck, R. 2002: *Globalization and Labour: the New 'Great Transformation'*. London: Zed Books.

Munck, R. 2011: 'Unions, globalisation and internationalism: results and prospects', in G. Gall, A. Wilkinson and R. Hurd (eds.), *The International Handbook of Labour Unions: Responses to Neo-Liberalism*. Cheltenham: Edward Elgar, 291–310.

Murillo, M. 2001: *Labor Unions, Partisan Coalitions and Market Reforms in Latin America*. Cambridge: Cambridge University Press.

Murphy, J. 2011: 'Indian call centre workers: vanguard of a global middle class?' *Work, Employment and Society*, 25, 3, 417–33.

Myloni, B., Harzing, A.-W. and Mirza, H. (2004). 'Human resource management in Greece: have the colours of culture faded away?' *International Journal of Cross Cultural Management*, 59, 4, 59–76.

Nadeem, S. 2009: 'Macaulay's (cyber) children: the cultural politics of outsourcing in India'. *Cultural Sociology*, 3, 1, 102–22.

(NASSCOM) National Association of Software and Services Companies n.d: *Annual Report 2011–12*. New Delhi: NASSCOM.

Nath, V. 2011: 'Aesthetic and emotional labour through stigma: national identity management and racial abuse in offshored Indian call centres'. *Work, Employment and Society*, 25, 4, 709–25.

Nichols, T., Cam, S., Chou, W., Chun, S., Zhao, W. and Feng, T. 2004: 'Factory regimes and the dismantling of established labour in China, South Korea and Taiwan'. *Work, Employment and Society*, 18, 4, 663–85.

Nichols, T. and Sugur, N. 2004: *Global Management, Local Labour: Turkish Workers and Modern Industry*. Basingstoke: Palgrave Macmillan.

Niforou, C. 2012: 'International framework agreements and industrial relations governance: global rhetoric versus local realities'. *British Journal of Industrial Relations*, 50, 2, 352–73.

Nilsson, M. 2012: 'Globalization and the formation of the political left in Latin America', in M. Nilsson and J. Gustafsson (eds.), *Latin American Responses to Globalization in the 21st Century*. Basingstoke: Palgrave Macmillan, 76–95.

Nilsson, M. and Gustafsson, J. (eds.) 2012: *Latin American Responses to Globalization in the 21st Century*. Basingstoke: Palgrave Macmillan.

Nishii, L. and Özbilgin, M. (2007) 'Global diversity management: towards a conceptual framework'. *International Journal of Human Resource Management*, 18, 11, 1883–94.

(NLC) National Labor Committee 2010: *China's Youth Meets Microsoft*. Pittsburgh PA: National Labor Committee.

Noronha, E. and D'Cruz, P. 2009: 'Engaging the professional: organising call centre agents in India'. *Industrial Relations Journal*, 40, 3, 215–34.

Novelli, M. 2007: 'Sintraemcali and social movement unionism: trade union resistance to neo-liberal globalisation in Colombia', in A. Gamble, S. Ludlam, A. Taylor and S. Wood (eds.), *Labour, the State, Social Movements and the Challenge of Neo-Liberal Globalisation*. Manchester: Manchester University Press, 185–203.

O'Brien, R. 2002: 'The varied paths to minimum global labour standards', in J. Harrod and R. O'Brien (eds.), *Global Unions? Theory and Strategies of Organized Labour in a Global Political Economy*. London: Routledge, 221–34.

O'Brien, R., Goetz, A.-M., Scholte, J.-A. and Williams, M. 2000: *Contesting Global Governance: Multilateral Economic Institutions and Global Social Movements*. Cambridge: Cambridge University Press.

O'Connell Davidson, J. 1998: *Prostitution, Power and Freedom*. Cambridge: Polity.

(OECD) Organisation for Economic Cooperation and Development 1996: *Trade, Employment and Labour Standards: A Study of Core Workers' Rights and International Trade*. Paris: OECD.

(OECD) Organisation for Economic Cooperation and Development 2007: *Offshoring and Employment: Trends and Impacts*. Paris: OECD.

(OECD) Organisation for Economic Cooperation and Development 2008: *Growing Unequal? Income Distribution and Poverty in OECD Countries*. Paris: OECD.

(OECD) Organisation for Economic Cooperation and Development 2009: *Is Informal Normal? Toward More and Better Jobs?* OECD Policy Brief, March.

(OECD) Organisation for Economic Cooperation and Development 2012a: *International Migration Outlook 2012*. Paris: OECD.

(OECD) Organisation for Economic Cooperation and Development 2012b: *OECD Employment Outlook 2012*. Paris: OECD.

Ohmae, K. 1999: *The Borderless World: Power and Strategy in the Interlinked Economy*. New York: Harper Collins.

Ohmae, K. 2005: *The Next Global Stage: Challenges and Opportunities in our Borderless World*. Upper Saddle River NJ: Prentice Hall.

Okpara, J. and Kabongo, J. 2011: 'Cross-cultural training and expatriate adjustment: a study of western expatriates in Nigeria'. *Journal of World Business*, 46, 22–30.

Ong, A. 1987: *Spirits of Resistance and Capitalist Discipline: Factory Women in Malaysia*. Albany NY: State University of New York Press.

(ONS) Office for National Statistics 2010: *Social Trends.*Volume XL. London: HMSO.

(ONS) Office for National Statistics 2012: *News Release: Census Gives Insights into Characteristics of London's Population*. London: Office for National Statistics, www.ons.gov.uk/ons/dcp29904_291554.pdf.

O'Rourke, D. 2002: 'Monitoring the monitors: a critique of corporate third-party labour monitoring', in R. Jenkins, R. Pearson and G. Seyfang (eds.), *Corporate Responsibility and Labour Rights: Codes of Conduct in the Global Economy*. London: Earthscan, 196–208.

O'Rourke, D. 2003: 'Outsourcing regulation: analyzing nongovernmental systems of labor standards and monitoring'. *Policy Studies Journal*, 31, 1, 1–29.

Ortega, B. 1999: *In Sam We Trust*. London: Kogan Page.

Paciello, M. 2011: *Egypt: Changes and Challenges of Political Transition*. MEDPRO Technical Report No.4, May, www.iai.it/pdf/mediterraneo/MedPro/MedPro-technical-paper_04.pdf.

Pai, H. H. 2008: *Chinese Whispers: The True Story Behind Britain's Hidden Army of Labour*. London: Penguin.

Palley, T. 2004: 'The economic case for international labour standards'. *Cambridge Journal of Economics*, 28, 1, 21–36.

Pangsapa, P. 2007: *Textures of Struggle: The Emergence of Resistance among Garment Workers in Thailand*. Ithaca NY: Cornell University Press.

Papadakis, K. (ed.) 2011: *Shaping Global Industrial Relations: The Impact of International Framework Agreements*. Basingstoke: Palgrave Macmillan.

Parkin, F. 1968: *Middle Class Radicalism*. New York: Praeger.

Parsons, N. 2013: 'Legitimizing illegal protest: the permissive ideational environ-ment and "bossnappings" in France'. *British Journal of Industrial Relations*, 51, 2, 288–309.

Parsons, T. 1937: *The Structure of Social Action*. New York: Free Press.

Parsons, T. 1951: *The Social System*. London: Routledge & Kegan Paul.

Partridge, D. 2011: 'Activist capitalism and supply-chain citizenship producing ethi-cal regimes and ready-to-wear clothes'. *Current Anthropology*, 52, S97–S111.

Patel, R. 2010: *Working the Night Shift: Women in India's Call Centres*. Palo Alto CA: Stanford University Press.

Patroni, V. 2008: 'After the collapse: workers and social conflict in Argentina', in M. Taylor (ed.), *Global Economy Contested: Power and Conflict across the International Division of Labour*. Abingdon: Routledge, 202–19.

Pattberg, P. 2005 'The institutionalization of private governance: how business and nonprofit organizations agree on transnational rules'. *Governance*, 18, 4, 589–610.

Pattee, J. 1999: '"Gapatistas" win a victory'. *Labour Research Review*, 24, 1, 77–84.

Pearce, R. (ed.) 2011: *China and the Multinationals: International Business and the Entry of China into the Global Economy*. Cheltenham: Edward Elgar.

Pereira, V. and Anderson, V. 2012: 'A longitudinal examination of HRM in a human resources offshoring (HRO) organization operating from India'. *Journal of World Business*, 47, 223–31.

Perrons, D. 2004: *Globalization and Social Change: People and Places in a Divided World*. London: Routledge.

Peters, J. 2011: 'The rise of finance and the decline of organised labour'. *New Political Economy*, 16, 1, 77–99.

Piazza, J. 2005: 'Globalizing quiescence: globalization, union density and strikes in 15 industrialized countries'. *Economic and Industrial Democracy*, 26, 2, 289–314.

Pilkington, E. 2012: 'Kansas prepares for clash of wills over future of unauthor-ised immigrants'. *The Guardian*, 2 February, www.guardian.co.uk/world/2012/feb/02/kansas-prepares-clash-unauthorised-migrants?INTCMP=SRCH.

Pollitt, C. and Bouckaert, G. 2011: *Public Management Reform: A Comparative Analysis – New Public Management, Governance and the Neo-Weberian State*. Oxford: Oxford University Press (3rd edition).

Posner, M. and Nolan, J. 2003: 'Can codes of conduct play a role in promoting work-ers' rights?' in R. Flanagan and W. Gould IV (eds.), *International Labor Standards: Globalization, Trade, and Public Policy*. Stanford CA: Stanford University Press, 207–26.

Poster, W. 2007: 'Who's on the line? Indian call center agents pose as Americans for US-outsourced firms'. *Industrial Relations*, 46, 2, 271–304.

Prakash Sethi, S., Veral, E., Shapiro, J. and Emelianova, O. 2011: 'Mattel, Inc: Global Manufacturing Principles (GMP) – a life-cycle analysis of a company-based code of conduct in the toy industry'. *Journal of Business Ethics*, 99, 4, 483–517.

Pritchard, K. and Symon, G. 2011: 'Identity on the line: constructing professional identity in a HR call centre'. *Work, Employment and Society*, 25, 3, 434–50.

Pun, N. 2004: 'Engendering Chinese modernity: the sexual politics of *dagongmei* in a dormitory labour regime'. *Asian Studies Review*, 28, 2, 151–65.

Pun, N. 2005a: *Made in China: Women Factory Workers in a Global Workplace*. Durham NC: Duke University Press.

Pun, N. 2005b: 'Global production, company codes of conduct, and labor conditions in China: a case study of two factories'. *The China Journal*, 54, 101–13.

Pun, N. 2007: 'Gendering the dormitory labor system: production, reproduction, and migrant labor in South China'. *Feminist Economics*, 13, 3, 239–58.

Pun, N. and Smith, C. 2007: 'Putting transnational labour process in its place: the dormitory labour regime in post-socialist China'. *Work, Employment and Society*, 21, 1, 27–45.

Pun, N. and Yu, X. 2008: 'When Wal-Mart and the Chinese dormitory labour regime meet: a study of three toy factories in China'. *China Journal of Social Work*, 1, 2, 110–29.

Pyle, J. 2006: 'Globalization, transnational migration, and gendered care work: introduction'. *Globalizations*, 3, 3, 283–95.

Quiggan, J. 2012: *Zombie Economics: How Dead Ideas Still Walk Among Us*. Princeton NJ: Princeton University Press (revised paperback edition).

Rainnie, A., Herod, A. and McGrath-Champ, S. 2011: 'Global production networks and labour'. *Competition and Change*, 15, 2, 155–69.

Ramumurti, R. and Singh, J. V. (eds.) 2009: *Emerging Multinationals in Emerging Markets*. Cambridge: Cambridge University Press.

Ransome, P. 2005: *Work, Consumption and Culture: Affluence and Social Change in the Twenty-First Century*. London and Thousand Oaks: SAGE.

Raworth, K. 2005: *Trading Away Our Rights: Women Working in Global Supply Chains*. Oxford: Oxfam.

Ray, L. 2007: *Globalization and Everyday Life*. London: Routledge.

Reitz, J. 2001: 'Immigrant skill utilization in the Canadian labour market: implications of human capital research'. *Journal of International Migration and Integration*, 2, 3, 347–78.

Resolution Foundation 2012: *What a Drag: The Chilling Impact of Unemployment on Real Wages*, www.resolutionfoundation.org/publications/what-drag-chilling-impact-unemployment-real-wages/.

Rigby, M. and Aledo, M. 2001: 'The worst record in Europe? A comparative analysis of industrial conflict in Spain'. *European Journal of Industrial Relations*, 7, 3, 287–305.

Rigg, J. 2007: *An Everyday Geography of the Global South*. Abingdon: Routledge.

Riisgard, L. 2005: 'International framework agreements: a new model for securing workers rights?' *Industrial Relations*, 44, 4, 707–37.

Ritzer, G. 2000: *The McDonaldization of Society: New Century Edition*. Thousand Oaks CA: Pine Forge Press.

Rivoli, P. 2009: *The Travels of a T-Shirt in the Global Economy*. New York: John Wiley.

Robertson, G. and Teitelbaum, E. 2011: 'Foreign direct investment, regime type and labor protest in developing countries'. *American Journal of Political Science*, 55, 3, 665–77.

Robinson, P. 2010: 'Do voluntary labour initiatives make a difference for the conditions of workers in global supply chains?' *Journal of Industrial Relations*, 52, 5, 561–73.

Rodríguez-Garavito, C. 2005: 'Global governance and labor rights: codes of conduct and anti-sweatshop struggles in global apparel factories in Mexico and Guatemala'. *Politics and Society*, 33, 2, 203–33.

Rofe, M. 2003: '"I want to be global": theorising the gentrifying class as an emergent élite global community'. *Urban Studies*, 40, 12, 2511–26.

Ross, A. and Hartman, P. 1960: *Changing Patterns of Industrial Conflict*. New York: John Wiley.

Ross, R. 2012: 'Clean Clothes Campaign', in G. Ritzer (ed.), *The Wiley–Blackwell Encyclopaedia of Globalization*. Chichester: Wiley-Blackwell.

Rothstein, J. 2012: 'When good jobs go bad: the declining quality of auto work in the global economy', in C. Warhurst, F. Carre, P. Findlay and C. Tilly (eds.), *Are Bad Jobs Inevitable?* London: Macmillan, 128–42.

RoyChowdhury, S. 2010: '"Class" in industrial disputes: case studies from Bangalore', in P. Bowles and J. Harriss (eds.), *Globalization and Labour in China and India: Impacts and Responses*. Basingstoke: Palgrave Macmillan, 170–88.

Royle, T. 2006: 'The dominance effect? Multinational corporations in the Italian quick-food service sector'. *British Journal of Industrial Relations*, 44, 4, 757–79.

Royle, T. 2011: 'Regulating global capital through public and private codes: an analysis of international labour standards and corporate voluntary initiatives', in M. Barry and A. Wilkinson (eds.), *Research Handbook of Comparative Employment Relations*. Cheltenham: Edward Elgar, 421–40.

Rubery, J. and Grimshaw, D. 2003: *The Organization of Employment: An International Perspective*. Basingstoke: Macmillan.

Salazar-Parreñas, R. 2001: *Servants of Globalization: Women, Migration and Domestic Work*. Stanford CA: Stanford University Press.

Salzinger, L. 2003: *Genders in Production: Making Workers in Mexico's Global Factories*. Berkeley CA: University of California Press.

Sassen, S. 1991: *The Global City: New York, London, Tokyo*. Princeton NJ and Oxford: Princeton University Press.

Sassen, S. 1994: *Cities in a World Economy*. Thousand Oaks CA and London: Pine Forge Press.

Sassen, S. 1996: 'Toward a feminist analytics of the global economy'. *Indiana Journal of Global Legal Studies*, 4, 1, 7–42.

Sassen, S. 2007: *A Sociology of Globalization*. New York: W.W. Norton.

Sauvant, K., Prakash Pradhan, J., Charterjee, A. and Harley, B. 2010: *The Rise of Indian Multinationals*. Basingstoke: Palgrave Macmillan.

Savage, M., Bagnall, G. and Longhurst, B. 2004: *Globalization and Belonging*. London: SAGE.

Sayim, K. Z. 2010: 'Pushed or pulled? Transfer of reward management policies in MNCs'. *International Journal of Human Resource Management*, 21, 14, 2631–58.

Scheuer, S. 2006: 'A novel calculus? Institutional change, globalisation and industrial conflict in Europe'. *European Journal of Industrial Relations*, 12, 2, 143–64.

Scholte, J. A. 2005: *Globalization: A Critical Introduction*. Basingstoke: Palgrave Macmillan (2nd edition).

Schuler, R., Jackson, S. and Tarique, I. 2011: 'Global talent management and global talent challenges: strategic opportunities for IHRM'. *Journal of World Business*, 46: 506–16.

Scullion, H. and Collings, D. 2011: 'Global talent management: introduction', in H. Scullion and D. Collings (eds.), *Global Talent Management*. Abingdon: Routledge, 3–16.

Seidman, G. 1994: *Manufacturing Militance: Workers' Movements in Brazil and South Africa*. Berkeley CA: University of California Press.

Seidman, G. 2007: *Beyond the Boycott: Labor Rights, Human Rights and Transnational Activism*. New York: Russell Sage Foundation.

Seidman, G. 2009: 'Labouring under an illusion? Lesotho's "sweat-free" label'. *Third World Quarterly*, 30, 3, 581–98.

Seidman, G. 2011: 'Workers' rights, union rights and solidarity across borders'. *International Labor and Working-Class History*, 80, 1, 169–75.

Senén González, C. and Medwid, B. 2009: 'The revitalization of trade unions and the re-emergence of industrial conflict in Argentina: the case of the oil industry'. *Journal of Industrial Relations*, 51, 5, 709–22.

Sennett, R. 1998: *The Corrosion of Character: The Personal Consequences of Work in the New Capitalism*. New York: W. W. Norton.

Shahrokhi, M. 2011: 'The global financial crises of 2007–2010 and the future of capitalism'. *Global Finance Journal*, 22, 3, 193–210.

Shalev, M. 1992: 'The resurgence of labour quiescence', in M. Regini (ed.), *The Future of Labour Movements.* London: SAGE, 102–32.

Shelley, T. 2007: *Exploited: Migrant Labour in the New Global Economy.* London: Zed Books.

Shen, J. 2007: *Labour Disputes and their Resolution in China.* Oxford: Chandos Publishing.

Shen, J. and Edwards, V. 2006: *International Human Resource Management in Chinese Multinationals.* London: Routledge.

Shin, K. Y. 2010: 'Globalisation and the working class in South Korea: contestation, fragmentation and renewal'. *Journal of Contemporary Asia,* 40, 2, 211–29.

Shorter, E. and Tilly, C. 1974: *Strikes in France.* Cambridge: Cambridge University Press.

Silver, B. 2003: *Forces of Labor: Workers' Movements and Globalization since 1870.* Cambridge: Cambridge University Press.

Silvey, R. 2003: 'Spaces of protest: gendered migration, social networks and labor activism in West Java, Indonesia'. *Political Geography,* 22, 2, 129–55.

Sklair, L. 2001: *The Transnational Capitalist Class.* Oxford: Blackwell.

Sklair, L. 2002: *Globalization: Capitalism and its Alternatives.* Oxford: Oxford University Press.

Slater, D. 1997: *Consumer Culture and Modernity.* Cambridge: Polity.

Smith, C. 2006: 'The double indeterminacy of labour power: labour effort and labour mobility'. *Work, Employment and Society,* 20, 2, 389–402.

Smith, C. 2008: 'Work organisation within a dynamic globalising context: a critique of national institutional analysis of the international firm and an alternative perspective', in C. Smith, B. McSweeney and R. Fitzgerald (eds.), *Remaking Management: Between Global and Local.* Cambridge: Cambridge University Press, 24–60.

Smith, C. 2010: 'Go with the flow: labour power mobility and labour process theory', in P. Thompson and C. Smith (eds.), *Working Life: Renewing Labour Process Analysis.* Basingstoke: Palgrave Macmillan, 269–96.

Smith, C. and Meiksins, P. 1995: 'System, society and dominance effects in cross-national organisational analysis'. *Work, Employment and Society,* 9, 2, 241–67.

Smith, C. and Pun, N. 2006: 'The dormitory labour regime in China as a site for control and resistance'. *International Journal of Human Resource Management,* 17, 8, 1456–70.

Smith, M. and Favell, A. (eds.) 2006: *The Human Face of Global Mobility: International Highly Skilled Migration in Europe, North America and the Asia-Pacific.* New Brunswick NJ: Transaction Press.

Smith, P. and Morton G. 1993: 'Union exclusion and the decollectivization of industrial relations in contemporary Britain'. *British Journal of Industrial Relations,* 31, 1, 97–114.

Snell, D. 2007: 'Beyond workers' rights: transnational corporations, human rights abuse and violent conflict in the Global South', in K. Bronfenbrenner (ed.), *Global Unions: Challenging Transnational Capital through Cross-Border Campaigns.* Ithaca NY: Cornell University Press, 195–211.

Som, A. 2008: 'Innovative human resource management and corporate performance in the context of economic liberalization in India'. *International Journal of Human Resource Management,* 19, 7, 1278–97.

Stalker, P. 2008: *The No-Nonsense Guide to International Migration.* Oxford: New Internationalist (2nd edition).

Standing, G. 2008: 'The ILO: an agency for globalization?' *Development and Change,* 39, 3, 355–84.

Standing, G. 2010: 'The International Labour Organization'. *New Political Economy,* 15, 2, 307–18.

Standing, G. 2011: *The Precariat: The New Dangerous Class.* London: Bloomsbury.

Stern, N. 2008: *The Economics of Climate Change: The Stern Review.* Cambridge: Cambridge University Press.

Stevis, D. and Boswell, T. 2007: 'International framework agreements: opportunities and challenges for global unionism', in K. Bronfenbrenner (ed.), *Global Unions: Challenging Transnational Capital through Cross-border Campaigns.* Ithaca NY: Cornell University Press, 174–94.

Stevis, D. and Boswell, T. 2008: *Globalisation and Labor: Democratizing Civil Governance.* Lanham MD: Rowman & Littlefield.

Stiglitz, J. 2002: *Globalization and its Discontents.* London: Allen Lane.

Stiglitz, J. 2007: *Making Globalization Work.* London: Penguin.

Stiglitz, J. 2010: *Freefall: Free Markets and the Sinking of the Global Economy.* London: Allen Lane.

Strange, S. 1996: *The Retreat of the State: The Diffusion of Power in the World Economy.* Cambridge: Cambridge University Press.

Streeck, W. 1997: 'Industrial citizenship under regime competition: the case of the European Works Councils'. *Journal of European Public Policy*, 4, 4: 643–64.

Tarrow, S. 1998: *Power in Movement: Social Movements and Contentious Politics.* Cambridge: Cambridge University Press (2nd edition).

Tarrow, S. 2005: *The New Transnational Activism.* Cambridge: Cambridge University Press.

Taylor, M. 2008: 'Power, conflict and the production of the global economy', in M. Taylor (ed.), *Global Economy Contested: Power and Conflict across the International Division of Labour.* Abingdon: Routledge, 11–31.

Taylor, M. 2011: 'Race you to the bottom . . . and back again? The uneven development of labour codes of conduct'. *New Political Economy*, 16, 4, 445–62.

Taylor, P. 2010: 'The globalization of service work: analyzing the transnational call centre value chain', in P. Thompson and C. Smith (eds.), *Working Life: Renewing Labour Process Analysis.* Basingstoke: Palgrave Macmillan, 244–68.

Taylor, P. 2012: '"The new normal"? Work and performance in an age of recession'. Paper presented to the Work, Employment and Society 25th Anniversary Conference. London, British Library.

Taylor, P. and Bain, P. 1999: 'An assembly line in the head: work and employee relations in the call centre'. *Industrial Relations Journal*, 30, 2, 101–17.

Taylor, P. and Bain, P. 2003: '"Subterranean worksick blues": humour as subversion in two call centres'. *Organization Studies*, 24, 9, 1487–509.

Taylor, P. and Bain, P. 2005: '"India calling to the far away towns": the call centre labour process and globalization'. *Work, Employment, and Society*, 19, 2, 261–82.

Taylor, P., Baldry, C., Bain, P. and Ellis, V. 2003: '"A unique working environment": health, sickness and absence in UK call centres'. *Work, Employment and Society*, 17, 3, 435–58.

Teague, P. 2003: 'Labour-standard setting and regional trading blocs: lesson drawing from the NAFTA experience'. *Employee Relations*, 25, 5, 428–52.

Teitelbaum, E. 2007: 'Can a developing democracy benefit from labour repression? Evidence from Sri Lanka'. *Journal of Development Studies*, 43, 5, 830–55.

Theobald, S. 2002: 'Working for global factories: Thai women in electronics export companies on the Northern Regional Industrial Estate', in D. S. Gills and N. Piper (eds.), *Women and Work in Globalising Asia.* London: Routledge, 131–53.

Theroux, P. 1986: *Sunrise with Seamonsters.* Harmondsworth: Penguin.

Thomas, M. 2009: *Belching out the Devil: Global Adventures with Coca-Cola.* London: Ebury Press.

Thomas, W. and Znaniecki, F. 1958: *The Polish Peasant in Europe and North America.* New York: Dover.

Thompson, G. 2010: '"Financial globalisation" and the "crisis": a critical assessment and "what is to be done"'. *New Political Economy*, 15, 1, 127–45.

Thompson, P. 2003: 'Disconnected capitalism: or why employers can't keep their side of the bargain'. *Work, Employment and Society*, 17, 2, 359–78.

Thompson, P. 2011: 'The trouble with HRM'. *Human Resource Management Journal*, 21, 4, 355–67.

Thompson, P. and Findlay, P. 1999: 'Changing the people: social engineering in the contemporary workplace', in L. Ray and A. Sayer (eds.), *Culture and Economy after the Cultural Turn*, London: SAGE, 162–88.

Thompson, P. and Smith, C. 2009: 'Labour power and labour process: contesting the marginality of the sociology of work'. *Sociology*, 43, 5, 913–30.

Thompson, P. and Smith, C. 2010: 'Debating labour process theory and the sociology of work', in P. Thompson and C. Smith (eds.), *Working Life: Renewing Labour Process Analysis*. Basingstoke: Palgrave Macmillan, 11–28.

Thrift, N. 1997: 'The rise of soft capitalism'. *Cultural Values* 1, 1, 29–57.

Tiano, S. 1990: 'Maquiladora women: a new category of workers?' in K. Ward (ed.), *Women Workers and Global Restructuring*. Ithaca NY: ILR Press, 193–223.

Tiano, S. 1994: *Patriarchy on the Line*. Philadelphia PA: Temple University Press.

Tilly, C. 1995: *Popular Contention in Great Britain 1758–1834*. Cambridge MA: Harvard University Press.

Tjandraningsih, I. 2000: 'Gendered work and labour control: women factory workers in Indonesia'. *Asian Studies Review*, 24, 2, 257–68.

Tonkiss, F. 2006: *Contemporary Economic Sociology: Globalization, Production, Inequality*. Abingdon: Routledge.

Touraine, A. 1971: *The Post-Industrial Society*. New York: Random House.

Tsai, C. J. 2006: 'High performance work systems and organizational performance: an empirical study of Taiwan's semiconductor design firms'. *International Journal of Human Resource Management*, 17, 9, 1512–30.

Tsogas, G. 2001: *Labor Regulation in a Global Economy*. New York: M. E. Sharpe.

Tsogas, G. 2009: 'International labour regulation: what have we really learnt so far?' *Relations Industrielles / Industrial Relations*, 64, 1, 75–94.

Turnbull, P. 2006: 'The war on Europe's waterfront – repertoires of power in the port transport industry'. *British Journal of Industrial Relations*, 44, 2, 305–26.

Tyner, J. 2004: *Made in the Philippines: Gendered Discourses and the Making of Migrants*. London: Routledge.

Tyner, J. 2009: *The Philippines: Mobilities, Identities and Globalization*. London and New York: Routledge.

Umney, C. 2011: 'The international labour movement and China'. *Industrial Relations Journal*, 42, 4, 322–38.

(UNCTAD) United Nations Conference on Trade and Development 2009: *World Investment Report 2009: Transnational Corporations, Agricultural Production and Development*. New York and Geneva: United Nations.

(UNCTAD) United Nations Conference on Trade and Development 2011: *World Investment Report 2011: Non-Equity Modes of International Production and Development*. New York and Geneva: United Nations.

UNESCO–UNICEF 2011: 'Delhi's *First City* magazine – migrants: voices of Delhi's silent majority', December 2011. Available at http://unesdoc.unesco.org/images/0021/002148/214828e.pdf.

United Nations 1990: Convention on the Protection of the Rights of All Migrant Workers and Members of Their Families. Available at http://www2.ohchr.org/english/law/cmw.htm.

United Nations 2005a: *Highly Skilled Migration*. Vienna: International Centre for Migration Policy Development.

United Nations 2005b: *Report of the Global Commission on International Migration*. New York: UN Population Division, Department of Economic and Social Affairs.

United Nations 2012a: *World Urbanization Prospects: The 2011 Revision*. New York: United Nations Department of Social and Economic Affairs.

United Nations 2012b: *Migrants By Origin and Destination: the Role of South to South Migration*. Population Facts, No. 2012/13. United Nations Department of Economic and Social Affairs Population Division, www.un.org/esa/population/publications/popfacts/popfacts_2012-3_South-South_migration.pdf.

Upadhya, C. 2009: 'Controlling offshore knowledge workers: power and agency in India's software outsourcing industry'. *New Technology, Work and Employment*, 24, 1, 2–18.

US Citizenship and Immigration Services 2013: 'Temporary (non-immigrant) workers'. Available at: www.uscis.gov/portal/site/uscis/menuitem.eb1d4c2a3e5b9ac89243c6a7543f6d1a/?vgnextoid=13ad2f8b69583210VgnVCM100000082ca60aRCRD&vgnextchannel=13ad2f8b69583210VgnVCM100000082ca60aRCRD.

Van der Velden, S. 2007: 'Introduction', in S. Van der Velden, H. Dribbusch, D. Lyddon and K. Vandaele (eds.), *Strikes around the World, 1968–2005*. Amsterdam: Askant Academic Publishing, 12–23.

Van Gelder, S. (ed.) 2011: *This Changes Everything: Occupy Wall Street and the 99% Movement*. San Francisco CA: Berrett-Koehler Publishers.

van Roozendaal, G. 2002: *Trade Unions and Global Governance: The Debate on a Social Clause*. London: Continuum.

Vandaele, K. 2011: *Sustaining or Abandoning 'Social Peace'? Strike Developments and Trends in Europe since the 1990s*. European Trade Union Institute Working Paper, No. 2011.05, Brussels: ETUI.

Varul, M. 2009: 'Ethical selving in cultural contexts: fairtrade consumption as an everyday ethical practice in the UK and Germany'. *International Journal of Consumer Studies*, 33, 2, 183–9.

Vertovec, S. 2009: *Transnationalism*. London and New York: Routledge.

Vieta, M. 2010: 'The social innovations of autogestión in Argentina's worker-recuperated enterprises: cooperatively reorganizing productive life in hard times'. *Labor Studies Journal*, 35, 3, 295–321.

Visser, J. 2006: 'Union membership statistics in 24 countries'. *Monthly Labour Review*, January, 38–49.

Vogel, D. 2008: 'Private global business regulation'. *Annual Review of Political Science*, 11, 261–82.

von Holdt, K. 2002: 'Social movement unionism: the case of South Africa'. *Work, Employment and Society*, 16, 2, 283–304.

Voss, E., Wilke, P., Sobczak, A. and Schömann, I. 2008: *Codes of Conduct and International Framework Agreements: New Forms of Governance at Company Level*. Dublin: European Foundation for the Improvement of Living and Working Conditions.

Wad, P. 2007: '"Due diligence" at APM-Maersk: from Malaysian industrial dispute to Danish cross-border campaign', in K. Bronfenbrenner (ed.), *Global Unions: Challenging Transnational Capital through Cross-Border Campaigns*. Ithaca NY: Cornell University Press, 40–56.

Wailes, N., Bamber, J. and Lansbury, R. 2011: 'International and comparative employment relations: an introduction', in G. Bamber, R. Lansbury and N. Wailes (eds.), *International and Comparative Employment Relations: Globalisation and Change*. London: SAGE, 1–35.

Waldinger, R., Erickson, C., Milkman, R., et al. 1998: 'Helots no more: a case study of the Justice for Janitors campaign in Los Angeles', in K. Bronfenbrenner, S.

Friedman, R. Hurd, R. Oswald and R. Seeber (eds.), *Organizing to Win: New Research on Union Strategies.* Ithaca NY: ILR Press, 102–19.

Wallace, J. and O'Sullivan, M. 2006: 'Contemporary strike trends since 1980: peering through the wrong end of a telescope', in M. Morley, P. Gunnigle and D. Collings (eds.), *Global Industrial Relations.* London: Routledge, 273–91.

Wallerstein, I. 1974: *The Modern World System.* New York: Academic Press.

Walsh, K. 2006: 'British expatriate belongings: mobile homes and transnational homing'. *Home Cultures,* 3, 2, 123–44.

Walters, B. 2010: 'Irish/Jewish diasporic intersections in the East End of London', in M. Prum (ed.), *La Place de l'autre Paris.* Paris: L'Harmattan Press, 53–67.

Ward, K. (ed.) 1990: *Women Workers and Global Restructuring.* Ithaca NY: ILR Press.

Ward, K. 2004: 'Going global? Internationalization and diversification in the temporary staffing industry'. *Journal of Economic Geography,* 4, 3, 251–73.

Ward, K. 2007: 'Thinking geographically about work, employment and society'. *Work, Employment and Society,* 21, 2, 265–76.

Warnecke, T. and De Ruyter, A. 2010: 'Positive economic freedom: an enabling role for international labor standards in developing countries?' *Journal of Economic Issues,* 44, 2, 385–92.

Warouw, N. 2008: 'Industrial workers in transition: women's experiences of factory work in Tangerang', in M. Ford and L. Parker (eds.), *Women and Work in Indonesia.* Abingdon: Routledge, 104–19.

Waterman, P. 2001: 'Trade union internationalism in the age of Seattle'. *Antipode,* 33, 3, 312–36.

Waters, M. 2001: *Globalization.* London and New York: Routledge (2nd edition).

Webb, B. and Webb, S. 1920: *A History of Trade Unionism.* London: Longmans.

Webster, E., Lambert, R. and Bezuidenhout, A. 2008: *Grounding Globalization: Labour in the Age of Insecurity.* Oxford: Blackwell Publishing.

Webster, E. and Omar, R. 2003: 'Work restructuring in post-apartheid South Africa'. *Work and Occupations,* 30, 2, 194–213.

Wells, D. 2007: 'Too weak for the job: corporate codes of conduct, non-governmental organizations and the regulation of international labour standards'. *Global Social Policy,* 7, 1, 51–74.

Wheeler, K. 2012: 'The practice of fairtrade support'. *Sociology – the Journal of the British Sociological Association,* 46, 1, 126–41.

Whitley, R. 2000: *Divergent Capitalisms: The Social Structuring and Change of Business Systems.* Oxford: Oxford University Press.

Whitson, R. 2007: 'Beyond the crisis: economic globalization and informal work in urban Argentina'. *Journal of Latin American Geography,* 6, 2, 121–36.

Wilkinson, B., Gamble, J., Humphrey, J., Morris, J. and Anthony, D. 2001: 'The new international division of labour in Asian electronics: work organization and human resources in Japan and Malaysia'. *Journal of Management Studies,* 38, 5, 675–95.

Willmott, H. 1993: 'Strength is ignorance, slavery is freedom: managing culture in modern organisations'. *Journal of Management Studies,* 30, 4, 515–52.

Wills, J. 2002: 'Bargaining for the space to organize in the global economy: a review of the Accor–IUF trade union rights agreement'. *Review of International Political Economy,* 9, 4, 675–700.

Wolf, D. 1994: *Factory Daughters: Gender, Household Dynamics and Rural Industrialization in Java.* Berkeley: University of California Press.

Wolf, M. 2004: *Why Globalization Works.* New Haven CT: Yale University Press.

Wolkowitz, C. 2006: *Bodies at Work.* London: SAGE.

Won, J. 2007: 'Post-socialist China: labour relations in Korean-managed factories'. *Journal of Contemporary Asia,* 37, 3, 309–25.

Woolfson, C. 2010: '"Hard times" in Lithuania: crises and "discourses of discontent" in post-communist society'. *Ethnography*, 11, 4, 487–514.

World Bank 2002: *Globalization, Growth and Poverty: Building an Inclusive World Economy*. Washington DC: World Bank and Oxford University Press.

World Bank 2003: *Unions and Collective Bargaining: Economic Effects in a Global Environment*. Washington DC: World Bank.

World Bank 2008: *World Development Indicators 2008*. Washington DC: World Bank.

World Bank 2011: *Multipolarity: The New Global Economy*. Washington DC: World Bank.

Wright, C. and Madrid, G. 2007: 'Contesting ethical trade in Colombia's cut-flower industry: a case of cultural and economic injustice'. *Cultural Sociology*, 1, 2, 255–75.

Xue, H. 2008: 'Local strategies of labor control: a case study of three electronics factories in China'. *International Labor and Working-Class History*, 73, 1, 85–103.

Yeates, N. 2005: *Global Care Chains: A Critical Introduction*. Geneva: Global Commission on International Migration.

Yeoh, B. and Willis, K. 2005: 'Singaporeans in China: transnational women elites and the negotiation of gendered identities'. *Geoforum*, 36, 2, 211–22.

Yildirim, E. and Calis, S. 2008: 'The impact of EU accession on Turkish industrial relations and social dialogue'. *Industrial Relations Journal*, 39, 3, 212–28.

Young, R. 2005: *Colonial Desire: Hybridity in Theory, Culture and Race*. London: Routledge (2nd edition).

Young, W. and Utting, K. 2005: 'Fair trade, business and sustainable development'. *Sustainable Development*, 13, 3, 139–42.

Yu, X. 2008: 'Impacts of corporate code of conduct on labor standards: a case study of Reebok's athletic footwear supplier factory in China'. *Journal of Business Ethics*, 81, 513–29.

Zachariah, K., Prakash, B. A. and Irudaya Rajan, S. 2004: 'Indian workers in UAE: employment, wages and working conditions'. *Economic and Political Weekly*, 39, 22, 2227–31.

Zhang, L. 2008: 'Lean production and labor controls in the Chinese automobile industry in an age of globalization'. *International Labor and Working-Class History*, 73, 1, 24–44.

Zimmermann, A. and Ravishankar, M. N. 2011: 'Collaborative IT offshoring relationships and professional role identities: reflections from a field study'. *Journal of Vocational Behavior*, 78, 3, 351–60.

Zlotnik, H. 1992: 'Empirical identification of international migration systems', in M. Kritz, L. L. Lim and H. Zlotnik (eds.), *International Migration: A Global Approach*. Oxford: Clarendon, 19–40.

Zontini, E. 2010: *Transnational Families: Moroccan and Filipino Women in Bologna and Barcelona*. New York: Berghahn Books.

Index